Biblio

HORATIO ALGER

OR THE AMERICAN HERO ERA

RALPH D. GARDNER

ARCO PUBLISHING COMPANY, INC.
New York

THIS BOOK

is for

MOTHER   NELLIE   DAD

and

THE BOYS

Published 1978 by Arco Publishing Company, Inc.
219 Park Avenue South, New York, N.Y. 10003

Copyright © 1964, 1971 by The Wayside Press

Library of Congress Cataloging in Publication Data

Gardner, Ralph D., 1923—
   Horatio Alger: or, The American hero era,
including Road to success.

   Bibliography: p.388
   Includes index.
   1. Alger, Horatio, 1832-1899—Biography.
2. Alger, Horatio, 1832-1899—Bibliography.
3. Authors, American—19th century—Biography.
I. Gardner, Ralph D., 1923—   Road to
success. 1978. II. Title: The American hero era.
PS1029.A3Z65   1978   813'.4 [B]   77-28059
ISBN 0-668-04466-7

Printed in the United States of America

CONTENTS

HORATIO ALGER, OR THE AMERICAN HERO ERA.

Preface

I REMEMBER, as though it were yesterday, the first time I met Horatio Alger.

It was near a village in Central Maine, late on a mid-summer afternoon in 1936. I was thirteen, and the famed author had been dead exactly thirty-seven years.

In the barn up a narrow path behind his house, a Mr. Spaulding stored and traded in such odd-assorted used furnishings as oil lamps, most of them without globes; high-backed rocking chairs, some with a single rocker, some with none; pitchers-and-wash-bowls, some cracked, some magnificent; brass bed-frames and the usual and unusual accumulations of local attics.

In a corner was a mound of books, many mildewed, mouse-nibbled or coverless. The first one to catch my eye was "Frank Fowler, The Cash Boy," by Horatio Alger, Jr.

Before scanning to the bottom of the first page, I became an Alger devotee and searched for others, finding a dozen more. It soon was evening and, as shadows spread through the unlighted shed, it became too dark to continue. Respectfully, I knocked on the side door of his cottage — as a sign requested — to call Mr. Spaulding and pay for the books.

I followed the tall, willowy proprietor to the out-building and pointed to my selection.

"How much do you charge for books, Mr. Spaulding?"

"A nickel apiece for the little ones," he answered, "a dime for big ones."

Algers were "little ones" and, having fifty cents, I chose ten with the most exciting titles or cover illustrations. The rest I replaced on the stack.

Mr. Spaulding picked up the three and handed them to me.

"Take these along," the kind Yankee said. "They're too nice to leave."

Thanking him, I asked if he found the books in the neighborhood.

"Not the Algers, sonny. They're mine. I read them all when I was younger than you are."

I planned — that summer and many times since — to go back, in hopes of finding other Alger treasures in the dusty pile. But more than a quarter of a century passed before, driving through New England, I made a side-trip along that lovely road in Maine.

Sentimental journeys often are best left untravelled. There was no trace of the old gentleman. I parked at a general store-post office, a mile away, and approached two elderly farmers who sat, talking, on a bench in front of the railroad station. I told them I was looking for the Mr. Spaulding who sold things in a barn back of his home.

"Spaulding?" the first man repeated the name slowly, digging deep into his memory.

"Wouldn't that be Newt Spaulding?" the second man wondered.

"No," the first corrected, " 'Twas Chase."

"Oh, yes. Chase Spaulding," the second agreed.

"He's dead," the first man declared.

"Many years ago," the second man added.

Perhaps this book should also be dedicated to Mr. Spaulding, with whom my adventure began.

The above lines were written in 1964 as a preface to *Horatio Alger; or, The American Hero Era*. That modest edition—some three thousand copies—soon sold out, and the book became recognized as "rare." Demand for it continues—in fact, increases—and when offered for sale through dealers' catalogues or at auction, it currently brings seven or eight times its original price.

This should not be too astonishing, considering the renewed

14

interest in Horatio Alger and his stories. Besides understandable nostalgia for durable, desirable products of distant times, perhaps the pendulum is now swinging back toward what Heywood Broun called these "simple tales of honesty triumphant," with manly, self-reliant heroes and inevitable happy endings.

While literary greatness cannot be claimed for Alger's writing, he nevertheless became America's all-time bestselling author, surely among the most influential this nation has produced. A number of his stories are once again in print. His works are today studied in universities. And the *name*, Horatio Alger, has taken on legendary meaning. It is used as a symbol, a figure of speech. As a handy synonym for spectacular rise to success, it has become a colloquialism.

This new volume is essentially two books in one: a *biography* plus the revised, updated *bibliography* of Alger's novels, short stories and poetry.

It is my sincere hope these pages will recall warm memories to readers who enjoyed Alger in years past. Also, that it might induce newer generations—to whom "a typical Horatio Alger story" may only be a frequently noticed phrase in news reports—to try one or two Alger tales. They may find unexpected delights in these unsophisticated but rattling good yarns that thrilled their grandparents long, long ago.

Ralph D. Gardner

New York, November 9, 1977

15

Top: Horatio's parents, The Reverend Horatio Alger, Sr., and Olive Augusta Fenno Alger. A Unitarian minister for a half-century, the parson was an outspoken abolitionist, and also served for many years as a Senator in the Massachusetts State Legislature. At bottom: Sister Olive Augusta Alger Cheney and her husband, Amos Parker Cheney. Herself a popular writer, "Gusti" was a life-long fighter in causes of temperance and women's suffrage.

At left: A daguerreotype of Horatio Alger, Jr., made on the occasion of his graduation from Harvard College, at twenty, in 1852. "Alphabetically speaking," Horatio often said, "I was the first scholar of my class." Scholastically he finished eighth among eighty-eight. Physically he was shortest, being but five feet, two inches tall. At right: An 1872 portrait when, at the age of forty, he was already well established as a busy, best-selling author.

Horatio Alger at the age of sixty, in 1892. More than a generation after creating "Ragged Dick," he still was a leading American writer of tales for young people. Although ever planning to lighten his work schedule, he continued producing about three novels each year.

During last three years of his life, 1896-1899, Horatio spent most of his time at the family home in South Natick, making only infrequent trips to his beloved New York. The author looks on (right), as his brother-in-law, Amos P. Cheney (left), and guest Louis Schick try to solve a word puzzle. Schick, who became a successful business man, was one of the many who, in their youth, enjoyed the assistance and friendship of Horatio Alger, Jr.

CHAPTER 1

"DEAR ADAMS"

"EARLY NEXT WEEK — Wednesday at the latest — I intend to send you the remaining parts of my story. I hope they are as acceptable to you as the first chapters, which you already received.

"Your encouragement is most welcome, and I share your eagerness awaiting Loring's decision whether to publish the story as a book. You know he was not too pleased with my last efforts.

"Frankly, this tale of life in the streets almost writes itself, as there exists in New York today an unruly horde of boys in straits so desperate as to seem unbelievable.

"Their plight first attracted me some years since, during a brief visit here. But now, with the Rebellion ended, their number increases daily. Most of them are homeless orphans, sleeping in cellars or alleyways. They support themselves as best they can, mainly as newsboys or bootblacks. Some engage as baggage carriers around the piers or run errands. Also, I'm sorry to tell you, many live by begging or by stealing, imposing upon smaller boys of their class, and other despicable ways. Still, there are enough good ones among them, given half a chance."

The small room in Bleecker Street suddenly became chill in the dusk of a mid-November afternoon, and the writer paused, briefly, to revive the smouldering flame in his fireplace. Adding the needed fuel, flames soon crackled with new energy, sending warmth and light to all parts of the lodging. He then turned up the wick in the lamp on his writing table.

The end of the year 1866 was rapidly approaching. Days already were noticeably shorter and, even at that moment, early snow fell silently on the roof-tops of New York, and carpeted the high-fenced backyards he could see from his third floor rear-window.

Returning to his letter, he wrote again.

"Note my new address," he continued. "These quarters are not nearly so comfortable as those I recently left on East Tenth Street, near University Place, but they are cheaper, and that is most important right now.

"When you have my final chapters, I hope you will be able to advance me some payment, which will be gratefully received, I assure you."

Re-reading the last sentence, and nodding his head in apparent agreement that his request was not improper, the writer ended his message,

"In haste, I am

Truly your friend,
Horatio Alger, Jr."

The letter, which started "Dear Adams:", was addressed to William T. Adams who, as Oliver Optic, was famed both as a magazine editor and writer of stories for young people.

Although he was ten years older than Horatio, they had been close friends for a dozen years, having met at the Alger home in Marlborough, before the war. Adams had long been a school teacher, yearning for the life of a writer.

Horatio had been until recently, pastor of the Unitarian Congregation at a village on Cape Cod. It was the calling selected for him by his father, a distinguished New England preacher, the descendant of generations of illustrious churchmen.

Yet, Horatio, like Will Adams, longed to write. Even as a child he composed stories, and long remembered the delight of seeing one of them printed when he was thirteen years old. Later, while still at college, during the period that followed, and all the months he occupied the pulpit at Brewster, Massachusetts, he had never stopped writing.

Adams was the first to taste success. He had already written several books and became a regular contributor to periodicals, primarily to Student and Schoolmate, a leading monthly for boys and girls. He encouraged Alger to submit short stories, and a number of these were published.

Through a rather recent development, however, Adams had been able to open for Horatio a greater opportunity. Having been appointed senior editor of the magazine, his increased duties prevented him from continuing to produce the serialized stories that were the featured attraction of each issue.

Alger, at about that time, had offered a number of articles on the rigors of street life in New York, suggesting as the title, "Among the Bootblacks." The idea had appealed to Adams, who promptly replied, asking if there was enough there to develop into six or twelve connected monthly installments.

"Yes, definitely!" Horatio quickly answered and, altering his original theme, had fervently set to work on a novel.

The manuscript had delighted Adams. He had engaged Alger for the job, adding his request that Horatio forward the balance of chapters at the earliest possible date as he, personally, was "keenly interested in learning the story's ending." The editor also had shrewdly taken the opportunity to offer to Aaron K. Loring, the publisher of some of Alger's earlier works, the book publication rights to the forthcoming — but as yet unfinished — serial.

*   *   *

After slowly going over the letter, Alger added a brief postscript.

"P.S.: I heartily approve of the title you suggest. It is better than mine. I agree my story should be called 'Ragged Dick'."

"Ragged Dick" was, for Horatio Alger, Jr., the end of one long road, and the beginning of another.

CHAPTER 2

THE ALGERS
OF BRIDGEWATER

THE LONG, WINDING ROAD that eventually led to "Ragged Dick" actually was embarked upon many years — as a matter of fact, more than three centuries — before that famous tale's author, Horatio Alger, Jr., had written its first paragraph.

Horatio's father, The Rev. Horatio Alger, Sr., had — during his own childhood — been carefully and most effectively tutored in the Alger family heritage. He was determined that this be passed on to his son. There never was a doubt in his mind but that he would have a son, one who would follow in his footsteps as a Servant of God and his fellow-man.

In The Reverend Mr. Alger, the family pride was well-enshrined. He would pass on the legend of an early ancestor, John Rogers, the first Protestant martyr burned at the stake by Queen Mary, at Southfield, England, in 1555. Then there were the Pilgrims. Of the 102 separatists from the Church of England who arrived aboard the Mayflower, founding Plymouth Colony in 1620, his son would be able to trace no less than fifteen ancestors. And seven of them were signers of The Mayflower Compact.

When Thomas Alger — the first bearing the family name to reach these shores — settled in New England during the Seventeenth Century, he still pronounced the name as *Auger,* in accordance with the rule of old English grammar that *a* before l was sounded like *au.* Consequently, in the earliest proprietary records of Taunton, Massachusetts, where he owned "a parcel of land that lieth at ye head of Thomas Linkon's land and ye land of Robert Crossman, as much as that place will afford," the name is listed as *Thomas Auger.* Thereafter, however, in all entries in the Old Colony registers, he is known as Thomas Alger.

Thomas, a farmer, became a friend of the Indians. He cleared fields from the forests and built a cabin in a meadow along a winding stream, known as Three-Mile River, that flows through the easterly part of Taunton. To this cottage he brought a wife in the autumn of 1665.

Accompanied by a small party of neighbors and friends, Thomas travelled to nearby Bridgewater on November 15th, to wed Elizabeth Packard who, with her parents, came as an infant from Wymondham, England, aboard the ship, Diligent, in 1638. They had two children — a son, Israel, and later a daughter, Deliverance. The children were named for a brother and sister of their mother.

In after years, Thomas added to his property, eventually moving with his family to a new home within the limits of Bridgewater. It is not known whether Thomas lived to see his children's families grow and considerably increase his original holdings.

He would have been proud to see his great-granddaughter, Patience, marry in 1732 into the family of John Quincy, the great-grandfather of President John Quincy Adams.

A pious man, Thomas might have been ashamed of his first name-sake who, on June 16, 1749, was publicly censured for a relatively minor breach of church discipline. According to the records, "Bro. Thomas Alger appeared before ye Church, and declared he was sorry he went out of ye Church Meeting as he did without order, inasmuch as it was a Violation of ye Rule and Order of ye Church, for which in the time of it he was not sensible of, and promised as he should be enabled to observe the Rules and Order of ye Church. Which ye Church Vot'd Satisfied with."

As years passed, the settlement grew and it was decided to construct a highway to replace foot-paths and lanes that connected the steadily increasing number of dwellings. The official order for laying out the new route stated that it be built "away from the old road over Flaggy Meadow Brook to the top of the hill. Then turning and going near by the house of Israel Alger, Jr., so down over the swamp by the side of a pond hole, and into the way to the bridge over the cove. So, westerly near Joseph Alger's house, and by the mile line to Cutting Cove Fence. And from the bridge a way to be laid over the slough by the west side of Israel Alger's meadow fence, and so by the east side of Thomas Alger's fence to John Field's land."

Until the Revolutionary War, Alger men were farmers, and most of their daughters married farmers. But, before the echoes of the first musket shots had faded, no less than eighteen descendants of Thomas Alger volunteered and quickly joined the ranks of the Continental Army. Daniel Alger, along with a number of his brothers and cousins (and their sisters' husbands) enlisted and served during the fighting in Rhode Island in Captain Nathan Packard's Company of Militia. Abner — a son of Mary Alger Hayward — was first an ensign in the Navy, later a captain in the Army. Sylvanus — a son of Bethiah Alger Lazell — was one of the Minute Men who marched from Bridgewater to Lexington on April 19th, 1775. He later was commissioned a brigadier general. His brother, Isaac, was a cavalry officer, and another brother, Edmund, was captain of a horse troop. In 1788, Edmund was a member of the Convention that met to adopt the United States Constitution.

Although a majority of the Algers remained at, or returned to, their farms after the War for Independence, their numbers eventually thinned. They drifted from the soil to business and the professions. Several were practicing law, some already making their names known in politics. A few became physicians. At least a half-dozen preferred the military life, serving with distinction in the War of 1812. There were teachers and writers, and ministers who occupied pulpits of the Universalist, Baptist, Congregational, Episcopal and, eventually, Unitarian denominations.

There were shop-keepers, tradesmen, commission merchants, bankers and industrialists. Algers operated iron foundries, textile mills and shoe factories. Among them were men of triumphant success and others doomed to bankruptcy and heart-breaking failure. There were rich and poor relations, and Algers who toiled throughout their lives to make ends meet, never exactly impoverished, but also never rising above the grayness of unceasing austerity.

Within the year after marrying his second wife, Susanna Snow, on Christmas Day, 1717, Israel Alger, Jr., aided only by his brothers, Joseph, Thomas, Nathaniel and John, built a sturdy two-story wooden frame house in a grove of elms. This was the loveliest part of his "twenty-acre farm on the Milstone Plain, near Old Cedar Swamp" on the north side of the Town River, in Bridgewater. The land had been a part of the original one hundred eleven-acre estate of Israel Alger, Sr., valued at "not less than £ 700."

In their comfortable home, to which a one-room wing had been added, Susanna gave birth to a son, James, on March 28, 1729. Here also, some two-score years later, James' son — named for his father — was born October 22, 1770.

Young Jamie was the pampered delight of his parents and of four sisters and a brother, Abiezer, who were from seven to eighteen years older. Three of the girls, Anna, Alice and Martha were wed while Jamie was still a child. Abiezer married Hepsibah Keith, in 1778, after serving as a militiaman during the war, and they moved to West Bridgewater. Phebe married in 1779, leaving home shortly before Jamie's ninth birthday.

So it was the youngest of James Alger's children who remained on the farm, working the fields and — but a few years later — eagerly clearing new pastures and cultivating orchards on recently acquired land in a part of town known as Scotland. Although not as tall as his father, Jamie grew powerfully broad-chested, with short though muscular arms, and fists like a pair of oak burls. His great strength — and the amount of work he could accomplish from "can-see 'til can't-see" — established for the mild-mannered, soft-spoken Jamie a reputation readily acknowledged from Freetown to Braintree.

"You're too easy-going," his closest cousin and childhood playmate, Abiel, often complained when both were young men.

"Watch out, or folks'll walk all over you." Jamie was never known to anger. But no neighborhood bully ever dared to test his temper.

Before he was twenty-one, Jamie fell deeply in love with slender, violet-eyed Hannah Bassett, a direct descendant, on her father's side, from William Bassett, and on her mother's side from The Reverend Robert Cushman, both of whom were among the Plymouth Pilgrims.

The couple wed, in April, 1791, in the First Congregational Church, at Bridgewater, a few days after Hannah turned nineteen. It being the Sabbath, there was no work to be done, so James — for this is what Hannah decided he should now be called — took his bride to inspect with him a three-acre meadow he had decided to buy.

In October, a son, Adin, was born in the old farmhouse, the second boy, Nahum, arriving two years later. By the time the daughter, Phebe-Cushman, was born in September, 1798, their ambitious, untiring father had — besides adding to his land — entered into a partnership with Col. Salmon Forbes to operate an iron furnace. The elder man had put up the cash, and James the brawn. The venture was profitable and, in the summer of 1802 — just about the time another son, Zenas, was born — the partners agreed to take over, from its retiring owner, the town's general store.

During years that followed, James — a deeply religious man — became a deacon of the church and increasingly active in affairs of his growing community. He also became a father again, for another child, a son — and the last of the Algers to be born in the old homestead on Milstone Plain — arrived on the chilly morning of November 6, 1806.

In honor of a noble ancestor, on the Bassett side, the infant was named Horatio.

Life at the Alger house was joyous during those early years of the Nineteenth Century. It was small enough to be agreeably warm during long, freezing winters, but sufficiently large to be quickly transformed — in the imaginative minds of Zenas, Horatio and their numerous cousins from neighboring farms — into pioneers' flatboats, frigates and occasionally into forests where Indians lurked.

During the sweet, warm months, the fragrant outdoors became their playground. But James insisted that all who came to play must also help with the chores. Bigger boys chopped wood and cleaned the barn. The little ones "learned" by watching father and his three hired helpers. The girls — in the kitchen richly aromatic with baking bread and juicy fruit pies — peeled apples and kneaded dough under gentle Hannah's vigilant direction.

But, for the adults, the times soon were to bring years of uncertainty and strife. The economic pressures of the Embargo Act, urged by President Jefferson and passed in Congress during December, 1807, were especially severe in New England. The decision to withdraw the entire American merchant marine from foreign trade quickly idled millions of tons of shipping at Yankee ports. Farm prices were sinking, and the existence of many regional industries was, at best, precarious.

In his home and at the Town Meeting House, James frequently gathered with other local leaders to discuss the situation and search for remedies. More and more often, these conferences took him to Boston, where he joined with those who urged quick conversion, wherever possible, to manufacturing. Their future, he predicted, lay more in the production of shoes and textiles than in merchant shipping.

In all arguments — for there were many who opposed James' views — he was sure of the support of his older brother, Abiezer, and especially of his nephew, Cyrus, whose age was closer to his own.

Abiezer had, years earlier, engaged in an iron foundry business in West Bridgewater. Now he also owned furnaces in Easton and Titicut, was prominent in regional affairs, serving as a justice of the peace and judge in the General Court.

But it was Abiezer's brilliant, impatient son, Cyrus, who, in 1809, established the main plant in South Boston. Some years earlier, while preparing for college, he gave up continued education as a waste of time, rolled up his sleeves, and moved into his father's foundry.

By the time he was ready for the Boston expansion, Cyrus' technical skill attracted the attention of General Aaron Winslow and T. H. Perkins, who underwrote the venture. From the beginning, the industry was a success, and Cyrus soon bought from the

South Boston Association additional land, including all the water-front property from the sea-wall to the channel. At his own expense, he began improving the area, repairing the sea-wall, constructing wharves, filling-in flats and parcelling land for building lots. He laid out gardens, widened streets and, after erecting the Sea Street Bridge, presented it to the city.

Meanwhile, the untenable friction in British-American relations exploded into the War of 1812. As in the Revolution, Algers served, joining in battles on land and sea, participating in the disastrous forays into Canada, and the triumph over Chief Tecumseh and his British-supported Indians. Cyrus Alger had secured for his South Boston Iron Company large government contracts for the production of cannon balls. Throughout the day and night the furnaces blazed red, their thick smoke blackening the skies over the city.

Horatio was eight years old when the war ended. It already was apparent that he would inherit his father's short stature, but not the older Alger's tremendous strength. The boy never shirked his many farm duties but, finishing them as quickly as he could, he retreated to his studies. His mother patiently taught him the primary lessons, and during the brief periods each year that the town could afford to hire a schoolmaster, Horatio was an avid pupil. By the time he was twelve there was little further benefit to be derived at the local one-room schoolhouse. He had moved rapidly from one row of benches to the next, and casually recited lessons assigned to students five years older than himself.

It was decided that Horatio should continue his education at home, and for this purpose a number of books were ordered. During the next three years he tutored himself in a variety of subjects, including Latin and French. When he was fifteen years old, two significant events came to pass. The first was that, as a last-minute replacement for a teacher who was engaged, but never reported for duty, Horatio earned thirty-six dollars as a substitute schoolmaster. The second was that he had made the Bible his constant companion. He could quote long passages by heart, and, in simple terms, explained to others the obscure meanings of lines they had often read but did not necessarily fathom.

In August, 1821, Horatio travelled to Cambridge, where he easily passed tests for admission to Harvard. During his four year stay at the college, his record was superior. He paid expenses by handling odd jobs, tutoring other students, and teaching at country schools during vacation periods. His tuition costs also were aided by special grants the college advanced to outstanding scholars.

Horatio received his Bachelor's degree with the Class of 1825, when he was eighteen years old. After teaching at Bridgewater throughout the summer recess, he returned in the fall to enter the Divinity School, from which he was graduated in 1829.

*　　*　　*

A dozen miles to the North of the college buildings and green fields of Cambridge, the centuries-old tranquility of the venerable town of Chelsea — lying close upon the unquiet shores of the Atlantic Ocean — was ruffled by voices of dissension in the Unitarian Church on County Road.

After ministering to the congregation for more than twenty-three years, the able Rev. Dr. Joseph Tuckerman could no longer conceal the reaction that had set in among a group of influential members of the parish, strenuously opposing departures from ancient orthodox doctrines in the direction of more liberal Unitarian views. Nevertheless, he was able to hold his group together during the next two years until, a quarter of a century — to the day — after his ordination, Dr. Tuckerman resigned on November 4, 1826.

His pulpit was briefly filled by The Rev. Ebenezer Crafts — who remained for several months — followed shortly by The Rev. Jonathan Farr, who preached for a year.

It was while The Rev. Mr. Farr was pastor that things came to a climax. As a result of energetic missionary efforts by Lyman Beecher, a leader of Evangelical forces in the region, a great number of parishioners were led to withdraw from the old church and establish the Evangelical Congregational Society. In 1828 the newly formed group voted to build a house of worship on a quarter-acre of land on the easterly side of the Salem Turnpike.

After the departure of Reverend Farr, it was decided, in April, 1829, to invite The Rev. John A. Williams to settle there, but he refused on account of ill health.

The committee then met again to discuss other possible candidates, but adjourned in complete disagreement. One was considered "too lax," another "overly puritanical." An apparently sterling possibility was "grossly unattractive," another "too pretty." Several were variously judged "too old," "a dreary speaker," "unsympathetic," "too expensive" or "not interested."

At the next meeting, one of the committeemen produced a letter received that day from Reverend Tuckerman, in which he relayed — without recommendation — his son Francis' advice that a former Harvard classmate, only recently out of Divinity School, fervently sought a pulpit. Probably, the message suggested, his price could be arranged at a very reasonable figure.

"Who is he?" asked John Payson, the committee's chairman.

"Horatio Alger, of Bridgewater."

"Probably very young," suggested Deacon John Fenno.

"Probably, too," interjected another, "we can engage him real cheap."

"The motion is made," the chairman hastily pronounced, "that the committee invite Mr. Alger to preach the Sabbaths during May, with the view that he settle with us as a Gospel Minister if he satisfies."

The motion was quickly seconded, with all present apparently voting in favor, and on the next day Horatio Alger was called to Chelsea.

CHAPTER 3

THE NEW PARSON

A SOAKING RAIN that started when mist rose from the marshes the previous evening, and lasted through the night, was still falling when the noon stage was due at Fenno's Corner. Travel was slow, over the muddy road from Mystic Ferry, and it would be late arriving.

In good weather, the coach's dusty trail was visible almost a mile distant, across the green foxtail fields of Old Cheever Farm. Today, May 4, 1829, it would only be seen rounding the Salem Turnpike bend, less than a hundred yards from its station.

But the arrival of a new minister was an event of great importance in the community, and several townspeople were on hand to join the church committee in greeting The Rev. Mr. Alger. In addition to Mr. Payson, Deacon Fenno and Squire Carpenter Staniels, a number of parishioners huddled together in the damp, drafty shed that provided poor protection against bad weather while awaiting the daily stage.

Other than committeemen, those who came to meet the parson were purely unofficial, but inevitably present when important incidents took place. Thanks to this group, other townsfolk could stay home, confident that one of them would presently drop by to convey the news, with few details lacking, and an abundance of personal appraisal included.

Mrs. Lavisa Slocum was the most assiduous of these news-gatherers, and her visit — generally around tea-time — invariably portended a strictly confidential account of current affairs. Her listeners charitably took into consideration that old Mrs. Slocum was so near-sighted that her descriptions often were vague, and so deaf that she was able to catch a word here and there only on her 'good days,' which became fewer and fewer during recent years.

"I remember the day Reverend Tuckerman arrived," Mrs. Slocum recalled, adding "Of course, I was only a child at the time."

"If I calc'late correct, Lavisa," Abner Tewksbury recalled, "you was then married already 'most ten years."

It being one of Mrs. Slocum's 'bad days,' the remark passed unheard.

"And what a grand manner he did have," she continued. "His hands were so delicate and his gestures so graceful. He had the eyes of a young poet, and that voice. Oh, my dear. How his voice stirred us girls. Me, mind you, being only a child at the time."

"If our Mr. Alger turns out half as creditable," John Payson remarked, "we will have made a fine choice."

"You say Mr. Alger has a fine voice?" Mrs. Slocum asked.

"Choice." Mr. Payson repeated. "I said 'choice'."

"Well, I'm glad you think so, Mr. Payson. I didn't know you'd heard him preach."

"I think they're coming," Abigail Stoughton said. She peered out of the shelter, inclining her head as she and the others could hear heavy wheels grinding the stony path someplace out of sight.

All moved expectantly forward to get the first glimpse of the stage as it rounded the turn in the road. Eventually they saw an outline moving slowly through the downpour. It was not the stage, but an ox-cart, returning from market. The group returned to the cabin.

"I'm told," said Abigail Stoughton, brightening, "that the new pastor is a bachelor. Is that correct, Mr. Staniels?"

"So I understand," the squire agreed.

"Well, well, Miss Abigail," Abner twitted the aging spinster, "I 'spect you're setting your cap for our young Reverend. Or are you planning to adopt him?"

The maiden lady pressed her thin lips, preparatory to answering the town wag, but from around the bend there sounded the distant rumble of hooves mingled with rattling harness and wheels. The familiar shout of Jacob Worth, the driver, left no doubt but that the stage was nearing and, seconds later, the coach — shiny wet — with four great horses snorting and steaming in the chill air, grated to a noisy halt at the station shed.

The lone passenger, weary from his journey and soaked through his dark, shapeless clothes, stepped down and, for a silent moment, parson and parishioners each contemplated the other.

The man who stood before them was thin, pale and shorter than they expected — only slightly over five feet tall. His nose was long and pointed, with wide nostrils. He had a large mouth set in a manner that gave the distinct impression it rarely curved into a smile, and sharp blue eyes that were stern and penetrating. Although he was not yet twenty-three years old, his hair was speckled with gray.

He stood very erect, like one trying to appear taller than his height, and unsmiling, but in a voice that was direct, authoritative and containing a surprising degree of warmth, he announced:

"I am Horatio Alger. Am I addressing Mr. Payson?"

The chairman of the church committee stepped forward, and, after introducing the minister to official and unofficial greeters, took him to his home, where board was arranged for the month-long probationary period.

The two men remained indoors through the day, 'drying out' and negotiating terms of the minister's engagement. These, apparently being satisfactorily agreed upon, The Reverend Mr. Alger spent the evening in his room, sipping hot tea and outlining his first sermon, which he titled "Go and Do Thou Likewise."

The rain ended during the night. The young parson, awakened by the first orange sunrays of morning, went to the window and breathed deeply of the fragrance of the new day and of his own new direction in life. From trees, barns and nearby meadows, birds announced the dawn with song and shrill signals as they dived low over wet fields in search of food.

After breakfast, Reverend Alger and Mr. Payson — joined by other committeemen — walked the short distance to the Unitarian Church.

It was originally built as town meetinghouse, about 1710, Carpenter Staniels explained.

"There used to be a tall steeple over there," the squire pointed to the front of the building. "But it got so rotted we tore it down and put up that cupola you see."

"But there is no bell," Alger noted. "Oh, we must have a bell."

Inside, there were private and public pews and, upstairs, galleries on three sides of the building. Facing these was the pulpit, directly opposite the entrance. During winter months, heating — which was never considered sufficient — was conveyed by an iron stove pipe that stretched the whole length of the ceiling, suspended by many wires. Under each joint in the pipe hung a little tin pail to collect the drippings from the smoke of the wood fire.

A good crowd filled the church that Sunday, as on following Sabbaths during The Rev. Horatio Alger's trial period. Early in June he was asked to continue supplying the pulpit through the summer, after which the final decision would be reached.

This was something of a disappointment to the parson, who expected that by the end of May he would be permanently settled over the congregation.

"I can tell you that they like you, Reverend," Deacon Fenno advised. "But some consider you a trifle young. They want to give you more time to prove you are the preacher to lead us during the years to come. I hope you will accept these conditions."

"Yes, I accept," Alger said, slowly. "But on August 10th I must have your decision."

During the term of trial, he learned much about Chelsea and its people. They found their minister to be both learned and practical. Although young, his dedication was unquestioned,

Rare editions by Horatio Alger, Jr. — earliest of which were published in the mid-19 Century — are highly valued by collectors. Some are almost unknown; others, like "Ragged Dick," still are nostalgically remembered.

Old timers fondly recall Alger paperbacks of their youth. "We read them all," they say. "When we finished a story it was swapped for other titles. I'll bet I had a hundred or more. All boys loved the Algers, and so did their sisters!" On cover of "The Erie Train Boy," Fred Fenton — the hero — offers a magazine to Joshua Bascom, a farm lad on his way to see the sights in New York City.

Paperbacks, which once sold from a dime to a quarter, often were reprints of novels published in more expensive hard covers. Earlier ones, however, were from serializations in popular story-papers. "Tom-Tracy," a fearless Alger hero, dives into Harlem River to rescue the daughter of Professor Martini, "a dancing master whose classes were drawn from prominent city families."

39

RISEN FROM THE RANKS

Colorful covers depict brave adventures or a humble start. In "Risen From the Ranks," Harry Walton, son of an impoverished New Hampshire farmer. wants to become a journalist. Calling upon the owner of the Centreville Gazette, he is hired as a journeyman printer at two dollars a week and board. At twenty-one years of age he is an influential newspaper editor and member of the State Legislature, soon to be elected to the Congress.

and long before his probation ended he was advising his flock in a multitude of their needs.

Always deeply studious, he quickly familiarized himself with the history of the community, from days long past when it was the home of the Pawtucket tribe of Indians, and known as Rumney Marsh. By the time white settlers arrived, about 1624, the number of Indians already was greatly reduced. In 1615 they had been attacked by the powerful Tarratine tribe, invading from east of the Penobscot. More fatal than war was the plague of 1616, which ravaged great portions of the region. In December, 1633, most of the remaining Indians — numbering about forty — and their chief, Wonohaquaham, named Sagamore John by the English, died of small-pox. Settlers took in and cared for the children, but many of them died soon after.

The young minister was particularly interested in the lore of their worship, which they apparently took seriously. They regularly came from as far distant as Saugus and the shores of Mystic River to attend prayers presided over by their powah, or priest, whom they called Passaconaway. The Indians believed that, after death, they went to the land of eternally pleasant southwest wind, where dwelt their great and benevolent god, Cautontowit. There they should enjoy perpetual pleasures, lush forests and good hunting and fishing without weariness.

In his free time, as well as in the course of duties, the minister roamed the countryside, now in the lush full bloom of summer and he soon knew the neighborhood from Winnisimmet to Pullen Point, and from Black Ann's Corner to McClure's brickyard.

There were some, among the townfolk, always eager to direct his attention to all manner of scandal. Sometimes the affected parties, themselves, sought his counsel. Occasionally, problems bordered on delicate matters that he, in the inexperience of his own extreme youth, had not previously encountered and which — to his best recollection — were not included in Divinity School manuals. In such events The Rev. Alger prayed for guidance and — so strong was his own belief — that he never for a moment doubted the practicable wisdom of his ultimate judgment.

On an oppressively hot afternoon in early August, as he was

leaving the home of aged, bed-ridden Miss Elizabeth Payson, he met Abigail Stoughton — bright-eyed and purse-lipped — who approached him with the air of one who had something urgent to report.

"I suppose, Reverend," she started, breathlessly, "You've heard about the goings-on down to Keayne's Farm?"

He had not, much to Miss Abigail's delight, for this was a tale she truly relished.

"Well," she began. "It's this Anna Keayne. Her father was such a gentleman, but that woman he married — Anna's mother, you see — well, sir, she was a fancy kind. And her father being Governor, no less. Well, sir, she lusted with any man that would have her. You get what I mean, Reverend?"

Reverend Alger was not sure he did, but he nodded and she hastened to continue.

"She drove him into an early grave right after which she — this fancy woman — takes up with a man named Pacy. But it's the daughter, Anna, I was telling of. Well, Anna started in so young — simply everyone knew about that child — that her grandfather, a most respected man, mind you, Reverend, wrote in his will instructions that Anna should 'have her carnal disposition subdued and reformed by strict discipline.' That's just how he wrote it in his own words, Reverend. He knew she was cut from the same pattern as her mother. And so did everyone else hereabouts. Oh, a fine article she was. Do you follow me, Reverend?"

Again he nodded, knowing Miss Abigail Stoughton would not be stopped.

"She was barely sixteen when she married this Edward Lane, a Boston man almost twenty years older than she, and right off, they had two children. Just like her mother she was, and I can tell you, Reverend, the poor man wouldn't claim the children as his own, even though the records show they are. For once Anna agrees with Mr. Lane, saying he can't beget children anyhow, and — bold as you please — she admits both children were given to her by Nicholas Paige."

"A tragic story, Miss Stoughton. Truly tragic. That is a lady in need of guidance."

"Exactly my point, Reverend Alger. That's the very reason

I'm standing here telling you this. It's shameful, and tragic, too, just like you say!"

"In other words, Miss Stoughton, you feel I can be of help," Reverend Alger suggested.

The spinster hesitated. "Help?" she asked. "Help who?"

Why, this tragic Mrs. Lane. Anna, you called her."

"Why, Reverend," Miss Abigail coyly raised the back of her hand to her mouth to suppress a giggle, "Anna, poor thing, is dead."

"Oh, I'm deeply sorry to hear that. When did it happen?"

"I'm afraid you simply don't understand, Reverend. Anna died in 1704. Why, that's a hundred and twenty-five years ago!"

∗　　∗　　∗

On August 10th, 1829, The Rev. Mr. Horatio Alger was invited to the home of Deacon John Fenno and asked by the committee to settle permanently as Minister of the First Unitarian Church of Chelsea. His salary would be four hundred dollars a year, including lodging. If he marries, the salary will be increased to five hundred dollars annually, but he will then arrange his own lodging, and at his own expense.

The terms were accepted, and the date set on which Reverend Alger would be ordained as pastor.

The business discussion ended, the gentlemen were served tea by Deacon Fenno's wife, Olive, assisted by their daughter, Olive Augusta. The young lady had on the previous day returned from Boston where, for some months, she was living with relatives.

When The Rev. Alger arose to be introduced, he estimated that Miss Fenno stood a good three inches taller than himself. Next he noted that, despite a colorless appearance — of which both Olive Augusta and her parents also were painfully aware — in her gray eyes as in her timid smile there was considerable charm. The Reverend Alger was not a romantic man but for the first time, he realized, he had met a girl who impressed him neither as once did his childhood playmates or cousins, nor even purely as a member of his congregation. He saw her in a way that even he could not explain to himself, other than than he wanted to see her again. To hear her voice; to walk with her. He found himself wondering if, perhaps, she might wish to discuss the Bible with him.

Lying in bed that night, he reviewed the day's happenings. He had been chosen to settle in Chelsea as Minister of the Church — the appointment for which he had studied so long and worked so hard—and this delighted the young man. He also thought of the girl, Olive Augusta, but still could not quite find, within his mind, the proper niche for the way he felt.

"Whatever it is," he thought, "I shall forget about it, at least for the time being. There isn't room for the likes of such dalliance in the future of a minister barely started on his career. Definitely, I will forget her!"

Although, on awakening, he found the plain, willowy maiden once more in his thoughts, strong will-power enabled him to dismiss her — and all other distractions — as it was the day on which he prepared his sermon. And this Sunday, he thought, fleetingly, she would probably be watching him from the Fenno pew, scarcely a few feet below his pulpit.

Olive Augusta was present at the services, arriving with her parents and sitting between them in their accustomed place. It was, of course, the first time she heard him preach, and was impressed with how much taller he appeared in the pulpit than when she stood beside him.

On September 2d, Horatio Alger was ordained, and the weeks that followed flew by like the flurry of autumn leaves that turned from red and gold to brown, and were falling from trees in Chelsea's gardens and orchards, in the woods and all along the winding roadside.

Except on the Sabbath he did not see Olive Augusta, and even then their contact was limited to a brief greeting. One Sunday in November she did not attend church, and her empty seat distressed him. Later, he asked for her, and Deacon Fenno said she had gone to Boston for a stay of several weeks.

The chill days that followed were bleak for Reverend Alger. He was irritable, often in a testy mood, and more and more his thoughts were of the girl.

Several days before Christmas the minister was called to

the Fenno home to attend a meeting of the church committee. It was the first time he had been there since August, the first time he saw *her*. Now she was gone and, instead, winter filled the house.

But when the meeting ended, and visitors were leaving, Deacon Fenno took the parson by the arm and said:

"Mrs. Fenno reminds me to ask you to join us for Christmas Dinner. We would be pleased to have you, Reverend, and Olive Augusta writes she is returning in time for the Holidays, so she will be here, too. Will you come?"

"Oh, yes sir. I'll come," Reverend Alger replied with delight, quickly adding, "Thank you, sir."

It later occurred to Deacon Fenno that this was the first time he had seen the minister smile.

CHAPTER 4

CHRISTMAS AT THE FENNO'S

CHRISTMAS WAS JOYOUS at the Fenno's big house. Olive Augusta had returned, in the company of two Boston cousins with whom she lately visited. For Reverend Alger she brought a heavy woolen shawl and, there before the crackling hearth, he tried it on, wrapping it around in a variety of styles, and posturing grandly, to the great delight of the young lady, her parents and the other guests.

The hearty, aromatic dinner included goose with rich stuffing, pudding and two kinds of pies. When the young parson led the small group in prayer, as they gathered at the table, he, himself, enjoyed a deeper feeling of thanks than he had ever known before.

The following Christmas — it was then 1830 — The Rev. Horatio Alger again joined the Fenno family in their festivities. He and Olive Augusta had recently become engaged, and their wedding date was set for the early spring. Also present for the holiday were a number of other Fenno children and a half-dozen noisy, frolicsome grand-children.

It was the first time Reverend Alger met most of them and that introduction, indeed, was one of the reasons for the gathering. The Chelsea Fennos were there, in addition to others who had just arrived, travelling by stage and ferry all the way from Boston.

The Fennos, actually, were relative newcomers to Chelsea, having joined the community only ten years earlier. Since 1804, Deacon Fenno had been a prominent merchant in Boston, and it was there that his six children — of which Olive Augusta was the youngest — were born. He bought Cheever Farm as a business investment, there setting up a plant to slaughter cattle for beef. For this he constructed a barn that served as a model for others later constructed in the area.

In the beginning, his son, Joseph, who managed the farm, occupied a new house on the edge of the turnpike, and the Cheever homestead was used as a vacation place by the family. As years passed, they spent more time at the farm and less in town, until the deacon eventually decided to turn his Boston store over to partners, and retire to Chelsea. From the start, he interested himself in the progress of the Unitarian Church and the village, soon firmly establishing himself as a leading citizen.

He arrived upon the scene about the time the original seven great farms of the region were being divided into smaller holdings, operated by descendants of owners or taken over by new settlers.

In 1820 there were 642 inhabitants, with the total increasing, but the number of negro slaves diminishing rapidly. A dozen years earlier there were still fifty or more in the area, but most of these — having reached old age — either received their freedom upon the death of former masters, or lived out their days as retainers on the land where some of them toiled since their youth. In a corner near the north side of the graveyard were simple markers indicating the graves of "Fanny Fairweather, aged 80; a native of Africa," "Job Warrow, a free negro on the roll of the Pullen Point Guards, aged 100," "Charity, slave of Nathaniel Oliver, aged 23 years," "Caesar, slave of Samuel Sprague, age near 100 years," "Margaret, negro woman, aged 84 years," "Jack, slave of Samuel Pratt, nearly 100 years old," "Fortune, negro man, of great age," "Sampson Bassett, a free negro, April 12, 1826, aged 86 years," "Parker Bassett, a black boy, Aug. 11, 1818, aged nine years, drowned in one of the clay pits."

47

*   *   *

For his daughter, Deacon Fenno built a simple seven-room, two-story house facing on County Road, conveniently near the church. Square and sturdy, with pegged oak beams and wide plank floors, the living room was dominated by a large brick fireplace. The outside was painted an unattractive durable brown, but the shutters were white, and at the rear was a shed to eventually shelter a horse and shay, when the minister could afford these luxuries.

The paint was barely dry and the rooms only sparsely furnished when Olive Augusta and The Rev. Horatio Alger moved in on their wedding day, March 31, 1831. Their new home soon became headquarters for much community activity, church meetings and Bible and literary discussions. The parson loved the duty of officiating, and his wife glowed in the pleasure of being aide to the scholarly and respected churchman.

There seemed to be no end to the little man's initiative and energy. Even before his ordination, he announced his intention to install a bell in the empty cupola above the church, backing up a plea for contributions with his own donation of five dollars. He campaigned vigorously for a post office, demanding it as a necessity for the progress of the town. He taught at the community school-room during summer months and, in his comfortable study, gladly gave extra instruction in a variety of subjects from French and Latin grammar to arithmetic and penmanship.

At the same time, his parish duties were carried out with a fervor — and occasionally a strictness — that caused some members of his congregation to give him the title of "Priest Alger." While he was a whole-hearted practitioner of the less puritanical doctrines — as prescribed by the Cambridge Divinity School — and he rapidly became known as a vigorous leader in the transition toward liberalization of prevailing orthodox views, he was, nevertheless, an austere and unwavering pastor.

As months passed, his seriousness increased, and he never ceased to affect the bearing that he believed a church official must possess; especially a very young one who, he feared, risked loss of respect if suspected of frivolity or unbecoming levity. He never raised his voice, actually lowering it when angered, and this proved effective in his preaching.

At the same time he was sensitive, infinitely dependable and available at all times to minister to his flock. No distance was too far, no blizzard too severe, to reach the bedside of a parishioner, or to cross icy fields to an isolated farmhouse where he was needed. This, above all, impressed his people, and all agreed they could not have chosen a finer leader.

✳   ✳   ✳

It snowed all through the night of Christmas Eve, 1831, and the big, wet flakes continued falling softly on Christmas Morning.

At the Holiday services, Reverend Alger was pleased with the large turnout, despite the weather. The worshippers understood — and readily excused — the brevity of his sermon, especially upon noting that Mrs. Alger was not present in church.

Olive — The Rev. Horatio had lately dropped the "Augusta" — was so big with a child that he feared it would certainly be born during his reading of the scriptures, and insisted she remain at home. He was worried and nervous, but assumed his feelings went unnoticed. What many did notice, however, was that, in his haste to end the ceremonies, he failed to close with the final "Amen." No one mentioned this as, departing, they shook the minister's hand and exchanged sincere wishes for a Merry Christmas. He wondered, though, why his parishioners guardedly chuckled as they turned up their collars and bent homeward through the storm.

As Olive assured him, the child had not yet appeared when the anxious pastor burst into the brown cottage and raced up the stairs to the bedroom.

"Relax a bit, my poor Horatio," Olive calmly suggested, "then go to father's for Christmas Dinner."

"Impossible," he said with finality. "You may - er- need me here. I'll stay."

His wife knew better than to argue with the obstinate man, but regretted that he would miss the feast to which he had been looking forward.

49

But within the hour, as the minister moved agitatedly about the unfamiliar regions of the kitchen, attempting to prepare tea for Olive, he heard distant sleighbells, the snow-muffled pounding of hooves and — above this — the joyous shouts of children. Moments later, Reverend Alger heard the booming voice of Deacon Fenno, as he reined his horse to a skidding halt. He and his oldest daughter, Sarah, were about to knock when the door opened.

"We've come to fetch you, Reverend," his father-in-law commanded cheerfully. "It's time for Christmas Dinner at the Fenno's!"

"Can't make it, Deacon. I just can't leave Olive alone."

"Of course you can't. I don't expect you to. That's why Sarah's here. She'll take over 'til you get back, and do a sight better job, for all that!"

Sarah, meanwhile, had laughingly brushed past the minister and was already stepping lightly up the stairs, toward her sister's room, her arms laden with gifts she brought from Boston, where she lived.

"Button up and let's go, son. Dinner can't wait and mother won't start without prayers." Then the large old man left the house and, outside, playfully admonished his grand-children to stop "G'dapping" the dappled mare.

"She'll take off with you and won't stop 'til Prattville," he warned. "Let's go, Reverend," he shouted toward the house. "It's cold out here. Darned cold. Damned cold. Let's go!"

"Do you really think I might, Olive?" the parson called from halfway up the staircase.

"Please go, Horatio, dear. I promise not to have the baby until you get home."

The Reverend wasn't sure Olive's flippancy was proper, but the gay, rapid chatter of the sisters convinced him his wife would be well-occupied during the brief while he'd be away.

Moments later he left the house, wrapping his shawl about his ears, and leaping onto the bench where he seated himself at the deacon's side. At a single crack of the slender whip, the mare lunged eagerly homeward, the children piping high-pitched pleas for greater speed.

The bells tinkled a jocund tune and, except for that and

mirthful noises of boys and girls, the countryside was silent and blissfully peaceful as narrow, shiny runners cut through the snow, and the mare, fitfully snorting bursts of vapor, drew the bright red sleigh ever closer to Fenno's Farm.

Soon all were seated around the table and, although his thoughts remained at the brown cottage, the minister savored with delight the heady aroma of roasts and sweets.

With all heads bowed in devout gratitude, Reverend Alger led the family in prayer.

"Well done, sir, truly well done," his fun-loving brother-in-law, Henry, declared as the simple rites concluded. "And I'm glad you didn't forget the 'Amen'!"

There was a good deal of laughter, but the hungry parson — who already was half-way through the first course — attached no particular significance to the remark.

CHAPTER 5

CHELSEA DAYS

CHRISTMAS PASSED and the year 1832 arrived with Olive and her husband still waiting. Sarah remained, primarily — she said — to prevent the minister from suffering a complete nervous breakdown.

She could hear him moving restlessly about the study long after his usual bedtime on Thursday night, January 12.

"Is Olive comfortable?" he asked his sister-in-law, as she prepared tea.

"She's feeling much better than you are," she answered. "What are you doing up so late?"

"My sermon just won't get started," he complained. "I've put it aside until tomorrow. In the meantime, I made up this list of names. How do you like the sound of 'James, the Third', after my father and grandfather?"

"How dynastic, Horatio. My, but that sounds important for a baby!"

"Perhaps; then do you like 'Robert Cushman', an ancestor on my mother's side? Or 'John Fenno', which would please your father. Yes, I do think 'John Fenno Alger' rings nicely." Then he repeated, "'The Reverend John Fenno Alger'. Excellent."

"Excellent, indeed," Sarah said, "assuming your son will be

a churchman. And," she added, "also assuming you will have a son. What names have you selected for a daughter?"

"I haven't," he replied, hesitatingly. "It never occured to me. Yet, I'm sure it will be a boy. I shall go right up to Olive and ask her how she likes 'John Fenno Alger'."

"Not just yet, Parson. Drink this tea while it's hot."

"Hot! It's scalding. Let it cool awhile."

"No time for that. Drink it down, I'm sending you on an errand."

"It can't wait 'til morning?"

"I'm not sure this one can. I want you to bring Eliza Peabody."

"The midwife?"

"Finish your tea."

"The baby is coming?"

"Not yet, but soon, I think."

Before Sarah finished the sentence, The Rev. Alger was out of the house, and running through the clear, freezing night to the Peabody house, a half-mile away. The experienced old woman quickly gathered her instruments and the two soon reached the minister's home, going directly to his wife's room.

Through the night, Sarah and Mrs. Peabody stayed at Olive's bedside, and as Friday, January 13th dawned, it appeared that there remained not many hours of waiting. The minister, barred from the chamber, refused to go to bed, and spent the time alternately trying to outline his Sunday sermon, and occasionally adding a line to the list of names he considered suitable for an Alger son. First one appealed to him, then another. Then a sound from upstairs would send him darting into the hallway.

Shortly after sunrise, Reverend Alger decided that a fitting topic and title for his sermon should be "Waiting." He wrote it at the top of a blank page and decided it was quite acceptable. Then, resting his head on his arms, he closed his eyes and dozed at his work table.

He had been sleeping three hours when, awaking with a start, he saw Sarah moving about the study, drawing curtains to let a flood of stark, white sunlight brighten the room.

"Good morning, Reverend," she greeted him cheerily. "Isn't it about time for you to visit your wife and son?"

Still half asleep, he asked first for Olive, then "A son, Sarah? You say I have a son?"

"Well, that's what you ordered, Horatio. Who would dare disobey you? Now go up to Olive. She just woke up, and I'm sure she'll want to introduce you to the child. I'll prepare breakfast."

The baby slept, but Olive was fully awake when the young father burst into the room. Seeing his family before him, the minister knelt to pray, and when he raised his head Olive saw tears coursing down his sunken cheeks. She was pale and still in considerable pain, but she put her hand over his and whispered, "I'm glad you have your son, my darling. I'm so happy it's a boy."

"I am, too, and as soon as you feel stronger we shall give him a fine name. I've made a list and you can choose the one you like best. I like 'John Fenno Alger', but if there's one you like better . . . "

"There is one I prefer, and I've already chosen a fine name for our son. I want to call him Horatio. That sounds wonderful to me." Looking down at the slumbering infant, she said, softly, "Sir Knight, I dub thee Horatio Alger, Jr."

*　　*　　*

The year of Horatio's birth was a busy and eventful one for the Algers. The minister — whose hair was now completely gray although he was barely twenty-six years old — had never ceased demanding that Chelsea needed a post office. Considering regular postal service as vital, he petitioned the Congress, addressed public gatherings and, even from the pulpit, predicted his pleas would not long go unheeded.

He was right, for on July 6, the Chelsea Post Office was established by order of Postmaster General Amos Kendall, the same document appointing The Rev. Horatio Alger as the town's first postmaster.

The added income, though small, was welcome and, during most months, duties were light. The Chelsea Post Office was housed in the Alger study. Mail arrived from Boston three times a week and the minister made prompt delivery, riding swiftly along the countryside astride a horse borrowed from Deacon Fenno.

As letters were received without stamps, it was the postmaster's job to collect postage. By the end of August, receipts averaged two dollars monthly, but as autumn approached, Reverend Alger was pleased to note a slight increase in revenue. To help her husband, Olive sorted mail, preparing it for distribution. She kept records and handled whatever the townspeople brought to the house for posting.

Throughout spring and summer, the pastor pleaded for the bell he wanted installed in the empty cupola. Sunday after Sunday he announced names of those who contributed, often hinting that he soon intended to name, from the pulpit, those who apparently did not think enough of their church to give to the fund.

"The bell must toll on next Easter Sunday," he repeated at services and committee meetings. "The First Unitarian Church of Chelsea must have its bell. Upon this I insist."

Then he would read the list of latest contributions. His father-in-law, Deacon Fenno, was a top donor, giving ten dollars. Brother-in-law John Fenno, Jr., equalled this, and other Fennos added lesser sums. Five dollar subscriptions were received from members of the Shurtleff, Staniels, Ellis, Stowers, Cary, Pierce, Sigourney, Floyd, Cutter, Green, Payson, Hall, Williams and Parkman families, and smaller amounts were eventually submitted by virtually every member of the community.

Some months later he reported a collection of $319.91. A bronze bell of rich, resonant tone was duly selected and purchased and, at an impressive ceremony attended by dignitaries from Boston and other towns, it was unveiled and summoning parishioners to services well in advance of the deadline date.

Immensely impressed with Alger's ability to get things done, he was nominated and — in November — elected to the State Legislature as its youngest member. There appeared to be no limit to the amount of tasks the minister could accept and handle most creditably. No member of his congregation ever wanted for lack of his attention. He satisfactorily fulfilled all duties, and still set aside time to enjoy the company of his wife and son.

Little Horatio was a frail child, slow in developing and, from infancy, was a constant cause of anxiety. He slept fitfully, frequently remaining awake and crying through the night. He was often feverish and uncommonly susceptible to colds.

When Horatio was two years old — this was shortly after the birth of his sister, Olive Augusta, in November, 1833 — he developed an extreme shortness of breath. Through the long nights, his mother sat at the child's bedside as he lay awake, wheezing and gasping for air. Unable to sleep, Olive prayed, asking that her child live through the night. Downstairs, in the silence of his study, Reverend Alger also prayed that his son be spared the dreaded lung fever, prevalent throughout the area. He fretted helplessly, both for the boy and for his wife's endless worry.

Spring finally arrived, and their son still lived.

He breathed more easily, and was able to sleep for longer periods. But the winter's illness left him so weakened that he needed constant attention, and few were permitted near him. Dr. Benjamin Shurtleff, who examined Horatio, diagnosed a bronchial congestion, but advised consultation with another physician.

The next day Olive took Horatio to Boston, where it was determined that the child suffered from a severe asthmatic condition. No effective remedy could be prescribed.

"But what can we do?" Olive implored.

"Pray," the doctor advised.

"We've been doing that, endlessly," the gentle woman answered.

"Thus far, then," the doctor commented, "your medicine has been better than any I can offer. The boy is delicate, and we know of no cure for his illness. You are doing everything possible and we can only hope he will increase his strength sufficiently to carry him through next winter. I think that, in time, he will improve. Until then, Mrs. Alger, you must continue being nurse as well as mother."

In March, 1836, when Horatio was four years old, a second son, James, was born to the Algers. Horatio was undersized, and had only recently started to walk. He was still unable to talk. Except for the companionship of his little sister, Olive Augusta — who was called Gusti, the name Olive being reserved for her mother — Horatio had no playmates. At family gatherings he was kept apart from the other children, his mother fearing he might catch their sniffles and coughs.

During the summer, Deacon Fenno died. Horatio, who didn't attend the funeral, would long remember his mother's deep sorrow, her black dress, and how — upon her return — she went to her room and remained there, all through the hot, rainy day. He could hear her sobbing, and he cried, too, though he knew not why. He tried to understand when, on the following day, she explained that "Grandpa has left us, and has gone to a wonderful, happy home in Heaven where some day we all shall meet him again." But, somehow, Horatio wished that Grandfather Fenno could have remained in Chelsea.

The sounds Horatio could utter, by the time he was six, were understandable only to Mother and Gusti. In the presence of most visitors he was shy and sat in silence, wishing they would leave. Those who did not know the child assumed he was half his actual age, and a very undernourished specimen, at that.

The only caller he greeted with enthusiasm was Ann-Montague Cary, a close friend of the Fenno family since their arrival in Chelsea. In recent years she had become Olive's confidante and was a frequent guest in the Alger home. The pleasant maiden-lady was locally famous for her chewy molasses candies and she always brought these to Horatio. While Olive was busy with housework, or attending Gusti and James, Miss Cary delighted Horatio with tales of the far-off Indies, where she was born in Grenada, in 1787. There, where her family was active in shipping, she spent her childhood. Her tales of the tropical islands, blue lagoons and merry, dark-skinned children who played the day-long in never-ending sunshine filled the boy with wonder. Often, when he was alone, he imagined himself racing joyously through those lush green surroundings. And, in these reveries, the emaciated little Horatio ran faster and laughed louder than all the rest.

The devoted, patient Olive and her husband were determined that Horatio should gain normal health, and doctors assured the parents that, but for his mother's dedicated attention, the child would not have survived the early years.

"When it is time for the boy to talk," more than one physician explained, "he will talk. First he must get his strength. The rest will come in good time."

A year later Horatio was talking, but he stuttered badly and this added to his self-consciousness. More than ever, he avoided contact with other children, though — from a distance — he observed them at their carefree games and never ceased to wish he could join them. From the garden at the rear of the Alger house, he saw boys and girls across the fields, running and shouting to each other. Because he needed sunshine, he would sit there while his mother read to him, and taught him the spelling and arithmetic that other youngsters learned at school.

Although he did not attend classes, Horatio was quick to learn. He did not enjoy working with numbers, but words fascinated him. In his loneliness, he developed a vivid imagination and was happiest when — alone with Mother and Gusti — he joyfully told them — speaking rapidly, despite stammer and stutter — little tales he created. These were adventures of sturdy young lads who played in nearby orchards. They swam across the creek to Hog Island, and daringly leaped from barn roofs into the soft, fragrant hay-mow. Horatio particularly liked to finish the story with an angry farmer chasing the naughty boys, and this inevitable ending always left Gusti giggling and clapping her hands in glee.

"'Oh, Horatio, that was a wonderful story," she would shout, throwing her arms about her brother's neck. Her eyes sparkled and her hair, tied in a long pig-tail, swung wildly as she hugged Horatio and begged for "just one more story."

Horatio and Gusti were inseparable, despite the difference in their ages. They were almost the same size, but the little girl's adoration made her brother feel as tall as a giant. They both shared their mother's fair complexion, gray eyes and light brown hair. Like their father, they were thin-lipped, their noses longish and somewhat pointed.

On Horatio's eighth birthday, his father gave him a volume of the New Testament, complete with a pronouncing dictionary and an explanatory key.

"This fine book was translated from the Greek by The Rev. Israel Alger, a cousin of your grandfather," he told the boy. "I read it many times over, and believe it helped fit me for the life of a minister. Now the book is yours. Learn well from it as you, too, will some day be a minister."

At about this time, the pastor took over his son's education, tutoring him in French, Latin, Greek and the Bible. Horatio was proving to be a brilliant student, and within a number of months could easily sight-translate long passages, write and converse with his father in the three languages. As Reverend Alger did, years earlier, Horatio memorized and could quote parts of the Bible, chapter and verse. When not studying, he read histories and texts saved from the minister's days at Cambridge.

Reverend Alger, feeling that a future minister cannot start his training too soon, decided Horatio was now old enough to accompany him on visits to parishioners and on short trips connected with church business.

As the boy's health had improved, although he was still subject to asthmatic attacks, it was agreed that this would not be harmful, and Horatio was eager to go. In a small one-horse carriage the minister now owned, father and son travelled the district, Horatio sometimes holding the reins and imagining himself driving a chariot or stage. His day-dreams often ended abruptly when the minister cautioned "Hold 'er in, son. Hold 'er. That's a mite too fast."

When they visited the aging Mrs. Mary Pratt, she enthralled Horatio with her eyewitness account of the Battle of Bunker Hill, which she observed in June, 1775, from the Malden side of the Mystic River. With sparkling eyes, the tiny woman retold, for the thousandth time, how untrained American troops bravely stood their ground in the face of fierce British attack. Young Horatio was a good listener and hung on to every detail, even when the story varied slightly from her equally exciting version of the previous visit.

Horatio always carried with him a freshly baked pie when calling on Old Mrs. Cheever. Years earlier, she dwelt in the family's stately gambrel-roofed mansion behind great mulberry trees, amidst a well-kept garden and acres of cultivated fields. The family had run down, and her husband — the last of the name — died a drunken ne'er-do-well, leaving his widow penniless. She was a dainty, lovely gentlewoman, beloved by everyone, and too old to learn. For a while it was feared there was nothing for her but the poorhouse.

This, the people of the town could not think of, and they built for her a small, one-room cottage where neighbors kept her comfortable and happy. She was never thought of as a pauper or object of charity, but as a delightful friend for whom it was a pleasure to provide. Children, sent by their mothers, brought her warm bread, cakes, pies and doughnuts and invitations to attend their Thanksgiving and Christmas celebrations. She was, traditionally, the honored guest at all local galas and festivities.

*   *   *

With Reverend Alger as perennial moderator, there were frequent meetings to argue the Chelsea school situation. Existing facilities and length of the term were inadequate; locating suitable teachers was an unending problem. A schoolhouse built in Winnisimmet years earlier had fallen into disrepair, was too distant for many children and unable to accommodate the growing number of pupils.

For a time, it continued to be used as a grammar school, with the primary class occupying temporary quarters in a room of the Tewksbury home and later in the town hall. When the schoolmaster suddenly departed, towards the end of 1839, Reverend Alger filled the position until, in March, 1840, Miss Sarah C. Swain — who was barely older than some of the pupils — took over as the new teacher.

It was decided, at a public assembly held in March, 1839, to build a new school — modern in every way — in which each student could have a separate desk, primary and grammar schools would occupy rooms of their own, and to be as nearly fireproof as possible.

The committee was most pleased with plans suggested by the Hon. Horace Mann, secretary of the Boston Board of Education. Land was purchased and the two-story structure completed in time for classes to begin in April, 1840. Miss Swain was the teacher and Horatio easily passed requirements for the upper grades. The school was named in honor of Dr. Benjamin

Shurtleff, who raised and contributed most of the money needed for the project.

The confinement of the classroom — and whatever discipline the teacher could muster — notwithstanding, most pupils preferred education to their farm chores. Attendance records were generally good, even during harshest months of winter.

During recess, children raced about the school yard until the monitor's bell summoned them back to their studies. After school, boys trudged slowly homeward to duties that waited, often stopping to play in the orchards at Copeland's Corner or to 'hunt' Indians in the marshes. In snow or icy weather they slid down the steep hill from the knoll atop which the schoolhouse stood, landing in the snowbank below. Nearby, the girls whispered secrets, enjoyed less strenuous games, or enthusiastically described dresses they were making from newly-arrived patterns.

Gusti, who was still in primary school, played with her close friends, Henrietta Green, Maria Hall, Mary Hannah Staniels, Charlotte Pinkham, Abbie Pratt — her cousin, Margaret Norwood Bailey Fenno — and one or more of the pretty Tewksbury sisters.

For Horatio it was more difficult to make friends. He was the smallest boy in his class, and he was the brightest, which — at first — did not tend to make him more popular. He could not keep up with the youths in their sports, and when he tried he wound up breathless, coughing and frustrated with his own frailty.

Unlike classmates, he always wore Sunday clothes, which his father considered proper attire for a minister's son. For this he was teased and ridiculed, until he tearfully persuaded Mother that he must be allowed to dress like the others.

"I cannot go back to school, Mother," he cried. "They laugh at my clothes and call me 'Holy Horatio, the parson's son'. I want to be like other boys!"

Mother seemed to agree, but Reverend Alger, entering the house as the discussion took place, did not share this view.

"But Horatio," he said, "you *are* a parson's son. One day you, too, will be a minister, and you cannot start too early to fight for what you believe in. Remember that more than one of your reverend ancestors fought — and some died — for what was right. You must prepare yourself to do the same."

"It seems obvious to me," Olive said furiously to her husband, "that Horatio doesn't consider clothes he wears worth becoming a martyr over. And if fighting and martyrdom are all that life in the church will hold for my son, he'd be better off as a merchant — like *my* ancestors!"

The minister, bewildered by his wife's attitude, retreated to his study, and the next morning Horatio wore jacket and trousers of inelegant cut, but — Horatio believed — better suited for school. He had taken the first step, he was sure, toward becoming a 'reg'lar', and winning acceptance of his classmates.

Between sessions he joined a group of boys who were planning to meet later to play 'Captain Lightfoot' in a nearby pasture. Horatio was delighted when he was invited to join in the afternoon's fun and, during the remaining hours of class-work, he glowed with unfamiliar inner warmth as he looked forward to the game.

Captain Lightfoot — a local bandit whose exploits had, in recent years, taken on legendary luster — was among the last of the highwaymen in the vicinity. His real name was Michael Martin, an Irishman by birth, and made a regular profession of plundering travellers on the turnpike. Some years earlier he established a reputation for gallantry while robbing Major Bray of twelve dollars and a gold watch. Mrs. Bray was with her husband, but the outlaw refused to take her jewelled brooch, declaring that he "never stole from ladies."

Shortly thereafter, he was arrested for horse stealing — a crime punishable by death — and was soon identified as the robber. After trial and conviction, he was confined to a lower cell in the East Cambridge jail, where no light nor air entered, except through three apertures in the wall, each about four inches wide and twenty long. He was bound to a ringbolt in the center of the cell, his left leg and right hand fettered by chains. One morning — shortly before his scheduled execution — "Uncle Nat" Cooledge brought the prisoner's breakfast, placing it upon the table. Martin dropped a pouch of tobacco and, in a feeble voice, asked the jailer to pick it up for him, claiming he was too weak to move. As the turnkey stooped, Martin struck him a violent blow on the head with the heavy iron shackles from which he had managed to free himself. Cooledge remained insensible on the floor for some minutes, as the convict rushed from the prison. He leaped over the high wall, racing across a nearby barnyard as roosters crowed and frightened hens scattered in every direction.

The noise, and Uncle Nat's call for help, attracted the attention of workers in a nearby cornfield. They chased and eventually overpowered Martin, two or three of his pursuers getting knocked down and battered during the brief battle. He was then returned to custody handcuffed and fettered with larger, stronger chains. A few days later he was hanged and buried in the paupers' graveyard. Captain Lightfoot had been dead more than a dozen years, but — along the now-peaceful countryside — his exploits lived on, memory better recalling his gallantry to Mrs. Bray than his many crimes.

After school the game was organized, Horatio running along as best he could to keep up with Samuel Sturgis Pratt, Abel Wright, cousin Will Fenno, Christopher Columbus Grover, Joseph Ingraham Hastings, Joshua Drummond Talbot, George Wiggin and several others.

Horatio, the newcomer to the group, received the honor of playing Captain Lightfoot, and the others had to find and capture him. This didn't take long, and Horatio soon found himself apprehended and being roughly shoved along by Josh Talbot, who relished his reputation of being the bully of the village. Horatio, acquiescent and eager to play, went along with the laughing, gleeful crowd. But when Josh produced a rope and tied it around the little boy's neck, Horatio started to wonder if this really was a part of the game. He said nothing, but it was Christopher Grover — a year younger than Joshua, but large and broad for his age — who told the bully he was playing too rough.

"Let's have a little fun," Josh grinned. "Nobody's going to get hurt."

A few of his friends agreed it would be good sport, but most of the youngsters sided with Chris, while Horatio stood there, wondering whether he was the hero or the victim.

"It's alright," Horatio kept repeating. "It's only fun. Really, I don't mind.

But there were tears in his eyes as the bigger boy tightened the noose around his neck.

"It's getting late," Christopher said, "and we'd better be getting on before dark." Saying this, he pushed Talbot aside and removed the rope. The bully angered at this interference, and was about to lunge back when Zachariah Hall, on whose property they were playing, appeared over the crest of the hill. The farmer hooted at the boys to scat. His dog barked ferociously, starting toward them, and all ran for the road.

No harm was done, Horatio thought. He had at last joined the others at play and, on the long walk home, his companions agreed he did well. He was delighted with their friendship, and felt he now was one of the 'reg'lars'.

That evening Horatio told of the day's adventure.

The parson was disturbed, feeling the boy allowed himself to take part in undignified pastime. "This will never make you a better minister," he criticized. "You'd have been better off studying."

Olive was horrified, thinking only of the possible danger.

Gusti loved the story, especially the part where the farmer's dog chased the boys.

CHAPTER 6

THE PARSON'S DEBTS

HORATIO'S PRECARIOUS HEALTH made him only an occasional pupil at Shurtleff School. The dampness of spring brought on new asthmatic attacks, leaving him bed-ridden for days at a time. He had no problem keeping up with class-work but — upon returning to school — was not permitted to take part in strenuous outdoor activities. It was during these periods that he sat wistfully on the sidelines, watching others running past and daydreaming great events of which he was the hero.

But when the day was clear and the air fresh and warm, the minister's son followed the boys on expeditions through the woods, or with them, sat on empty nail kegs watching sparks fly as Silas Clapp, the blacksmith, hammered red-glowing metal into horseshoes and buggy parts.

It was, strangely enough, on expeditions in search of Indian relics that Horatio became a leader. Between Sagamore Hill and the old burial ground he had, during a previous lonely wandering, discovered an ancient Indian dwelling place or fort. To it he gladly led his friends, suggesting to them the most likely spots to unearth Indian shells, arrow-heads, fishhooks and other implements that pre-dated the earliest settlers.

Many of the boys found wampum, some lucky ones digging

up tomahawks and other weapons. One day in June, Horatio found a ceremonial pipe which, having centuries earlier been carefully wrapped in deerskin, was remarkably well preserved.

Joshua Talbot was determined to own it and tried to persuade Horatio to give it to him. He refused and, when the bigger boy attempted to take it, Horatio fought back, receiving a bloody nose for his struggle. Christopher Grover immediately leaped to his aid, dumping Joshua on the ground and handing back to the pummelled Horatio the treasure he had found. The bully glowered at Horatio and shook his fist at him, but made no further effort to take the pipe.

Later in the afternoon the boys came upon a pile of bones that included some nearly complete skeletons, and a number of them proudly carried off sinister-appearing Indian skulls.

Journeying homeward, Horatio gave his relic to Christopher, who wasn't certain he should accept the gift.

"Why don't you keep it, Horatio?" he asked. "It's a wonderful pipe."

"I'd rather you have it, Christopher," he answered. "My father probably would fear I was smoking it if he found it about me."

Being the first scholar in his class, Horatio gladly helped others with their homework. He excelled in every subject and could explain a lesson with great clarity. His willingness and ability to show the way to others eventually won for him a number of admirers, as well as the spelling prize at the examination held just before summer vacation.

With members of the school committee and many parents present, Horatio correctly spelled every word in the test. He became nervous and stuttered badly, causing considerable laughter among the children and some visitors. But when the contest ended, Horatio Alger, Jr., was announced as the winner, and he proudly carried home the prize, a small, slender book whose title was "True Heroes."

Reverend Alger had become increasingly disturbed by news, from Bridgewater, of his aging father's illness. James, already well over seventy, developed what doctors called "an organic affection of the back." The old man — once so powerful — could no longer stand erect and had become unable to manage his farm. The minister urged his parents to sell their property and to make their home with him in Chelsea. He had recently bought several acres of fields and was interested in some additional plots. He explained to his father that he needed his advice and help in farming the land, and upon this premise James and Hannah decided to come, arriving early in August.

With a yoke of oxen and an occasional helper, the parson tilled the land, managing to eke out sufficient produce to feed his family. He labored long hours, but weariness was never apparent.

After months of toil and hope, the soil gave a fair quantity of corn, beans, squash, pumpkins and other vegetables; trees were heavy with apples and pears, and a variety of large and luscious berries grew in profusion around the edges of the fields. With Hannah's help, Olive preserved much of this for the months ahead. Whatever surplus could be gathered was bartered — either at John Wright's Grocery or Fenno's Corner Store — for other household needs. And, as he believed proper, Reverend Alger carried a portion of his harvest to the almshouse and also gave quantities to needy parishioners.

Greatly distressed because her work in the kitchen was unfinished, Olive — upon everyone's insistence — retired to her bed about noon, on October 24th, and before sunset gave birth to another daughter, her fourth child. To honor her devoted companion, who had — in fact — aided in the delivery, the infant was named Ann-Montague Cary Alger, and the spinster's joy was as complete as if the child was her own.

A little less than two years later, the fifth and last of the Alger children was born on a hot morning in August, 1842. The third son was named Francis after the minister's cousin, who already was a noted industrialist and explorer, a prolific writer on mineralogy and a director of his father's South Boston Iron Company.

The passing months brought with them hard times for the

Alger household. The parson's debts increased as his family grew, and he could not manage on his income. The elder James was now a bedridden invalid in constant need of medical care, and Hannah became increasingly feeble. Her memory was failing and when she wandered from the house she was frequently unable to find her way back.

Gusti became her mother's assistant in the kitchen and, unable to continue even part-time services of a hired man, Horatio helped his father with the planting. For a while it appeared the coming harvest might, by cutting down on family needs, enable him to pay off part of his indebtedness. But one morning, when Horatio and the parson reached their fields, they found locusts — by the millions — pouring out of the earth. By noon the countryside was black with shrilly-chirping, ravaging insects and all attempts by farmers to disperse them by banging tin pans and beating the bushes were unsuccessful. On the third day, the invaders — as if by a signal — arose with a mighty flutter. For moments they hovered in the sky over Chelsea like a great dark storm cloud, and then they were gone.

But with them went the crops and hopes of many despairing farmers. It was a disaster from which the entire region would not soon recover.

There was even more bad news in store with the unexpected notification that, upon expiration of his current term as postmaster, the appointment would not be renewed. Shortly thereafter, he was succeeded in office by Abel Bowen, who operated a new post office in the Winnisimmet district.

Olive shared the minister's low spirits as they sat at the kitchen table, one evening, reviewing their financial situation.

"I've fallen behind considerably in payments on the land," he said. "Taxes are in arrears, and we are in debt to a number of tradesmen." Summing up his problems, Reverend Alger added, "The house needs paint and repairs, and the roof leaks. I wish I could see a way out of this tangle."

"Perhaps," his wife suggested, "the church committee would recommend an increase in your salary."

"I've already asked for it but was told it's impossible. I'm afraid our parishioners are not rich, for the most part, and I was advised it wouldn't be wise to push the point just now. As it is, the treasurer owes me over a hundred dollars, but he is still unable to collect it to pay me."

The next morning, Adam Bennett, the butcher, called and urgently requested payment of his bill. It amounted to only twenty five dollars, but the minister's stock of ready cash was reduced to five. To give this on account would have left him penniless.

"I don't think people ought to buy meat if they can't afford it," said the butcher, bluntly.

"The parish is owing me more than the amount of your bill, Mr. Bennett," said the perplexed minister. "Just as soon as I can collect the money. . ."

"I need it now," said the butcher, coarsely. "I have bills to pay, too, and I can't unless my customers pay me."

"I wish I could pay you at once," said Reverend Alger. "Would you take an order on the parish treasurer?"

"No. He's so slack it wouldn't do me any good. Can't you pay me half right now?"

"I've got only five dollars on hand, Mr. Bennett. I can't give it all to you, but I'll divide it with you."

The butcher grumbled, but took the small amount offered.

"These things try me a good deal," the minister told Olive, with a sigh, after the departure of his creditor. "Do you think we could economize any more than we do?"

"I don't see how. I've lain awake nights thinking if it would be possible. It just isn't. We couldn't pinch our table any more without risking health."

"I'm sure you're right."

"Why not call on Mr. Ferry, the treasurer, and see if he doesn't have some money for you?"

"Yes, I'll try that, but it probably will be of little use."

The minister was right. The treasurer handed him two dollars.

"It's all I've been able to collect," he said. "Money is tight, Mr. Alger, and everybody puts off paying."

"Still," the minister emphasized. "Something will have to be done. I have considerable debts to settle."

"Well," the treasurer pondered, "the annual church donation party isn't due for three months. Perhaps I can persuade the committee to hold it within the next few weeks."

Olive was indignant when her husband reported to her the results of the meeting.

"How do they expect us to live?" she demanded, angrily.

"They think we should manage, somehow. Besides, Mr. Ferry feels the donation party will help."

"I suppose it will amount to about as much as the others did. People will bring provisions, most of which they eat themselves. When it's over we'll be richer by a dozen pin-cushions, half-a-dozen pies, a bushel of potatoes and a few knick-knacks for which we have no earthly use."

"I'm afraid, Olive, you're getting cynical."

"But you know it's true. The worst of it is that we are expected to be grateful for what is only an additional burden."

Adding to the humiliation of the Alger family was the amount of comment and gossip that the minister's distress provided for the town's idlers.

"What's this?" asked the inquisitive Polly Grove greeting Jacob Worth as he unloaded parcels from the baggage compartment of the stage.

"For the parson," he answered. " 'Pears to be a book from Boston."

"Him with a houseful of books! Land sakes, he must be crazy. Nobody but a minister would want so many books as that. And it's a clear waste for him to be spending money so. If he didn't waste on books, his wife could dress a little more decent. Why, the man's got at least a hundred books already, and yet he needs another."

"I guess his wife don't complain, Polly," the stage driver answered, "and it's no affair of mine."

"Nevertheless," she continued, "I'm sick of that old bombazine she's worn to church the last three years. A stranger might think we stinted the minister."

"Precisely, Mrs. Grove," said a voice behind her. "That's exactly my opinion."

"Oh, Dr. Shurtleff, is that you?" said the old lady, turning.

"What's left of me. I've been making calls all afternoon and

I'm about used up. So you think we're stinting our minister?"

"No, I don't," she said emphatically. "I think we pay him handsome. Five hundred dollars a year is more'n some of us get. That, and a donation party, too!"

"Deliver me from the donation party," said the doctor, hastily. "I look upon that as just another of the poor man's trials. I'm glad it isn't the fashion to help doctors that way."

"The doctor's got queer notions," Mrs. Grove muttered as he walked away. "If folks all talked that way, mebbe the minister will get discontented. But as I say to Rachel Gardner, there's more to be had, and more attractive ones, too. I sometimes think The Rev. Mr. Alger's outlived his usefulness here. A new man might kinder stir up the people, and make 'em feel more convicted of sin."

Olive Alger was the topic of conversation at a ladies' committee meeting to plan the donation party.

"Mrs. Alger is looking pale and careworn," said Hattie Kent to Almira Hadley. "Don't you think so?"

"She hasn't much energy about her," replied Squire Simon Hadley's wife. "If she had, the minister would get along better."

"I think she's no sort of manager," said Mrs. Bennet. "She runs her husband into debt by her shiftless ways."

"I think you're mistaken," said Huldah Pratt, quietly. "I know her well and I consider her an admirable manager. She makes a little go as far as she can; as far as any one of us could."

"I only know my husband can't get his bill paid," the butcher's wife went on. "He went to the house to get twenty five dollars they owe, and only got two dollars and a half. Seems to me there must be poor management somewhere."

"The trouble is," Mrs. Pratt said. "That Mr. Alger's salary is too small. How do you expect him to support his family on such an amount as that?"

Returning home that evening, Mrs. Hadley reported the conversation to her husband. Squire Simon Hadley, who owned considerable land in the town, held mortgages and notes on Reverend Alger's property. He was well aware that installments were long overdue, but he was not a mean person and refused to press the minister for payments. His wife, who was known for her parsimony, strongly objected to her husband's "pampering the min-

71

ister." She bitterly recalled the days — twenty years earlier — when Olive's family was the wealthiest in town. Her own family, until she wed Squire Hadley, had comparatively little and she long envied the Fennos' position and abundance. She deeply relished the present turnabout in their circumstances, and allowed no opportunity to pass but that she brought this to Olive's attention.

"Mrs. Pratt asked how we could expect them to live on five hundred dollars a year," she said, "but Mrs. Bennett claims it's just poor management on Olive Alger's part, and I'm inclined to believe it."

"I passed their house recently," the squire recalled, "and noted that it is in need of repairs."

"It's good enough for the Algers," she answered. "Ministers shouldn't be too particular about their earthly dwellings. I believe in ministers being unworldly, for my part."

"But it does look rather bad, and I understand the roof leaks."

"A few drops won't hurt the furniture she's got," said Mrs. Hadley, contemptuously.

"Nevertheless, a coat of paint would do the house considerable good."

"It will do no good," she said, positively. "It won't make the house any warmer, and will only conduce to the vanity of the minister and his wife."

"I really never thought either of them vain," her husband answered.

"You only look to the surface," his wife said in a tone of calm superiority. "I go deeper. You think, because Mrs. Alger can't afford to dress well, that she has no vanity? I read her better. If she had the means she'd cut a dash. You may depend upon it."

"There's one thing I can't understand, Almira," said her husband. "Why are things worldly in them that are not in us?"

"Because you are not a minister, nor I a minister's wife. They should set their hearts on things above."

"Shouldn't we?"

"Not in the same way. They should be humble and not self-seeking. They must set a good example to the parish. Does Mr.

Alger pay off his debt to you regular?" she asked, suddenly changing the subject.

"Tolerable."

"You mean he is in arrears!"

"I can't tell exactly without looking at the books," said the squire, evasively.

"I understand. You don't want to tell me. I dare say he must be owing half a year's payments plus interest. I think it shameful for a minister not to pay his debts," said Mrs. Hadley in acid tones.

"Suppose we had five children and all our clothing and household expenses to be paid out of five hundred a year. The parson lost his postmaster's income, and his job in the Legislature barely covers the expenses it involves. A minister can't make a dollar go farther than other people."

"He can give up luxuries and vanities."

"Our pastor indulges in very few of those," he answered, shrugging his shoulders.

"I don't know about that. I saw Olive Alger in the store the other day buying granulated sugar, when brown sugar is cheaper and does equally well."

"I believe we use granulated sugar, Almira," said Squire Hadley, his eyes twinkling.

"You are not a minister."

"And I shouldn't want to be if the sinners are to get all the good things in life, and the saints have to take the poorest."

"Call yourself a sinner if you like, but don't call me one, Mr. Hadley," said his wife with some asperity.

"Ain't you a sinner?"

"We are all sinners, if it comes to that, but I consider myself as good as most people. How much did you say Reverend Alger is owing you?"

"I didn't say," the squire answered.

"Keep it a secret if you please. All I say is that it's a duty you owe your own family to collect what is honestly due you. I'd certainly collect it, if I were a man."

"Yes, Almira," he agreed with a sigh. "I'm certain you would. However, to please you, I'll attend to it shortly."

Since the donation party had been decided upon, it was a

prominent subject for discussion around the town. Though designed to provide substantial assistance to the pastor's family, it also was considered a festive occasion — a sort of ministerial party — and thus was regarded by all as a social event.

At four o'clock on the afternoon of the party, guests began to arrive. The house had been arranged for the gathering, and The Rev. and Mrs. Alger awaited their visitors.

"Is it necessary for me to be here?" asked Horatio.

"It would hardly look well for you to be away, my son."

"I'll stay if you wish, father, but it humiliates me. It looks as if we were receiving charity."

"I confess I get the same impression," the minister answered. "But it may be a feeling of worldly pride. We must try to look upon it differently."

"Why can't they give you the value of their presents in money, or by adding it to your salary?" Horatio suggested.

"They would not be willing. We must accept what they choose to give, and in the form in which they choose to give it."

The first to arrive was Mrs. Ada Pulsifer, who gave the minister a hideous pin-cushion.

"I made it with my own hands," she said complacently. "As the apostle says, 'Silver and gold have I none, but such as I have give I unto thee'."

"Thank you, Mrs. Pulsifer," said the minister, trying to look pleased, but failing.

The next to arrive was Lavisa Slocum, carrying in a basket a couple of dyspeptic-looking pies and a loaf of bread.

"I thought you might need 'em for the company," the deaf woman shouted at Mrs. Alger.

"You are very kind, Mrs. Slocum," the hostess replied. She was quite resigned to the immediate use of the gift.

Next came Margaret Breck, with her family. She, too, contributed some pies and a cake, but of better quality than her predecessor. Close behind her followed Clarissa Bass, the primary school teacher, bearing aloft a gorgeous pin-cushion, which she presented with a flourish.

"It'll do for your best room, Mrs. Alger," she said. "Oh, I see you've got one already," eyeing Mrs. Pulsifer's offering disdainfully.

74

"And I expect several more," said Olive, smiling faintly. "We are generally well remembered with pin-cushions."

The next two guests donated a bottle of cheap cologne and a small edition of English poems, in such fine print as to make perilous reading for a person of any except strongest eyesight.

A dozen arrivals that followed were laden with provisions. The ladies' committee took charge of these, and spread a large table, on which all foodstuffs were placed.

While this was going on, Almira Hadley arrived with a dress pattern for Olive. It was cheap calico of large, garish design, and very repugnant to the taste of the minister's wife. Olive's heart sank within her as she accepted it. The squire's wife got it at a bargain at the village store, where it had lain unsold on the shelves for several seasons.

"Dress goods are always acceptable," she said with the air of one conferring a great favor. "I'm sure you'll look lovely in it."

And Olive was obliged to thank her benefactor.

"Brother Alger," said The Rev. Mr. William Langworthy, minister of the Evangelical Congregational Church, in a cheery voice, "I hope I do not intrude. The fact is, I couldn't keep away. Please accept a small gift from your Congregational Brother," and he placed in the pastor's hand a five dollar bill.

"Thank you, Brother Langworthy," said Reverend Alger, grasping his hand cordially and adding, in a lowered voice, "I see you understand what I need most."

"I ought to," the visitor replied with a knowing smile. Deacon Uriah Prouty entered next.

"I've brought you a bushel of apples, parson," he said. "My boy'll carry them around the kitchen. This is a joyful day for you. Your house overflows with the bounties of Providence."

Reverend Alger knew better, correctly assuming food brought in would be eaten before the company departed. But he didn't say this, as it would have seriously offended his callers, who felt the minister's family could not be grateful enough for their gifts.

Hattie Kent, arriving with her young daughter, handed the minister an envelope containing ten dollars.

"Properly," she explained, "it isn't a gift at all, but a small part of what we owe you."

The next gift — and equally acceptable — was two dollars given by Miss Hannah Haven, the new teacher who took over the grammar school when Sarah Swain left to get married. "I wish it could be more," she apologized.

The minister brightened up, not only because the cash was so badly needed, but because the donors' words indicated appreciation, and a proper estimate of the donation party. They helped him to bear the patronizing manner of Mrs. Bennett, the butcher's wife, who handed Mrs. Alger a small bag of sausages.

"Times is hard, I know," she said. "Why, my husband has so many bad bills, and so much trouble collectin' money. . ."

The parson was painfully aware that he was one of the debtors who found it hard to pay his bills, and he knew that Mrs. Bennett's speech was meant as a hint.

Supper was by this time ready, and the ladies and gentlemen eagerly filed out to the tables. It was, doubtless, the consciousness that they were engaged in philanthropic action that increased their appetites. At any rate, there was very little left when dinner was over. All present seemed in excellent spirits, and congratulations poured in upon the minister and his wife who, it apparently was thought, were in great luck.

"Guess this'll put you well on your feet, parson," said Deacon Prouty, a little huskily, for he had stuffed half of a large doughnut into his mouth. "The people have come for'ard very liberal today."

"Yes," agreed the minister, unenthusiastically.

"Reminds me of the land flowin' with milk an' honey," resumed the deacon.

"So he thinks," thought Reverend Alger. On ordinary days there was small appearance of plenty on his frugal board and, as guests ate everything they brought, there seemed no chance of immediate improvement.

Eighteen forty three ended and 1844 began with no relief in sight from the minister's unbearable and increasing indebtedness. Reverend Alger, though not yet forty years old, appeared aged beyond his years, and his wife's face was lined with care.

With Horatio again suffering severe bronchial attacks, which recurred frequently throughout that winter, Olive rarely left his bedside, except to tend the constant needs of her father-in-law, James, who clung tentatively to the thread of life.

Dr. Shurtleff was a frequent caller at the Alger home, but refused to accept payment. When Olive asked the kind physician how much was owed, he invariably replied, in an inconsequential manner, that he hadn't time to figure his fees.

Although a number of creditors considerately avoided insisting upon payments, others harrassed constantly, some of them resorting to legal action. Toward the end of March, the pastor requested a meeting of the church committee, for the purpose of discussing his distressing financial situation.

"This meeting shall be brief, gentlemen," he started. "The parish owes me well over a hundred dollars, and refuses to increase my annual salary although that increase is long past due. At the same time I'm pressed for payment of debts. I ask that you instruct the treasurer to immediately pay me in full, and to raise my income, starting April first, to $750.00 annually."

After discussing the matter among themselves, they advised the pastor that, while the sum they owe was being liquidated as rapidly as possible, increased salary was out of the question.

"In that case," Reverend Alger said slowly, taking an envelope from his pocket, "I must regrettably hand you my resignation. I have received a call to the West Parish Church of Marlborough, and I mean to accept it."

During weeks that followed, the bankrupt parson's land was assigned to various creditors. The minister and his wife watched as the little brown cottage, which had been their home for thirteen years — and in which their five children were born — was sold at auction. After paying off every dollar he owed, little cash remained.

"But it will be enough to get us started in our new parish," Olive said, making a great effort to appear cheerful.

"The good Lord will provide," Reverend Alger said philosophically, as the family left Chelsea forever, "and I feel all is for the best."

CHAPTER 7

A NEW HOME
IN MARLBOROUGH

A YEAR PASSED and it was a good one for the Alger family, marred only by the death of Grandfather James and — several weeks later — of his beloved Hannah.

The minister took over the reins of the Marlborough Unitarian Church with renewed vigor. He was satisfied with the salary arrangement — $750.00 annually plus twenty cords of wood (enough to supply household needs for a year) delivered to his door — and parishioners were pleased with a leader who, from the start, appealed to them as "a doer; not a talker."

"I suppose we made the right decision," Mrs. Corrina Morse said one day to Levi Bigelow. "He seems a good preacher, alright, but he just ain't quite as tall as I wish he was."

"Well," answered Mr. Bigelow, the master of Robin Hill District School, "If that's his only *shortcoming*, I'd judge his settlement with us will be successful."

Free at last from the hardships of his last years at Chelsea, Reverend Alger also was relieved by the change in Olive. Cheerfully, she busied herself organizing their new home, looking after the children, and fulfilling the endless duties of a parson's wife.

The inland climate apparently had good affect on Horatio. His attacks of bronchial asthma were much less frequent. Although still undersized, he started gaining weight and was able to attend school regularly.

Upon arriving in town, the Algers for a short time lived in rented quarters, but soon moved into a lovely white clapboard-sheathed frame house. It was two stories high, set back a distance off the Boston Post Road, and occupied an acre of land within walking distance of Reverend Alger's church.

It was bigger and more comfortable than the cottage at Chelsea, containing nine rooms, a large attic, and low-roofed cellar ideal for keeping foodstuffs fresh. Outside was the stable and privy.

The kitchen also served as dining and living room. During the winter it was warm and comfortable, with its large fireplace, brick hearth and the aroma of good things cooking. In the corner stood a heavy loom which Olive learned to operate, and she, in turn, taught Gusti and Annie to spin cloth for clothing, bed quilts and blankets. The parlor was used only on special occasions, and the parson turned the downstairs bedroom into a study.

In the garden were trees that, in their season, became laden with great English cherries. Some branches extended almost to upstairs windows and Olive always feared the children would fall, reaching for fruit. Shrubbery and flowers lined both sides of the walk, and in the spring, — assisted by James, Annie and Francis — Olive planted daffodils, jonquils, sweet William and other varieties. An old fashioned white rose bush spread between the parlor windows, and cinnamon roses could be seen behind the shed. At the rear of the house grew apple trees, a pear tree and a patch in which flourished red, white and black currants, rhubarb, asparagus, quince and grape vines. The soil of Marlborough was fertile, and there always was abundance from the earth.

Nearby were dwellings of the Sylvester Bucklin, Martin Stowe, Joseph Draper and Richard Farwell families. Opposite, across the meadow, lived James Woods, who operated a malt house. To it, residents of all parts of the community brought their hams to be smoked. On the outskirts of town was Daniel Brigham's tannery, and on the main street — along the Common — was located Samuel Chipman's cabinet maker's shop, Woodward's provision store in which his wife ran a bakery, Dr. Hild-

79

reth's and Squire Draper's offices, and Capt. Asa Thayer's brick hotel.

On the opposite side of the road, slightly to the south, stood a number of residences and barns, and beyond these was Gates Academy, where Horatio went to school.

A few days after the family moved to Marlborough, a small notice in the local newspaper advised that "young people seeking admission should present themselves at Town Hall for examination. They should bring with them pencils, slates, a reader and Colburn's Mental Arithmetic."

The schoolhouse was a square one-room building whose walls the storms since 1827 had beaten without producing any decided effect. Through panes encrusted with accumulated dirt, the light filtered in upon a scene presided over by Obadiah Wheelock Albee, the principal. Tall, slender and slightly bent, Albee had directed the institution since 1832, the year he graduated from Brown University.

He was unmarried when he came to Marlborough, and boarded at a large house where some pupils also were accommodated. A year later the teacher wed the proprietor's niece, after which they occupied their own home.

Gates Academy was intended for the relatively few in the region who wished to continue their education, for a small fee, beyond grammar school. Most of the students came from surrounding farms, many travelling considerable distances to attend classes. During severe winter months, however, a number of them boarded with families near the school.

The Academy received its name from Silas Gates, former owner of the Williams Tavern, who contributed most of the money for the building. His ancient inn — which had been raided by Indians in 1676, and whose guests included Washington, Franklin, Lafayette, Jeffrey Amherst and other prominent travellers — was a well-known stage stopover on the route from Boston to New York.

Entering the Academy for the first time, Horatio compared it to the new Shurtleff School he recently attended in Chelsea, and was not favorably impressed.

It was characterized by extreme and severe simplicity. There was a noticeable need for paint, and no decorations were apparent. In the classroom, there were no pictures on the walls but, instead, a formidable expanse of blackboard. In front of the teacher's high stool and desk stood a venerable box stove with a rusty funnel reaching to the ceiling like a Doric column. Three long tables — their tops carved by the jack-knives of successive occupants — were arranged in U-shape around it, and behind these sat the students.

Accustomed to the strict discipline and enforced silence of Shurtleff School, Horatio was awed by the great latitude Mr. Albee allowed. There were no rules against whispering. Boys and girls could leave their seats without permission, and could study together with their neighbors if they preferred. The school-master respected and made large allowance for individual tastes and opinions. He took it for granted that his pupils came to learn, and did not require constant watching.

In 1845, Marlborough was largely agricultural — and oxen still outnumbered horses three-to-one — but with industries starting to make their importance felt in the area. In and about the town were shoe factories, a hat manufacturer and a plant producing organs, melodeons and similar musical instruments. The population was increasing steadily, many newcomers being Irish and French-Canadian immigrants who came seeking employment in the factories. Those who could not find jobs generally moved on, towards Worcester and beyond, where paper mills, cotton and woolen mills were developing. The ever-expanding railroads always needed laborers, and some women took work as domestic servants.

Among farmers money was scarce, and the little that came in was put aside for taxes. All food and most necessities were raised on their land. Sheep were sheared and the wool washed, carded, woven and made into clothing right in the home. Hides were taken to the tannery, where the tanner was paid with a share of the leather. Logs were brought to the sawyer and a portion of the lumber left for his services. Grain was ground by the miller, who took his fee in meal. Every farm had its own cider press. A few surplus products were traded at the general store for other needed items. Many farm implements and pieces of furniture were home made, the menfolk being proficient at a number of skills.

Women were busy the day-long making butter, cheese, soap, candles, gathering herbs, drying fruit and vegetables, nursing and raising children in addition to usual household duties. They helped the aged and the sick — tuberculosis and typhoid fever were prevalent — and cared for neighbors at childbirth. In their free time they knitted, made rag carpets and stitched samplers with their daughters.

As the churchman of the community was among its most learned citizens, entitled to added respect by virtue of wisdom, Reverend Alger was highly and affectionately esteemed. He became a minor shareholder in Gates Academy, an officer of Marlborough Savings Bank and a member of the three-man school committee.

The selectmen allowed these committeemen a stipend for their periodical visits to the ten schools in the area, some of them a considerable distance from the town. Based upon mileage covered, the minister's income averaged between thirty and fifty dollars a year, considerably more than sums given to David B. Goodale or L. E. Wakefield, his fellow superintendents. Although townspeople often cited this as an indication of the reverend's dedication, cynics pointed out that clergymen were always poor, and this probably was Mr. Alger's way of earning extra cash.

One of the committee tasks was to interview prospective teachers, and issue certificates to those found acceptable. Women were hired for summer sessions, and men for the winter. Summer classes were filled mainly with younger children, their older brothers and sisters being needed to help with the farm work. But during winter, schoolrooms were crowded and a master's discipline often needed.

The male instructors frequently were university students. As a large number of them paid their own tuition, most colleges allowed a three-month recess to give them opportunity to take teaching positions in rural areas. Women who taught on a permanent year-around basis often were aging spinsters; conscientious but poorly educated, neither overly loved nor appreciated by their scholars. Summer temporaries generally were recent graduates of a nearby district school, sometimes younger than a number of their pupils.

Classes around Marlborough were held in typical rural red-painted schoolhouses, with a dusty yard up front and, in the rear, an outhouse for boys and one for girls.

Year-end examinations, held in May, were festive occasions attended by parents and friends. The three superintendents were guests of honor, and they conducted oral testing in a number of subjects. As the event must never be marred by a failure that would embarrass a young scholar, those who faltered were subtly helped out of their dilemma by a committeeman.

After the exercises one of them spoke, generally dispensing complimentary remarks about the teacher, and reminding students of the advantages of the education they were receiving.

Occasionally Horatio accompanied his father on the examining circuit, the parson convinced this was an essential part of the boy's training for the ministry, and for the day he would be on a school committee. When Reverend Alger addressed an assembly, he frequently made reference to "my own son who, like yourselves, attends one of Marlborough's fine institutions of learning."

Horatio, who sat priggishly behind his father on the platform — a defenseless target for the class spitball marksman — squirmed miserably as all eyes turned toward him. He wished he could disappear or run from the room. Once he became so nauseous that he swallowed hard to keep from vomiting before the parson ended his lengthy speech.

The program ended with presentation of merit awards to virtually everyone in the class. Those who could not get them for excellent grades received the small cards for good conduct, effort or cleaning blackboards. No one was disappointed, parents were proud and all present — especially committeemen — had by this time worked up an enormous appetite for picnic lunch in a meadow across the road.

CHAPTER 8

IN SUMMERTIME

ON THE OUTSKIRTS OF MARLBOROUGH, flowing in a southerly direction through blue fields of slender flax, winds a narrow, slow-moving river known as the Assabet. Here, in the shade of overhanging boughs of willow and birch trees, Horatio's classmates whiled away shimmery summer mornings, fishing for yellow perch and long pickerel that lay motionless among weeds and rocks at the bottom of shallow pools along the shore.

During the first days of vacation, local ponds and streams were an irresistible lure to boys exhilarating in new-found freedom from studies and class routine. They awakened earlier than usual to finish morning chores and then, barefoot, hurried to favorite secret spots where fish were bigger and hungrier, and particularly fond of fat night-crawlers the young fishermen threaded over their hooks.

Horatio occasionally joined his friends. He tagged along after them to the stream, to Gates Pond, on exploring trips to the top of Shoestring Hill and through the woods around Spoon Hill.

Although the pastor's son accompanied the other boys, he rarely joined in their fun. He was only a fair fisherman, his catch generally being smaller than his comrades'. Once, discretion abandoned, he left his clothes on a mossy bank and dove, naked, into the lake. He couldn't swim and, although the water reached only to other boys' shoulders, it was well over Horatio's head. They pulled him out, coughing and choking, and he never tried it again. One day, delighted with his friend, Edward Bigelow's invitation to build a raft and navigate it across Bartlett Pond, Horatio waded, caught a chill and spent the rest of the week in bed. So, for the most part, Horatio sat in the background, watching more robust lads doing things he could not. He yearned to, like them, have a strong, sun-tanned body that glistened in bright sunshine as they splashed in the creek. He wanted to climb to the highest branches of ancient, spreading oaks and to once win the race up Slygo Hill, where low-bush blueberries grew large as grapes, and children collected them in buckets.

The Fourth of July was a day of sheer joy, starting with muster of the Marlborough Rifle Company on Union Common. Traditionally, parents gave boys and girls a penny to spend as they pleased and, at Jacob Fairbanks' store, this was generally invested in licorice, spicy barley candy or red and white peppermint sticks.

The militiamen, resplendent in dark gray uniforms decorated with shining brass buttons and black piping, marched in formation to the Spring Hill meeting house, then to the church, preparing for the parade.

This event always attracted the town eccentric, a woman known as Mrs. Crazy Crane. She followed closely behind the troops as they drilled, keeping perfect time and when the band played, she danced ecstatically before assembled onlookers. She wore a pink cambric dress with matching stockings, high-heeled slippers, and colored steamers flying from her hair, wrists and ankles.

She was harmless and nobody ever tried to stop her, but treated her with respect. While she danced she often sang and, smiling with pleasure, bowed low to the crowd's applause when the music stopped. Almost everyone knew that she lost her reasoning, years earlier, as a result of cruel treatment by her husband, Jabez Crane, and his sisters. After the procession, she quietly departed and was rarely seen in town until the next patriotic celebration.

At mid-day there were family outings around the lake, followed in the evening by oratory. One year Daniel Webster was the speaker, attracting crowds from as far off as Boston and Worcester. Then there was a concert on the Common, and a fireworks display that started as soon as it was dark enough. Before it ended — in a spectacle of dazzling skyrockets, American flags and eagles — many children had fallen asleep in their wagons and father, driving home through the darkness, drowsily complained that he'll never be up in time for milking.

✳ ✳ ✳

Williams Tavern, which had lately come to be called Gates House, was the most exciting place in town when the daily stage was due. Children played nearby, listening and then shouting with delight at the sound of the coachman's distant horn. Minutes later it arrived and all became hurry and bustle.

Word was passed in to the kitchen as to how many would be seated for dinner, the mail pouch was dropped and passengers alighted, stretching and stomping the dust from their clothes. They glanced about and then entered the inn, looking very serious and important to the boys and girls who watched them in awe. While they ate and rested, fresh horses were harnessed and an occasional piece of cargo loaded or unloaded. The travellers soon returned to their places in the coach, and the driver mounted his box. Then, at the crack of a whip, they quickly resumed the journey toward the world of mystery and adventure that lay beyond the hazy green ridge of Maynard's Hill.

With their friends, the Brighams — who were related to Mrs. Elizabeth Gates — James, Annie and Francis Alger were sometimes permitted to wander through the wondrous house with indoor wash rooms, many chambers, and a huge loft where hired help slept. Outside were dairy rooms, barns and an old buckboard which the youngsters took turns driving to imaginary far-off lands.

Throughout the day, teamsters halted heavily loaded drays

at the inn. They were jovially greeted by their host, Silas Gates, Jr., who particularly enjoyed preparing special hearty meals for these robust men.

Sometimes they let boys carry to their teams pails of water from the well, and hitch canvas feed-bags over the heads of the huge horses.

On Sunday afternoons the road in front of the tavern was jammed with chaises of young gentlemen — from Northborough, Southborough, Eastborough, Framingham and other adjoining villages — who took their sweethearts riding in the country. Here they paused for refreshment and discreet wooing before turning about and leisurely heading homeward at sundown.

Something always seemed to be happening at the Gates House. There always was so much to see.

Like many of her friends, Gusti put vacation time to profitable use braiding straw and selling it to local merchants. With girls who lived nearby — Augusta Brigham, Elizabeth Boyd and the Proctor twins, Harriette and Eveline — she set out to find the best fields of rye. Pooling their funds, they would buy as much as they could carry, the farmer cutting and binding the bundles.

Mrs. Brigham helped cure the straw, spreading it to dry in the warm sun, then bleaching it over a large barrel in which smouldered a crock of crushed brimstone. Working eleven strands at a time, each child could produce almost eight yards a day, earning three cents a yard. It also was acceptable as barter in most of the shops. Fay and Witherbee's was among Gusti's good customers, using braid to manufacture bonnets and decorative straw-flowers. At Lambert Bigelow's store it was sewed into baskets and other useful items.

In huckleberry time almost everyone picked several quarts a day, and later there were tangy clarkberries and checkerberries, and the woods were abundant with black walnuts, chestnuts and button-nuts.

Narrow paths hidden between low-hanging branches, the smell of damp earth beneath a carpet of fallen leaves, wooly caterpillars and the distant drumming of a red-headed woodpecker struck deep to the marrow of a growing boy during the last delicious days of summer. Why, he wondered, must this all end so soon?

CHAPTER 9

THE PHILOLOGIANS

"CAN ANYONE," Obadiah Albee asked his pupils on the day the fall term started, "tell me the meaning of 'philology'?"

Only one girl raised her hand but, when called upon, incorrectly recited a definition of "philosophy." There were no other volunteers.

"'Philology'," the teacher explained, "is made up of two Greek words, 'philos' and 'logos'. Together they form a word that means 'love of learning'. When I was at college we had a group known as the Philologian Society. We met regularly to debate topical issues. How many of you would enjoy meeting here one evening each week for such a lyceum?"

Almost all the students indicated they could make arrangements to attend, and they enthusiastically discussed the project when class was dismissed. As they were leaving, Mr. Albee asked Horatio to remain.

"Why didn't you raise your hand, Horatio?" he asked. "I know you could have defined 'philology'. After all, you are the class linguist," he added, a trace of a smile crossing the deep lines in his thin face, "and you've told me that Greek is your favorite language."

"I guess, sir," the boy stammered, "It's because I'm not fond of speaking in class if I don't have to."

"Why?"

"Because I stutter and the others laugh."

"I don't agree with you, Horatio," the principal said. "It's hardly noticeable. Your speech improved tremendously since you first came to Gates. Tell me, in your Greek lessons, what did you learn about Demosthenes?"

"He was the famous orator of Athens."

"Yes. I think he was the greatest of all times, but in his youth he was small and frail, his voice was weak and he stuttered so badly that no one could understand him. Do you know what he did to correct this?"

"I read he practiced talking slowly and distinctly with pebbles in his mouth. He declaimed by the shores of the Aegean Sea, shouting so his voice was heard above the waves."

"Exactly, Horatio, I very much want our Philologian Society to become *your* 'Aegean shore'. Our debates will give you the chance to speak on many subjects. I'm sure your speech will continue to improve, and the other students will learn much from what you can tell them."

At the meeting held the following week, Edwin Heard — one of the older boys — was elected president of the Gates Academy Philologian Society, and the evening's subject was "whether expectation of reward is a greater incentive to exertion than fear of punishment."

As they did the previous year — when there was an evening course in ornamental penmanship — each boy and girl brought a tallow candle to help illuminate the room. A few carried metal candlesticks, but most of them used either a small block of wood or potato with a hole gouged out to insert the candle.

The classroom was strange and unfamiliar in the dusk, and flickering candles lighted up some three dozen young faces with an orange glow, projecting magnified shadows that danced on the walls behind them. The perimeter of light added a touch of coziness to the room, but the corners and ceiling were hidden in the purple distance.

The discussion passed pleasantly, and it soon was nine o'clock, the hour of adjournment. Horatio did not take part in

90

the first session, but was assigned to argue in the negative at the next program, when the topic would be "has intemperance wrought more havoc than war?".

The cool air of early autumn was clean and refreshing, and all breathed deeply of its goodness as they left the stale climate of the schoolhouse. For some minutes they stood around in small groups, complimenting the debaters and bidding each other good night. Then, in couples and fours, boys and girls strolled in the various directions of their homes. Their voices and gay laughter grew constantly fainter and soon became a part of the silent darkness. Then Horatio, who walked home alone, heard them no more, and the only sound was the crunching of his footsteps on gravel and fallen leaves.

Reverend Alger was displeased to hear from Horatio, in the morning, that at the coming meeting he would represent the team upholding intemperance.

"But you know it's wrong, don't you?"

"Yes, father, drunkenness is not right."

"It's also a sin."

"I know it."

"Then how can you speak in its favor?"

"Mr. Albee assigned it that way."

"Can't you ask him to let you argue against intemperance?"

"No, father. I must do the best I can with the assignment. But don't fear. I shall never take up drinking, myself."

The pastor shook his head in bewilderment.

"What sort of minister will you make," he wondered aloud, "when from the start you plead in favor of sin?"

He shrugged his shoulders and retreated to his study. But the breakfast conversation had provided him with a good topic for Sunday's sermon. He would let parishioners know that drinking — and what it must lead to — is evil!

Horatio carefully prepared his material. Alone in his room, he rehearsed what he would say. Articulating slowly and clearly, he repeated troublesome words until his jaws ached. He prayed the Lord would overlook his position in the argument but, at the same time, not desert him when he would be trying so hard to talk without stuttering. When he had his remarks sufficiently organized, he presented his case before Mother, Gusti and the other children. Father refused to listen, declaring that no view which seeks to justify sin could be valid, and he had no time to waste on invalid theories.

On Sunday morning, Reverend Alger hammered away at the intemperate habits of some of his flock, and Horatio sat listening, ears burning and conscience searing him with the guilt of the damned.

But Wednesday evening he stood before his fellow-Philologians and, in the uncertain candlelight explained that, although he had never been in a war, he believed nobody ever really enjoyed one whereas, right around Marlborough, he noted persons deriving genuine pleasure from their intemperance. At worst, he reasoned, liquor can destroy the individual. War ravages entire nations.

His speech was slow and belabored. Twice he faltered but apparently managed to conquer the stammer by pausing briefly, and then continuing at an even slower pace than before. His opponent in the debate was George Manson who, Horatio thought, was more fluent and delivered a far more logical view than his own.

Horatio finished and returned to his seat with the conviction he had done nothing to strengthen his side. He still felt that way after all essays were read, and his team was judged the winner. Anticipating the parson's displeasure, the boy was only slightly pleased when, at dismissal, he shared in congratulations, and would rather have been with the losers.

Regardless of the debate's conclusion — and whether or not Horatio attacked or defended — Reverend Alger believed his sermon hit close to a number of targets, and he was determined to strike again.

So, speaking from the pulpit the next Sabbath, and on others that followed, he upbraided the town's general store proprietors, pointing out that rum was their largest-selling commodity. He rebuked tavern-keepers, townspeople who flaunted drunkenness in public, he chided farmers who hid bottles in the barn and noted the presence of a number who required constant doses of liquor, supposedly for medicinal purposes. If this transgression did not end immediately, he declared, he intended to post a list of sinners.

Reverend Alger had, for the first time since settling in Marlborough, succeeded in agitating and angering many among his congregation.

✳   ✳   ✳

"Where's James?" Horatio asked, seeing his brother's chair unoccupied at dinner.

"He won't be down tonight," Mother answered.

"Why? Isn't he well?"

"Our Father. . ." the parson began to pray, and all conversation ceased.

"Why wasn't James at supper, Gusti?" Horatio asked his sister when the family left the table.

"He's being punished. He and the Coolidge boys were annoying Granny Beeler again, so she came and complained to Papa. He was furious, and told James to stay in his room and repent. I'm going to take a plate of meat up to him," the girl said, and added as an afterthought, "but I'd better wait til Papa goes inside."

Granny Beeler — who preferred to be known as Doctress Beeler — was always considered a stranger in Marlborough, although she occupied her house on Hildreth Street ever since Captain Thayer moved out to take over his hotel. She was a self-fashioned healer (children shouted "Healer Beeler!" when they saw her on the street), claiming cures for cancer, ulcers, tumors, scrofula and every other type of disease.

A large, masculine sort of woman with heavy hands and a dozen hairs bristling from her chin, she could neither read nor write, but prescribed all manner of roots and herbs as "nature's remedies." Her secrets of life-long health, she hinted, came from Indians who raised her from childhood.

Her home was always filled with sufferers, some of them apparently ailing dreadfully. Many travelled from Quincy, Abington and more distant places for treatment. They wore plasters and poultices as they left the clinic, most of them carrying small packets of odd medicines.

"Boil these in two quarts of water," she instructed. "Add a pint of rum and drink a half-glassful three times a day."

93

Her advice was the same for all callers, and some were convinced she accomplished wonders.

Granny was rarely seen without a clay pipe which, she said, warded off sickness. She apparently also found substantial doses of rum to be helpful, and it was on this ingredient that she and Reverend Alger widely disagreed. She became a relatively wealthy woman and owned a horse and buggy in which she periodically drove to see patients in other communities.

The woman's great pleasure was a lovely daughter, Rachel, who married and lived near Lowell with her family. When they came to visit, once each year, she put off professional duties, passing the time buying gifts for her grand-children and happily driving them about in her wagon.

But Granny's arch-enemy was George Rowe, the town lounger, who overlooked no opportunity to torment her. Once — after she tired of his repeated visits for free treatment of imaginary ills — they quarrelled and she pushed him out of the house. After that he spent his days devising ways to provoke her. She eventually had him arrested. At his trial, in Concord, several townspeople appeared to testify in Granny Beeler's behalf. She was a kindly and likeable person, despite her dubious profession, and Rowe was known as a nuisance and trouble-maker. He was sentenced to a short term in jail, after which he ceased to bother her. But, whenever possible, he would persuade children to taunt and harass the old quack.

"Persecuting any fellow-being is un-Christian, James," the pastor scolded his son after Granny left his study. "I leave it to the Coolidge boys' parents to punish them, but I want you to remain in your room and seek forgiveness for the wrong you've done. Mrs. Beeler is a strange person, and I don't like what she does, but it's not our job to pass judgment and carry out the penalty. She could properly have boxed your ears, and I'm sorry she didn't. If you ever bother her again — or if anyone else comes to me with such a complaint — I'll do it myself. Now, get upstairs!"

With gray skies and endless formations of geese honking

high overhead, their wings beating against the wind and long necks thrust forward in south-bound flight, the good year of 1845 was drawing to a close.

Horatio, Gusti and James were busy with schoolwork; Olive was agreeably occupied with her household and caring for Annie and Francis. The town was growing and so was Reverend Alger's congregation. Church duties seemed infinite, but so was the pastor's dedication and effort. His schedule was filled with weddings — he officiated at numerous marriages of newly-arrived French-Canadians, conducting ceremonies in their own language — and the church-bell slowly striking at sunset spread news that on the morrow he would conduct a funeral.

It was customary to toll the age of the deceased, and the bell often struck eighty or ninety times. Sometimes, however, it sounded only once or twice, announcing the death of a child, and all who heard it were saddened by the message.

As a year-end project, Mr. Albee proposed to the Philologians the publication of a paper consisting of writings originally presented at weekly debates. It was in connection with this journal that Horatio had his first editorial experience and his contribution — a thesis that Washington was a greater man than Napoleon — appeared alongside articles on the pro and con of corporal punishment in schools, more opportunity at home or in the West, the abolition movement and other subjects covered during the past term.

For another eighteen months, until recess for summer vacation in 1847, Horatio continued at Gates Academy.

A few days before classes ended, the principal asked him about his plans for the future.

"I hope to enter Harvard in a year, after which Father expects me to attend the Divinity School.

"You don't sound over-anxious to become a churchman," Albee observed.

"I'm not," the boy answered, "but it's what Father always wanted for me."

"What would you rather do?"

"I'm not positive. Maybe I would prefer to teach or become a journalist. However," Horatio added, philosophically, "if I'm to be a minister I'll try to be a good one."

"I'm sure, Horatio, you'll be successful, whatever you decide to do. But that isn't my purpose for wanting to talk with you. I've come to the conclusion there isn't much more that Gates Academy —or I — can offer you. You are further advanced than any of my students — considerably farther even than classmates older than yourself. After this term there could be no further benefits for you from continued attendance."

"On the other hand," Horatio suggested, "I'm still not ready for college."

"I agree. You could do well reading and preparing yourself for university life. I'll gladly recommend a number of courses, and you can continue your language studies. I don't doubt that you'll be ready to take the tests next summer. Discuss this with Reverend Alger and see what he advises."

The parson's main anxiety — when he and Horatio talked of the future, that night — wasn't his son's preparation for Harvard, but how they would pay for it.

Your tuition and board will be almost three hundred dollars a year." he estimated.

"That's a lot more than you can afford on your salary, Father," Horatio replied. "But I'm not worried. I could teach during vacations and make up some of my expenses."

"We'll work it out and I'll arrange to pay at least a part of it, son. And perhaps the college will allow you a grant from their beneficiary funds."

"As you always say, Father, 'the good Lord will provide'."

"Well," the minister said with a faint smile, "let's hope so."

The days quickly passed as Horatio continued his education at home. A part of his time was occupied accompanying the minister on short trips around the parish, and assisting him in official tasks. When the winter school session started, Horatio applied for and got a job taking care of the District No. 2 Schoolhouse. Between six and eight o'clock each morning, he swept the classroom, cleaned the stove, started a fire so the building would be heated when pupils arrived, and chopped enough wood to keep a fire going through the day. His earnings for the term amounted to $26.87.

In the evenings, Horatio read. After finishing every book in the minister's study — these included Jacob Abbott's "The Young

Christian," Cooper's "The Prairie," Longfellow's "Poems" and others — he borrowed several from Mr. Albee. The kindly teacher offered J a r e d Sparks' "Life of Washington," Dickens' "Oliver Twist" and a number of works of Walter Scott. Horatio's closest companion, Edward Bigelow, loaned him Dana's "Two Years Before the Mast" and Hawthorne's "Twice-Told Tales." From another friend's bookshelf came a story by Washington Irving and The Rev. J. L. Blake's "Historical Reader," which traced world events from the Creation to the Battle of New Orleans.

Sometimes, when the youth finished a book, he wanted to write. And the lines he put on paper most often were p o e m s. Longfellow was Horatio's idol and many efforts were clumsy imitations of the master. His verses were short; when he ventured on long compositions he soon became bored, bringing them to an abrupt ending. Most of his works did not satisfy him, and were discarded. What he couldn't complete at a sitting generally was abandoned. Only rarely did he consider his poetry worthy of presentation and these few he recited, with appropriate gestures, before the gathered Alger family.

Mother always seemed pleased, primarily because Horatio's stutter had virtually disappeared. Father said some p i e c e s showed deep religious feeling, and Horatio occasionally saw him nodding approvingly during the performance. Gusti grimaced, saying most of them were too sad, and James — when he exclaimed that one poem about a boy hero was "Bully!" — was cautioned by the minister to mind his language in the presence of his mother and sister.

In the spring of 1848, when Horatio was sixteen years old, he received a letter from Cambridge. Signed by the Clerk of Harvard College, it acknowledged his application for admission and directed that, on August 17th, he appear for examination.

CHAPTER 10

HARVARD DAYS

TWO TIMID BOYS WANDERED through University Hall, searching for the examination room. One of them was Horatio; the other was Henry Gardner Denny, slim, bespectacled and very near-sighted, who was a year younger. They had, only minutes earlier, met in the registration office, and were now on their way to take the entrance tests to Harvard College. Finding the study hall, where they were instructed to report, they took seats near each other and waited.

Several — most of them appearing slightly fearful — were already in their places and some were still arriving. Near the front, a swarthy-complexioned, foreign-looking person shuffled about, opening windows, dusting benches with a red bandana he took from his pocket, and smiling affably at each youth who entered.

"Here, janitor," one newcomer called to him, "where do we put our hats?"

"Please let me take it for you, sir," the man answered in a heavy accent. With mischievous twinkle in his dark eyes, he added, "I'll return it to you later."

Promptly at nine o'clock the odd-looking fellow, perspiring profusely in the mid-August heat, closed the door. Small, fat and sloppy in appearance, he was a comical sight to behold and several in the room laughed audibly at his oddly-pronounced English. His oversized shoes — scuffed and unshined — bright blue yarn socks, inches-too-short trousers almost bursting at the waist and open-necked, collarless shirt caused one youth to suggest that "he looks more like a rag-picker than a porter."

"Perhaps it's President Everett in disguise," another whispered. "I think the old bug is going to speak."

"Gentlemen," he said pleasantly, "On behalf of Harvard College I greet you and wish you success in the examinations you are about to take. Those who pass will know me better. I am Professor Evangelinus Apostolides Sophocles, instructor of Greek. Please start now with Exercise A, and there will be no more talking. You may go when you are finished."

The tests lasted two days, about eight hours each day, leaving candidates fairly wilted, and many doubtful whether they passed. Horatio Alger was accepted, however — as was his friend, Denny — and together they went through preparations for their college careers. In spare time they explored the area that would be their home during the next four years.

Cambridge was a pretty, sleepy village, its narrow winding paths shaded by over-arching trees, bordered by hedge-rows of lilac and syringa. On one side, land sloped to the lazy waters of the Charles River, with its clumps of pollard willows everywhere. Beyond pleasant country roads stretched northward-lying farms, their newly cut fields filling the summer air with a delicious, fresh perfume. To the west, approached on one side by Love Lane, was Fresh Pond.

The College Yard — surrounded by stone posts connected by iron chains — consisted of some ten structures arranged about a rolling green meadow shaded by towering elms. There was a new library made of stone in Gothic style, living and recitation halls, the Dane Law School, Lawrence Scientific School, a small gymnasium and an old office building. Outside Hollis Hall stood the ancient College Pump from which students carried water to their quarters. The rooms, themselves, were simple enough and most were bare of homelike decorations. As many students worked to pay their way, few could afford luxuries. The dreariness of winter evenings, however, was dispelled by the cheer and warmth of cavernous, open fireplaces that added a touch of comfort to each chamber.

Harvard Square was hardly more than a village green, surrounded by a church, an inn and a number of residences where some of the students boarded. Here the new classmen lounged in their free moments, contemplating an atmosphere of dignity and quiet little disturbed by hourly arrivals and departures of the Cambridge-Boston Omnibus. After enrollment formalities were finished, young men climbed aboard the wagon — there were seats inside and also on top — and rode, relaxed and happy, to fabled Boston Town. The stage started at the ringing of a bell under the seat nearest the door and, to the merry chatter of its passengers, horses pulled the car along the route to Scollay Square.

Through Reverend Alger's efforts, and with the help of his friend and classmate, Professor Oliver Wendell Holmes — who was dean of the Harvard Medical School — Horatio was appointed President's Freshman. This was a part-time job running official errands for the head of the school, for which he received forty dollars for the year and rent of his dormitory room.

His roommate, in the building known as Holworthy Hall, was George Lovell Cary, a tall, gaunt, sensitive scholar whose family owned factories in Medway. Across the corridor lived Joseph Hodges Choate and his brother, William Gardner Choate, of nearby Salem. They planned to follow the law profession of a number of their distinguished relatives who preceded them at Harvard. The only other freshmen in the building — all easy prey for the pranks of upper classmen — were Samuel Foster Haven, Jr., and his companion, Francis William Hilliard. Henry Denny's parents decided that, because he was younger than most of the others, home surroundings would be preferable, and he lodged with a private family.

Classes started in September. Days soon grew shorter as hours of study lengthened and, from first Chapel call at six a.m. until evening, there was little leisure time except on Sunday afternoons.

Besides the odd but learned Professor Sophocles' Greek lectures, the "Men of the Class of '52," as they called themselves, attended Henry Wadsworth Longfellow's classes in modern languages, Louis Agassiz' course in geology, Edward Tyrell Channing's sessions in rhetoric and oratory, and Charles Sumner's political science seminars.

Every afternoon, after classes, Horatio reported to President Edward Everett's office where, when not delivering messages, he studied and prepared lessons for the next day. His duties ended at supper-time and he generally went directly to Commons, in the basement of University Hall. The dining area was divided into two parts, a more expensive bill of fare — consisting of beef and pudding — being served on one side, while a cheaper menu was offered on the other. Horatio ate with a group in the lower-priced section, which Joe Choate always referred to as Starvation Hollow. Some of those who were among the regulars at the evening meal included James Bradley Thayer, son of an impoverished Whig editor, who since childhood did chores for his board and now lived a meager existence while preparing himself for a law career; William Robert Ware — nicknamed Billy-Bobby — who had lung fever as a child and boasted of a romance when he was nine years old, and Darwin Erastus Ware, handsome and popular, a generous friend to all and an ardent anti-slavery man. He found outspoken allies in Henry Denny and Jerome Bonaparte Kimball, and they talked abolition at every opportunity.

"Alger," President Everett called, as the youth reported for work one afternoon in mid-December, "who was the fellow seated beside you at Chapel this morning?"

"Do you mean Thayer?" Horatio asked.

"He has an ugly scar — a sort of bald spot — on the left side of his head."

"Yes, sir, that's Thayer. The scar is from a burn he got when he was a child."

"The temperature was well below freezing and he wasn't wearing a coat. I've noticed him coatless several times. Would you know why?"

"I think, Dr. Everett, that he doesn't have one."

"That's what I think."

The President quickly wrote Thayer's name on an envelope he took from his pocket. He handed it to Horatio, asking him to deliver it.

Jim Thayer was studying before the fireplace when Horatio burst into his room in Massachusetts Hall.

101

"Say, Jim," Horatio panted, breathless from hurrying across the campus and climbing the stairs, "Here's a note from Everett. Maybe he's making you a professor."

"More likely I'm being bounced," Thayer said nervously as he tore open the envelope.

It contained thirty dollars and a one-line message: "Get a coat!"

✳   ✳   ✳

Early in 1849, The Hon. Edward Everett — he had been a Unitarian minister at 20, a professor of Greek at 21, Governor of Massachusetts from 1836 to 1840 and United States Minister to England between 1841 and 1845 — decided to resign as President of Harvard. Soon afterward it was announced that Professor Jared Sparks, the eminent historian, would succeed him, and plans for his inauguration added excitement to remaining months of the term.

The ceremony took place Wednesday, June 20th, lasting most of the day with students' open house festivities continuing noisily through the night. In the morning there was a procession of undergraduates, faculty, government, state and local dignitaries, alumni, college overseers, ex-Presidents Quincy and Everett, and innumerable invited guests. Official events ended with a private reception at Gore Hall, while students embarked on the revel that left many wandering unsteadily across the Yard when the few who were able hurried to Chapel the next morning.

For Horatio, the day's mail had brought a special added reason for celebration. A poem and short story he recently sent to The Pictorial National Library — a Boston Monthly — were accepted for publication, and full payment of two dollars was enclosed.

CHAPTER 11

THE STRANGE DISAPPEARANCE
OF
DR. PARKMAN

HORATIO ALGER'S SOPHOMORE YEAR at Harvard began with the assignment of familiarizing new class members with the college routine and three· of them became his close friends. Addison Brown, who was a freshman at Amherst, worked in a shoe factory to pay his expenses. Charles Carroll Vinal had been teaching since leaving preparatory school, and William Henry Waring — a recent graduate of Union Academy at Kinderhook, New York — came from Brooklyn where he lived with his grandfather in a mansion surrounded by spacious grounds, exquisitely maintained gardens and a stable of thoroughbred horses.

Horatio's roommate was Samuel Pearse Jennison, but the term had scarcely begun when he left, in September, to become principal of a school at Concord, New Hampshire, and at the same time read for the law in the office of a prominent judge. Brown took his place and he and Horatio remained roommates throughout their undergraduate days.

The group also included three newcomers from the South: Josiah Collins, Jr., bearded and courtly, from Scuppernong, North Carolina; Frederick Percival Leverett, Massachusetts-born but raised in Beaufort District, South Carolina; and Guignard Scott, of Woodville, Mississippi.

Some time after the semester started, the class was joined by Paul Revere, a Bostonian descending form French Huguenots; the namesake and grandson of the midnight rider of the American Revolution.

"Horatio, I'm in luck!" Addison Brown exclaimed jubilantly as he joined him at Commons one evening in mid-November. "I got a job."

"As what?" his roommate asked, "Professor of Boot Repairs?"

"Even better. I'm to play the organ at morning chapel, at a salary of two dollars a week. I'll soon be rich!"

"I've got more news for you, Ad," Horatio said, pulling two small envelopes from his pocket, "We've been invited to join the Institute of 1770."

The Institute was a literary and debating society, and Horatio read aloud from his card that the season's first meeting would be held Friday evening on the ground floor of Massachusetts Hall.

"Great. Really Great," Brown grunted happily between mouthfuls of stew that he ladled from a platter in front of him. "I say that this is going to be a real exciting year."

"Watch out it doesn't get too exciting, men," Henry Kemble Oliver suggested, taking his place at the table. "Look at those nuts, Denny and Ware, working over the poor Southern lads. What will they ever think of our Yankee hospitality? Hey, Denny," Oliver called to his chum across the dining room, "take abolition talk out to the Rebellion Tree and let's have some quiet at this banquet."

Denny — the gentlest, friendliest lad in the college — was becoming uncontrollable on the subject of slavery, and his new Southern classmates often bore the brunt of his attacks. The comic part of it — Sid Willard pointed out — was that Denny, Collins and Scott were closest companions and, after his evening political tirade ended, their conversation drifted to more agreeable subjects.

The meal finished, Oliver hurriedly scraped food leftovers from his comrades' plates onto a paper.

"You see, Horatio," Addison Brown explained, "our young

scholar is so fond of slum-chowder he takes some along in case he gets hungry during the night."

"Fond of slum-chowder, hell!" Oliver exclaimed, emptying one dish after another. "I just took in another tenant and if I don't bring supper there'll be such screeching and hooting around midnight they'll send the sheriff from Boston!"

Nature-loving Oliver had a peculiar liking for owls, and he now kept three in his room. In warmer weather he caught frogs for their dinner in a marsh at the far end of the campus, but a recent cold snap apparently drove them deep into hibernation.

"Just one chirp, Oliver," Brown — his dormitory neighbor — threatened, "and you and your big birds will camp by the river."

"Like you said, Ad," Horatio reminded his roommate, "this is going to be a real exciting year!"

The excitement Addison Brown predicted — but of a far more sinister sort — fell swiftly and unexpectedly over the Harvard Yard, and lasted many weeks.

It arrived with the early dawn of Sunday, November 25th. On a morning too chilly and damp for outings, a number of small boats were being rowed through the thin mist of the Charles River. Men, dimly seen, could be heard calling from one skiff to another, and curious onlookers, standing along both banks, spoke in low tones as they watched. Soon many students, attracted by the unusual activity, joined the steadily increasing crowd, asking what the men were searching for. Had someone drowned? Was this a college hoax?

Before noon the astounding news broke like a thunderclap and, within hours, everyone was talking about the strange disappearance of "Chin" Parkman.

Dr. George Parkman — called "Chin" because of a pugnaciously protruding jaw, which jutted all the more when he wore his conspicuously large false teeth — was a Boston aristocrat known to all. Tall and thin, always somberly attired in a long black frock coat, high collar and stovepipe hat, he was a familiar figure hurrying about town, at the university and at exclusive clubs. Having long since retired from medical practice in favor of business and finance, he supplied the land upon which the medical school was built. The Parkman Chair of Anatomy, occupied by Professor Oliver Wendell Holmes, was named in his honor. He was the brother of Reverend Francis Parkman and his nephew, Francis Parkman, Jr., who graduated at Harvard five years earlier, had already won acclaim for his recently published "The Oregon Trail," a monumental record of his Western journey through wild Indian country.

From information passing among spectators at the dredging, Horatio and friends who joined the throng gathered that the prominent Dr. Parkman had been missing since Friday. At any rate, he did not return to his home at Number 8 Walnut Street for lunch as he invariably did. By evening his worried family notified police and the search was on. All day Saturday they probed through cellars, alleyways and abandoned buildings, and in the morning started dragging grappling irons along the bottom of the shallow river.

By mid-day he still had not returned, nor was his body found or a single clue uncovered. Later there were rumors he had been seen in a distant part of town, but another source claimed, just as certainly, that Parkman was at precisely the same time at the railroad station, boarding a Southbound train.

On Monday the story covered front pages of all newspapers, and rewards were offered for information as to his whereabouts. Reports mentioned that Professor John W. Webster, a lecturer at the medical college, called at Reverend Francis Parkman's home Sunday afternoon to say he saw his brother Friday, apparently shortly before he vanished.

"We had an appointment at my laboratory," Professor Webster explained. "I owed Dr. Parkman $483.00, and he came to collect. He was in a great hurry and, as soon as I repaid the debt, he rushed out with the money in his hand."

This gave considerable support to a police theory that Dr. Parkman had been attacked by thieves and murdered. They began their investigation at the medical school, calling first upon Ephraim Littlefield, the building porter.

"Yes," the janitor recalled, "I did see Dr. Parkman, probably Friday. But it's hard to tell for sure. He frequently came for Professor Webster."

"They were friends?" the inspector inquired.

"I wouldn't call them that. Dr. Parkman was always trying to collect money from Professor Webster. When it wasn't ready he got mad.

"You were present during these discussions, Mr. Littlefield?"

"Once, but I don't think more."

"Then how do you know Dr. Parkman *always* came to collect money from Professor Webster."

"Well, sir, Webster most often didn't have enough cash to satisfy him and there was a lot of hollering. Anyone could hear it, it was so loud."

Professor Holmes, who lectured in the room above Webster's laboratory, corroborated these statements, saying he occasionally heard noisy discussion coming from the floor below.

During the next few days, the police kept watch on Littlefield, and the janitor, in turn, decided to look into some unaccustomed activities of Professor Webster.

He noted Webster staying later than usual in the laboratory and at night heard his footsteps — they were slow, as though carrying something heavy — descending the basement stairs. Past Littlefield's sleeping quarters he was moving in the dark. Moments later he opened the heavy iron door to the private vault where chemicals for his experiments were stored. From within came sounds of water running and — after an hour or more — the gate again grating open and closed. Then the professor's tread, lighter and faster than before, mounting the staircase.

On Thursday, November 29th — Thanksgiving Day — Littlefield was alone in the building, and decided to investigate. He couldn't unlock the door, so, with sledge hammer, crowbar and chisel, he pounded the brick wall. Fearful that Webster would suddenly come upon him — wondering how he would explain the damage — he worked all day and through most of the night.

Early Friday morning he broke through and, holding his light forward, peered into the chamber.

The first thing he saw was parts of two dismembered legs, splashes of blood on the floor, and other parts of a body over which water from the sink was dripping.

Frightened and horrified, he reported his discovery to the

city marshal, and a squad of police was immediately sent to Professor Webster's home, where he was arrested for the murder of Dr. George Parkman.

Faced with the evidence, Webster tried to shift blame on to Littlefield. Then, shortly after being placed in a cell at the police station, he attempted suicide by gulping a dose of strychnine concealed in his vest pocket. Falling upon the cot, he suffered a series of violent spasms but, having apparently taken an insufficient quantity of the poison, he soon recovered.

Professor Webster, middle-aged, heavy set, with rheumy, myopic eyes and graying mutton-chop whiskers, was an unlikely suspect, and many doubted he was the killer.

However, a motive was soon established. With an apparent zest for lavish living and entertaining, Webster quickly squandered an inheritance received from his father. His salary, twelve hundred dollars a year, wasn't enough to support his wife and three daughters, and borrowing became necessary.

Yes, he borrowed, Webster admitted. But that is not a crime. Parkman was a hard, relentless creditor, and he hounded the professor daily to repay. Webster, often interrupted during an experiment by Parkman's abrupt entry, resented this interference and his words were heated and loud. However, this also was not a crime.

Quickly collecting his senses, Webster laughed, ridiculing the suspicion that the body was Dr. Parkman's.

"Of course there is a cadaver," he explained. "I'm always conducting tests on human organs. That's what I do as a teacher at the university.

He stuck to this alibi and it became the task of the state prosecutor to prove that the remains uncovered in the vault actually were parts of George Parkman.

A month later there still were those who believed Parkman would turn up, alive. Others thought his corpse would be found, either floating in the harbor or someplace far from the city. Among those who knew John Webster, it was impossible to conclude that the kind-hearted, fussy, dull, bumbling college instructor was capable of murder!

When trial was set for March, 1850, Webster's family and friends asked Rufus Choate — an older cousin of Horatio's classmates, Joe and Bill Choate — who was an acknowledged leader of the American Bar and a skilled examiner of witnesses, to undertake the defense.

After studying evidence, the attorney would agree only if Webster pleaded guilty, in which case he believed he could persuade the court that the crime was manslaughter, not murder. The professor, however, stubbornly insisted he was innocent, and Choate declined.

The trial, which lasted eleven days, attracted nationwide attention. In addition to intensive coverage by local newspapers, special reporters were sent from New York by the Herald, the Daily Globe and a number of others. Charles A. Dana, right-hand man to Horace Greeley, handled the story for the Tribune.

Dana, thirty-one years old, with a full bristly brown beard, a cordial manner and thick dark hair brushed well forward to conceal baldness, was very much at home around the college. He had entered Harvard in 1839 but was ordered by physicians to abandon studies, two years later, to save his seriously affected eyesight.

Horatio, in connection with chores as part-time messenger in the college office, assisted Dana — as well as other reporters — in their efforts to track down information and locate persons about the campus who were connected with Parkman or Webster.

An estimated sixty thousand spectators filed in and out of the courtroom and gallery to watch proceedings. The testimony seemed endless with witnesses minutely questioned, their statements filling volumes.

Littlefield spent several hours in the witness box, describing meetings between Parkman and Webster. A couple of days before Dr. Parkman disappeared, the porter said, Professor Webster casually mentioned he would be storing some remains from the dissecting room. The next day, Webster sent him on an errand to Massachusetts General Hospital for a quart of blood. He remembered, positively, seeing Dr. Parkman in the neighborhood of the college the day he disappeared, but cross-examination made clear he did not see him enter.

On Friday evening and Saturday, Littlefield continued, Webster remained in the laboratory at uncustomary times. During this period, the furnace was in continuous operation, and he heard water running in the sink.

At this point the witness was excused.

The defense called an impressive roster of acquaintances and faculty members to testify as to the type of man John W. Webster was. He was well-respected, they affirmed, and of fine character. Harvard President Jared Sparks took the stand, as did Oliver Wendell Holmes.

Thus far, the case was largely based upon hearsay but, as the trial drew to a close, the prosecution introduced surprise evidence. Closely re-examining the furnace in the medical college laboratory, they found fragments of false teeth. They also located a trunk in which was uncovered — buried in tanbark — several parts of a human body.

An expressman testified he had, during that week, delivered a shipment of tanbark to Professor Webster.

Then the state introduced its star witness. He was Dr. Nathan C. Keep, a friend of both men, who made the teeth for Dr. Parkman. Tearfully — for he realized his testimony would condemn the prisoner — the dentist fitted fragments from the oven into a mould from which they were made.

Chief Justice Shaw, skillfully charging the jury, carefully explained the nature and value of the circumstantial evidence that had closed about Professor Webster. It had not been conclusively proved, he pointed out, that the two men were together at the time of the alleged murder.

Nevertheless, on the eleventh day, the jury pondered and in less than three hours returned — about midnight — with their verdict.

"*Guilty!*"

The professor was then sentenced to death by hanging, execution to be carried out the last Friday in August.

One morning, early in May, Professor Webster asked for paper and pen, saying he wished to make a full confession. He then spent most of the day writing in the dim lamplight of his cell.

He started with the request that his court statement, declaring utter innocence, be withdrawn. He then documented the crime, from the first time he applied to Parkman for a loan, until the doctor's final visit.

110

Bedevilment by Dr. Parkman began the moment the first note was due, and Webster was unable to meet it. Repayment of the loan, and subsequent ones totalling about three thousand dollars, were slow and at one time he gave Parkman a mortgage on his personal property.

The constant harassment was unnerving, he claimed, leading to an unusually bitter exchange between the men some weeks before the fatal Friday. Webster was preparing chemical ingredients for an experiment, when Dr. Parkman appeared behind him. He neither heard him enter, nor as he approached, and was unaware of his presence until Parkman demanded, "Webster, are you ready for me?"

"No, Doctor, I'm not ready," the professor replied.

There was loud discussion, Parkman accusing him of dishonorable evasion and threatening legal action. Webster promised he would have money for him the next day.

"Very well. I'll be here. And something must be accomplished tomorrow!" Parkman said, furiously, as he strode from the room.

Webster was always in arrears. In the belief that it would hasten his collections, Parkman occasionally attended the professor's evening lectures, taking a seat in the front row from where he tormented and confused his debtor by jutting at him his prognathous jaw and large, shining teeth.

At nine o'clock on the morning of November 23rd, Webster called at the Parkman home, asking his creditor to call on him at one-thirty.

"He came," Webster wrote, "between half-past one and two. I was removing some glasses from my table. He moved rapidly down the steps and followed me into the laboratory, immediately addressing me with great energy.

" 'Are you ready for me, sir? Have you got the money?' "

"I replied: 'No, Dr. Parkman,' and was then beginning to state my condition and make an appeal to him. He wouldn't listen, but interrupted with much vehemence, calling me 'scoundrel' and 'liar' and went on, heaping upon me bitter epithets. He threatened to get me out of my job. I kept trying to pacify him, but could not, and soon my own temper was up."

Webster became infuriated by the sting of his words and

111

menacing gestures and, in a fit of rage smashed his skull with a heavy stick that lay nearby, the blow instantly killing Dr. Parkman. In panic, the confession continued, he thought only of getting rid of the body.

After burning clothes, papers and other possessions, he dismembered Dr. Parkman's body with a surgical knife, disposing of the parts as had already been brought out at the trial.

On the day of execution, Dr. Webster appeared calm. He had sent a note to Littlefield, apologizing for attempting to throw suspicion on him, and one to Reverend Francis Parkman, expressing deep contrition. Then, outwardly serene, he was led to the gallows and hanged.

CHAPTER 12

THE CLASS OF '52

PROFESSOR CHARLES SUMNER left Harvard, in 1850, to campaign for a seat in the United States Senate as a Free Soil-Democratic coalition candidate. The son of abolition parents and himself long a champion of unpopular causes, he had become a leading voice in the bitter struggle to end slavery. Elected, Senator Sumner took his seat early in 1851, beginning immediately to indict and combat the Fugitive Slave Law.

Throughout New England, the talk was abolition. Horatio was swept along by Henry Denny's tirades against slavery and became his dedicated ally in classroom discussions, Commons and dormitory arguments and at debates of the Institute of 1770. Alger, Denny and Darwin Ware were known as a battling triumvirate, often helped by Jerome Bonaparte Kimball, Andrew Washburn and Samuel Miller Quincy. The Junior Class had been joined by two new students from Baltimore, and the secessionists welcomed the support of David Churchill Trimble and William Duncan McKim. Francis William Hilliard, although born and raised in Massachusetts, frequently expressed preference for the Southern cause.

Returning home to Marlborough for end-term vacation, Horatio found the community aroused against the Compromise of 18-

50, that Daniel Webster and Henry Clay recently succeeded in having enacted into law by the Congress. "But it hasn't prevented war," many claimed. "It's only postponed it!"

Anti-slavery pamphlets and tracts by John Greenleaf Whittier were being widely circulated. Mr. Albee quoted from them to his classes at Gates Academy and Gusti Alger — now almost eighteen and a teacher at the Robin Hill District School — had become an outspoken disciple of William Lloyd Garrison.

Garrison, the crusading anti-slavery editor from Boston, accepted Reverend Alger's invitation to speak at the West Parish Unitarian Church, and his fiery attack on New Englanders who — because of economic benefit or apathy — tolerated compromise, brought criticism upon the minister from some members of his congregation. Stronger comment came from several churchmen who advised Reverend Alger to confine his efforts to the Lord's work and leave politics to legislators. Some sought to point out Biblical justification of slavery while others suggested an attitude such as his was embarrassing to all of them.

Reverend Alger, however, rubbed his hands gleefully at the tempest he created, hurled rebuttal at his critics and joined with The Reverend Theodore Parker, another Unitarian preacher, as a pastor of abolition. Even in the church, he said, it was too late for neutrality. As he predicted, ministers of many denominations were soon declaring their position, most of them emphatically against slavery in the South and new territories.

Denny chuckled when Horatio told him of the excitement going on at home.

"It's going to be a great fight," he said, cleaning the lenses of his small, silver-rimmed spectacles, "and I want to be in it. Don't you?"

"For sure," Horatio agreed, "Everyone knows there's going to be a war. Back home most men are joining the town militia. There's nothing like getting ready!"

Henry Norris felt the same way and, early in the Senior year, arranged with the First Corps of Cadets, of which he was a member, to borrow rifles from their armory. With these he drilled a group a few evenings each week on the banks of the Charles River. Horatio and Denny — both of them short and slender —

struggled clumsily with the heavy, outdated weapons. Sam Quincy — grandson of a former Harvard President — quickly learned the manual of arms, and Calvin Page and Charles Francis Dana handled the oversized antiques with ease. Dana, who spent several childhood years abroad, attended German schools where military training was part of the curriculum. Several of the southern boys joined the "Musket and Marching Club" — political strife did not affect close friendships between classmates from North and South — demonstrating conspicuous skill and familiarity with firearms.

During their last year as undergraduates, a number of organizations and competitions took up much of the students' spare time. Horatio Alger, along with a number of others, joined the Harvard Natural History Society, of which Henry Oliver was president. The whole purpose of the club, explained Sam Thorndike — the elegantly mustached class comic — was "to provide a home for Oliver's blasted owls." Horace Coolidge agreed, adding "Now we *all* go down to Fresh Pond to dig up bugs and frogs for their dinner!"

Early in his Senior year, Horatio — who stood eighth, scholastically, in the class of eighty-eight — was elected to Phi Beta Kappa. He also became a founding member of the Alpha Chapter of Psi Upsilon. Addison Brown warmly recalled the fraternity from his Freshman days at Amherst, and joined several others in petitioning the faculty to grant a charter.

As in previous years, Horatio easily won Bowdoin Prizes for Greek Prose and these sums — forty to fifty dollars — helped pay his tuition. Now he was assigned to prepare a Greek dissertation for the annual public exhibition. This netted another sixty dollars, which was immediately put aside for next fall, when he would enroll for graduate study in the Divinity School.

Final weeks of the Class of 1852 passed swiftly and eventfully. Horatio, who tried to assume the role of a sauntering, sophisticated Senior, was admonished for excessive unexcused absences from morning prayers; Paul Revere — admitting taking part in a campus prank, but refusing to name accomplices — was suspended, but returned in time for graduation; many accompanied the Boat Club excursion to Lake Winnipesaukee, New Hampshire, to cheer Sid Willard, Tom Curtis and Jonathan

Dwight, crew members of the Harvard boat, Oneida, in the first Harvard-Yale Regatta.

Tuesday, May 4, 1852, was declared a half-holiday so students could participate in Boston's welcome to Louis Kossuth, exiled leader of Hungary's fight for independence from Austria. On the eve of his departure for England, he was escorted about the College Yard by President Sparks and Professor Longfellow, and was later the honored guest at a reception given by Mrs. Charles Russell Lowell, at her home on Quincy Street. Horatio, Charles Vinal and a number of the seniors attended, and Kossuth — eloquent though threadbare — was cordially greeted as a conquering hero.

After final examinations, full attention was turned to graduation. Horatio was elected Class Odist, and his verses, to the traditional tune of "Fair Harvard," were sung by the celebrants at Class Day.

The festivities began after chapel services on June 25th. The morning was gray and humid, with dark, threatening clouds hanging low overhead. But, although many carried umbrellas, it did not rain.

The first event was a series of readings in Professor Longfellow's lecture room at University Hall. Then the procession to the President's home where they were greeted on the lawn by Jared Sparks, and toasted with lemonade served from a punch bowl given in 1701 by the Hon. William Stoughton. At noon, exercises resumed in the chapel with prayers and dedications. Joe Choate read the class poem, and Addison Brown played the organ.

A luncheon at Harvard Hall was presided over by Mrs. Sparks, and the banquet tables — extending nearly the entire length of the room — were loaded with delicacies and ornamented with arrangements of colorful flowers.

Many young ladies of Cambridge were invited to the outdoor dancing that started late in the afternoon, and continued through the evening. After a formal dinner, "Auld Lang Syne" was sung around the Rebellion Tree, and floral wreaths fashioned by the women were given to each member of the class.

The Commencement ceremonies, in July, were almost anticlimatic, with seniors busily packing and preparing to return to

116

their homes. The graduates, their guests, and numerous invited dignitaries, filled pews of the First Church at Harvard Square.

Despite intolerable heat, they sat through a program that included forty-one speeches, dissertations and essays, interspersed with seven lengthy musical compositions. The talks ranged from Henry Brown's "Literature of Iceland," and Darwin Ware's "Pythagorean Theory of Numbers with Reference to the Problem of Science," to Josiah Collins' "Works of Fiction as Weapons of Controversy" and Gorham Thomas' "Prospects of Australia."

Horatio appeared seventh, and — to the joy of his parents, who came with Obadiah Albee to attend the graduation — he flawlessly delivered the English Oration, "Cicero's Return from Banishment." As he spoke — clearly and with splendid gestures — Olive's eyes filled with tears, Mr. Albee beamed with pride at the accomplishment of his former stuttering, tongue-tied student, and Reverend Alger, amid nostalgic memories of his own departure from Harvard, twenty-three years earlier, was satisfied that his oldest son had the makings of a minister.

In the afternoon, Denny and a number of the others received friends in their rooms, and at night the Class Supper was held at Winthrop House in Boston.

The dinner finished, each man stood to announce his future profession, and retold favorite college experiences. There were happy reminiscences of futile attempts to put the campus bell out of action, of the odd disappearance of Professor Agassiz' trilobite fossil, and of the time Professor "Potty" Channing hid behind a door listening, while students, believing he had not yet arrived, joked about his heroically-proportioned pot-belly.

They recalled freshman days, awesome upper-classmen, midnight goings-on at Holworthy Hall's Old East Entry, and the reassuring sight of Edward Everett, Henry Wadsworth Longfellow and Charles Sumner, arm-in-arm, crossing the College Yard in the bright moonlight.

Before adjourning, the Class of 1852 toasted the years to come with goblets of Madeira. Each wished the other well and all then returned to the College Yard and preparations to leave Cambridge in the morning.

CHAPTER 13

AFTER GRADUATION

THE WORCESTER DIRECT LINE, which stopped to discharge passengers at Feltonville, seven miles from Marlborough, left the Boston Railway Station a few minutes before noon. Horatio boarded early, took his seat in the half-empty coach and gazed dreamily out of an open window as the cars rattled out of the yards. He carried with him only a green carpet bag, having that morning turned his heavy trunk over to Sawin, the expressman.

After long days of study for examinations, graduation ceremonies and festivities, the young man was alone at last. The train moved slowly, halting frequently, but the city was soon far behind and the green hills of home only a little more than two hours away. It was a warm, sunny afternoon and even through gusts of smoke and cinders, Horatio could inhale exhilarating farm smells of hay, livestock and fresh-turned earth.

A week after returning to Marlborough, Horatio took over as teacher at a district school for the summer term. Some free time was spent assisting his father, as preparation for forthcoming studies at the Divinity School, but more and more he was developing a strong appetite for writing.

He preferred poetry, but some themes, he found, were more easily moulded into short stories. He wrote these in a notebook and read them to his pupils. They weren't received with great enthusiasm, but Horatio increasingly felt that he would rather be an author than a preacher. He was reluctant to discuss this with Reverend Alger, but his ambition soon became well known to Olive and Gusti.

Unexpectedly, he was offered the assignment of preparing a history of Middlesex County, and immediately accepted. This would, Horatio reasoned, also allow time for other writing, and he impulsively cancelled plans to return to Cambridge and theology.

It was a bitter disappointment to his father, but the minister reluctantly agreed when Horatio promised that, if he could not become self-supporting as a journalist within a year, he would resume training for the ministry.

Throughout the autumn and winter, Horatio searched through volumes of faded, barely legible records. From documents and family bibles he slowly and tediously constructed a story of the community. Among bales of long-forgotten land grants, deeds and personal papers he sorted the dull facts from which county histories were constructed. Occasionally, however, he chanced upon considerably more spirited material. Although unsuited for inclusion, he studied these chronicles — the earliest notes composed in ancient English style of speech and spelling— of long-forgotten persons and events. Starting with records left by earliest Puritan settlers, and continuing through later arrivals of Scotch-Irish and French, there were references to acts of treachery, shrewdness and double-crossing, admixtures of native Indian blood, bastardy, divorces, house-burning, murder and punishment. The best tales, Horatio decided, were the ones he couldn't print!

In the evenings he turned, with greater enthusiasm, to what he considered 'his own' projects. He produced articles by the dozens, hopefully sending them to various publications in Boston and New York. For months not a single piece was accepted, and the greater portion of the Alger family's mail consisted of rejected stories being returned to the young author.

Success, of a sort, arrived early in April, 1853, when his poem, "A Chant of Life," appeared in the Boston Transcript. The next month two items were published, a poem, "A Welcome to

119

May," in Peterson's Magazine, and another, "The Cottage by the Sea," in Gleason's Pictorial Drawing Room Companion.

After the first outburst of Horatio's unbounded delight at seeing his efforts in print, there followed a disappointing wait for payments that did not arrive. Upon inquiring, Horatio was advised that works of new, unknown writers were used without compensation. Seeing their stories, a memo on Transcript stationery explained, should be sufficient reward. A more hopeful letter was received from Maturin M. Ballou, the editor at Gleason's. They would publish the few Alger tales on hand without payment, he stated, but Horatio would receive two dollars apiece for any they accepted in the future.

Several appeared during months that followed, but it soon became apparent that their earnings could not make Horatio self-supporting. In June he was notified that, for the time being, no more funds were available for the county history and — almost with a feeling of relief — the tedious job was abandoned.

"Horatio," Gusti said to her brother, "this morning I heard Papa saying it was time he talked to you about going back to Cambridge."

"I've been expecting it, Gusti," Horatio answered, with resignation. "I haven't had much success."

"But you've started. I know you don't want to be a minister. Why don't you tell him that?"

"I can't. He allowed me to work as I pleased through this year, and I must keep my part of the bargain."

After dinner, the young man entered the parson's study.

"Father," he announced, "I shall soon be leaving for the Divinity School."

"I really think it's what is best for you, Horatio. On the other hand, I'm sorry you couldn't realize your wish to make a livelihood at writing. My great hope always has been for you to enter the church. However, your mother has been very stern with me, these past months. She is only anxious that you be happy; that you do what satisfies you. Am I wrong, Horatio, in wanting you to carry on *my* work?"

"I know you want what's right for me, Father, and I shall become a minister. However," he added, "I mean to keep writing at the same time."

In August, 1853, Horatio enrolled for the theological course and, for a time, was happily reunited with Henry Denny, Charley Vinal and other classmates who returned to Harvard to continue at the graduate schools. But in November he abandoned Cambridge again, having taken a position as assistant editor of the Boston Daily Advertiser. At the beginning he liked the work but later became dissatisfied when administrative tasks took up most of his time. Accordingly, he was quite willing to accept, in June 1854, a teaching job at Charles Winston Green's Potowome Boarding School for Boys at East Greenwich, Rhode Island.

His duties were greatly satisfying and during this period he frequently considered giving full attention to teaching Greek and Latin. He enjoyed companionship of youths, and had ample time for writing. During his stay at Potowome, virtually everything he wrote was printed in Gleason's and in a new periodical, The Flag of Our Union. Before the end of 1854, Maturin Ballou resigned as editorial chief of the Gleason publications to start his own magazine. It was established as Ballou's Dollar Monthly (although the selling price was fifteen cents) and from the earliest issues, there appeared short stories signed "By Horatio Alger, Jr."

Horatio was slowly drifting from poetry, and produced an endless stream of brief tales, most of them bearing a significant moral lesson. His name was becoming familiar to readers of a number of story papers and magazines, and his rates increased to about five dollars per story.

With the damp November weather, Horatio suffered an attack of bronchial asthma that left him bedridden for a week, and a physician urged him to return to Marlborough and remain there until after Thanksgiving.

"Prepare Father," Horatio wrote to Gusti, anticipating the pastor's vexation with him for having left the Divinity School. He had not been home in more than a year, and was apprehensive of their meeting.

"Papa is prepared," she replied promptly, "better prepare yourself!"

But when Horatio returned to Marlborough, the Reverend Alger scarcely indicated displeasure. As a matter of fact, he said, he still believed his son would complete the course and eventually find satisfaction in a parish. Horatio was disturbed to discern his father's weariness, and noted how much he aged since he last saw him.

He never ceased fighting against intemperance and slavery, Olive explained to her son, and the strain of battle was exhausting him. His features were etched with deep lines, and his step was slower. But in the pulpit his energy still swelled within him, and he damned sinners who returned pathetic, trembling runaway slaves to Southern masters, just as — Sunday after Sunday — he condemned parishioners who sold liquor, and those who bought it.

Side by side with Obadiah Albee, the minister demanded a personal liberty law to replace the Fugitive Slave Act. Soon, even those who agreed with them tired of their attacks, and they antagonized a number of influential citizens who opposed their views.

The Wednesday evening after Horatio arrived, the Mechanics Institute — a group that met to hear lectures on topical subjects — presented a temperance discussion featuring a talk by William Taylor Adams.

Adams, thirty-two years old, had for more than a dozen years been a Boston school teacher. Using the pen-name, Oliver Optic, he became a popular writer, his articles appearing regularly in a number of story papers. The handsome young man, who wore a full mustache that connected with carefully-trimmed side whiskers, came as a guest of the minister, staying at the Alger home. He had delivered a powerful sermon at the church, some months earlier, and townspeople were eager to hear him again.

Gusti, now twenty years old, tiny, with mischievously sparkling eyes, a rare, delicate complexion, pointed nose and small mouth that gave her a bright sparrow-like appearance, greeted Adams affectionately and held his arm as they walked through the streets of Marlborough. She introduced him to Horatio, and the two men immediately became warm friends.

They had much in common, both being teachers and writers, although Adams already achieved some journalistic success, and Horatio was only a beginner. They talked of their hopes, greatly enjoying each other's company until Gusti called to warn that it was time to leave for the meeting.

Reverend Alger introduced the speaker, who delighted the

audience with adventurous tales of Sam Houston, the fearless Texas hero. The famed warrior and frontiersman, he said, was — until his marriage in 1840 — a heavy drinker. Upon reforming, however, he substituted religion for liquor and soon became a devoted leader in the struggle against intemperance.

Later, over cups of steaming tea, Horatio and Adams chatted late into the night. Horatio proudly produced clippings of his published works, and Will Adams — as he read them — became increasingly captivated by their style and rapid pace.

"I'd like to see these in a book!" he said, enthusiastically.

"So would I," Horatio quickly agreed, "but there's no line of publishers waiting at my door."

"There will be," Adams predicted. "This is sturdy stuff. I think it can't miss!" Then, seized by an idea, he added, "Let me take this down to Brown, Bazin, in Boston. They've got a book of mine on the presses right now, and maybe they'll be interested in your work, too."

When Adams departed, the next morning, he carried with him the bundle of stories. Gusti and Horatio took him to the railroad, the young lady — claiming she could do anything a man can do — driving the carriage.

"You'll hear from me about these," Adams promised as he boarded the train to Boston. "I'll drop it off at the publishers today or tomorrow."

"I hope they like it," Horatio said with a smile.

"Don't worry, they will!"

Puffing clouds of thick gray smoke, and to the clanging of a bell, the cars moved slowly toward the hills. Soon, only the smoke trail was visible. Then it, too, disappeared.

Early in December Horatio returned to Potowome, not fully recovered and with frequent discomfort. Unable to sleep, he often sat up through the night, writing, and he continued to send off considerable quantities of stories to a number of publications.

He had no news from Adams, but in January Gusti received a letter from her friend in which he mentioned that Brown, Bazin & Company would soon make a decision. About a month later, the same mail brought to Horatio a letter from Will Adams with the welcome news that the book idea was accepted, and one from the publisher asking him to call to discuss arrangements.

Before the end of that week, he visited their offices on Washington Street and terms were easily reached. The book would include poems and stories submitted, and they asked for several more to fill out the volume. It was decided the title should be "Cousin Bertha's Christmas Tale," after one of the short stories in the collection. Long before publication however, this was changed to "Bertha's Christmas Vision; An Autumn Sheaf."

Before hastening back to the railway station, Horatio called upon Will Adams to thank him.

"Let's run over to Parker's to celebrate," his friend insisted. "This is a double celebration, for your book and mine!"

The Oliver Optic tale, "The Boat Club; or, The Bunkers of Rippleton," had only recently been published. But sales were increasing steadily, and the author was speeding production of new stories for a series.

Horatio remained at Potowome until spring, 1856, when he left to take charge of the academy at Deerfield, Massachusetts, for the summer session. He enjoyed teaching, and employers knew him to be a learned and conscientious instructor. Students did well in the company of this gentle, mild-mannered man. He was no disciplinarian, and could not be strict with boys, but they generally became so fond of him — he was a notoriously generous marker — that stern measures were unnecessary.

The timid little instructor also was vain, and it didn't take pupils long to realize that to mention having read and enjoyed his latest story was to win his friendship and gratitude.

"Bertha's Christmas Vision" had been in print for some months, but it received little notice and sales were poor. It did, however, bring Horatio to the attention of John Townsend Trowbridge, the busy editorial writer of True Flag, who was eager to turn his efforts to full-length novels. Trowbridge showed the book to James R. Elliott, a partner in the firm of Moulton, Elliott and and Lincoln, publishers of the weekly magazine. Elliott already knew Alger's work, and agreed he might be the right person to handle some of Trowbridge's duties.

Accordingly, in September, when the term ended at Deerfield, Horatio was engaged as a writer of unsigned editorials. He worked three days a week at True Flag, on School Street, sharing a desk with John Trowbridge. They were close companions, Horatio Alger greatly appreciating the opportunity arranged for him, and Trowbridge pleased with the relief from burdensome labor that his new assistant cheerfully provided.

Renting an inexpensive room in Boston, but a short walk from the office, Horatio settled down to city life. He divided spare time between tutoring and composing, and before the year ended, a number of articles were published in the Boston Transcript, the New York Daily Sun and other journals.

It was, at the start, a pleasant situation but it did not last. Early in 1857 the general business situation worsened. A number of industries failed; unemployment rose steadily. For Horatio, the depression was first felt in the notification, by periodicals that had been buying his stories, that — because of losses in earnings — they must discontinue these purchases. Shortly afterward, some of the students he tutored were obliged to discontinue, and in May Horatio lost his job at True Flag.

"My writing career is stalled," he wrote to Gusti, "but I am not discouraged. I am thinking of going to New York where, perhaps, I can situate at one of the newspapers. It may be just the thing. If nothing else, I could take a school, but I've also thought of returning to finish at Cambridge. It would please Father. What is happening at home?"

His sister's reply arrived early the next week.

"Of first importance," she wrote, "James has left for the gold fields of California. He went last week and, doubtless, it will be ages before we hear from him. You know how he is, and none of us chould change his mind. We had all we could do to keep Francis from going, too. When he was gone, Mother wept. She has her hands full with Annie, who has been abed for some days. Her cough gets no better. Father is as always, and so am I."

Horatio had dinner with Will Adams, a few evenings later, and told him of the letter. Adams always asked for Gusti, and did not conceal his warm friendship for the high-spirited young lady.

The conversation soon drifted to other matters, primarily the discouraging prospects for a journalist during these hard times.

"I can hold out," Adams said. "But it means I still can't quit teaching. I tell you, Horatio, I'd give a lot to write full-time. Some day I shall; you mark my words."

"It's what I wish for you and me, both," Horatio agreed.

A message from James French & Co. a month later, sent Horatio hurrying to that publishing house. Knyvet Lowell, the editor, greeted him cordially, inquiring if he could anonymously handle a rush assignment.

For the first time in several years, Horatio — nervous and over-anxious — was embarrassed by a fit of stammering, but recovered fast enough to assure him he was immediately available.

Rudd & Carleton, a New York publishing house — the editor explained — had just issued a slim volume of satirical verse by William Allen Butler. Entitled "Nothing to Wear," it was reprinted from Harper's Weekly, where it won wide and favorable reception.

"This book," he said, handing it to Horatio, "should do rather well. In substance," he continued, "it's a comical peep-through-the-keyhole at high society; Paris gowns, Tiffany diamonds, fancy dress balls. That sort of thing. We want to follow this up with a reply along the same lines, playing up woes of the idle rich. You know: lots of money, lots of time, but nothing to do. Do you follow me?"

Returning to his room, Horatio read Butler's book, and then wrote steadily for the greater part of five days. He drank gallons of black coffee and slept only when too exhausted to see what he was putting on the paper before him.

He finished shortly after sunrise on a humid, sweltering day in mid-July. Taking the manuscript immediately to the publisher, Horatio arrived before the office opened. Waiting in the corridor, he read over his lines, making changes and repeating stanzas aloud to himself in the empty hallway.

Mr. Lowell eventually appeared and promptly set to reading the poem Horatio placed on his desk. The humor of it pleased him. He nodded his head approvingly at its tempo, and remarked that the millionaire's son, Augustus Fitz-Herbert — who was the central character — as well as the hangers-on, snobs and situations into which Horatio injected them, were exactly what he had in mind.

A month later the book was displayed in libraries and stationers' shops along Washington Street. It was titled "Nothing to

Do: A Tilt at our Best Society," and was issued only slightly ahead of several other "Nothings," — all follow-up to Butler's work — that were hurriedly printed by enterprising publishers.

With a check for twenty-five dollars in his pocket, Horatio Alger left James French & Co., and — after stopping at a restaurant for a hearty breakfast — went directly to his lodging, where he slept through the day and night, until the next morning. Upon awakening, he examined the week's growth of beard and decided to let it remain. Several days later, however, he tired of it and shaved all but the mustache. It was light brown, sparse and scraggly, and Horatio tugged at it constantly, in the hope that would make it grow faster.

During the last week in July, Horatio joined some twenty-one of his Harvard classmates for a fifth anniversary reunion. Some of them were already making their mark in various fields. Several only recently left graduate schools and a few still attended classes at Cambridge. Looking at the faces that lined both sides of the long table, Horatio felt that, in the years since leaving the university, he accomplished less — and could show less —than most of his chums. A half-dozen had married and among the group were business men, lawyers, physicians and ministers. If he had followed his father's advice, he thought, he would now be a parson like Bill Leverett, Frank Hilliard and a number of others.

As impulsively as he left the Divinity School, almost five years earlier, Horatio decided to return and complete the course. It would take almost three years, he estimated, so the sooner he started, the sooner he'd be on his way. He still was not positive he could devote his life to the church, but in his mind found various justifications and assured himself that, like other preachers, he would continue writing.

The next day Horatio made arrangements to return, in August, to the College Yard and theological studies. Upon registering, he was relieved to learn he could receive funds from the Hopkins Charity — the same grants that enabled his father to attend Divinity School — and he would be relatively free from financial stress.

"I have made up my mind to go back, Father," he wrote to Reverend Alger, "and this time I stay to finish. You can depend upon that!"

CHAPTER 14

POLITICS AND PROBLEMS

THE RELAXED ATMOSPHERE of Cambridge offered welcome relief to Horatio and he occasionally wondered why he waited so long to return to the Divinity School. His routine was much easier than during undergraduate days; there were fewer hours of class-work, a less-rigid schedule and an abundance of leisure.

In his free time, Horatio continued to write, but many of his stories were rejected, newspapers and magazines still unable to afford outside contributions. Returned manuscripts were put aside. He had little doubt but that they eventually would be published. But for the present, he decided, he could earn more by coaching younger students, and he set himself up as a private tutor of classical languages.

Letters from Gusti arrived regularly, and from these her brother learned of new dissention in Marlborough caused by construction of two railway spur lines that connected the town with Boston. The North Branch Railroad, already in operation, was owned by Mark Fay and several members of the Bigelow family, all of them communicants of the West Parish Church, over which Reverend Alger presided. Friction and conflict simmered even before the recent completion of the rival South Branch Line, sponsored by an East Parish group. Amidst increasing bitterness, the litigation was taken to district courts where it lingered for many months.

For a while attention was diverted from the railroad rivalry when a runaway slave, on his way to freedom in Canada, was found and turned over to the law. The Negro, who said his name was Rush — it wasn't known if that was his first or last name — had almost made good his escape from a plantation near Savannah, Georgia.

Returning to his shack after a day of labor on the roads, Rush found his infant alone and weeping, his wife having during his absence been sold to another land owner. Grief-stricken and unable to learn where the woman had been taken, Rush became infuriated, savagely battered the overseer and, seizing his little daughter, ran all night through the woods.

Occasionally receiving help — and frequently hiding from search parties — they avoided towns and villages, sleeping in forests and traveling slowly after dusk. Rush generally was on the verge of starvation, living on berries and bringing what food he could find to the baby girl. During several days of rain both became sick and feverish and, on the night they crossed the North Carolina-Virginia border, they were too weak to travel further.

The child coughed continuously as Rush held her in his arms in the darkness. When, after some hours, the coughing stopped, the fugitive dozed for a while, awakening shortly before dawn. The infant, now silent and motionless, was dead. As the sun rose, Rush buried his daughter, prayed over her tiny grave and then continued his flight to the North.

In captivity again, after more than two months on the escape route, Rush was nursed back to health. But the law must be upheld, the court ruled, and he was soon on his way back to the South and slavery.

Many in the community were infuriated by what they termed gross injustice, and Obadiah Albee led a movement to impeach the judge who handed down the decision. In this he had the support of Reverend Alger who — at the same time — was deeply embroiled in a heated exchange with The Reverend John H. Hopkins, Episcopal Bishop of Vermont, who was an outspoken anti-abolitionist and an apologist for slavery.

The runaway slave issue was still being argued as the elections of 1858 approached, and there were many who wanted to nominate Albee for the State Legislature. He declined, saying he could not spare the time from Gates Academy, and urged supporters to choose Reverend Alger instead. This was done, and the pastor elected despite those opposed to his views on temperance, and who believed he should stick to preaching and keep out of politics. Because of the parson's earlier service, as delegate from Chelsea, he was designated Patriarch of the Massachusetts House of Representatives.

During the winter recess of 1858, Horatio returned to Marlborough to teach the session at a district school, earning $71.37 for the season. With the extra cash he saved over the past two years, he planned a trip to Europe after finishing the theology course. But for the present, until he went back to Harvard in January, he was content to teach, to relax at his parents' home and occasionally assist the parson.

The West Parish had for generations been settled by the Bigelow family, and they were for two centuries active in every aspect of the community's growth and development. Unfortunately for Reverend Alger, his impulsive and often unstatesmanlike outbursts brought him into headlong conflict with members of that close-knit clan.

Probably unintentionally, he sorely offended his friend, Levi Bigelow when, in the official capacity of school superintendent, he visited him at Robin Hill District School, of which Levi had long been the greatly-respected principal. Although versed in many subjects, especially mathematics (he was also a land surveyor), Levi's forte and great pride was ornamental penmanship. Dexterous handling of the quill had won for him widespread reputation, and he passed on to students his skill at beautifully styling delicately shaded swans, peacocks, eagles and doves. In joyous anticipation of the minister's visit, he prepared to show some of his pupils' finest work.

The pastor scarcely noticed the splendid array when he entered, and proceeded to call on boys and girls to recite. Waiting patiently for the right moment, Levi, with a broad smile, proudly directed Reverend Alger's attention to the artistic exhibit, while youngsters held their breath, awaiting the appraisal by their guest.

He put on his spectacles and stepped back a few paces, squinting eyes slightly and rubbing his chin. For several seconds he examined the Spencerian and Old English specimens, and then remarked, "Mr. Bigelow, some of these birds look as though they haven't finished hatching out of their eggs!"

His humor — if it was so intended — missed its mark by far and, a moment after the parson left the building, the schoolmaster brought his cane angrily down on the top of his desk and announced, "Class dismissed!"

Barely a month later, embarking upon a campaign to enforce stricter Sabbath observance, Reverend Alger aimed his wrath at Levi's son Leander Bigelow. Word reached him that Leander — a farmer — generally loaded his wagon on Sundays, in order to get an earlier start to market Monday morning.

As the minister reprimanded the young man from the pulpit, various Bigelows exchanged surprised, disapproving glances. Reverend Alger, a number of them decided, was carrying his nonsense too far!

Within the year Leander moved from the West Parish, having bought a larger farm some distance from the town. One day, Reverend Alger — driving along the road — saw Leander plowing a field. Pulling up his horse, the pastor called out to his former parishioner, "Halloo, Mr. Bigelow. Glad to see you. What are you doing these days?"

"Still farming," was the reply. "Not half so profitable as preaching or stealing, but it's a damn sight more honorable. Giddy-ap!"

After being ineffectively shuttled from one court to the next, the legal battle between Marlborough's competing North and South Branch Railroads was handed over to members of the State Legislature assembling early in 1859.

With Reverend Alger as their representative, Mark Fay, the Bigelows and other North Branch stockholders — as well as most West Parish residents — were confident they would win.

For some reason, however, the majority voted in favor of the South Branch, leaving the minister and his constituents stunned and defeated.

A few days later, on April 12, 1859, Reverend Alger — sensing deep resentment and increasing dissatisfaction with his efforts and policies — offered his resignation. It would take effect three months later, and the Church Committee set to finding a successor.

Having lived for fifteen years in Marlborough and now reaching well into middle-age, the minister was saddened at the prospect of leaving, and his family regretted his decision.

By early July, however, no replacement had been chosen and Reverend Alger was asked to remain on a temporary basis. This was agreeable to him, especially as — when news of his resignation became known — he was offered an excellent pulpit if he could wait a year to take over. The Rev. William G. Babcock, minister of the First Unitarian Church at South Natick, sixteen miles away, would retire in 1860, and he and his congregation were unanimous in their desire that Reverend Alger move in at that time. To show their sincere interest in his leadership, the contract was arranged many months in advance, made binding by a cash payment the parson considered most acceptable.

In the meantime he maintained his rigorous pace at West Parish Church, even assisting in selecting the new minister. Duties as school committeeman continued, and he still travelled to the State Capitol to attend meetings of the House of Representatives.

Although the pastor assured himself and his family that the year prior to settling in South Natick would be a period of long-needed relaxation, he became more deeply embroiled than ever in Marlborough's problems and activities.

One year hence the town would celebrate the bi-centennial of its incorporation in 1660, and Reverend Alger became chairman of the arrangements committee. The Shenstone Tree Planting Society, which he founded a few years earlier, was growing, and would soon issue a monthly publication, which he must help produce.

Equally time-consuming, but far less pleasant, was the minister's involvement in the heated controversy centering about his close friend, Obadiah Wheelock Albee. A movement was set in motion — and rapidly gaining momentum — to tear down the outdated Gates Academy and build a new public high school. Underlying this plan was an effort to replace Mr. Albee with a younger principal; a man who could bring to Marlborough latest trends and practices of education.

Virtually all agreed the improved institution was a necessity. There was division of opinion as to whether Albee or another should take charge. But the source of increasing friction was the extremes to which some townspeople went to discredit Albee and make him appear as an inept relic whose replacement was long overdue.

All this went on without so much as the acknowledgment of Obadiah Albee. He refused to speak out in his own behalf, and his unwillingness to get into the fight exasperated Reverend Alger.

"As long as they want me, Parson, I'll stay," he said. "If they've finished with me, I'll go. Maybe it *is* time for a new chap to bring in fresh ideas, eh?"

After centuries as a slumbering hamlet, Marlborough was growing steadily, and changes were noticeable. Main Street lengthened in both directions, lined with many stores and professional offices. In addition to food and clothing shops were taverns, millinery rooms, dressmakers, hardware, bootmakers, furniture and dry goods shops; a barber, dentists, doctors, lawyers, a photographer and agents for everything from sewing machines to farm equipment. A newspaper, The Marlborough Mirror, was now issued weekly, informing old and many new residents of regional events.

It was primarily among the newcomers that those opposed to Albee's continued administration found support. They saw only the stooped, aging schoolmaster, and knew little of the dedicated scholar who befriended and inspired nearly three decades of Marlborough youth.

"If he would talk to the people," his many friends declared, "he could convince them. But he won't lift a finger to help himself!"

"Who has the time?" Albee asked in reply, "with a new term starting and our nation being torn apart by the slaveholders? I advise you not to spend energy on me. More important things must be done."

As the year 1859 drew to a close, the dispute continued to spread, but Obadiah Albee still remained silent. The time was rapidly approaching, however, when he must make his own feelings known.

When Reverend Alger suggested organizing the Shenstone Society, its single purpose was to add beauty to streets of the expanding township, especially in less attractive new districts — populated mostly by immigrants — sprouting around the factories. Shade trees and shrubs were planted each spring, with gratifying results.

Its members — including a number of East Parish people — so thoroughly enjoyed their monthly meetings in the church vestry that they decided to continue them through autumn and winter. For these gatherings, various entertainments were provided, programs consisting of musicales, group singing, readings and declamations, with the evening often highlighted by a humorous recitation. As the group was named after William Shenstone, the Eighteenth Century English botanist who also was a poet, all were encouraged to present their own original verse.

By early spring, editors were enthusiastically preparing the first issue of their monthly publication, the Shenstone Laurel. In addition to news of local interest and literary contributions, the journal was made self-supporting by regularly filling two of its four pages with advertisements for such patent medicines as Dr. McLane's Vermifuge for Worms; Wistar's Balsam of Wild Cherry for Coughs; Fleming's Cephalic Pills to cure headaches, and Oxygenated Bitters guaranteed to end liver and bilious complaints, acidity, flatulency, dyspepsia and loss of appetite. There also were offers of fresh Vermont butter at less than twenty cents a pound; "ladies' capes and sacks in the latest approved styles of 1860;" an engraving depicting "Daniel Webster's Great Speech for the Union!!" — cheap at $1.25; harnesses, carriage trimmings, "1,000 yards of dress goods;" a blacksmith "wanted immediately — none but an American need apply;" and an assortment of "Mrs.

C. W. Cottings straw bonnets, boulevard hats and shaker hoods at very low prices."

There was news at last from James. He had reached California, travelling the long overland route, and struck out for gold fields in the high Sierras.

"It's almost two years since I left home," he wrote, "and you probably wonder if I'm still alive. . . Life is rough in these mountains, but it agrees with me. There are some up here who have been panning for ten years or more, and have nothing to show for their hardship. I've been able to put up a little, 'though probably not more than if I followed a trade at home. But this is a vast and different world than you know, and I shall remain for a while. . ."

Francis Alger, now eighteen years old, was determined to leave Marlborough to make his own way. He occasionally spoke of going West to search for his brother and to make his own fortune as a miner. But now that James had been heard from — and his report of rugged existence in the camps was unappealing to Francis — the young man decided to seek his future in the city.

He first thought of going to New York, but his parents persuaded him that prospects were better in Boston. There he would find progress easier, the minister suggested, and he had relatives to help him get settled. This seemed agreeable, and Francis soon left for Boston. Horatio found him a room in Franklin Street, and the Fennos arranged employment in a men's clothing store. Although he was not aggressive, Francis had a pleasant personality and became a successful salesman.

Gusti's letters sadly told of Annie's worsening lung fever and coughing spells. "If only she could be someplace where there is constant sunshine," she wrote to Horatio, "it would surely do her some good. As it is, she appears weaker every day. Momma is, of course, distressed, and so is Papa, even though he says nothing."

As for herself, Gusti said, she continues teaching and has written some sketches which she sent to periodicals, so far without good results.

"Papa's great pleasure, at this time," she continued, "is the realization that you will soon finish at the Divinity School and become a preacher. With all his worries, I'm glad he has this to look forward to."

Wednesday, June 13th, 1860, was set as the date of the Bi-Centennial Celebration of the Incorporation of Marlborough, and by mid-May plans for the parade, speeches and related public observances were well under way.

Reverend Alger — Chairman of the Committee on Arrangements, and also holding the post of Chaplain — lost no time in dismaying planners by scheduling morning church services as a part of the day-long program, and insisting that contingents of Antiques and Horribles — a generally boisterous merry-making association — not be permitted to join in the procession. After several days of useless and frustrating argument, a compromise was reached. There would not be any special church services, but Reverend Alger would lead the celebrants in prayer, and the Antiques and Horribles would conduct a separate march late in the afternoon, well after the official morning parade had ended.

The Marlborough Mirror filled almost eight columns of its issue of Saturday, June 16th, with a report of the event, the detailed story appearing next to an item, headlined "Garibaldi in Sicily," and starting: "Garibaldi, the Italian patriot, has gone from Piedmont to Sicily, to aid in the revolutionary movement there."

"The day of the Bi-Centennial Celebration, pleasant as one could wish," the newspaper stated, "was ushered in by the firing of one hundred guns and the ringing of bells. All the night previous, an occasional toot told of the gathering cohorts of the Antiques and Horribles, who were raising their courage to the martial music of fish horns. At an early hour, after promenading the principal streets, they assembled on Liberty Green," where they conducted their own mock observance.

The official procession, starting promptly at ten o'clock, was led by the Marlborough Rifle Company, marching smartly to the beat set by Gilmore's Drum Corps. Next came carriages containing committeemen, orators, the town's four oldest citizens and a number of invited guests.

Then followed marching societies, Free Masons, Sons of Temperance, and Hall's Boston Brass Band. There were delegations from the other boroughs and neighboring communities —

most of them carrying colorful banners — followed by volunteer fire-fighting contingents.

"Dressed in uniform, which consists of red jackets, blue pants and the New York style of fireman's hats," the article continued, assembled crowds cheered the "Torrent Engine Company No. 1, Wide Awake Hose Company of Milford, Yankee Engine Company No. 5, Niagara No. 3, Tiger Associates of Worcester, Okommakamesit Engine Company and Eureka Fire Brigade of Feltonville."

The newspaper estimated that some twelve to fifteen thousand persons jammed the town to take part in the event. "1,400 excursion tickets were issued on the Agricultural and Worcester Railroad," it was noted, "and 600 from Feltonville."

Under sunny, cloudless skies, the procession moved forward from the East Common along streets decorated with flags, streamers and bunting. Banners stretched "from Mr. Stowe's blacksmith shop to C. B. Whitney's shoe manufactory; from Mr. Lewis Howe's to Mrs. Andrews' Boarding House, and a campaign flag fluttered between the homes of Deacon William Stetson and S. A. Chipman.

"Among many private residences, we note Squire Hollis Loring's, displaying English and American flags in neat festoons, showing the dates 1660 - 1860; Thomas Corey's finely draped with bunting, and William Dadmun's, superbly decorated in front with evergreens, flowers, etc. Public buildings were trimmed with streamers and the shields of several states, and the Ordway Hall Oyster Saloon displayed American and Irish flags and a sign declaring 'Ireland must be free in 1860'."

After completing the winding route through Marlborough, the procession arrived at a huge tent set up on Ockocangansett Hill, where ceremonies were held. The heat soon became oppressive within, and swarms of buzzing flies added to the discomfort of spectators who — some seated; many standing — listened to a half-dozen speeches. After the talks, the assembly heard a hymn specially written for the occasion by William Cullen Bryant, and a choir sang a piece, titled "Bi-Centennial Ode," that Horatio composed at Reverend Alger's request.

"Immediately after the orations closed, about two o'clock," the Marlborough Mirror reported, "the ranks re-formed and proceeded to a large pavilion near the depot, where J. B. Smith had prepared one of his best feasts. He had seats and plates for about 1,600, and the tent was well filled."

After the Antiques and Horribles performance in the late afternoon ("a most ludicrous affair, which, though not part of the Committee's programme, will not soon be forgotten"), "a concert, never excelled in this town, was given by Hall's Boston Band, Gilmore's Band and the Marlborough Cornets. The latter never played better. Fireworks closed the festivities and, at a late hour, the meeting was adjourned one hundred years."

Shortly before the Algers moved to South Natick, a month later, Obadiah Albee resigned as principal of Gates Academy. Declaring that he agreed with those who believed it was time for a younger man to replace him, the teacher said he wanted to retire to his nearby farm home and enjoy a life of leisurely reading. He did this, but also continued to devote much time to the community. He was appointed to fill the vacancy in the State Legislature, created by Reverend Alger's departure, and in this office drafted the law which guaranteed sanctuary to any slave who might escape to Massachusetts. He also became a director of the North Branch Railroad and a trial justice in municipal court. In his spare time he took over the parson's duties as the Shenstone Laurel's editor and chief contributor.

His was, he often said, a very active retirement.

CHAPTER 15

A TRIP ABROAD

DURING THE LAST DAYS of July, 1860, Horatio graduated from the Divinity School, leaving immediately for his family's new home at South Natick. A busy month lie ahead, for in September he was leaving for Europe with his former Harvard classmate Charley Vinal — who also recently completed the theological course at Cambridge — and his cousin, George Fenno, of Boston.

The three young men had been planning the voyage for over a year, and Horatio arranged with the New York Sun — in whose columns his writing had already appeared — to mail them regular news reports from abroad. He offered the same correspondence to the Marlborough Mirror and, between the two newspapers, was assured of payments averaging almost five dollars a week.

He loved South Natick from the moment he stepped from the Wellesley Stage that arrived in front of Bailey's Hotel.

Across the square stood the First Unitarian Church and downhill, over a wooden bridge that spanned the Charles River, was the parsonage, still in the disarray of resettlement by its new tenants.

More beautiful, by far, than his childhood home at Chelsea,

near the sea, and in a community much smaller and quieter than Marlborough, Horatio was from the start delighted with the serenity of the village.

Natick, the town center — two miles distant — was a busy crossroads of traffic between Boston and Worcester, and a production center of the finest hand-made shoes in the country. It was here that Henry Wilson — who in 1855 was elected to the United States Senate — first opened his modest pegging shop and, even in the nation's capital, he was still referred to as "the Natick cobbler." It was a title he relished and often used to describe his humble beginnings.

But South Natick, the heart of a farming community, rested tranquilly on a slight rise of shore at the side of the river. The original site — named Neataug, after the tribe of local Indians — was planned in 1650 by The Reverend John Eliot, a dissenting minister who came from England.

In his efforts to benefit the inhabitants, who were being sold liquor, cheated and mistreated by newly-arrived immigrants, Eliot persuaded The Queen's Great and General Court to vote the region out-of-bounds to white men. He laid out three streets, dividing them into lots for houses and gardens. At their midst, near an ancient oak beneath which Eliot preached to the Indians in their own language, he directed the construction of a circular fort. This building also served as a school-room on weekdays and a house of worship Sundays, with an upstairs loft used as storage for furs and articles made for sale at nearby markets.

Behind the fort, which eventually became the First Unitarian — or Eliot — Church, and whose pulpit was now occupied by Reverend Alger, a graveyard known as the Old Indian Burial Ground was situated. The last tribesmen had departed by 1763, and the cemetery became the resting place of generations of settlers who eventually took over the land.

The church, splendidly white with green-painted roof and high, tapering spire, was a brief walk from the parsonage, with its grassy lawn, long picket fence and spacious porch that faced on Pleasant Street. It was a comfortable two story structure and Horatio's room, on the second floor, overlooked the river through a leafy grove of elms across the road. In the morning the water's surface glistened in bright sunshine, and Horatio delighted to awaken to the sound of the stream slowly passing over a low dam beneath the bridge.

Olive and Gusti were hard at work organizing the household. Annie insisted on helping, but she tired easily and spent afternoons resting in the garden. Sometimes Gusti sat with her, reading aloud the dialogues she was writing, a few of which had already been published.

Reverend Alger was always busy, getting to know his parishioners and keeping up with new duties. Horatio assisted him, and on August 17th travelled to Chicopee where he preached the Sabbath and presided over the congregation during an absence of the regular pastor.

Soon after returning home, Horatio packed and departed for Boston where Charley Vinal and George Fenno were waiting and, together, they completed final arrangements for their ocean trip. The morning after arriving in the city he called at the office of the Literary Companion — a new Gleason publication that printed some of his short stories — and offered a number of recently completed pieces. A selection was made, for future use, and it was suggested that he now sign his works "By Rev. Horatio Alger, Jr." It would enhance the periodical's high moral character, the editor explained. Enthusiastically, Horatio agreed, pleased to combine his new role as churchman with his overwhelming desire to be an author.

A few days later, on September 5th, the three companions boarded the Cunard ship, Arabia, and at high tide sailed from East Boston Harbor on their way, at last, across the Atlantic to England.

"Our voyage was rather disagreeable," Horatio wrote in an article that appeared some weeks later, "and we were all heartily glad to reach Liverpool last Sunday morning at 2 A.M. We remained 'til Monday afternoon, seeing a few sights and doing a little shopping. We each bought a small knapsack strapping over the shoulders, and capable of containing a couple of pounds of clothing. Then, booking our carpet bags to London, we started through the Kingdom as travelling students."

By rail, carriage and often walking, they first toured Wales, visiting castles at Conway and Caernorvon; Mount Snowden "whose scenery strongly resembles the White Mountain region," the nearby slate quarries and ruined cities "full of strange, grotesque buildings, Roman relics and thousand year-old churches."

After hiking to Holyhead through fields in which "the harvest season has just begun. . .we took the night boat and the next morning stepped on the quays at Dublin, where I am stopping at Price's Hotel on Sackville Street, opposite Nelson's Pillar.

"Dublin is a very gay and handsome city," Horatio reported, "with plenty of dress and fashion. Yesterday we went into the Lord Lieutenant's palace, and in the evening attended the Theatre Royal where Mario and Grisi are at present singing in an Italian opera."

Their travels continued, by jaunting cart and donkey-drawn wagon, through the beautiful Irish countryside. Leaving rugged coastal towns far behind, Horatio, Charley Vinal and George Fenno slowly covered miles of narrow roads bordered by mossy piled-rock fences. Farmers waved to them from hillsides and women and children came out of tiny thatched-roof cottages to greet them as they passed.

After spending two days enjoying the beauty of the Killarney lakes and surrounding mountains whose high peaks were always hidden in mists, the friends started "for Belfast by rail, whence we go by water to Glasgow, and shall probably spend several days in Scotland."

From the highlands, south through the midlands, they reached London on a cold, damp morning in November. Their hotel room was always chilly, and they would have left immediately, but for the necessity "to examine the many magnificent landmarks about the town. Fortified with a hearty breakfast of porridge, kippers and tea, we set out each morning in a different direction and soon knew the place as intimately as Boston, to which there is occasional similarity."

Three weeks later they crossed the English Channel to France. Horatio, anxious to try his knowledge of the French language in native surroundings, appeared on deck before dawn, eager for a first glimpse of the Normandy Coast. But heavy fog prolonged the night, and a steady, freezing drizzle crusted the deck with a thin, icy glaze. Morning and daylight came at last, but land still lay in the unseen distance behind an off-shore haze.

A few hours later the fog lifted. The vessel moved slowly into port and by noon passengers were disembarking, most of them going directly to the railroad terminal, from where the Paris Express was soon scheduled to depart.

It rained continuously for three days, and Horatio, coughing and feverish by the time he reached Paris, was confined to his lodgings for almost a week. Frustrated and impatient, he sat at a small table, writing and yearning to burst forth upon the fabled city which still seemed distant even though he could hear its noises and breathe its musty, late autumn air. His small room overlooked a courtyard behind the Rue de Surene, and Horatio gazed dreamily out the window, watching tradesmen deliver supplies to the scullery door. Every morning a boy chopped wood for kitchen fires, and shortly after noon Horatio saw the heavy charwoman who cleaned the upstairs chambers cross the yard carrying his lunch. This most often consisted of a deep bowl of soup, thick with vegetables and sometimes also containing a chunk of beef. There was a length of light-baked, crusty bread — frequently still warm and aromatic — and an apple or pear.

Late in the afternoon, Charley and George returned with breathless reports of wonderful things they saw, promising Horatio that when he felt better they would give him a deluxe tour of Paris. By the weekend the sun shone, and Horatio was well enough to go out. They visited the Madeleine Church, Tuileries Gardens and Champs Elysees. The next day Notre Dame, the Louvre and island cities of the Seine.

By the beginning of the following week Horatio had fully recovered and crisp weather filled him with vigor and high spirits. The three young men climbed the steep hill of Montmartre, visiting Pere la Chaise Cemetery on the way up, and pausing to rest at Sacre Coeur.

"From this place," Horatio wrote, "the view is so breathtaking as to be difficult to describe. The city spreads endlessly beneath us, crossed by wide avenues lined with venerable trees. Parks and public gardens abound. Boulevards are crowded the day-long with busy people, carriages and omnibuses. Here and there the River Seine appears, then winds out of sight, only to reappear unexpectedly. Along its banks some fishermen always can be seen, while small boats move silently in both directions, carrying food and other supplies to and from the countryside, and beyond."

As much as they wished to remain in Paris, Horatio and Charley Vinal were amenable to George Fenno's urging, early in January, 1861, that they continue on their journey to Italy. The weather had become increasingly cold and cheerless, and the prospect of warm, sunny climate was appealing.

Agreeing to return to Paris on the way home, they travelled next to Marseilles, remaining for a week in the French port on the Mediterranean.

"Skies are blue and weather agreeable," Horatio reported. "At home we could enjoy this only briefly in the spring, but here it is mild many months of the year."

Italy was a thrilling experience for Horatio and his Harvard classmate, Vinal, as they visited places that, during their undergraduate days, Professor Longfellow had described in warm and affectionate detail. Italian was one of Horatio's favorite subjects and now, in Rome at last, he felt that he long knew magnificent structures and monuments he was seeing for the first time.

"I have the impression," he noted, "that I've been here before. All is familiar and, from the moment we arrived, I believe I could have given accurate directions to a stranger. How this will amuse Longfellow!"

Travelling slowly southward, Horatio recorded details and sent them, in an article, to the Shenstone Laurel.

By February he had enjoyed a moonlight cruise on the Mediterranean, ascended Mount Vesuvius, explored "Pompeii, Herculaneum and Stabili, three cities destroyed by the famous eruption of A.D. 79," and apparently ate quantities of "large, golden oranges, some of which were fourteen months on the trees, and in flavor excelled any I'd ever eaten."

After bargaining and persuading a driver to lower his rate from ten to four-and-a-half piastres, Horatio described the twenty-five mile carriage ride from Naples to Sorrento. He recalled that they "left about nine o'clock one pleasant morning, proposing to arrive in time to dine at six. The road is an excellent one, skirting the bay through nearly its entire extent.

"Foreign-looking people were engaged in various occupations which they freely pursued out of doors, while others had no earthly business but to stare at passersby. The villages are so different from our own. The varied landscape, with Vesuvius smoking menacingly in the background, possesses beauty that has not been overrated, and every foot of it is classic ground."

The next day the tourists "decided upon an excursion to Il Deserto, a convent on the summit of a lofty hill. The landlord promised to supply donkeys for the expedition.

"In coming down the mountain, Charley and myself were some distance in advance of the rest of the party. We kept on, not suspecting we lost the way, until we came to the edge of a ravine we hadn't seen before. Turning the donkeys about, we retraced our course nearly a mile. Here three paths branched off, but we were uncertain which to take. Charley suggested we trust to the donkeys' instinct, but they were firmly determined to offer us no help whatever.

"At last we guessed at the road, and after a time overtook a priest. I summoned up sufficient Italian to ask him the direction but, unfortunately, couldn't understand his voluble answer. In perplexity, I switched to Latin, and then my early devotion to Andrews and Stoddard's Latin Grammar served me in a way I could hardly have dreamed of in my schoolboy days."

Two weeks later, Horatio, Vinal and Fenno were back in Paris, arriving during a soaking snowfall. The next morning, February 22d, they visited the Palais Royal and, returning through Rue St. Honore, unexpectedly came upon the funeral procession of Augustin Eugene Scribe, the revered dramatist and Academician, who had died at the age of seventy.

Asking bystanders to point out noted persons, Horatio made careful notes and later prepared a report of the event that was published in the North American Review.

All traffic was halted, he wrote, "by a dense crowd gathered in front of the Church of Saint Roch. The center of the street was filled by a long procession, stretching from Place Vendome to the portals of the church, which was draped in funereal black.

"This ancient edifice, beneath which repose the ashes of Voltaire, and which witnessed, during the last century, some of the most frightful atrocities of the French Revolution, was this day the scene of a striking and, for many reasons, remarkable ceremony.

"The most prominent men in France were assembled within its walls to pay a last tribute of respect and affection to one who, for nearly half a century, held possession of the French stage, achieving in that period a long list of brilliant successes, hardly interrupted by failure.

"Pall-bearers were Monsieur Dumas, President of the Municipal Board of Paris; Vitet, Director of the French Academy; Thierry, Director of the Theatre Francais, and Auguste Maquet, President of the Club of Authors and Dramatic Composers. The Academy was represented by its most distinguished members, among them Cousin, a striking figure with white hair; Thiers, author of 'The Consulate and the Empire,' the Duc de Broglie and others.

"Actors, attached to four leading theatres of Paris — Theatre Francais, Opera, Opera Comique and Gymnase — appropriately paid homage to the author in whose fame they so often participated. The Minister of State, the Minister of Public Instruction, Count de Walewski, Monsieur Baroche, President of the Council of State, and numerous others of the imperial government lent dignity to the occasion.

"Notwithstanding a drizzling rain which fell through the greater part of the day, not less than three thousand persons, embracing those of social and literary eminence, took part in the services and followed the remains of Scribe to their last resting place.

"Selecting a favorable point for observation, we watched with interest the shifting figures in the procession as, with slow steps and subdued demeanor they passed before him. Poets, philosophers, savants, novelists, dramatic writers, diplomats and cabinet ministers — representatives of the wit, wisdom, science, imagination and statesmanship of France — met today for a common purpose, and were moved in common sorrow.

"Not they alone, for even the workman in his ragged blouse, who sometimes on fete-days occupied a cheap seat in a minor theatre, suffered a personal loss. As the funeral car passed, he doffed his cap and remained standing with uncovered head, murmuring in regretful accents, 'Scribe est mort!' "

*   *   *

During Horatio's final weeks in Paris the weather improved steadily, making daily walks to distant parts of the city pleasantly exhilarating. By mid-March, several mild, sunny days encouraged cafe-owners to set up, outside their shops, the iron tables and chairs that, since the dreary days of late autumn, were stacked in cellars or backyards. Then the tempo of the great metropolis slowed, and Parisians joyously returned to the sidewalk terraces, there to talk, argue or peacefully read newspapers in the bright afternoon sunshine over sips of dark coffee or light wine.

The evening before departing for England and a home-bound steamer, Horatio and Charley Vinal strolled along the left bank of the Seine. George Fenno, who preferred to finish packing and get to bed, did not accompany them. Reaching Boulevard Saint-Michel, they entered one of the street cafes, occupying a table with a fine view of passing traffic.

They had hardly taken their places when, directly behind them, a familiar voice called their names.

"If this is a Class of '52 reunion, may I join?" asked George Sohier — whom they hadn't seen since undergraduate days — as he swung his chair to their table.

It was a delightful surprise for the former classmates, and they sat late into the night retracing their paths since leaving Harvard.

Sohier, even as a student, was a frequent invalid and lately, he told Horatio and Charley, his condition had worsened. They remembered that, even at twenty, he seemed aged and weary, and throughout winter terms his eyes were inflamed, the result of a painful rheumatic condition. Now, with gray hair and pale, drawn features, he appeared old beyond his years.

"For a time I practiced law," he said, "but this trouble kept recurring, and I had to give it up. Doctors urged a long rest abroad, and when I reached Paris I decided to stay. This is my home now, but I get back to Boston every year or two, during the summer."

He wanted to hear news of college friends, and was pleased to learn of their success and accomplishments.

"Hank Oliver was here last fall," Sohier recalled. "He attended medical school in Vienna, and was on his way home. I asked if he still kept those blasted owls that used to keep us awake nights."

The chums laughingly remembered Oliver's searches for frogs in the marsh at the far end of the Harvard Yard, and how he collected scraps from Commons to feed his pets.

It was after midnight when they parted.

The following day Horatio, Charley and George started their homeward journey, remaining briefly in London before continuing to Liverpool, where they put to sea on April 5th.

During the long crossing — throughout which continuous rain forced passengers to remain below deck for days at a time — the three young men passed the hours contemplating their future after returning to America.

For George Fenno there was little speculation. He would resume duties at his family's mercantile business from which, he feared, he had already absented himself too many months

"But this has been a fine trip," he declared, happily, "one I shall always remember. Most likely I won't have the chance to do it again."

Charley Vinal still looked forward to a month of leisure, after which he planned to settle over the Unitarian parish at North Andover, a commitment made before leaving for Europe. The days would pass slowly, he anticipated, for he was eager to begin as minister.

Only for Horatio was the future clouded and uncertain.

"I'll probably assist my father," he surmised, "until I receive a call to take over a church. But I'm in no hurry. I still hope to devote considerable time to writing and, perhaps, even after ordination, I can continue to do so."

"Maybe you'll be sent to Indian Territory, Horatio," his cousin suggested. "You'd find plenty to write about out there."

"Or to California," Charley added. "You can make a fortune mining when you're not preaching."

"For the time being, Boston or New York would do nicely thank you," Horatio said with a smile. "You fellows are apt to fall into bad habits if I'm too far out of sight!"

Monotonously, the voyage continued for two weeks, and none regretted reaching port the morning of April 19th, 1861.

Approaching the pier, passengers crowded along the rail

to watch hectic activity on shore. Naval vessels, getting up steam for hasty departure, were taking on provisions. Blue uniformed troops stood guard while, for some distance along the wharf, what appeared to be several battalions of soldiers, carrying rifles and field packs, stood in formation waiting to board the ships.

"What's happening?" one of the crewmen called over the side to a team of stevedores working below, "Is there going to be a parade?"

"Parade, hell," a dock worker shouted back, "The South has seceded. Fort Sumter's been fired upon. We're at war!"

CHAPTER 16

CIVIL WAR DAYS

THE EVENING HORATIO RETURNED to South Natick there was "A Call to Arms Rally" at the town hall, summoned in response to President Lincoln's appeal for 75,000 troops to crush the Rebellion.

For several days, large signs had been posted on fences and barns. There was a notice in front of Bailey's Hotel, others in store windows and at the post office. Most of the townspeople were present, and the room was filled long before the meeting was called to order.

There were a number of speakers, including Reverend Alger, whose remarks were frequently applauded.

Orators noted "the feeling which now animates every patriotic breast," and guaranteed that the community "will do its share in supplying the talent and spirit requisite to meet the crisis in a manner conforming with the ancient glory of the Good Old Commonwealth!"

Between speeches a cornet band "played inspiring airs, and with 'Yankee Doodle,' 'Hail Columbia' and other well-chosen tunes, contributed to swell the grand chorus of freedom which now is rolling throughout the land." A local weekly newspaper went on to report that, following the playing of these selections, "there was often and hearty hand-clapping."

Announcements, greeted by cheers, were made of a local resident being appointed a naval officer; the hook and ladder company was postponing construction of a new truck house "so those funds can be put to the call of the country, and go forth to defend our honor against traitors and thieves arrayed in arms against us!," and the Stars and Stripes was now "waving gaily atop the Wellesley and Worcester stages."

After a final speech — ". . Let every man who has strength to lift a musket, shoulder it and march; let every man who has a dollar to give, give it. . . ." — twenty-five were asked to volunteer for military service and suggestions made to provide uniforms for a rifle company, and grant a one hundred fifty dollar bounty to each recruit.

Some in the audience opposed the payment, claiming it would increase taxes and that "our people don't need to be hired to fight for their country. . .their patriotism can't be bought."

But the motion was overwhelmingly approved and, to the applause of the assembly, young men from various sections of the hall — Horatio Alger, Jr, among them — stepped forward to put down their names for enlistment.

A few days later, in an atmosphere of celebration, they started for Boston for induction into the Grand Army of the Republic. Most of them carried a few personal belongings wrapped in handkerchiefs or in neatly-tied parcels. After repeated and affectionate farewells to families and neighbors, they climbed into farm wagons and, to the music of fifes, trumpets and drums, left for the railroad station, followed a good part of the way by joyous, shouting children.

Early the following week, the village council received a request for a substitute volunteer. Horatio — his asthmatic condition being discovered during medical examination — was rejected as physically unfit. Despondent, and feeling he was being deprived of a great adventure, he remained for a few days in the city before returning to the parsonage at South Natick.

Without enthusiasm, he accepted a job as junior associate to his father and, until summer, also preached regularly at nearby Dover, where the regular pastor, declaring there would be

151

greater need for God on the battlefields, resigned to join in the expected move Southward by General McClellan's Army of the Potomac.

Early in July the Algers received long delayed mail from James, advising he'd given up mining as "too much digging for too little gold," and moved to San Francisco, taking employment as assistant to an optometrist. "If this surprises you," he wrote to his parents, "what will you think when I tell you that, November 15th last, I married the former Miss Elizabeth H. Ward!"

Another letter, addressed to Horatio, was from Henry Denny, his close companion of college days. It advised that the Civil War was breaking up his law practice and partnership with Harvard classmate, Sidney Willard.

"I have not a bit of time," Henry exclaimed, "for anything other than war work. The army turned me down because of my eyes, but they can't keep me out of the fight. At present," he continued, "I am collecting funds to aid families of John Brown and others killed in the tragedy at Harper's Ferry. Also, I am encouraged that I shall receive an appointment to accompany our troops in the field as an agent of the American Unitarian Association.

"Sid, on the other hand," he continued, "will soon be in uniform. He applied for a commission, which he gets as soon as he raises the necessary men to follow him in the ranks. Signing up the needed number has not been easy, due to considerable lethargy here, and dissatisfaction with the way the war is being run."

Horatio immediately addressed a note to Willard, assuring willingness to join the militia, and mentioning his earlier rejection.

"Come on down," his friend quickly replied. "It's worth a try."

Before the end of the month Horatio was back in Boston, lodging with the Fennos and, during hot afternoons, marching and learning manual of arms, with Sid Willard as drill-master.

Despite exhausting heat, those were exhilarating days for Horatio. He already felt close to the battle and little doubted but that he would soon be ready to avenge the recent Union defeat at Bull Run, and then march on the Confederate capital at Richmond. Before the middle of August, Willard filled his quota, presenting his roster to the Adjutant General. He was appointed a captain in the 35th Regiment of Massachusetts Volunteers and, with his men, reported for duty. Physical examinations were progressing in hasty, superficial manner, and Horatio had, of late, been enjoying excellent health. He believed his chances were good. But, placing the records he carried upon the desk of a Medical Corps sergeant, the soldier asked, without looking up, "Were you ever previously rejected?"

"Yes," Horatio Alger answered, his hopes suddenly dropping. "Why?"

Horatio answered truthfully. He was told to bring his file to the officer-in-charge who, noting the recruit's asthmatic condition, wrote across the paper, "Excused from military service."

The next day Horatio sent a brief message to his father. He was not immediately returning to South Natick, he decided, as to do so after being turned down by the army twice would be humiliating. Rather, the young man decided, he was returning — for the time being — to Cambridge. A number of tutors were needed to replace those who had gone off to war. There he would await the call to a pastorate, and resume writing in his spare moments.

For months Horatio, moody and restless, withdrew from his friends, rarely venturing far from his room near the College Yard. He had little of his usual enthusiasm for teaching Latin and Greek, and could not write anything worth offering for publication. When, in the spring of 1862, he was offered the pulpit of the Unitarian Society at Alton, Illinois, he abruptly declined.

"I couldn't impose myself upon those good people," he wrote to Gusti. "In my present frame of mind I'd fail and, in the end, be once more rejected."

A few weeks later, when Horatio returned from an evening walk by the riverside, he found Henry Denny waiting at his door.

"Rather than risk sleepless nights awaiting a reply," the caller announced in exaggerated tones intended to be humorous, "I came out here to personally invite you to the ten-year reunion of the Class of '52. That's the class of which you, my lad, claim to be a member."

Horatio laughed heartily at the comical performance and, greeting his friend warmly, led the way into the darkened room.

153

Moments later it was cheerfully lighted, and a pot of tea aromatically brewing for the visitor.

"Really, Alger, you can't refuse," Denny continued. "The Choates are coming and so is Oliver. I've written to Vinal and he asks if you'll be there. Frankly, I said you'd attend, so don't let me down."

"So it's already ten years. I was hardly aware of it." Horatio said slowly, "Of course I'll be with you."

The dinner, in July, was held at the Union Club, with ten present. Joe Choate, practicing law in New York, was congratulated on his recent marriage. His brother Bill, now a county commissioner and President of the Salem Common Council, had become noticeably heavier. Oliver was a physician, recently appointed to the staff of Massachusetts General Hospital, and Vinal — "sorrowful-eyed as ever," Oliver said — was comfortably settled over his parish at North Andover.

Adam W. Thaxter ("It's 'A. Wallace Thaxter'," he always corrected those who called him Adam) also attended. As dramatic critic for the popular Saturday Evening Gazette, he was esteemed by actors and audiences, and had, himself, written a number of successful plays.

Others at the table included Charley Bonney, practicing law in the great whaling center of New Bedford, who was a specialist in marine and admiralty cases; Sam Thorndike, who left College before graduation to accompany classmate Bill Hooper on a trip around the world, was practicing law in partnership with Ed Pratt, another member of the Class of '52, and Bill Williamson — whom all greeted by his nickname, The Belfast Giant — also an attorney, was President of the Young Men's Democratic Club of Boston, and a frequent lyceum lecturer at Faneuil Hall.

After the meal Thorndike sang "Our Heroes," and proposed a toast to the memory of Charley Upham, a classmate who recently died. An ode was written for the occasion by Thaxter, and sung by all. Then Bonney, standing, raised his glass of Madeira to "Our absent classmates in the field. May the Lord cover their heads in the day of battle."

Henry Denny, as Class Secretary, next gave news of the men with whom he maintained close contact. Of great interest were reports on those in the War — hearts and prayers were with classmates fighting for both the North and South — and Denny read these first.

Sam Jennison was a lieutenant, stationed in Indian Territory; Sid Willard, promoted to major, had seen action at Arlington Heights, wrote that he wished "Uncle Sam would allow his majors to walk. . . Nature never intended me for a horseman, I hate the beasts!"; Russell Williams — who became a plainsman and Indian trader at White Cloud, Kansas, after graduation — was a naval ensign, serving in the Union's Mississippi Squadron; Horatio Whittemore was examining surgeon at Fort Sewall; Charles Stedman was a medical officer aboard the gunboat Huron; Josiah Porter, the first in the class to volunteer, was a captain under General Patterson, described the battering suffered by Union forces in the Shenandoah Valley; Paul Revere, soon after promotion to Major, was wounded and captured at Ball's Bluff. There was hope he would soon be sent home in an exchange of wounded prisoners. Ben King was a private in the 44th Massachusetts Regiment, the same unit in which Robert Ware was surgeon.

There also were reports from classmates battling for the Confederacy. Guignard Scott had, soon after the outbreak of hostilities, enlisted in the 28th Mississippi Cavalry, under General Armstrong; Bob Fowle was with the Alexandria Rifles; Dave Trimble enlisted but, due to ill health, still hadn't seen much action; Almon Spencer was an artillery sergeant under Bragg; Fred Leverett joined the Beaufort Volunteer Artillery, but was transferred to the 9th South Carolina Infantry; Bill McKim was a captain taking part in a number of engagements; Josiah Collins and Edwin Fay had enlisted, but there were no reports of their whereabouts.

"Thank God they're all alive," Denny concluded, putting down the papers.

It had turned out to be a most pleasant evening, in the company of old friends and, upon leaving, Horatio thanked Denny for digging him out of hibernation.

"Well, Horatio," Vinal said as they left the Union Club, "have you turned those piles of notes you made in Europe into a couple of novels? I remember that, on the boat, you couldn't wait to get started."

155

"I guess the Rebellion changed that," Horatio replied. "I've been feeling so rotten — not being able to get into the fight — that I had no mind for writing nor, for that matter, teaching or preaching."

"I don't agree with you at all. For one thing, there's no shame in being rejected, And you're a minister, Horatio. Perhaps the Lord meant for you to stay behind. He may have greater need for you in a church than on battlefields. Accept the call, Horatio. That's how you can fight. Until you get your church," Vinal added with a faint smile, "write a book so people won't think you wasted time in Europe."

Horatio's spirits were considerably higher, that night, than when he crossed the bridge to Boston hours earlier. Before retiring, he pulled from his trunk sheafs of notes made during his now almost forgotten journey and, reading them while he sipped tea from a favorite large cup, thin threads of ideas began to weave a story in his mind. He slept well, better than at any time since returning from abroad during the early war days of April, more than a year ago.

The seasons changed and, except for an occasional soldier — a visitor or old graduate — seen crossing the College Yard, the war seemed far from Cambridge. After a summer and autumn of frustrating setbacks for Federal armies, with tremendous losses sustained by both sides, there were long weeks of stalemate, with little news to boost morale at home. Field leaders of the North complained more bitterly of hindrance from politicians in Washington than from enemy attacks. Enlistments sagged, and abolitionists increased pressure on President Lincoln to go on record with legislation to end slavery.

On the floor of Congress, Senator Sumner demanded immediate emancipation, and Horace Greeley, in his New York Tribune, backed him up with editorials urging strong measures. The President, already determined to issue the proclamation freeing slaves in Confederate States, waited only for the right moment, advising critics that "my paramount object in this struggle is to save the Union. . ." and asking their patience and forbearance.

More directly affecting civilians in the North than the proclamation of Emancipation which, on January 1, 1863, made the slaves "forever free," was the military draft signed into law the following March. By summer, when the first men were called, bloody riots threatened Boston and raged for three days in New York. Claiming that the Conscription Act favored the wealthy, who might evade service by paying a three hundred dollar penalty or hiring a substitute, unruly groups — led by brawlers and drunken hoodlums — raged through streets in packs of hundreds.

Stores, public buildings, factories, homes and newspaper offices were burned and looted, Negroes were beaten and killed and Federal troops, hastily moved in to restore order, were attacked with guns, cobblestones, torches and clubs.

When the terror ended, conscription resumed, and Horatio received notice to report for army duty. But for the third time he was sent away, classified as physically unfit, and resigned to his unacceptability to fight in the Civil War. For whatever satisfaction it offered him, no less than thirty-five Alger relatives were serving, a number of whom already had been killed in action. The youngest of these was Nahum Francis Alger who, before his fifteenth birthday, joined as a drummer-boy, and had already been following troops into battle for a year-and-a-half. Warren Alger was another. Enlisting April 19, 1861, he was in the Battle of Ball's Bluff, captured at Richmond — escaped — in action at Gettysburg, taken prisoner again — escaped again — eventually wounded and recaptured. He died at Andersonville Prison. After Warren's death, his mother, Susan Saunders Alger, served as a nurse, tending sick and wounded at military hospitals.

Horatio's cousin, The Rev. William Rounseville Alger, nine years older and minister of Boston's Bulfinch Street Church, shared his anxiety to get closer to the fighting but reconsidered when his congregation appealed to him to remain. "At first I didn't like it any more than you do," he told Horatio, "but I came to realize I could, perhaps, accomplish more here at home. Don't think I wouldn't rather be down there with Grant or Meade, especially when I go to meet the trainloads of wounded. I console myself that other Algers are on the battlefield, and try to do the best I can for families of other men at the front."

With his intense hope to participate in the war abandoned, Horatio turned his full attention to writing. He would accept the next call to settle over a church, he assured himself, and would in the meantime write for lonely pickets huddled about distant campfires, and for those who wait at home.

Based primarily upon combat reports he read in newspapers, Horatio began to turn out poems and short stories with enthusiasm and determination. The Boston Transcript used them and the New York Sun, after receiving the first, asked for more. One of the first, "Song of the Croaker" — a rhyme about a philosophical old frog who lived in a swamp near a battlefield — won favorable comment when published in The Rebellion Record, and was reprinted in other periodicals. He followed this with "Last Words," "Gone to the War," and others.

Between war themes, Horatio developed plots he previously outlined in his European notebooks. He recorded his vivid recollection of the funeral of Eugene Scribe, and added details of the illustrious dramatist's career. Finishing a lengthy article after thirty hours of continuous work — except to heat a pot of tea, he rarely paused until the job was done — he delivered the manuscript to the office of the influential North American Review. A few days later he received a note from James Russell Lowell, the editor, advising it had been accepted for publication in the magazine's October issue.

He had already begun the creation of a more ambitious product — a novel — and the good news inspired his labor. In the style of romances currently featured in popular weeklies, Horatio composed a tale of life in Paris slums. His heroine was Marie Bertrand, after whom he titled the story. The villain was her father, Jacques, a criminal and fugitive from the law. Marie, left years before to shift for herself, had nevertheless blossomed into radiant, innocent young womanhood. Industriously, she toiled as a seamstress, earning barely enough to survive. Against the background of city and countryside, characters kind and evil moved the narrative along at a rapid pace. And all turned out well in the end.

Horatio was pleased with the result and, on an impulse, departed for New York to offer it to Moses M. Beach, Editor of the New York Sun. Beach had previously published anonymous Alger articles and it was, in fact, he who authorized Horatio to serve as foreign correspondent in Europe.

But they had never met, and this — Horatio decided — was a good time to get acquainted.

CHAPTER 17

A VISITOR IN NEW YORK

THE NIGHT BOAT FROM BOSTON docked near Fulton Street shortly before six a.m. on a warm autumn morning in 1863, and Horatio had his first glimpse of New York as the sun rose over the East River. South Street was already filled with workers busily unloading newly arrived vessels and preparing others to sail with the tide. From the Battery, as far uptown as Horatio could see, ships' masts and smoke stacks towered above the buildings, with the booms of many square riggers extending overhead across the wharves.

The pungent air smelled of fish, fresh from the ocean, produce grown on Long Island farms, and small livestock, all shortly to be displayed at the city's markets. Pushcarts were stocked and quickly departed. Wagons, pulled by giant horses, rattled noisily along the waterfront, and passengers arriving on early ferries from Brooklyn moved rapidly to their employment.

Darting between the many men laboring on the piers were hordes of ragged, barefoot children intent on earning their breakfast by carrying luggage or guiding out-of-town travellers to their hotels.

"Smash yer bag, Major?" a boy about twelve years old

asked, aggressively reaching for the small parcel Horatio carried.

"No thank you," he answered, surprised and amused, "I wouldn't want it damaged."

"Hokey," replied the lad, impatiently — his eye already searching for another customer — "I don't mean smashed. I mean *smashed!* I mean *carry* yer bag. It's me line o' business, Major. Here, yer better let me take it."

"It's actually very light," Horatio resisted. "I can carry it quite easily. Why do you call me Major?"

" 'Cuz yer look important. Ye ain't a major or a senator? C'mon, lemme help yer. Things is mizzable at home. All the kids is sick and me stepfather'll whup hell outa me if I don't bring some money. I been out all night an' ain't made a shilling."

"Really, I don't need help," Horatio said, kindly, "but I'll give you ten cents if you'll tell me how I get to The Sun office."

"I'll take you there for twenty-five, Major," the boy counter-offered with a business-like air. "Yer better let me, or ye'll get lost sure."

"Very well, lead on," Horatio instructed. "Is it far?"

"Not very. I know a short-cut."

"Does your short-cut pass a restaurant? I haven't had breakfast, and get the impression you could use some, too."

"Yer right there, Major. I was just headin' for Delmonico's when I saw you. I eats there reg'lar."

Horatio laughed, appreciating the youth's quick humor. "I doubt if we'll find them open at this hour," he said, looking at his watch.

"Hokey, what a watch!" the boy exclaimed. "Is it real gold?"

"Yes, it is."

"You must be real rich, Major. I bet it cost you a pooty penny."

"It probably was expensive," Horatio agreed, "but it cost me nothing. My parents gave it to me when I graduated college. It belonged to my grandfather. Perhaps one day you'll get a fine watch, too."

"Not much chance. I got no family to gimme, and I ain't about to be adopted by a rich man, unless yer willin'."

"What about the family you mentioned before?"

161

"No, I ain't got none. Never did. I say whatever'll fetch the customer."

Horatio pitied the young rogue, but was getting hungry and brought the conversation back to the subject of breakfast.

"Oh, there's Toomey's Saloon on Chatham Street," the boy suggested. "We can buy a beer and eat herring and pickles free."

"I'm in the mood for something heartier," Horatio suggested.

"Then it's Pat's on Nassau Street. They got the bulliest beef and 'taters in town for ten cents. It's just t'other end of this alley."

Minutes later they were seated in a basement restaurant patronized mainly by laborers. The food was plain, but portions generous at low cost.

Horatio had just finished the meat platter and sat for a few moments, silently looking at the tattered child facing him.

"Do you always work around the Fulton wharves?" he asked.

"Only sometimes. I was sleepin' in a hallway there and decided I could pick up a few cents to start the day."

"Don't you have a home?"

"None to speak of. There's a crate with some straw in a yard back of Pearl Street, but a big feller beat me to it, so I was bummin' it last night. Sand boxes is swell, 'cuz yer can get it up all around yer. But in winter nothin beats them steam gratin's. Oh, Major, they's just like a featherbed."

"What is your usual line of business, when you're not 'smashing baggage'?"

"That depends. In the morning and evening I sell newspapers. Sometimes I run errands. I pitch pennies good and can always make a meal that way. But many's a night I bum it in the cold. It's real elegant," the boy said, with a philosophical smile, "but I'm goin' to retire soon's me fortune's made."

Breakfast finished, Horatio and his guide resumed their walk to the corner of Fulton and Nassau, near Park Row, where The Sun was located. Streets now were considerably more crowded than an hour earlier. Omnibus and stage traffic jammed the main thoroughfares, and everywhere clerks and businessmen hurried to their offices and shops. To Horatio it seemed very noisy and a little confusing. He was glad he had the boy to show the way.

Approaching the publishing house, they passed a small store that displayed an assortment of inexpensive jewelry, clocks and watches in its window. Horatio, excusing himself, entered and returned in a few minutes with a shiny, nickel-plated Waterbury watch.

"This is, for you," he said pleasantly, handing it over.

"You ain't kiddin', Major?" the boy asked incredulously, his large, dark eyes wide with surprise and excitement.

To Horatio, who delighted in giving, the youth — seemingly aged and hardened by his rough way of life — suddenly became a child again, and his dirty faced flushed with pleasure as he clutched in both hands the treasured gift.

"I hope you'll some day own a real gold one," Horatio said, paying the twenty-five cents agreed upon, and preparing to enter The Sun office.

"Well, if I'm ever gonna, I'd best get started," the boy declared. "I'll run 'round the corner and spend this quarter on a stock of mornin' papers. Maybe by next week I can invest me earnin's in Erie shares."

"I hope so. Then, the next time we meet, you can invite me to Delmonico's."

"No. I gen'ally take me special guests to dinner at the Fifth Avenoo Hotel. Then I'll sport yer to an evenin' at the Old Bowery, huh?"

Both grinned happily as they parted on the steps of the building and, as Horatio walked through the wide entrance, it occurred to him that he didn't even know the street boy's name.

Climbing two flights of stairs to the newsroom, Horatio was impressed with a general sensation of urgent activity. The pace of Boston journals, with which he was more familiar, was slower. Here were dozens of men, hastily coming and going, with an air of imperative dignity. No one spoke loudly, yet the place crackled with the drone of many voices giving or receiving instructions. Reporters discussed assignments with their editors, and young messengers were carrying copy and proofs between desks, and to the composing room on the floor below.

Although windows were open, the atmosphere was stale, and odors of perspiration, tobacco and discarded food scraps mingled with scents of ink and newsprint permeating from the basement pressroom.

Press deadline was at hand, a secretary explained, and

Moses Beach would be unavailable until noon. Horatio was asked if he could conveniently return later, at which time the editor would be pleased to have him as his luncheon guest. Agreeing to do so, Horatio decided to explore the neighborhood until his appointment.

He first walked to Broadway, now lively with traffic and throngs. On every corner newsboys shouted headlines, the vendors often pushing younger competitors aside when customers approached. Waiting for a momentary lull in the confusion of carriages, stages and trucks, Horatio crossed over to City Hall Park where he rested on a bench and watched the passing crowds.

Along the gate which surrounded the park, bootblacks and men and women peddlers of a variety of products chanted of their services and wares. There were numerous soldiers and sailors in uniform and, as mid-morning approached, a stream of fashionable ladies, many of them carrying daintily-wrapped purchases, paused to look into shop's windows. The unending swarms of city-dwellers paid scant attention to provincially-dressed country folk, and to immigrants in costumes of foreign lands.

Up and down the avenue Horatio saw tall buildings, and many former homes apparently converted to commercial use. There were endless rows of retail stores, elegant hotels and a number of theaters.

With an hour remaining before his meeting, Horatio walked east and soon found himself on Centre Street. As he did in Paris and London, Horatio kept a note-book handy, and recorded interesting sights. He "walked about a quarter of a mile," he scribbled, until he "came near to the Tombs," the old city jail "which is situated at the northwest corner of Centre and Leonard Streets, fronting on the first. It is a grim-looking building, built of massive stone." He didn't "quite go up to it, but turned off, and went down Leonard Street in an easterly direction.

"Leonard, between Centre and Baxter, is wretched and squalid, not as bad perhaps as some others — for example, Baxter Street — but a very undesirable residence." He stopped "in front of a dilapidated brick building of six stories. The front was defaced, blinds were broken and on the whole looked miserable and neglected. There is a grocery kept in the lower part, and the remaining five stories crowded with tenants, two or three families to a floor. The street is littered with discards in a broken-down condition, and odors far from savory rise from garbage piled here and there.

"Pale, unhealthy-looking children with dirty faces, generally bare-headed and bare-footed, play about, managing with the happy faculty of childhood to show light hearted gayety, even under the most unpromising circumstances."

Returning to The Sun, Horatio was jovially greeted by Moses Beach, short, stocky and gray-haired, who proceeded to show him around the editorial room introducing him as "the author of those splendid articles from Europe." It being a mild, sunny day, he suggested they walk up Broadway to Pfaff's Restaurant, a few doors above Bleecker Street. On route, he pointed out such famous landmarks as P. T. Barnum's American Museum, A. T. Stewart's department store, newspaper offices along Park Row, and shops of various booksellers and publishers. Downtown in the distance, he indicated the spire of Trinity Church while north, the steeple of Grace Church dominated the uptown skyline.

Charley Pfaff's German cuisine, Beach explained with the enthusiasm of a lover of fine cookery, was favored by the writing fraternity. It was here that journalists gathered, as did Thomas Bailey Aldrich, Walt Whitman, Bayard Taylor and George Farrar Brown, who was better known by his pen-name, Artemus Ward. William Dean Howells — at the time serving as President Lincoln's consul at Venice — made the tavern his New York headquarters.

In a quiet corner, over second cups of black coffee, Horatio presented to Moses Beach the manuscript of "Marie Bertrand," and waited breathlessly for a reaction.

Pausing only to light a cigar and call for more coffee, Beach read sheet after sheet of the novel. For almost a half hour he said nothing, then, putting down the papers, he re-lit his cigar and looked across the table at his guest.

"I think it's a good yarn, Alger," he said, "but I can't use it."

The author's face showed deep disappointment.

"We've gotten away from long tales," Beach explained, "and now concentrate on stories that run complete in a single issue.

There are already too many weeklies specializing in serialization, so we stick to reporting news, and to articles related to current topics." Then, struck by a sudden thought, he asked, "Have you shown this to anyone else in town?"

"No," Horatio quickly answered. "I came down here expressly to offer my story to you."

"I have an idea. Let me take you to Street & Smith. Maybe we can convince them to consider this for their New York Weekly. Come, we'll try."

Walking rapidly downtown, the two men soon reached the office in Frankfort Street, and Moses Beach asked an attendant to take his card to his friend, Francis S. Smith, the firm's co-publisher and editorial chief.

Moments later they were invited into Smith's private rooms, welcomed by the tall, adventurous-looking man with full brown mustache, and seated before his cluttered desk.

Beach briefly explained the purpose of their visit, describing Horatio as his valued contributor. Smith, an alert seeker of new talent, and impressed with the recommendation, appreciated the opportunity to read "Marie Bertrand."

"Are you staying in the city?" he asked.

"Yes, I remain through tomorrow," Horatio replied.

"Excellent. Then, as I suppose you're anxious to receive my verdict, I'll read your story at home this evening. Can you return at ten in the morning?"

Horatio assured him he would be prompt, and a few moments later departed with Beach.

"If you'll want a place for the night," the Sun editor suggested, "there are any number of rooming houses on Duane Street. No luxury, but inexpensive and comfortable."

When they parted, Horatio immediately set to arranging his lodging. This was easily accomplished and, as it was only mid-afternoon, he left his quarters to continue touring the lower part of the city. This time he headed south toward The Battery, exploring Wall Street and other narrow streets and alleyways in that district. Soon he approached Bowling Green, where mansions of former decades housed foreign consulates and steamship companies. Before turning back he paused for some minutes at

166

Castle Garden, once a fort, later an amusement palace, and for the past several years a depot for reception of immigrants.

As Horatio retraced his steps up Broadway, with the sun sinking fast beyond the New Jersey hills, hordes of office workers and shop clerks poured into the streets, homeward bound. All public conveyances quickly became packed beyond capacity, and the shouting and swearing of teamsters added to the deafening rattle of traffic. Yet, above this din could be heard the clear, compelling cries of newsboys, hawking their evening editions.

"Rebels attacking at Chattanooga!" they yelled, "Union troops under siege!"

Near Duane Street, Horatio entered a restaurant and ordered his evening meal. Then, fatigued after a long, busy day in New York, he went directly to his room, retired early, and slept soundly through the night.

When he awakened, early the next morning, wheezy, discordant sounds of a musical instrument were heard from the street below, and Horatio parted the curtains to investigate. He saw a small boy — perhaps ten years old, but emaciated and undersized — standing at the curb, disconsolately squeezing a concertina as he begged charity of passersby. He was shoeless, and wore only a faded shirt and patched, oversized trousers tied at the waist with a rope.

Raising his eyes to scan upper windows, the child quickly spotted Horatio. Attempting to smile cordially, although it appeared wan and pathetic crossing his pinched, yellowish face, he played harder and louder and greeted Horatio in Italian:

'Prego, signore," he called, "Prego." Then he extended his hand upward, hoping for a contribution.

Horatio left the window, reappearing a moment later with some coins, and tossed them to the boy. Bowing, the young street musician nodded appreciatively as he continued playing and walking slowly toward the corner in search of alms.

At ten o'clock Horatio entered the offices of Street & Smith, and announced his appointment.

"You're very punctual, Mr. Alger," Francis Smith greeted him as he approached the editor's desk.

"Thank you, Mr. Smith. Actually, I'm very anxious to learn your decision."

"Fair enough, sir. Street & Smith is buying your story! Is that what you wanted to know?"

"Indeed it is," Horatio quickly replied, and found himself stammering for the first time in years. Then, regaining composure, he added, "I'm so pleased you find it acceptable."

The meeting lasted ten minutes, and Horatio left in a jubilant mood, having been told he'd receive half payment in a week, and the balance when the story appears, probably in about three months time.

"Have you anything else to offer us?" Smith asked, as he escorted his new author through the hall.

"I hope to, very soon."

"Excellent. Be sure to send it to me. I'm eager to read your next story."

Business successfully completed, Horatio decided to spend the remainder of the day enjoying the exciting city, and leave on the evening train.

He walked north on Broadway, turning left at Waverly Place. Then, continuing to Washington Square, Horatio became entranced by its serenity and long rows of beautiful colonial houses. He next wandered about Greenwich Village and the quiet side-streets between Fifth and Sixth Avenues. Here, he believed, he would some day like to live.

Back on Fifth, he took the omnibus as far as the reservoir, at Forty-second Street, getting a glimpse of the marble-fronted Fifth Avenue Hotel at Twenty-third. From the stage terminal, Horatio went up Fifth Avenue — admiring palatial homes — and eventually arrived at the entrance to Central Park, at Fifty-ninth Street.

After following paths a short distance toward the interior, where he seated himself on a lakeside bench to admire the bright autumn foliage, Horatio made his way to Madison Avenue, and boarded the horse-cars to Madison Square. Arriving there after a pleasant ride down the fashionable residential thoroughfare, he strolled through tree-lined adjacent streets, admiring handsome brownstones, many of which were dwellings of persons prominent in New York society.

Glancing at his watch — and surprised to note how late it had become — Horatio asked directions of a passing coachman, then hurried off in the direction of Grand Central Depot, where he reached the cars only moments before departure.

As the locomotive steamed northward, Horatio Alger leaned back in his seat, content with results of the journey, and wondering if, perhaps, his career, his happiness and his future were not to be closely tied to New York. Barely an hour parted from the teeming, noisy city, he now thought only of returning.

CHAPTER 18

THE CALL

BY THE TIME "MARIE BERTRAND" appeared in New York Weekly, starting in January, 1864, Horatio sold a story to Harper's Monthly, a number of his earlier works were being reprinted, and he was busily writing "Frank's Campaign," about a lad who carries on at the farm while his father is fighting the Civil War.

For the setting of "Rossville," one of "the little democracies which make up our New England States," he recalled scenes around Marlborough, while incidents connected with the call to arms — the citizens' rally, volunteers and the departure of troops — were his own memories of events at South Natick during the days following his return from Europe. Horatio depended on news bulletins of the disastrous Battle of Fredericksburg to fill in details of the crossing of the Rappahannock River, and subsequent battering of Federal troops and the wounding of Henry Frost, the hero's father.

"I am obliged to leave my story incomplete," Horatio wrote in a final paragraph. "The Rebellion is not yet at an end." But, assuring readers that, while it lasts, "neither Frank nor his father will abandon their different spheres of duty," he hastily ended the narrative and mailed it to Street & Smith.

A week later the manuscript was returned, rejected, with a

note from Francis Smith apologetically explaining that he and his partner, Mr. Street, decided to pursue a hands-off policy on subjects related to the war. He hoped, the message continued, that Horatio might soon offer something more acceptable.

That afternoon, with "Frank's Campaign" under his arm, Horatio took the tram into Boston, and headed directly to the offices of Student and Schoolmate, a monthly magazine for young folks. His old friend, Will Adams, who recently became its editor and chief contributor, had previously asked Horatio to submit articles, and he already printed a number of Gusti's dialogues.

Barely glancing at the sheaf of papers, Adams shook his head, saying he was unable to use anything of such great length. Each issue featured but one serialized novel, he explained, and he was its author. Not only was the story completed for the current year, he continued, but installments for 1865 were also ready for publication.

"Give me some poems and shorts, Horatio," he advised. "That's what I need most. In the meantime, bring this" — he tapped his fingers on the manuscript — "to Aaron Loring."

"Loring?" Horatio asked. "The bookseller on Washington Street?"

"Exactly. He's also publishing now, and wants some good adventures for boys. He told me he will issue girls' books by Laura Caxton, A. D. T. Whitney, Virginia Townsend and is also arranging with Louisa May Alcott to put out a volume of her collected magazine pieces."

Will Adams wrote a message across the back of his card and handed it to Horatio. "My friend, Mr. Alger," it said, "may be the juvenile writer you said you needed."

"Take this to Loring," Adams said, "but don't wait too long. He may be signing up another author right now."

At 319 Washington Street, opposite Doane's Oyster House, Aaron Kimball Loring had for several years presided over his Up-Town Bookstore and Select Library. The location along Boston's Publishers' Row was ideal and, from his stock, patrons could select works of a great variety of American and English authors.

They could buy books or, if preferred, borrow them for two cents per day. An impressive rack of domestic and foreign periodicals stood near the entrance and, at the rear of the shop, he arrayed a selection of the "most fashionable stationery in the city." To a distinguished clientele, A. K. Loring also served as host and confidant, and the establishment was known as a meeting place of prominent intellectuals.

Six years older than Horatio, and only slightly taller, he now enthusiastically discussed with callers his exciting new venture. His first book — "Faith Gartney's Girlhood," by Mrs. Whitney — only a short time in circulation, was receiving excellent critical notices, and sales were brisk.

"What I'm looking for now," he frequently announced, "is a book for boys to equal it." Oliver Optic would be ideal, but Will Adams — to whom that pen-name belonged — was under contract to Lee & Shepard. "If I could find another like him," Loring often wished.

Horatio, therefore, arriving with Adams' introduction and recommendation, was graciously received by the mild-mannered, courtly little bookman.

"Didn't I read something by you only recently?" Loring asked, when the two sat to talk in his comfortable office. "Perhaps," Horatio answered, flattered that his stories had come to the publisher's attention. "My 'Job Warner's Christmas' appeared in last month's Harper's, or you might have seen my article on Eugene Scribe in The North American Review for October."

Returning to the purpose of Horatio's visit, Loring asked him to leave the manuscript of "Frank's Campaign," which he would study at the earliest opportunity. "I've read dozens," he frankly admitted, "but still haven't found exactly what I want."

Almost a month passed before Horatio heard again from A. K. Loring, and then he received a brief note asking him to come in for a further discussion the following Monday.

All weekend a blizzard raged, and the tram ride into the city was long and cold, with strong winds and slippery roads adding to the hazards. There was little traffic on the street as Horatio approached the shop, and Loring was surprised to see him enter, brushing snow from coat and trousers and finally unwinding a long shawl he had wrapped around his head.

"Good Heavens, Mr. Alger, forgive me for pulling you out in this weather," he apologized. "I scarcely believed you'd get through."

"Nothing could keep me away, sir. I'm so keen to know what you think of my novel, I'd have pushed through snow twice as deep."

"I like it rather well and discussed it with our friend, Adams. He persuaded me that I would not be the loser for publishing it, and I'm inclined to suggest an arrangement."

A. K. Loring then proposed to Horatio that he would agree to print "Frank's Campaign," allowing a royalty of five cents per copy, and he would give him ten free copies of the book. Accepting fifty dollars as an advance, Horatio was pleased with the contract, and, upon leaving the Up-Town Bookstore, waded through high drifts to Student and Schoolmate, two blocks down Washington Street, to tell Will Adams of his good fortune.

The months ahead were filled with eager anticipation, as Horatio awaited publication of his book. He considered it his first major effort, and began to believe that writing for young people might be more rewarding than either the moralistic or semi-sophisticated short stories he produced during recent years.

Another indication of this was the interest in another effort, "The Young Hero," written earlier, but just reprinted by D. Appleton & Co., of New York, in their immensely popular Railway Anecdote Book. A short piece describing the bravery of a poor farm lad, Horatio constructed a simple plot around the widowed mother's inability to pay the rent. With but three days to raise the money, her son, Henry — "who was a stout, handsome boy of twelve" — is crossing fields to ask a neighboring farmer to hire him to rake hay. Passing near a railroad bridge, he discovered that, "whether because it was badly constructed, or for some other cause not apparent," it had given way "and must inevitably cause the destruction of any train which should attempt to cross it."

With the whistle already hooting in the distance, Henry "placed himself between the rails. . .waved his hat, threw up his hands and, in every possible way endeavored to attract the notice of the engineer.

" 'They'll stop rather than run over me,' he thought. Yet, the feeling of his own personal danger, in case they should think him not in earnest, blanched his cheek.

" 'Never mind,' he said, resolutely; 'better risk my own life than let so many perish without warning'.

"Will the reader picture himself in the terrible situation in which our hero stood," Horatio asks, "in the way of a train travelling at the rate of twenty-five miles an hour, waving his hat frantically, and exposed to the hazard of not being able to get out of the way in case he failed to succeed in stopping the cars!"

But the youth holds his ground, and the engine grinds to a halt barely "two rods distant." Someone exclaims "Good Heavens, we have been saved from a terrible fate," Henry faints, and when he comes to, grateful passengers have passed the hat, collecting three hundred dollars to reward his bravery.

One of them, "a merchant doing business in the city," goes to Henry's mother, tells her "I want a lad for my counting room. I have taken a fancy to your son, and if you will intrust him to me, I will take care to advance his interest as far as may be in my power.

"Henry is at this moment a junior partner in the firm," the tale concludes, "and his mother and sister are raised far above want. Mrs. Hall is justly proud of the son to whose boyish intrepidity all their present prosperity is due."

Perhaps not originally, but in a manner which made readers ask for more, Horatio formulated the plot wherein a poor boy, through an act of daring, places his foot firmly upon the first rung of the ladder of success, which is fully and satisfyingly achieved at story's end.

Continuing as a tutor at Cambridge, and writing late into each night, Horatio welcomed the mild, early spring that followed the harsh winter. Because of his heavy schedule of work, and a siege of sniffles — a result of his trip to Boston, several weeks previously, to meet with Loring — he had not lately enjoyed the social life, nor seen any of his old friends.

In the same mail that brought him a check in payment for a second article printed in Harper's Monthly, Horatio received from Henry Denny the annual notification of their class meeting.

It was an evening of relaxation he always looked forward to, and attended whenever possible.

The 1864 Reunion of Harvard, '52 was held on a warm June night in the private rooms at Parker's, with fourteen college chums present. At the ending of the previous year's event, all raised their glasses in a wish for a speedy end to the War, but as they again met to recall happy moments of the past, merriment was quickly turned to sadness by Secretary Denny's report of those who fell in battle.

Among men with the Union forces, Sid Willard was the first to die, being struck by a ball during the Battle of Fredericksburg; Robert Ware, Surgeon of the 44th Massachusetts Regiment, himself suffering from fatigue and exhaustion while treating others, was victim of typhoid pneumonia; Paul Revere, taken prisoner and later exchanged, returned to duty only to be severely wounded at Antietam. He recovered, rejoined his old regiment — in the meantime having been appointed colonel — and led his men into the Battle of Gettysburg, where he was killed.

William Sturgis Hooper, shortly after promotion to captain, died of tuberculosis; Henry Downes, a private in the 124th Illinois Volunteers, succumbed to malarial fever, and Sam Haven Jr., serving with the 15th Massachusetts Regiment, fell at Fredericksburg.

Among classmates who marched with the Armies of Confederacy, Guignard Scott was killed in action during a cavalry charge in Tennessee; Fred Leverett, who served as Senior Surgeon alongside Lee and Longstreet, contracted a fatal disease while tending wounded Confederate soldiers within Union lines, and Bill McKim was buried at Chancellorsville.

After Denny led the men in silent prayer for their dead comrades, Bill Williamson suggested they join him in a Class Ode written by Adam Thaxter. They did, and tears coursed down their cheeks as, to the traditional tune of "Fair Harvard," they sang:

". . .Yet all are not here. Shenandoah's green vale,
    Potomac's blue waves break in view,
And there are our brothers who shrink not nor quail
    To honor and loyalty true.

On the field of the fray, in the keep of the South,
'52 has her patriot sons,
And her canoneer stands by his battery's mouth
Where the swoll'n Chickahominy runs.
In the ranks of the foe are our classmates of yore,
And to them we send greeting tonight,
For we love the warm hearts that we cherished before
Our land was ablaze with war-light.
In sorrow, not anger, their names we recall,
And long for the hour of the end,
When one grasp of the hand says 'Oblivion for all,
Dear Brother — bold Southron — true friend!' "

As the evening drew to a close, and the group made ready
to leave, Denny announced he was temporarily withdrawing as
Class Secretary. His commission as agent of the American Unitarian Association had been approved, he said, and he soon must
leave for assignment with the Army of the Potomac. When the
Rebellion ended he would, please God, greet them all once more.

Amidst wishes of good luck and speedy return, someone began to parody a popular song with the words, "When Denny
Comes Marching Home Again, Hurrah! Hurrah!" In a moment
all joined in, and the meeting adjourned on a note of laughter
and cheer.

*   *   *

Three months later, returning to Cambridge after a vacation
at South Natick, Horatio visited Loring and was effusively welcomed by his publisher. The first edition of "Frank's Campaign"
— issued about a month earlier — was completely sold out, and a
larger printing was coming off the presses. When could he have
another novel, Loring asked, and was pleased to learn it was already started and being rushed to completion.

A few evenings later Horatio was invited to the home of The
Rev. William Rounseville Alger and, after dinner, the minister
led the way into his study.

"I have welcome news for you, Horatio," he started. "A pastor soon will be needed at the First Parish Church, at Brewster.

I took the liberty to suggest your name and it has been agreed that you supply the pulpit during a trial period. Then, as I know you will satisfy, you shall receive a year's contract."

Seeing an expression of uncertainty crossing Horatio's face, he hastened to add that he advised Reverend Alger of this great opportunity, and the parson had immediately replied, expressing great satisfaction that his son would, at last, occupy a place in the church.

His outlook completely occupied with ambitions for a writing career, and work under way on a second novel for Loring, Horatio was momentarily jolted by this sudden, unexpected turn in events.

After some moments of hesitation, he decided that this was, after all, the call he awaited, and for which he had been years in preparing. Thanking William for his kind efforts, Horatio asked when he would be expected to move to Brewster.

"I should think a month would be sufficient time. When you write, they will tell you exactly. And, Horatio," the minister added, sensing what was in his cousin's mind, "I believe you'll discover this to be a lovely and quiet place to write your books. You'll be pleased to know the committee was already familiar with your name, as author of "Frank's Campaign," and its high moral tone was one of the deciding factors in your favor."

CHAPTER 19

CAPE COD DAYS

ON A MILD, CLEAR INDIAN SUMMER day, five weeks later, Horatio arrived at Brewster, on Cape Cod. He was taken directly to comfortable lodgings near the church — gleaming white in bright afternoon sunshine — which was set back on a broad, rising glade, and whose steeple towered gracefully above surrounding elms.

Horatio was captivated by the beauty of brilliant autumn foliage, and his senses sharpened to the ocean's salty perfume that, in fresh breezes, mingled headily with fragrant bayberry and balsam from shadowed pine forests.

Nestled in a secluded inlet on Cape Cod Bay, the village originally was known as Satucket, and later Harwich. It eventually was renamed by descendants of Elder Brewster, who settled there after arriving at Plymouth. Along the sandy shore, dunes drifted in ever-changing patterns, and tall, reedy grasses bent at the whim of capricious winds.

Horatio's congregation was comprised, to a large extent, of families of deepwater shipmasters some of whose square-riggers put to sea in the foreign trade, while others were whalers who sailed from nearby Wellfleet to the distant hunting grounds of the killer, sperm and humpback herds.

Brewster was a prosperous community, some of whose residents lived in gracious Georgian mansions as well as square colonials and story-and-a-half cottages with low eaves and severe salt-box design.

After preaching for some weeks on a probationary basis, Horatio was engaged, on November 26th, at a salary of eight hundred dollars a year. With his parents, Charley Vinal and cousin, Rev. William R. Alger present, he was ordained over the Unitarian Church at Brewster on December 8th.

From the start, Horatio was considered to be an acceptable, but far from ideal leader. He was eager enough to help, but not particularly knowing of their needs. He didn't know as much about life at sea as any sailor's five year-old son, and did not seem quick to learn. He got off a good sermon, it was said, but never fully comprehended the thoughts of worried wives when threatening clouds of a Nor'easter heavily burdened the far horizon.

To Vinal, who had already achieved a fine reputation as a clergyman, Horatio wrote of his problems.

"My people are kindly and good," he said, "but in character more austere than any I've known. I believe they would prefer a parson of their own cut; one who was a seaman before becoming a man of God. I keep trying to understand their ways, but they say I am 'a purely Boston preacher,' meaning, I suppose, better suited to a city parish than to their needs."

They had decidedly little appreciation for their parson's humor and, on the rare occasions he tried to interject a light note to illustrate a point, the lack of response was chilling.

Sitting in at a meeting to arrange a social, Horatio recalled a story he first heard as a child in Chelsea, when similar preparations were being made.

"In the midst of a conversation," he began, "one oyster suddenly asked another, 'Where are we?'

" 'In a bowl of stew,' the other oyster replied.

" 'But where is this bowl of stew?' the first asked.

" 'At a church supper,' he was told.

" 'Well, then why are we *both* here?' "

Horatio fared no better when, on receiving a letter from Henry Denny, who was at the battlefront, he read excerpts to his parishioners.

"An unlucky private in one of the New York Regiments was

179

shot on the way to Atlanta," he quoted from Denny's letter, "and the chaplain arrived at his side just as a surgeon was removing the ball from a small hole back of his shoulder. The boy was lying, face down.

" 'Ah, my poor son,' said the chaplain, mournfully, 'I'm very sorry for you. It's bad to be hit, especially in the back.'

"The wounded lad then turned over and, pointing to the wide opening above his arm, exclaimed, 'The devil, Chaplain, lookee here where that ball went in!' "

As church duties often were light, there was time for writing and, before the year ended, a short story was published in Frank Leslie's Illustrated Newspaper, and two poems in Student and Schoolmate. But Horatio confined his main effort to the novel for Loring. "Frank's Campaign" was already in its third printing, and the publisher was hoping soon to receive the new manuscript.

Horatio started by constructing the title, "Paul Prescott's Charge," after which he proceeded to piece together a tale. He worked to create a brave young hero and, from the first page, determined to set at least part of the action in New York. He was charmed by the great city's literary possibilities, and meant to use it lavishly in his story.

Like Frank Frost, Paul Prescott was competent and ready to pitch into a rugged task. But, at thirteen, Paul is left an orphan. In addition to making his way and, at the same time fending off evil-doers, he has burdened himself with a deathbed promise to his father to repay a five hundred dollar debt. On the morning of his father's funeral, the pompous Squire Newcome — "in the right of his position as Justice of the Peace, Chairman of the Selectmen and wealthiest resident of Wrenville" — has Paul packed off to the poorhouse.

Soon wearying of cruel treatment dispensed by the loathsome keeper of the poor, Paul plans his escape, and walks most of the hundred mile distance to New York.

". . .It was in the morning that Paul came in sight of the city," Horatio wrote. "He climbed up into a high tree, which, having the benefit of an elevated situation, afforded him an extensive prospect.

"He got into Broadway, and walked on and on, thinking that the street must end somewhere. But the farther he walked the thicker the houses seemed crowded together. . .Paul at last sat down in a doorway, and watched with interest the hurrying crowds that passed before him. Everybody seemed to be in a hurry, pressing forward as if life and death depended on his haste. There were lawyers with their sharp, keen glances; merchants with calculating faces; speculators pondering on the chances of a rise or fall in stocks; errand boys with bundles under their arms; business men hurrying to the slip to take the boat for Brooklyn or Jersey City — all seemed intent on business of some kind, even to the ragged newsboys who had just obtained their supply of evening papers, and were now crying them at the top of their voices.

"Perhaps it was not altogether strange that a feeling of desolation should come over Paul as he recollected that he stood alone, homeless, friendless and, it might be, shelterless for the coming night."

In winter, when fields were white, the tall pines crested with snow and brooks laced with ice, Horatio wrote in his quiet room, creating for Paul new crises and triumphs. It was almost spring when he brought the adventure to a close, writing, "And now, dear reader, it behooves us to draw together the different threads of our story, and bring all to a satisfactory conclusion."

A few days later the completed manuscript was on Loring's desk, with plans under way for speedy publication. For his second book, Horatio asked for — and received — a royalty of ten cents per copy, the same amount that Loring offered to Louisa May Alcott.

Since the first days of 1865, an announcement of the end of the war was momentarily expected. Sherman had marched through Georgia, to the sea, cutting a broad swath of devastation from Atlanta to Savannah. Next, he turned his forces Northward, seeking to link-up with Grant's armies. The Confederacy was disintegrating and falling back on all fronts. General Hood's attempted counter-attacks in Tennessee faltered and crumbled, and on April 1st, after defeat at Five Forks, Virginia, Lee's routed divisions hastily abandoned Petersburg and Richmond.

With troops exhausted and beaten — many units were without rations or ammunition and, behind the lines, hungry civilians rioted for food—Lee, broken-hearted and gravely concerned over the future of his men and beloved South, surrendered to Grant, on April 9th, at the little railroad crossing of Appomattox Courthouse.

The news, so long awaited, created a sensation in the North and, with torchlight parades, speeches and bonfires there were wild celebrations of victory everywhere. But less than a week later, on April 15th, President Lincoln lay dead, the victim of an assassin's bullet, and millions who had so lately overflowed with jubilation now wept and mourned their great loss.

Soon rich, cream-colored yucca lilies bloomed about gardens and countryside, and wild plum blossoms unfolded during the spring nights. Beside nearby Stony Brook, almost hidden by ancient shading trees, Horatio discovered the grist mill where, for two centuries, Cape Cod farmers ground their corn.

Quiet, with only the turning water wheel or occasional flutter of a bird's wings to break the silence, Horatio came daily to sit on the bank of the shallow pool. It was an ideal place to think and write, and 1865 was a busy year for him. Will Adams had asked for a number of short stories and he worked rapidly to finish them and move on to his next novel. As a matter of fact, he had two new projects already begun. One would be a romance for older girls, and the other a tale for adults.

The first he titled "Helen Ford," after the heroine, a dutiful daughter whose song recitals support her father, an impractical inventor trying to design a flying machine. The second, "Timothy Crump's Ward," concerns the family of a poor, honest cooper, and what happens to the household when a baby girl is abandoned at their doorstep.

When "Paul Prescott's Charge" was issued, about mid-summer, it was readily accepted by the many youths awaiting Horatio Alger's new book. It soon went into a second edition, and Loring was asking for more.

By October, however, members of the First Parish of Brewster were wondering whether, perhaps, they had had enough of their "writing parson." He was so occupied with his stories, they complained, that he virtually relegated church duties only to spare moments. This was brought to Horatio's attention and, for a short while, he gave more time to his congregation.

But he was obviously unhappy about it, and resented every hour away from his fiction characters, with whom he had become deeply involved. More than once he was tempted to resign, for he now realized he wasn't able to continue as pastor and writer, and properly handle both jobs. But, having promised his father he would attempt to become a successful minister, he kept trying, though failing.

In November the church committee voted not to re-engage him and, in accordance with terms of his contract, they gave him three months notice. Horatio more or less expected this and gladly would have departed at once, but for the obligation to remain.

During this terminal period, he gave greater energy to parish work than in many previous months, possibly to show he harbored no bitterness, but more probably because of the thankful relief that the end of his assignment was in sight.

He would miss Cape Cod, the pretty village and its friendly folk. But most of all, Horatio thought, he would regret leaving the cool, grassy banks of Stony Brook and its old grist mill, where he scribbled in happy haste, and came to the irrevocable conclusion that, for better or worse, he would pass all of his future years as a writer.

CHAPTER 20

RAGGED DICK

BEFORE LEAVING BREWSTER, in March, 1866, Horatio completed the manuscripts of "Helen Ford" and "Timothy Crump's Ward," and went directly to Boston to turn them over to A. K. Loring.

But the publisher was not overly enthused with either of them. He currently was circulating books for girls written by a number of accomplished women authors, he said, and did not need another. Regarding the adult novel, he wished the author would turn it over to another house, and, for him, continue only his output of juveniles.

A long discussion followed, with Horatio trying to explain why these were better than his previous books, and would surely reach greater sales. Loring was neither impressed nor completely persuaded, but agreed, at length, to print a small edition of each on condition that Horatio accept lesser royalties and submit another manuscript — of a story for boys — in time for Christmas publication.

Grousing and displeased with the arrangement, Horatio next called upon Will Adams, in search of sympathy. But from Oliver Optic, no such support was forthcoming.

"Aaron is right," Will told his friend. "He's got some of the best girl's writers already working for him, and the adult story isn't in his line. Really, Horatio, you should be very pleased. I doubt if my publisher would be half so generous with me."

"You make me feel better already, Will," Horatio said with a smile. Then he took from his bag the short stories written for Student and Schoolmate, and handed them to Adams.

The editor studied each piece for some minutes, tugging frequently on the right side of his mustache, and occasionally grunting approval of what he read.

"These will do fine, Horatio," he said. "You are becoming an important contributor to our magazine. If you supply me with a few more of these before the end of summer, I think you can be represented in every issue this year. I'm glad of it, too, as my chores have increased, and I need dependable people whose copy won't take up my time."

And Horatio was dependable. His assignments were submitted on schedule; the stories enjoyed by a wide age-range of children, causing many young readers — and their parents — to write letters of praise, asking that others "from the same pen," appear in the very near future.

"Shall you go back to your rooms in Cambridge?" Adams asked when Horatio announced he had given up his pulpit in favor of devoting full time to writing.

"No, Will, I'm on my way to New York. I'm now quite positive I can support myself as a writer, and in those exhilarating surroundings, I can produce better than ever before. I feel it already, and ideas keep popping about, within, just calling out to me to get them on paper!"

"In that case, Horatio, I must not keep you another moment. I'm in need of your articles, so get yourself situated in New York and send them on to me as fast as you can."

During the remainder of the afternoon, Horatio visited briefly with his brother, Francis, and then called upon Henry Denny who, back from the wars, was re-established in his law practice, had been appointed justice of the peace, and was active on a half-dozen charitable and welfare committees.

Taking the night train to New York, Horatio slept little, savoring visions of his return to the great city which, although he had known it for but two days, he had, nevertheless, come to love and admire.

Arriving in the morning, he boarded a downtown horse-car. His first task was to secure lodging, and he hoped to find suitable quarters near Washington Square. From Broadway, west to Sixth Avenue, he went through one street and then the next, applying wherever a sign indicated rooms to let. Rates in this district were higher than he expected, but when, by mid-afternoon, he was shown a spacious second-story front room in Tenth Street, near University Place, he found it irresistible, and engaged it at once.

The rent was more than he planned to spend, but he had put up some money that he could draw upon, temporarily. In two months time he expected royalty payments from Loring and, shortly afterwards, his two new books would be issued. In the meantime other small amounts were due him from a number of periodicals. If he lived sparingly, he estimated, and set to work producing stories in greater quantities than ever before, he would have no difficulty. If necessary, he could continue tutoring, especially mornings, as he preferred to write during silent hours of darkness.

Allowing himself a weekend of relaxation, and to become accustomed to his exciting new surroundings, he spent the days walking about the city. He retraced paths of his first visit, two-and-a-half years earlier, and explored areas he didn't see before.

Then, at last, Horatio was again ready to write. He had become a fidgety perfectionist who needed all materials at hand. There were two floor-to-ceiling windows in his room and he moved his writing table in front of one of them, placing it first one way, then another, so as to get greatest benefit from the daylight. His heavy lamp — by which he most often labored — was close by his left hand, a neat pile of paper always at his right, with ink and a dozen pens directly before him.

In a peculiar manner of working, he quickly sketched out ideas of several different themes he had in mind, then moved erratically from one story to the next, writing a number of lines or pages, and temporarily abandoning it when he suddenly came upon an innovation suitable to one of the others. Horatio somehow fancied this was a faster method of writing, and that he accomplished more than if he struggled a single narrative through to completion. Even if it was faster, it was hazardous, for Horatio occasionally misplaced his characters, and some of the stories were stranded mid-way, never to be resumed.

At the same time he was rushing the novel for Loring — which was to be titled "Charlie Codman's Cruise" — he worked on more than a half-dozen short stories and, by summer, had sent three to Student and Schoolmate, at least four to Gleason's Literary Companion and one to Our Young Folks, a new monthly edited by John T. Trowbridge, who, a decade earlier, was Horatio's associate at True Flag.

Unexpectedly, but for happy purpose, Horatio left New York, late in June, to return for a few days to South Natick. He had been summoned by his father, with the surprising advice that Gusti — thirty-two years old and, until recently without prospect of marriage — had accepted the proposal of their neighbor, Amos Parker Cheney.

The next mail brought more news, this time directly from the bride-to-be. Mr. Cheney, she informed her brother, was a shy, lumbering giant, four years older than herself, who needed looking after "for he's frightfully clumsy." He stood close to six feet, three inches, she said (Gusti, herself, measuring but five feet with hair piled in a bun), and earned a good living as a tree nurseryman.

So, on June 28th, in the First Unitarian Church at South Natick, Horatio proudly gave his sister away in marriage as Reverend Alger performed the ceremony. Horatio and Amos immediately got on like lifelong friends. His brother-in-law seemed even larger than described and, with clear blue eyes, reddish-brown hair and full, bright red beard, he reminded Horatio of Stonewall Jackson or a hardy plainsman of the West, rather than a well-read, soft-spoken breeder of fruit and ornamental trees, plants and flowering shrubs.

He was slow and easy-going; the diminutive Gusti was fast, quick-witted, and possessed an inflexible will. They were opposites in almost every respect — except in that it was apparent they were deeply in love.

"I know I'm like I am," Amos readily admitted, "and Gusti's like she is. But she suits me fine just that way!"

Loring released "Timothy Crump's Ward" in August, and "Helen Ford" several weeks later. The adult novel appeared without the author's name, the publisher fearing it would confuse and disappoint young readers who had become Alger enthusiasts. Sales of both books were meager, and "Timothy Crump's Ward" was dropped after appearing in only a single hard-cover edition, and briefly in Loring's paper-wrapped Railway Companion series. "Helen Ford" was moving slowly but Loring kept it in print, shrewdly estimating it might attract girls to Alger's next book.

Based upon the performance of these two, Loring was somewhat apprehensive of "Charlie Codman's Cruise," when he received the manuscript in October. Nevertheless, he was counting upon it for Christmas trade, and rushed into print. It appeared to Loring to be made of the same stuff as Horatio's first books — both of which were still selling — and he hoped it would equal their success.

Horatio, in the meantime, was running low in funds. Royalties on his first books dwindled, and none were yet due for the pair just published. The periodicals, which eagerly accepted his short stories were, nevertheless, unable to pay impressive sums, and even their small remuneration was usually delayed in arriving. At the same time, Horatio was reluctant to seek pupils for tutoring, for he had chanced upon a theme that suggested new and exciting possibilities, and he meant to give it his full attention.

Among the pathetic, nomadic class of street boys, Horatio had discovered — virtually everywhere in the city — material for a number of stories, and he quickly prepared for Will Adams the tale of a ragged bootblack, a lad of unknown origin, whose only home had been Manhattan's back alleys and gutters.

"There appears to be an endless supply of material here," Horatio suggested to Adams, "for there also are newsboys, luggage carriers and messengers who exist by wits and initiative in a dozen different ways."

Horatio remembered them well from his first visit to New York, but now their number had multiplied to the extent that

they often crowded the streets of Lower Broadway, and the surrounding area.

"Their increased ranks are greatly a result of the war," he
wrote. "Their parents may have been killed or simply took the opportunity to abandon them. Some, apparently, were left where
their mothers had them.

"Among the older boys are a number who ran away from
farm homes to serve as drummers and foragers with the troops,
and many of the children — there are girls among them — followed the armies, becoming mascots or begging or stealing to
live. At any rate, they somehow made their way to the city, and
now accept constant struggle as a part of their daily lives."

Horatio's idea was tremendously appealing to Will Adams,
who answered by return mail.

"This may answer my current problem," he replied. "Can
you, instead of writing various short stories about your street
arabs, prepare a single one to run through six or twelve issues,
starting January? Since becoming chief editor I haven't had time
for my usual serialization. In fact, I would welcome passing the
burden along, and am wondering if you are willing to supply my
place.

"If so," Adams continued, "re-write and expand your story —
which I return for this purpose — and send the first chapters to
me within a week, if possible."

Horatio, receiving this favorable response — and delighted
with the great opportunity so casually presented to him — turned
immediately to his desk, composing during the remainder of the
afternoon, and through the night. He titled the series "Among
the Bootblacks," and before the end of the week sent off to Boston sufficient material for three installments. Then he continued
writing at a frantic pace.

On November 1st, he received further news.

"Horatio, this is your finest!" Adams' exultant letter began.
"It's exactly what I hoped for, and now eagerly await the final
chapters, as I am keenly interested to learn the ending.

"I managed to insert a brief note in our current issue, announcing that these sketches of street life in New York will start
in January and continue through July. If you are able to sustain
the narrative to December, please do so.

189

"Note that I changed the story's title, and it will be called 'Ragged Dick,' after your hero.

"This morning I gave a set of proofs to Aaron Loring, recommending that he publish 'Ragged Dick' as a book, following serialization. As soon as I hear from him I will, of course, advise you of his decision."

Several days later, Horatio put aside his work for several hours, during which he moved to less expensive quarters on Bleecker Street, several blocks away. The room, up three flights with but a single window looking out upon a row of backyards, was smaller, darker and less comfortable than the chamber he left on Tenth Street. But it was half the price, and as his savings were nearly depleted, he was determined to economize wherever possible. When he could afford it, he would return to something more elegant. For the time being, however, this must suffice.

Settling back to writing, he was pleased to find the room quiet and, with a few stout logs on the fire, agreeably warm and cozy. It was a good place to work, he decided, away from distracting noises of passersby, traffic and peddlers.

That night the weather suddenly turned colder. There were frequent snow flurries and, during the frosty days that followed, Horatio rarely left his work table. Constantly, while writing, his thoughts turned to the thinly-clad, barefoot waifs of the streets. Then, determined that his story direct attention to their plight, he toiled harder to make "Ragged Dick" a success.

Late Saturday afternoon he paused at his labor for a few moments of relaxation and, as he sipped tea from an oversized cup that he cherished and kept with him since college days, he wrote again to Adams. He thanked the editor for his recent kind words, advised that remaining parts of the story would go forward to him shortly, and discreetly asked for partial payment which, Horatio added, "will be gratefully received, I assure you."

Then he continued writing, rapidly — rarely hesitating or making changes or corrections — but glancing occasionally at the manuscript which, as the story neared completion, grew higher and higher in a neat pile at his elbow.

✳   ✳   ✳

On Tuesday — with the end in sight — Horatio noted that Ragged Dick, "dressed in his new suit, surveyed his figure with pardonable complacency.

". . .'My lucky stars are shinin' pretty bright now,' " he said.

Having graduated from the streets to a responsible position in his benefactor's counting house, but keeping his shoe-blacking box "to remind me of the hard times I've had when I was an ignorant bootblack and never expected to be anything better," Horatio assured his readers that "Dick's great ambition to 'grow up 'spectable' seemed likely to be accomplished, after all."

As Dick's chum, Fosdick, put it, "A young gentleman on the way to fame and fortune."

In the afternoon, the papers were carefully wrapped in a sturdy bundle and carried to the post office. Then, his story dispatched, Horatio Alger breathed deeply of the chill November air and walked briskly toward Sixth Avenue where — just as Ragged Dick would have done — he entered a restaurant and ordered a large, steaming bowl of oyster stew.

CHAPTER 21

FAME AND FORTUNE

"RAGGED DICK" was a sensation!

Within a week after the first installment appeared in the January, 1867, issue of Student and Schoolmate, the story attracted more enthusiastic mail than any previous feature. Children, parents, teachers and ministers complimented the magazine and the author, and subscriptions increased as never before.

No one was more delighted with Dick's success than Will Adams, and he quickly signed Horatio to write a sequel, so the installments should continue through 1868. A. K. Loring, who at first was hesitant about publishing the book, now eagerly contracted for the privilege, and wanted Horatio to create a series of tales of street life in New York.

Gleason's was soon asking him for more stories, as was Ballou's, New York Weekly and other periodicals. Horatio was invited to lecture and serve on committees; his opinions were solicited, and his judgment valued. Boys wanted to know when his next story would begin, and many asked if the characters were real, because they seemed so lifelike.

Between replying to letters, filling requests for autographs and moving to a more attractive front room in the boarding house on Bleecker Street, Horatio set to work on "Fame and

Fortune," in which he related further adventures of Dick and his companions. He finished in June, and left immediately for a vacation at South Natick.

Gusti and Amos met him at the railroad station and they drove directly to the parsonage, where Olive and the minister were waiting in the garden. It was cool and pleasant and, for Horatio, a welcome relief from the city's heat.

Gusti soon prepared lemonade and the family sat on the porch, talking, throughout the summer evening, happy to be together again. Earlier in the day, Horatio told them, he had called upon Francis who was leading a happy bachelor's life in Boston, without the slightest inclination to settle down. Annie, who now was continually bedridden except during occasional warm, sunny hours of afternoon, retired before her brother arrived, and he was anxious to see her in the morning. She slept in the downstairs bedroom, and all spoke softly, not to awaken her.

Olive and Reverend Alger appeared weary to their son, and he was glad that Gusti and Amos agreed to make their home with his parents. The giant Amos, clumsily bumping into furniture and often ducking to avoid hitting his head against door-tops, was wonderfully attentive to his wife as well as to her parents. Gusti ran the household — her mother being completely occupied with Annie — and still found time to write. Using her full married name, Olive Augusta Cheney, she had become a popular contributor to a number of periodicals.

All were delighted with Horatio's success, and even the parson — though still regretting his son did not remain a churchman — was pleased he had at last found his place in literature. He believed that the years of theological training would still be put to good use in writing.

On pleasant summer mornings, Horatio often walked along the river, accompanied by a number of children. In the afternoons he crossed the road from the parsonage, carrying a small folding chair, and sat, writing in a shaded grove of trees overlooking the nearby waterfall and the length of the Charles River.

Part of each day he sat beside his beloved youngest sister, reading to her and describing wonders of New York. She was

193

pale and thinner than the last time Horatio saw her and, as each day wore on, she became increasingly exhausted by constant coughing. Nothing more could be done, physicians counseled, but to "give her love and attention for the while she is still to be with us."

As the sun set, the large pitcher of lemonade was set out upon a wicker table on the porch, for guests almost always gathered at nightfall. Among neighbors and parishioners stopping by to pay respects to the minister was Senator Henry Wilson. With Congress in recess, he relaxed at his Natick home, and became a frequent caller.

Horatio's favorites were Harriet Beecher Stowe, the famed author of "Uncle Tom's Cabin," and her husband, Prof. Calvin E. Stowe, who were spending the month but a short distance up the road. Professor Stowe, on the faculty of the Harvard Divinity School, sat in a comfortable rocker looking patriarchal and sage. With full white beard and steel-rimmed eyeglasses high on his forehead, he preferred to talk little, leaving most of the conversation to his wife. Harriet was currently working on "Old Town Folks," a new book with Natick as its setting, and many townspeople — to whom she assigned fictitious names — as the characters. She fell in love with Natick years earlier, before she ever came to the place, when she and her husband were still living in Ohio, and he would retell stories of his family home.

"The old town is a pleasant spot," he often said, "with its snug comfort and sociability. All day long the streets are quiet, and one can hear the murmur of the tiny waterfall on the Charles River."

He brought her to his village when they moved to Brunswick, Maine, and later to Andover, where Professor Stowe was teaching, and now she was able to return even more frequently.

On those evenings, by candlelight on the Algers' porch, she sometimes read portions of her story, everyone chuckling over the thinly-veiled portraits of Sam Lawson, the local do-nothing; Major Broad, the aging dandy who married a young girl; Mump Morse, who led the church choir, Boston Foodah, Joe Steadman, Patty Sawin and others whom she had sharply observed. The model for her main subject — Horace Holyoke — was her husband, as she remembered him in years gone by, and the professor relished her lines about his youthful adventures.

Sometimes, when there were no visitors, Horatio and Amos crossed the bridge to Bailey's Hotel, there to discuss current affairs with the evening loungers.

Shortly before Horatio went back to New York, there was a letter from James, and all gathered about to hear the news. With usual brevity he merely advised that he divorced his first wife, remarried, and had become a partner in the San Francisco optometry shop where he had for several years been employed. He wished he could return home for a visit. "Perhaps," James wrote, "when the trans-continental rail connection is completed, this will be possible."

*   *   *

Impatiently awaiting Horatio's return was the eminent Charles Loring Brace, wealthy social worker and a founder of the Children's Aid Society, who for many years dedicated his efforts to improving the lot of the city's homeless waifs.

He read with keen interest the early chapters of "Ragged Dick" and, during a recent visit to Boston, asked his friend, The Rev. William Rounseville Alger, if he was related to the story's author. The minister quickly told him about his cousin, and suggested they meet.

"Exactly what I have in mind," Brace said, "I may be able to put him in the way of material for more stories."

When Brace departed, he carried with him a letter of introduction, and held it in his hand as he knocked heavily upon Horatio's door.

"So, I find you at home at last, my friend," Brace exclaimed with unintentional brusqueness, when the door opened. "I called previously, but you were always out."

"Please forgive me," Horatio said, unclear as to what was wanted, "I've been away and got back only this morning."

"Ah, then that explains it," Brace nodded, smiling broadly and walking into the room without waiting to be asked.

"Oh, yes, please do come in," Horatio said, after the caller

195

had already entered. He was still puzzled as to the purpose of the intrusion.

Removing his coat, as though he intended to remain awhile, and seating himself comfortably in Horatio's favorite overstuffed chair, he handed over the letter William had supplied.

Horatio sat at his work table, turning the chair toward his visitor as he read. Then, looking up, he took note of the large man with bald head, full beard and small, twinkling eyes. They grinned at each other and, in that instant, became warm friends.

"Young man," Brace began, "I can't sufficiently tell you how very important your story is to my work. 'Ragged Dick' has called the attention of many, many thousands to a situation most of them didn't know exists, and that many simply ignore. May I ask, sir, if you are familiar with the Newsboys' Lodging House?"

"I've heard of it," Horatio answered, frankly, "but know little more."

Charles Loring Brace then told him, very briefly, about the home, its purposes and problems. He described his own connection with the institution and, coming to the point, asked the author to visit the place with him.

"There, Mr. Alger, you will find sufficient material for a hundred 'Ragged Dicks,' and we can make it all available to you. But I want you to see for yourself. Can you come along with me now? Come, take your hat. My carriage is waiting and we can be there in a quarter of an hour."

Horatio, impressed with the older man's persuasiveness and vitality, followed him down the stairs and to the street.

The Newsboys' Lodging House — or The Lodge, as its inmates called it — occupied a loft on the top floor of The Sun Building. When the two men entered, a number of begrimed and tattered youths were lined up at a desk, checking in for the evening. Brace introduced Horatio to Charles O'Connor, a red-headed Irishman who had served in England's Crimean Army, and who now supervised all activities at the lodge. Mrs. O'Connor was the matron and house mother to the smaller boys.

Horatio was led to a small corner room, which was O'Connor's office. There they were seated, and Brace described the premises.

"On this floor," he began, "we have beds for seventy five boys, a dining area, classroom, washroom and small infirmary. The classroom also serves as a chapel and reading room. The boys pay six cents a night for a bed and locker, and an additional six cents if they want breakfast.

"When I first came to the city, I was pained by the sight of great numbers of these children sleeping about the streets at night, in boxes or under stairways. I remember one cold night seeing some ten or a dozen little homeless creatures piled together trying to keep each other warm over a grating outside The Sun office. There also used to be a mass of them at The Atlas, sleeping in the lobby and cellar, until printers drove them away by pouring water on them.

"Occasionally, an unusually enthusiastic street preacher would come along, but they'd chaff and hoot at the poor fellow and he'd soon quit in disgust.

"I asked where these boys went, when it was too cold to remain on sidewalks, and no one seemed to know until, one day, a newspaperman undertook to show me, and we found a crowd of them in back of a gin shop, all drunk, even though it was already morning.

"I was determined to provide some sort of shelter and went to the Children's Aid Society, which we organized a year earlier, in 1853. They soon raised a thousand dollars with which we obtained and equipped this loft. The first night — that was in March, 1854 — the place filled with a motley gang of young toughs, many of them apparently having come only to make a disturbance.

"But, somehow it worked out, and we're still in business. Trouble is, we could use space for a hundred more."

Brace paused to reflect for a moment, then continued:

"As you might expect, these kids are a fighting, gambling bunch, with the little ones continually plundered by the larger. I'd say they average in age from five to fifteen years.

"You shouldn't fool yourself, Mr. Alger. We've got lads cunning and sharpened by all the friction of street life. Some are merely young, ignorant and friendless, but many have already

197

tasted fruits of vice and crime. They've put in time at Black-well's Island and are very much at home in the Five Points. Their friends often are the forlorn prostitute and mature criminal.

"But, fortunately, some have strong conscientious feelings, and a desire for goodness. Even they, however, are exposed to every species of temptation, driven by innumerable currents of passion, desire and bad habits; liable tomorrow to commit some act which should ruin them utterly.

"Nearly all started life with every circumstance against them. For the short time we have them here, we try to offer a small measure of kindness and home life. We don't always succeed, but we try, knowing that tomorrow a third of them will disappear, and never show up again."

Rubbing his large hand back on his bald head, Charles Loring Brace then explained how the Children's Aid Society occasionally finds homes for the little ones and employment for older boys.

"Some time ago," he continued, "we started sending large parties of youngsters to the West. The Society places them with farmers settling in newly-opened territories, and others in factories, shops, telegraph offices or with the railroads. They generally succeed, once they settle down, because they're shrewd and the self-reliance acquired in their rough way of life appears to have made them efficient and equal to anything they undertake."

Brace and O'Connor then showed Horatio through the rooms, as the young lodgers stared suspiciously at the short, timid-appearing newcomer. He looked harmless enough, but they were always wary of missionaries and "prayin' men" brought in to lecture that toss-penny, street-fighting, and hanging around cockfights and pot-houses is the path of sin.

After his first visit, Horatio returned almost daily to the Newsboys' Lodging House. It became his office, workshop and laboratory. Charles O'Connor set up a spare chamber where Horatio could write, and a bed was soon installed so he could remain overnight. The boys — young, yet worldly — fascinated him, and he listened for hours to their street adventures.

Copies of Student and Schoolmate were supplied, and those

who could read described Ragged Dick's trials and triumphs to the others. They were impressed and awed with the kindly, naive author who wrote so understandingly of newsboys and bootblacks. They came to accept Horatio as one of themselves, and treated him with great respect. Some, quickly discovering he was a soft touch, brought him sad tales of disaster and urgent need, and went off fifty cents or a dollar richer for their inventiveness.

For all their hardship, Horatio learned, they were a merry, light-hearted lot, spending every penny they earned, and devoted to performances at cheap theaters along The Bowery. They were generous, ready to share with a poorer boy. Most of them observed a unique code of honor: they repaid debts and wouldn't poach upon another's customary beat. If ever they did — or someone entered their territory — summary justice was administered with fists.

A few acknowledged a vague sort of religion, but most knew nothing of God. This wasn't surprising, Horatio considered, upon discovering that many of them did not know their own names.

They were familiar to each other mainly by nicknames, usually ones that were short and practical, and most often indicated a physical peculiarity, special talent, personality trait or background. To an outsider it was confusing, but O'Connor said he learned quickly, and soon Horatio, too, recognized the boys who were called Mickety, Round Hearts, Fat Jack, Pickle Nose, Cranky Jim, Dodge-me-John, Stud Horse, Shanty, Tickle-me-Foot, Know-Nothing, O'Neill the Great, Professor and Pompey.

Others were Skinny, Whitey, Slobbery, Bumlets, Kelly the Rake, Snitcher, King-of-the-Crapshooters, Limpy, One-Lung-Pete, Dutch, Cat's Eyes, Soggy Pants, Toothless, Humpy, Bloodsucker, High Bridge, Country and Jake the Oyster.

One of these youngsters, who explained to Horatio that he was a "a timber merchant in a small way, sellin' matches," provided the author with the theme for his next story, and he promptly set to work on "Mark the Match Boy."

✳ ✳ ✳

As much as Horatio enjoyed writing and the success it was finally bringing him, he often wished to continue tutoring, especially in the mornings, when he was not generally in the mood to compose. Furthermore, in tallying his finances, Horatio decided that additional funds would be welcome. His income as an author comfortably covered present needs, he estimated, but left little for savings or emergencies. And he was already thinking of a second voyage to Europe.

He mentioned this casually to Charles Loring Brace and had forgotten the conversation when, some months later, the busy, energetic philanthropist asked if he was still inclined to take on a teaching assignment.

Assuring him he would, assuming it could be fit into his writing schedule, Brace arranged a meeting between Horatio and Joseph Seligman, head of the prominent New York banking family, who needed an instructor for his children.

Isaac and George were the first to become Horatio's pupils, and he went regularly to their home on Fifth Avenue to conduct lessons. They soon became devoted to their instructor, and found his easy-going, good-humored manner greatly conducive to learning. Part of the time was passed studying grammar, literature, Greek and Latin, and at least once each week Horatio would take them strolling through nearby streets, or Madison Square Park, after which they adjourned to an ice cream parlor.

The parents were as fond of the tutor as their children had become, and Horatio was a frequent visitor at evening gatherings at the Seligman home. From the moment "Ragged Dick" appeared in book form, Horatio Alger was a best-selling author, and his name known to all who met him. Whenever he attended a social event, books were brought for him to autograph, which he did with great pleasure.

When, in 1868, Will Adams became proprietor of another publication, Our Boys and Girls — also known as Oliver Optic's Magazine — Joseph H. Allen, the owner of Student and Schoolmate, asked Horatio to continue the features that highlighted each issue. He was willing, but on condition he be free to deal with other periodicals, as well, because he was now turning out stories faster than Student and Schoolmate, alone, could print them.

Accordingly, when he was approached by Maturin M. Ballou, Horatio agreed to write for his Monthly Magazine and two — "Luck and Pluck" and "Sink or Swim" — were serialized during 1869 and 1870. In the meantime, producing more adventures in the style of "Ragged Dick," he completed "Rough and Ready," "Rufus and Rose" and "Ben the Luggage Boy."

Early on the morning of Thursday, April 7th, 1870, Horatio was awakened by an American District Telegraph messenger knocking at his door. It was a wire from Gusti, advising that Annie was in a coma from which the doctor believed she would not regain consciousness. It was a message Horatio expected for some days, as letters from home indicated his sister's strength was rapidly ebbing. Nevertheless, he was shaken by the news, when it came, and left immediately for South Natick.

When he arrived, late in the evening, little Annie had already been dead for several hours, and Horatio assisted Amos in making arrangements. The simple funeral, with only family and a few close friends present, took place in the parsonage two days later, after which the frail body, free at last from lifelong illness and pain, was laid to rest in the old cemetery behind the church. The brief services were conducted by The Rev. S. D. Robbins, a long time friend of Reverend Alger.

The house seemed silent without Annie. Her room was now empty. There was no longer a child for Olive to care for, nor a sister who sat, listening intently as Gusti read to her in the garden on warm, sunny afternoons.

For several days Horatio was listless, and could not settle down to his work. When he returned to New York he went directly to the Newsboys Lodging House, where he lavished affection and attention upon the homeless waifs, buying them gifts of shoes, clothing and sweets, and handing over money for boot-blacking supplies, newspapers and other needs of their trade. Any who happened to mention they had younger sisters, were sure to walk off with an extra gift of cash.

*   *   *

A long-time benefactor of the Newsboys' Lodging House was Phineas T. Barnum, and Horatio was first introduced to him by Charles O'Connor shortly after the great showman opened Barnum & Wood's Hippodrome, in 1868, at the corner of Broadway and Thirteenth Street.

Horatio remembered his American Museum, having seen the imposing flag-bedecked, illuminated building on Ann Street when he briefly visited New York in 1864. That landmark was burned out, however, the following year, as was his next location, above Spring Street where he had combined forces with Van Amburgh's Menagerie.

After the second fire, Barnum decided to retire, but was wooed back into business by George Wood, who frankly admitted he preferred having the wily exhibitor as a partner, rather than lose sleep fearing he would return as a competitor.

In addition to providing occasional employment, P. T. Barnum regularly sent to the lodge free tickets for performances. A large, corpulent man with bulbous nose, high, round forehead and bushy eyebrows, he was known to all the streetboys, and they tipped their caps respectfully as, in his familiar, ornate carriage, he drove past them along Broadway.

One or two times each year he visited the Lodging House and lectured on temperance, morality and the limitless opportunities that abound throughout the nation. He urged migration Westward in groups organized by the Children's Aid Society, enticing listeners with his own recollections of clean, wholesome life in the abundant lands of the Mississippi Valley, and beyond.

Barnum grew fond of Horatio and, when Horatio moved to 26 West 34th Street — a fashionable neighborhood conveniently near the Seligman home — they rode uptown together in the black-lacquered brougham with its polished silver appointments. After delivering the author to his door — which created for Horatio considerable prestige among fellow residents of his brownstone dwelling — Barnum continued uptown to his mansion at 438 Fifth Avenue, situated upon the crest of Murray Hill at 39th Street.

During these rides, and at other times they were together, the enterprising, egotistical Barnum urged Horatio to use his spectacular productions as the background for a story, offering to place all facilities at the author's convenience.

"It will have tremendous appeal for your young readers and also their parents," he predicted.

An excellent suggestion, Horatio said, and he agreed to write a novel with such a colorful setting at the earliest opportunity.

With a dozen or more tattered urchins in tow, Horatio frequently enjoyed an evening at the Hippodrome. Acts were diversified and periodically changed, so it was always a dazzling, exciting experience. In the Grand Lecture Hall there were preliminary presentations that included educated dogs, a family of trained bears, jugglers, ventriloquists, living statuary, tableaus, colorfully-costumed gypsies, albinos, giants, midgets, magicians and glass-blowers.

The main entertainment, which followed an intermission during which performers sold photo post cards, was either a family-type play of high moral calibre or lively minstrel show filled with banjo and tambourine music, popular songs, jokes and dances.

One of the most successful attractions — at least as far as inmates of the Newsboys' Lodging House were concerned — was a performance by several chiefs of wild Indian tribes. They had been to Washington to visit the President, Barnum claimed, and the showman persuaded their official guide to bring them to New York where he would present them to people of the great city.

As they trouped onto the stage to "receive the citizens who congregated to do them honor," P. T. Barnum personally introduced them to the public. Explaining they understood no English, he called upon War Bonnet, Lean Bear and Hand-in-the-Water, Chiefs of the Cheyennes; Yellow Buffalo and Yellow Bear of the Kiowas; Jacob, of the Caddos, and White Bull, an Apache.

"That wiry little fellow, Yellow Bear," Barnum declared with broad gestures, "has killed many whites as they travelled through his land. He is a sly, treacherous, blood-thirsty savage who would think no more of scalping a family than a butcher would of wringing a chicken's neck!"

Patting the warrior familiarly upon the shoulder, which

caused him to look up at Barnum with a pleasant smile, and stroke his arm in a simple, loving manner, the host continued:

"He has no doubt slain scores of white persons, and is probably the meanest black-hearted rascal ever to come out of Indian Territory. If this villain understood what I was saying, he would scalp me in a moment, but, as he thinks I am complimenting him, I can safely state the truth to you that he is a lying, thieving, murderous monster.

"He has tortured to death poor, unprotected women, murdered their husbands, brained their helpless little ones. And he would gladly do the same to you or me, if he thought he could escape punishment. This is but a faint description of the character of Yellow Bear."

Then Barnum gave him a patronizing pat on the head and the chief, with happy grin, bowed to the audience, as much as to say the words were quite true, and that he was thankful of the high praise so generously heaped upon him.

After a week as star attractions, one of the tribesmen discovered that people paid money to see them. This he hastily communicated to the others, and there was an immediate murmur of discontent. Their dignity had been offended and, seeing a disagreeable gleam in their dark, flashing eyes, P. T. Barnum remained absent from the Hippodrome until he was assured they departed for their homes in the West.

Horatio passed July and August of 1870 with the Seligmans at their summer home at Long Branch, on the Jersey Shore. He continued tutoring — three more Seligman children, Isabella, Edwin and Alfred, had become his pupils — and at the same time he was hard at work on a new assignment.

Members of the Seligman family and a number of their friends were exploring possibilities of sponsoring a young people's monthly magazine to benefit the Hebrew Orphan Asylum, a charity to which they were generous donors. The institution's printing establishment, which provided training and cash savings for the orphans, would handle publication, and the learned Louis Schnabel agreed to become editor.

When Horatio Alger was invited to contribute an article, as his name would immediately enhance the project, he readily assented, generously offering to provide the main story, which would be serialized over the first twelve numbers. Thus, he spent part of each day writing "Paddle your own Canoe; or, the Fortunes of Walter Conrad." Occasionally, at tea-time, the children and a number of their playmates gathered about and listened raptly as their beloved story-teller read to them an exciting chapter he just finished.

Cooled by gentle breezes, that summer by the sea passed pleasantly and all too quickly. Soon after the vacationers returned to the city it was announced that the new story paper would be known as Young Israel, and its first issue was scheduled to appear in January.

Francis Shubael Smith said he was offended because Horatio had not recently presented any material to New York Weekly. Expressing prerogative as an early patron, Smith reproved the author when they met for lunch at the Astor House, and asked for a new Alger novel. Horatio chuckled at the mild reprimand, and promised the next story he completed. He was now busily preparing "Abner Holden's Bound Boy," he advised, and would deliver it to Street & Smith within a month.

With the "Ragged Dick" Series concluded, and "Luck and Pluck" Series well under way, Loring reported that there still was a tremendous demand, among young readers, for tales of street life. Accordingly, Horatio started to labor simultaneously upon two stories, "Tattered Tom" and "Paul and Peddler."

"Tom," despite the name, was a girl, and Horatio created her upon the insistence of Isabella Seligman, who complained bitterly that her tutor wrote only about boys. He had, as a matter of fact, often seen emaciated little girls, clad only in tattered discards, shifting for themselves and, in competition to survive on the streeets, they were as rowdy and untamed as the boys. Assuring Loring that this would not be purely a story for girls — as was "Helen Ford" — but would contain all the pepper and hurrah of his popular boys' stories, he moved rapidly ahead, and pages of manuscript were soon piling high on his desk.

In November, A. K. Loring moved from his old shop at 319 Washington Street and, by the New Year, settled in larger quarters at Washington and Bromfield, one of Boston's busiest corners. His climb as a publisher was meteoric. Horatio Alger emerged as his best-selling author, closely followed by Louisa May Alcott and several others. Although Miss Alcott's "Little Women" and "An Old Fashioned Girl" were issued by Roberts Brothers, the four books released earlier by Loring enjoyed moderate success and were now doing splendidly in the wake of enthusiastic public reception of "Little Women."

His Select Library occupied the entire ground floor, with publishing offices upstairs. To handle increased activity in various departments, and so that he could devote greater attention to book production, Loring elevated one of his clerks, George W. Dillingham, to the position of assistant. So it was with Dillingham — tall, slender and energetic — that Horatio now corresponded and forwarded chapters as they were hurriedly completed.

CHAPTER 22

PHIL THE FIDDLER

TIME AND AGAIN Horatio recalled the barefoot ragamuffin who played beneath his window in Duane Street, when he first came to the city during the war. He frequently saw other Italian street musicians, out in all weather, at all hours of day and night. They scratched tunes on battered violins, squeezed accordians, or banged upon triangles and tambourines. Some carried no instrument, but sang loudly to be heard above the traffic's clatter, while others went as ordinary beggars, either singly or leading a cripple.

They were strangely different from friendly, laughing Italian bootblacks who came to Lodging House, or who toiled to help their impoverished families get settled in this new land, thousands of miles from sunny Naples, where they were born.

As a matter of fact, Horatio thought when he once determined to write an article about them, something was peculiar about their obviously evasive manner. They spoke no English, seemed completely bewildered by their surroundings, and appeared frightened by anyone who approached them.

When Horatio met one, he handed over a coin, but, starting a conversation, received no reply. Then, as Horatio addressed him in imperfect but clear Italian, the child would become terrified and quickly move away.

To the inquisitive author, this didn't make sense, nor did the disinclination of other Italians to talk about these pathetic, undernourished — often badly bruised — guttersnipes. At that time Horatio prepared to probe deeper. However, another assignment was undertaken, the mystery of the wistful little sidewalk musicians set aside, and his research had not been resumed.

But when, in the humid mid-summer of 1871, a noonday crowd gathered around an incoherently shrieking child on Park Row, Horatio suddenly found himself engulfed at the core of a criminal practice that was bestial, heart-rendingly tragic and, for himself, extremely perilous.

Early editions of afternoon newspapers had just reached the streets, and newshawkers raced in every direction, shouting headlines of "The Scandal in City Hall," "Boss Tweed and Tammany Corruption Exposed," and "Multi-Million Dollar Fraud in New Courthouse." The public had been jolted by reports of incredible political roguery that The New York Times revealed a few days earlier, and now was being pursued by other journals.

In the din of this excitement, few heeded what appeared to be just another barefoot street boy sobbing hysterically as he fled, panic-stricken, through the snarled tangle of drays and horse cars, attempting to escape from a dark, evil-appearing brute who — vehemently cursing in Italian — followed scant yards behind.

The lad — who was perhaps eight or nine years old — darted first one way, then another. He bumped into several persons before a well-dressed, impressive-looking gentleman grabbed his thin, fleshless arm and, with determination, held him until the hooligan arrived.

"A thief, no doubt," the self-righteous citizen smilingly remarked to a passerby, after he released his grip and continued on his way.

Within seconds a curious throng collected to see the boy mercilessly beaten until he collapsed on the ground, after which his burly persecutor viciously kicked him about the body and face.

Those who moments before surmised this was a scamp receiving a deserved thrashing from his father, or a peddler whose fruit he had stolen, now implored the man to cease the pounding. Two pressmen from The World eventually restrained him and, breathing heavily, he ordered the youngster, whom he called Paolo, to stand up and go with him.

But little Paolo, his eyes closed and a trickle of blood flowing from his mouth, lay motionless, barely breathing. His tormentor, frightened by what he had done, turned and disappeared, unnoticed.

"Is the kid dead?" a woman apple seller asked.

"It looks like it. Best fetch a copper." But the policeman usually stationed at a neaby corner had also departed.

Finally, a passing messenger suggested the child be taken to the Newsboys Lodging House. "They'll know what to do," he said.

Reaching Fulton Street, a few minutes later, Paolo was carried to the infirmary and a doctor sent for. Neither O'Connor nor anyone present knew the helpless victim.

"He looks like them Italian players," someone remarked.

Horatio, who was writing in his corner room, heard voices and shuffling in the corridor, and opened his door to investigate. He followed the men to the bed where they carried the limp form and, looking down at Paolo, became sickened. After a few moments the boy stirred slightly, his pale lips trembled and moved. He hadn't strength to talk, but Horatio bent low to catch words he was trying to utter, and heard him whisper in Italian, "No, padrone, no! Don't beat me, padrone!"

For a brief moment he opened his dark, swollen eyes — they were filled with fear and terror — then they closed and he lapsed back into unconsciousness.

Minutes later Paolo died, not only from inhuman punishment, the physician declared, but also from starvation. His frail body was a mass of scars from burns and frequent lashings, and Horatio wondered if other helpless children were being forced to share this suffering.

Although he quickly realized no help would be received from Italian street boys he met — they became obviously frightened when queried on the subject — Horatio now was determined to track the story to its source. Charles O'Connor joined in these inquiries, learning little, but soon realizing that, since he and Horatio took up the matter, Italian boys stopped coming to the lodging house, and avoided him on the streets. Police were singularly closed-mouthed. Several indicated they had their hands full with thousands of street arabs of every description and weren't mindful of any particular group.

"But it smells like dirty business, Mr. Alger," one patrolman hinted. "Take my advice and keep far out of it."

Horatio suspected the officer could have told more, but chose not to.

Shortly after returning to his uptown rooms one evening, Horatio received an unexpected caller. The man, who spoke with an Italian accent, was dignified and courtly although his foreign-cut clothes, while neat, appeared old and worn. He was short and dark-haired, with a neatly trimmed, pointed beard.

Entering, he bowed in a gracious old world manner, introducing himself as Alfonso Cerqua, superintendent of the Italian School at the Five Points.

"Mr. Alger," he said softly, rapidly approaching the purpose of his visit, "you appear to be asking questions about the young street musicians. Is there something I can tell you?"

Horatio brightened at the prospect of enlightenment, quickly told of the tragedy of Paolo and of his subsequent inability to gather any significant information about these children.

"This doesn't surprise me, sir," Mr. Cerqua said with a faint smile. "You tread on very dangerous ground. I should start by warning you that, if you continue, your own life may be in danger."

"You mean I'm dealing with criminals?"

"I mean you are dealing with murderers!"

"Who are these murderers, Mr. Cerqua?"

"They are the padrones — the masters — of the tiny slaves you are asking about."

Horatio sensed his visitor's hatred for the persons he mentioned, and asked:

"Do you think these padrones may already be aware that I'm planning to write a story of their crimes?"

"I'm sure they know. If it has come to me, it came as quickly to them."

"Then what would be the purpose of turning back?" Horatio wondered aloud, adding, "Have you no fear for yourself, coming here to see me?"

"Of course, sir, I have fear. But I am no vegetable. I will help anyone willing to battle against tyranny. I'm proud to say I marched at the side of Garibaldi in the Alps, through Sicily, and on to Naples. Now America is my country, and I wish to see no tyranny here, especially among those from my own homeland. I think I'm not too old for one more fight!"

"How did you hear about me, Mr. Cerqua?"

"In the Five Points and Mulberry Bend, my dear Mr. Alger, news travels fast, even when it is beneath the surface. As you have probably noticed, most Italians will give you no assistance. Please do not blame them, for they are afraid. Not only for themselves — for which I cannot blame them — but also for the lives of their families in Italy. The influence of "the system" reaches far. They hesitate at nothing. They have not yet been stopped and, very frankly, I'm not sure you and I are the ones to do it.

"But first, let me give you the background of this padrone system. I can answer questions later.

"The terrible crimes against these children," he began, "do not start on the streets of New York, but in the vineyards and huts of Naples, where most of them come from.

"Men posing as agents of American farmers and businesses persuade parents to turn over to them their children, promising a better life in the United States. Need I explain that these poor people — knowing only poverty and hunger — are happy for the opportunity to provide something better? But every case is not the same. Sometimes they pay toward expenses, such as transportation and schooling. Most cannot pay, and just hand sons and daughters over to the strangers. When it isn't easy to convince parents, they are given a small sum. I guess you'd say they are selling their young ones into slavery.

"Of course, a very pretty picture is painted for these ignorant people. They are told their children will live in good homes, become educated and, before long, will be shipping gifts and money to their families, or sending for them to come to America.

"Sometimes many from a community depart together amid music and celebration. Everyone thinks they are going to a better life, so they are happy. It is only long after that the truth is revealed.

"You see, the padrones do not operate only in New York. They are in Philadelphia, Chicago, San Francisco and other places. Mr. Alger, neither you nor I know the full extent of the horrors imposed upon these bewildered, helpless boys and girls. Perhaps I know more than you, who are familiar only with those who roam about as musicians. There are others in worse circumstances, but I will describe that later.

"In general, they live as prisoners. Most are starved and many die within a few months after they arrive. The clothes of those who perish then are given to others, for they come in great numbers.

On the streets they are not alone, for padrones — or older boys who started as beggars but became as cruel as their masters — are always nearby. The children never know when one is watching, and being caught talking to anyone means a whipping and no supper — such as it is — when they return in the evening. The penalty is the same, incidentally, if they do not bring in enough money. And padrones are not easily satisfied."

At this point Alfonso Cerqua paused, and Horatio asked why the youngsters do not escape.

"Ah," Cerqua said, raising a hand in despair, "there is so little chance. Occasionally one tries, but they almost always are caught. As they speak no English it is difficult to be understood. They can't travel far, and if seen on the streets they will be tracked down. Unfortunately, most other Italians also dread the padrones, and will not give refuge. Everyone wants to help, and some do, but it is a risky affair. Pity the child who runs away and is brought back. He is whipped to death before the others, after which they are all quite docile and obedient."

"What about police and the law?" Horatio asked, obviously agitated and shocked by these revelations. "Our nation is founded upon justice, not intimidation."

"I think it's easier for you to say that, Mr. Alger. Many of

212

my countrymen have an inborn fear and hatred of police, and hesitate to go to them. Because of their ignorance, they are afraid. They are told police will not protect them, and those they report will have immediate revenge. In our district, sir, an overturned pushcart or a battered infant is enough to make almost anyone think twice before going to the police.

"Officers of the law, incidentally, don't prefer the climate of the Five Points, and are rarely seen there. When they show up, it's generally only to be paid off for minding their own business, after which they depart and don't interfere any more.

"To get back, for a moment, to the training I mentioned these unfortunate little prisoners can expect:

"As I said, you see only the wandering street musicians. You probably aren't aware that any who show promise are taught to become thieves and pickpockets. Then they graduate to burglary. There are many places of prostitution around Old Brewery, and in a number of these is considerable demand for little girls the padrones provide. Can you see the tragedy of it, Mr. Alger? Even for those who survive, what future is there? Only lives of crime and wickedness. Eventually the penitentiary, or worse.

"My own main interest is in properly teaching immigrants to become good Americans, and the great benefit I can offer them is to continue at my school. The padrones already have no love for me, for they know I'm not easily scared off. I carry on my battle against them by educating my people; instructing them to read and write, and explaining this land can only be what they make it.

"While I don't know how much additional help I can give you, I shall keep in touch, nevertheless. But there is a man who wishes to share your effort, and I recommend you meet him. He is Giovanni Secchi de Casale, editor of our local newspaper, Eco d'Italia. They've tried to stop him, but without success. He hates the padrones and fearlessly writes editorials about their crimes. He also is impatient with the timidity of our own people. Attempts were made to bribe him, threaten him and ruin his press, but he hasn't ever been stopped for long. When a couple of his deliverers were beaten, and others quit, he distributed newspapers himself, demanding and getting policemen to accompany him. Now the padrones try to stop people from reading his editorials, but somehow they are being circulated, and those who can read are telling others.

"Mr. de Casale is looking forward to seeing you. Would you like him to visit you here or at the Newsboys' Lodging House?"

"Neither," Horatio replied, "I prefer to call upon him at his office. Then I can tour around the neighborhood, as I'm not too familiar with it."

"Are you serious?" Cerqua asked. "You'll never leave the Five Points alive!"

"In that case, Mr. Cerqua," the little author said with a smile, "I'll leave you my notes, so that you may finish this story."

A few minutes later the school superintendent departed. Horatio had quickly developed tremendous respect for the courage of the man who, he noted, was not an inch taller than himself!

Charles Loring Brace was revolted by the report of Paolo's death. He favored Horatio's determination to document the evils of the entire padrone system, but urged extreme caution. O'Connor fearing trouble, insisted upon going along into the slum district.

The foray was also joined by Horatio's friend, Nathan D. Urner, a Tribune reporter who specialized in human interest features. Himself a man of formidable structure, he fancied the forthcoming adventure, as did his employer, Horace Greeley, when Urner asked for the assignment. The bewhiskered owner of the newspaper was a veteran of battles against oppression and skullduggery, and he now was eager to awaken the public to the tragedy of these children enslaved in the heart of the city.

Urner was the one most familiar with the "Bloody Sixth" Ward, of which the Five Points was the worst part. He had covered vice, riots and murders there, and other news events, mostly of a criminal or violent nature. The district was the collecting point of outcasts from all corners of the world and those who were able, took their families out of its filth and turmoil as soon as they could afford better surroundings. In addition to swarms of Italians were Irish who fled famine and hardship in their native land, Jews from ghettos of Eastern Europe, and the indigent, unwanted dregs of a dozen nations, including Chinese, Germans, Gypsies, Spaniards and Portuguese, as well as freed Negro slaves from the South.

Every street was plundered by gangs and cutthroats. There was constant friction between groups of newly-arrived foreigners, their differences settled by brawls, beatings and killing. From Chatham Street to Canal, and east of The Bowery almost to Broadway, life after dark was dangerously uncertain, and police, when they appeared, patrolled the crooked, poorly lit streets and alleys in pairs.

Before going to the office of Eco d'Italia, where they hoped to find Mr. de Casale, its editor, Nathan pointed out sewers of human degeneracy they passed along the way. Vilest of these was the Old Brewery, an abandoned rat and vermin-infested distillery scheduled for early demolition. But in the meantime, dozens of men and women derelicts occupied, rent-free, every available space, from its splintering, rotting passages and lofts to water-flooded cellars and vats. There were no doors; windows were shattered or entirely fallen away. In the narrow, cobble-stoned street, residents, airing themselves in sunlight that seeped down between closely-spaced buildings, called to the three investigators. Drunken harridans obscenely offered themselves for a price, and a couple of the men reached towards them as they passed. One sot, trying to raise himself from where he reclined along the side of the structure, smiled sheepishly as he unsteadily fell back to a squatting position. Another, who approached them menacingly, was roughly pushed aside by Urner. Children — some of them naked — played noisily amidst garbage and rubble, oblivious to the squalor around them.

Gang hangouts and barrooms — many of which sold women in addition to liquor — were everywhere, and Urner pointed out the establishments of Dusty Bob, Poughkeepsie Jake, Phil Maquire, Abe Florence, Sloppy Mag Unsky, Fanny White and Eliza Pratt. These were the dens, the reporter said, where "Bill the Butcher" Poole whipped his enemy, Wally Mason, so severely he never recovered, and was himself stomped to death in a rough-and-tumble fight with John "Old Smoke" Morrissey. Here Jim Irving — who, like Morrissey, later became a member of the Legislature—and Jack Somerindyke chewed each other's mutton in a punching, gouging, biting affray that was long remembered. Tim Heenan and Charley Lozier were well-known hangers-on recently shot to death; William Farley, who liked to be called Reddy the Blacksmith, and Jack Hilton, alias the Limerick Boy, were carved into small portions, and more than one evening's entertainment ended in the hanging of a less fortunate customer.

Soon they approached the Mulberry Bend block and the Italian sector. It was set low in a hollow and, at the far end, turned sharply off into a warren of tumbledown tenements that, in places, were constructed three deep with hardly enough passage between them for a cat to squeeze through. Inhabitants, nevertheless, knew how to get around by a maze that led beneath houses, over low sheds and through holes in wooden fences and brick walls. These lanes had no official names, but were known as Bottle Alley, Bandit's Roost and Ragpicker's Row and, in their shadows, the sharp stiletto was thrust — or the heavy club bashed brains — as regularly as goods was stolen from neighborhood shops and pushcarts.

In the basement of one of these dwellings was the printing plant of Eco d'Italia, and the headquarters of Giovanni Secchi de Casale, its owner. When eventually they found it and entered its cramped space, the editor — who was industriously cleaning his press — came forward to greet them.

"If one of you is Mr. Alger," he said with a smile, "I am expecting you." Horatio then stepped forward and introduced himself and his friends to the valiant journalist, a tall, broad-shouldered man with dark skin, thick white hair and light gray eyes.

Soon they were seated around a work table cluttered with page proofs and hand-written sheets. Mr. de Casale poured for them small cups of thick, black coffee and welcomed the men who, he said, were at last joining his fight. He told them of horrors endured by the beleaguered children held in bondage by cruel padrones, but added little Horatio had not already learned from Alfonso Cerqua. De Casale read them editorials he wrote on the subject, as well as one he was planning to feature on the front page of his next issue.

"Sooner or later," he said, emphasizing each word, "my people will learn it is wiser to stand and battle, than to close their shutters and pray evil-doers will leave them unharmed. My hardest job is to explain to them that they will not be abandoned, but will eventually unite all who come to know of these shocking conditions."

"It's my hope, Mr. de Casale," Nathan Urner said, "that I may be of some help to you in this respect. I've been authorized to report on these crimes in the Tribune, and we mean to print the full story."

"And you, Mr. Alger. Do I understand you will create a novel from this situation?"

"That is my plan."

"But you write for children. Is this a story for boys and girls?"

"There is no reason it cannot be. However, I would very much like to talk to these unfortunate children. I feel the success of my book depends on aid I receive from young people involved. Then I write realistically, in their own words. Can I meet with one of these street musicians, Mr. de Casale?"

"Not a simple thing to arrange, sir," the editor replied, "without endangering the life of the informer, as well as your own. Those bound to padrones will be too frightened, and actually I have no way of approaching them without risking their safety." He sat for some seconds in silent thought, then added, "It won't be easy, but let me try. I have friends who may be able to help, and I shall speak with them today."

Advising Horatio he would soon be in touch with him, Mr. de Casale saw his visitors to the street. As they walked slowly through the wicked paths of the Five Points, loungers on sidewalks and in doorways stared at Horatio, Charles O'Connor and Nathan Urner, and they had the feeling their steps were also being followed by eyes hidden behind closed shutters.

When they reached the corner of Fulton and Nassau, there was commotion in the street, and even more in the hallway outside the lodging house. Sensing something wrong, O'Connor ran ahead, bounding up wooden stairs two and three at a time. Even before Horatio and Nathan followed him to the top floor, they smelled the nauseating fumes of a stench bomb.

Nobody knew who delivered it, or how it was placed in

the dormitory but as the three men — along with a number of newsboys and bootblacks — went about opening doors and windows, the usually mild-dispositioned O'Connor was working himself into a temper, swearing what he would do to the culprit, if he ever caught him.

The men wondered whether this was a prank by one of the boys, or an attack connected with their excursion to the Five Points.

"Perhaps," Nathan suggested, "it was meant as a warning."

When Horatio returned to his quarters in Thirty-fourth Street, later that evening, he tripped over something as he entered the darkened room. Lighting the desk lamp, he was dismayed to find the place in complete chaos. Papers and the contents of his bureau were strewn about, furniture overturned, clothing, bedding and upholstery cut to shreds, and the notes he made during Alfonso Cerqua's visit were gone.

For almost two weeks there was no word from de Casale, and Horatio began to worry he may have fallen victim to vengeful padrones. Then, one day in late August a youth in his early teens called at the lodging house and asked to see the author.

"I am Mario," he announced in heavily accented English. "Signore de Casale sends me."

"Good," Horatio said, relieved to be hearing at last from the editor. "Do you bring me a message?"

"Si, signore. He says 'a little bird has left its cage. As soon as a new nest is prepared you may see it'."

"Excellent. I shall await further news." After a moment of thought, Horatio said to the youth, "You are brave to come. Aren't you afraid?"

"No," he said with a careless laugh, "my parents fear, but our priest told them it is alright. They listen to him."

"Can you tell me anything else?"

"I know nothing else, for Signore de Casale thinks it's safest for me that way. But I think I return in one or two days."

"Do you live near the Eco d'Italia office?" Horato asked.

"In the same house, upstairs. But soon we move. My father has vegetable cart since we come to this country, but now he will take a small shop uptown and we can live by the store. Much nicer than Mulberry Bend."

"And I suppose you go to school?"

"To Signore Cerqua. He teaches me English so one day I am a professor, too. We need many," he said, a trifle sadly, "to help all the Italians who come to this country."

When Mario departed, Horatio went directly to O'Connor's apartment to tell him the news. Mrs. O'Connor opened the door, greeting him maternally, for she considered the author one of her 'children,' as she referred to street boys who lived in the dormitory. Then the matron returned to her rocking chair, and resumed mending a shirt for one of the boarders.

Her husband sat in the next chamber — the one he called his office — discussing a forthcoming departure of children for the West with his friend and predecessor, Christian Tracy. Tracy, lean and slightly bent at the shoulders, was a man of few words, who preferred to listen. He puffed contentedly on the pipe that was his constant companion, watching clouds of smoke drift through a beam of light above the table lamp. He had been a carpenter, and the first superintendent of the Lodging House. With the help of a few newsboys and bootblacks, he did most of the construction work himself.

But when the Children's Aid Society started resettling youngsters in healthier areas out West, Tracy was placed in charge of the operation, and had been managing with dedication — and success — for several years. In a week another group would leave for Missouri, and he was in New York to outfit the travellers, and accompany them on this journey to new homes.

Although he was a native of the city, and returned two or three times each year, he now considered himself a plainsman, and wore rough leather knee-boots, a bright red bandana and broad-brimmed hat.

"Charley, I think we're in luck!" Horatio said, and told of the message just received from de Casale. "If I understand it correctly," he continued, "one of the street musicians escaped and, as soon as they hide him in a safe place, we'll have a chance to talk with him."

Shortly after dinner, two evenings later, Mario returned and Horatio sent a messenger across the Square for Nathan, who was waiting impatiently at his desk in the Tribune Building. He arrived a few minutes later — puffing after climbing six flights of stairs — with the gleaming eyes and set jaw of a master sleuth. In his belt he carried two pistols — Mr. Greeley kept them locked in a cabinet in his office for reporters to carry on risky assignments — and he handed one of them to Horatio.

"There were only two, Charley," he apologized to O'Connor, "but don't worry, you're well protected."

"I'm not bothered about that," the superintendent said, slowly. "I'm just wondering if there's apt to be another accident here, like last time. I hate to leave the place unguarded."

"What the hell do you mean, 'unguarded'?" Tracy grunted. "I'm sittin' right here, ain't I?"

He knew about the stench bomb attack, and was warned it might happen again.

"Just let them try." He smiled, unhurriedly refilling his pipe. "Now, I think you fellers better take off," he suggested. "I get just a bit nervous watching you toy with them Colts."

O'Connor put on his jacket and, taking up a stout walking stick, was ready to go.

"Will we see Mr. de Casale?" Horatio inquired, when they were in the street.

"No, signore, he feared he might be watched. But Signore Cerqua is waiting for you."

"Where are we going?" Nathan asked, noting they didn't turn off in the direction of Mulberry Bend.

"To a lady's store at the corner of Clinton and Rivington Streets," Mario whispered. She is looking after your 'little bird.'"

"A lady's store at Clinton and Rivington," Nathan repeated, thoughtfully. After a few moments of silence he tapped the guide lightly on the shoulder and asked, "Son, would you by any chance be taking us to Mother Mandelbaum?"

"Si, signore. That is the name they told me."

"Wow!" the newspaperman exclaimed loudly, in surprise.

"Shhhhh!" O'Connor hissed, looking behind to see if they were being followed. "What's got you so heated up?" he wanted to know.

"Only that if we're not murdered by padrones, we still may wind up in jail. Mother Mandelbaum is one of the most notorious crooks in the city! She runs a dry-goods store as a front, but actually operates in partnership with every thief and shoplifter in town.

"Mother — that's what everyone calls her — is known as The Queen of Fences," Nathan continued, "but police have never been able to put her out of business, probably because half the force is on her payroll.

"I've known her a dozen years. She came from Germany and opened this little store. She was a keen business-woman, but apparently found receiving stolen goods more profitable. Mother specializes in silks and other fine fabrics, and I've heard she's got storage rooms all over town. She is suspected of being the brain behind a dozen big robberies but this could never be proved.

"I covered one of her arrests, and the district attorney thought this time he had her, sure. But along came Howe and Hummel, her lawyers, and in fifteen minutes she was free and planning the next job.

"One way or another," Nathan chuckled, "this will be an interesting assignment."

Horatio was startled by this disclosure, and wondered what sort of fearsome Amazon he was about to meet. His mind briefly recalled the hulking, unsavory Granny Beeler whom children taunted and plagued years ago, during his boyhood in Marlborough.

The sun was setting as the group walked along Rivington Street, and evening shadows enveloped the quiet residential section inhabited mostly by German immigrants. Lights began to flicker uncertainly in a number of dwellings and tenants sat on stoops, relaxing after the heat of the summer day.

Shades were drawn over windows of the dry-goods and haberdashery shop at 79 Clinton Street, and Mario said they were to go around to the back of the three-story frame building. Before he could knock, the door was opened by Alfonso Cerqua, and he motioned to them to enter quickly and in silence.

The schoolmaster, nervous and perspiring, breathed a deep sigh of relief as he led them into a comfortable living room, and a moment later Mother Mandelbaum entered through a draped archway.

She immediately recognized Nathan Urner and hugged him

affectionately, asking if he came to write another story about her in the Tribune. Contrary to what Horatio expected, she was a short, buxom woman of middle age, with gray hair neatly tied in a bun and a face upon which was wreathed a benign maternal expression.

She greeted each of the men graciously, as though they came on a social visit, and told them cake and coffee would be ready in a few minutes.

Cerqua, now a bit more relaxed, explained that the street musician they would meet had for months been awaiting an opportune moment to escape. His chance came unexpectedly a few days before, when he was told to spend the morning playing his violin in Brooklyn. He was aware that one of the older boys followed him to the ferry and stood watching for some minutes after he went aboard. However, the overseer departed before the boat left the dock, and the young fiddler followed a moment later. Knowing he would not be missed for several hours, he hoped to cross over to New Jersey, and continue Westward until he was far beyond the reach of his master.

With no money, he decided to hurry uptown, to a neighborhood where he was not likely to be discovered, and play long enough to earn the fare across the Hudson. Fortunately, he met Mario and his father, who were wheeling their pushcart toward Houston Street. He became momentarily panic-stricken when Mario recognized him, but, in response to the peddler's friendly smile, approached them to ask their help. Mario's father quickly agreed to shelter the ragged beggar in the empty store he rented, where he soon would establish his fruit and vegetable business.

In the meantime, Mario — having read Giovanni de Casale's condemnation of padrones in Eco d'Italia — hurried to tell the editor of the boy who fled from his cruel guardians.

De Casale acted quickly, and the next night the street musician was moved to another hiding place. That afternoon he had been brought in a closed carriage to Mother Mandelbaum's home, where he washed away the filth of his former life, and was provided with nourishment and clothing.

"And all this time," Cerqua concluded, "we can suppose

his former 'employers' are looking all over Brooklyn for their missing musician."

"Can we see him now?" Horatio asked, anxious to hear the runaway's story.

"Ach, he still is sleeping, poor child," Mother Mandelbaum said. "Let's first have some nice warm kuchen — I made it myself — then I'll wake him up."

She left the room and returned, a moment later, carrying a tray of cakes, which she served to her guests. Seating herself next to Horatio she chatted amiably, asking the author what he was planning to write about the little fiddler.

"Such things as they are doing to children, these animals," she shook her head vigorously in disgust, "you should tell people it's a crime. And you too, Nathan, meine liebchen," she turned playfully to the reporter, "write a fine story and get them all thrown into The Tombs, where those no-goods belong."

O'Connor heard someone moving about in another room, and Mother calmly explained it was some friends who were in the house to make sure no uninvited callers disturbed her young guest. Two of the gentlemen entered, and Nathan recognized them as Shang Draper and Fat Owney Dobbs, a couple of citizens he last saw at the police lineup.

"The kid is up now, Marm," Shang advised, and Mother said it was alright to bring him down.

A few minutes later the boy was heard coming down the stairs, accompanied by a protector assigned by the hostess. He was now different in appearance from other street players, having exchanged his rags for a neat suit and new shoes. He was nervous, but smiled happily when he saw Mother, and went immediately to her side.

Although undersized for his age, he was a handsome lad, about twelve years old. He had a dark complexion, black hair and shining brown eyes. Horatio and Nathan made notes as Cerqua spoke to the boy in Italian, telling who the men were, and the purpose of their visit.

"My name is Filippo," he responded in Italian to their questions, which Cerqua translated. "I came here a year ago from Calabria. My parents are peasants, and very poor."

He spoke affectionately of his mother and little sister, who remained in Italy, but his voice cracked with bitterness when he told how his father, for a small sum, sold him into slavery. Mother Mandelbaum wept as he continued, telling of cruel treatment by the padrones. Almost as soon as he arrived in New York, and went out on the streets as a beggar, he began to plot eventual escape. Like other little slaves, he knew the terrible consequences of being caught and brought back. But he made up his mind to leave, at any risk, when his best friend, a sickly boy, died after a beating received for not bringing in enough money at the end of a day.

When Alfonso Cerqua suggested the boy had spoken enough for one evening, O'Connor asked where Filippo would go next, and how he would be kept safe from searchers.

"He can stay here," Mother Mandelbaum replied, "or I can move him further uptown. Then, when they give up their hunt, I can send him on to friends in another city."

"I think I have a better plan," the superintendent said. "Filippo can now return with me to the Newsboys' Lodging House. There we will give him good protection and, in a few days he'll leave for the West with a group of our boys. He'll be placed with a good family in Missouri, where he'll be far from the padrones."

All agreed this was a fine idea, and Filippo was overjoyed when the school teacher explained O'Connor's proposal. Mother Mandelbaum sent one of her men out and, in a few minutes he returned with her carriage. Soon the youth, with Horatio, O'Connor and Urner, was on his way to temporary refuge on Fulton Street. He was more confident than he had been earlier, and looked forward to the adventure of his trip across the country.

Tracy was waiting up for them, and remarked dryly that they probably didn't meet bandits, as he heard no shooting. His own vigil passed without incident.

Filippo — whom Horatio decided should henceforth be called Phil — was taken directly to O'Connor's apartment where he remained until the end of the week, when the group would board the train to begin the journey westward.

During days before departure, Horatio — who welcomed this opportunity to improve his Italian — gave Phil primary lessons in English, meanwhile continuing to collect information on the boy's former life. He made notes on the dilapidated hovel in which forty children lived in cramped quarters; how they played until midnight in saloons, where they were sometimes forced to drink with surly, drunken patrons; and how, in freezing winter, they dreamed of their faraway homes on sunny slopes by the blue Mediterranean.

In a few days Phil was gone, and Horatio never heard from him again. While he remained in New York, the boy was not bothered by padrones who, even if they saw him, would not recognize their former slave carefully groomed and wearing a neat, new suit. There was no reason for concern, Charles O'Connor declared as the party left for the West, for Christian Tracy vowed to "keep a special eye on the kid, all the way."

For three months Horatio wrote continuously, sending chapters off to his publisher as soon as one was completed. He titled his new book "Phil, the Fiddler; or, the Story of a Young Street Musician."

When it appeared, the following spring, it caused an uproar in New York and other metropolises, and reaction was immediate. Newspapers began paying special attention to crimes against "the little white slaves," and day after day quoted Horatio Alger as their authority. Nathan Urner's news articles also hit hard at the system, and were widely reprinted.

Units were formed, pledged to rub out the evil, and politicians and police officials could no longer turn their backs. Arrests were made, followed by convictions and stiff penalties. Slowly at first, but with momentum increasing daily, padrones were hauled off to jail or, tipped off that arrest was imminent, fled the city, abandoning their helpless charges to shift for themselves.

At the beginning there was no one to help these children, and many continued at former trades as beggars and street musicians. Various charitable groups quickly pleaded that the welfare of Italian waifs was not their obligation, they being severely pressed to meet needs of their own charges.

For months, as committees and city departments struggled,

the situation drifted, with no aid in sight for the unfortunate —
now homeless — children. Relief finally was offered by Henry
Bergh, the philanthropist who organized the Society for Prevention of Cruelty to Animals, several years earlier, primarily to
bring to justice owners caught starving and beating their horses.
For the time being, Bergh suggested, his people would arrange
what assistance they could to feed and shelter these urchins.

Then he embarked upon a more direct project — one that
would permanently protect youngsters, at the same time assuring prosecution of scoundrels who imposed upon them — and
speeded foundation of the New York Society for Prevention of
Cruelty to Children. Bergh was a tireless fighter and, with the
aid of Horatio Alger and strong editorial support from Nathan
D. Urner, badgered and hounded the Legislature until this protection was enacted into law, and wanton cruelty to children
became punishable as a criminal offense.

CHAPTER 23

THE BUSY, HAPPY YEARS

NEW YORK, IN THE 1870's, was a busy, happy place for Horatio. He wrote constantly, supplying new serialized novels to Student and Schoolmate, Young Israel and New York Weekly. He was receiving top prices for his stories, plus royalties rising to twelve-and-a-half percent. A. K. Loring issued his books as fast as they became available, usually three or four each year, with young readers always impatient for the next one.

"Phil, the Fiddler" was quickly followed by "Slow and Sure," "Strive and Succeed," "Try and Trust," "Bound to Rise," "Brave and Bold," "Risen from the Ranks," "Julius; or, The Street Boy out West" and many others.

During three seasons Horatio enjoyed the social bachelor life in the city. During summer months he was the respected, successful author and country gentleman in South Natick.

Because of his deep friendship for the Seligman family, he continued tutoring their children. Although he was continually sought after to serve on committees, and his daily mail was filled with all manner of invitations to elegant affairs, he always felt more relaxed in the company of his boys — especially news-boys and bootblacks of the Lodging House — and much of his time was spent with them. They were the inspiration for his work, a source of information, and severe critics to whom he recited new adventures he was creating for the youth of a growing nation.

His volumes were collected by young people in every State and Territory, libraries had double rows of Algers — as his works were generically known — and they were recommended by ministers and Sunday school teachers.

In 1872, while "Phil, the Fiddler" continued to make news every time another wretched padrone was apprehended or brought to trial, Horatio rolled up shirtsleeves to assist Charles O'Connor in moving to larger quarters. They had long since outgrown the dreary loft atop the old Sun Building, and O'Connor urged Charles Loring Brace to ask the Children's Aid Society to take over the lease of the Hotel Shakespeare, located nearby at 244 William Street.

This was done and the transfer got under way. With a crew of volunteers, Horatio puffed and struggled under the weight of mattresses and beds he helped carry down long flights of stairs and load on drays lined up at the curb. O'Connor directed evacuation, Brace took charge at the receiving end, and Horatio was "team captain" commanding newsboys, bootblacks and baggage smashers who carted, pushed, lifted and dragged equipment and supplies that included lockers, dining room tables, gymnasium apparatus and medical cabinets.

The spacious new seven-story place — known to all as "the hotel" — was a dream-come-true for the street boys. Instead of the dormitory, there now were only one or two double-decker bunks to a room. There was a pleasant recreation lounge, classrooms in which they learned reading and writing two evenings a week, a library and a chapel where, on Sunday mornings, Horatio — who was given the official title of Chaplain — conducted services for all who wished to attend.

On the third floor, next to O'Connor's apartment, Horatio had his own corner room, which he comfortably furnished with carpets, drapes, pictures and a few extra chairs and lamps.

There was a party a week after they moved in, and the menu featured a chicken dinner. Then the boys put on a noisy but well-received entertainment after which they enjoyed cake and ice cream that Mother Mandelbaum supplied, insisting her gift remain anonymous. Horatio and O'Connor were the only ones who knew who the donor was, but the unknown friend was loudly cheered after the refreshment.

The celebration carried over to the next day, when Horatio herded boys onto a ferryboat and took them to Brooklyn. They were the guests of P. T. Barnum, who opened his Mammoth Travelling Museum, Menagerie, Caravan and Hippodrome — to which Dan Costello's Celebrated Circus was added — under three acres of canvas that could hold nearly ten thousand spectators. Brooklyn, where he would spend a week, was the first stop of his summer tour that would be transported by hundreds of men, horses, vehicles and railroad cars.

Horatio was as delighted as were his boys with the din and music and hurrying throngs. A brass band was playing as they reached their seats, and a moment later the tent's great flaps parted and a grand procession began. Led by teams of elephants and camels, a massive tableau appeared. Announced as the Temple of Juno, it was thirty feet in length, gilt and carved all over, and studded with many mirrors. Upon an elevated platform, beneath an elaborately plumed oriental canopy, sat the circus queen, attended by gods and goddesses in mythological costumes.

The parade continued, consisting of seventy cages, wagons and chariots, drawn by 250 horses. There were wild animals the boys had never seen before, clowns, acrobats, trapeze artists, strong men, tumblers and lithe, yellow-haired maidens in ballet costumes who cavorted lightly on the backs of splendid white steeds. There were trained seals, ponies and dogs, as well as a ferocious gorilla and lions whose roars terrified the audience. Then the huge arena filled with arabs and bedouins of the desert, Roman legionnaires, knights and heralds of King Arthur's court, chanting African warriors and bejewelled Eastern princes and bashaws of olden times.

One breathtaking spectacle followed another, and the audience cheered lustily as, in the grand finale, a troop of United States Cavalry charged across the ring with bugles blaring and swords drawn, then circled around several times, waving American flags.

For Horatio and his young friends, it was a joyous, unforgettable afternoon.

✳   ✳   ✳

On the way to South Natick, for his summer stay with his family, Horatio spent a day in Boston to discuss future projects with A. K. Loring. George Dillingham greeted him, saying "Let's go down to the boss. He's probably in the coffee shop."

Horatio had heard about, but not previously visited, the restaurant his publisher opened in the basement of his book store, with a special entrance in Bromfield Street.

"It will become Boston's literary meeting place," Loring predicted, "and the public will come to meet authors I'll entertain there. The book department will have new customers, and my lunch room shall provide handsome profits of its own."

"I hope the boss knows what he's talking about," Dillingham remarked, dubiously. "He spends all his time down there and people are asking if he's given up books for the sandwich business."

The publisher rushed to the door, when Horatio entered, welcoming him with the affability of a maitre d'hotel, and led him to a table, introducing him on the way to others who sat about talking and reading newspapers.

Between dispensing five cent cups of coffee or glasses of cold sarsaparilla, he sat with Horatio and Dillingham to discuss the writer's forthcoming novels. From time to time he left to greet new arrivals, returning each time to exclaim he had established a phenomenal new enterprise, jokingly adding that perhaps he should abandon book selling and concentrate on food.

"Along Washington Street they're saying he's already done that," Dillingham whispered the next time his employer moved away to serve another party.

"The place is very crowded," Horatio remarked, noting that almost every space was filled.

"Yes," Dillingham agreed, "it's always crowded, but almost everyone is eating on the cuff."

Shortly before Horatio arrived at the parsonage, there was

news from California that James' wife had given birth to a baby girl, and the infant named Annie after his late sister. Olive and the minister were overjoyed, and longed to see their new granddaughter.

There was exciting conversation in South Natick, that summer, and Horatio frequently was asked to retell his perilous adventures among the padrones. As the report passed from one to another, details became increasingly harrowing, and embellished with richly imaginative descriptions of fist fights, narrow escapes from raging, dagger-wielding Italians, and of Horatio and his friends fearlessly advancing against the bandits with pistols drawn and ready to fire.

The villagers also were whispering about recent writings of Harriet Beecher Stowe who, with her husband, was vacationing at his family home.

She had issued a highly controversial book on the incestuous romance between Lord Byron and his sister. The volume was a vindication of Lady Byron, who gave Harriet the information, and many townspeople thought the subject could just as well have been left alone, especially by one of their neighbors.

There were some among the local folk who were especially sensitive about her work since she wrote, in Christian Union, a much publicized editorial defending her brother, The Rev. Henry Ward Beecher, for marrying a divorced woman to a dying man with whom she had been living in sin.

Titling her article "Christ and the Woman," she revived some incidents of the well-known scandal. The groom was Albert D. Richardson, a reporter on the staff of the New York Tribune, whose mistress had been the wife of Daniel McFarland, the man who shot him, and was serving a prison term for his crime.

The sympathetic author claimed Reverend Stowe was being unjustly criticized for what actually was a godly act of mercy, and went on to justify Mrs. McFarland's adulterous life, urging readers to excuse it, as Christ pardoned Mary Magdalen.

On the veranda at Bailey's Hotel, the evening talk was mostly politics, especially about Senator Henry Wilson, who had just been nominated as running mate to Grant in the November presidential election. There were fireworks at the Republican convention in Philadelphia, with a reform group led by Carl Schurz bolting to join forces with Democrats supporting Horace Greeley. Posters began to appear everywhere, and in the tap room men harmonized the new campaign song about riding to victory with "The Man on Horseback and the Natick Cobbler."

Horatio was back in New York before the election, busily working on new novels and a group of short tales he agreed to write for Gleason's Monthly Companion. There seemed to be no end to his output and he always was delighted with the favorable reception his stories received.

Wherever the author went he was asked for autographs and called upon to speak out for causes of every description. He was timid, and reluctant to stand before an audience — always afraid he might falter and stammer — but readily signed checks for virtually every solicitation he received. His generosity, when he thought charity was involved, led him to be swindled by raisers of funds of questionable nature. Horatio often neglected to ask the name or purpose of their appeal, but contributed, believing he was alleviating suffering of orphans and invalids, or helping to feed starving children in distant nations.

His munificence toward hard-pressed street boys was known to them and, over the years, hundreds benefited from his kindness. The pleas of many were false, but Horatio gave anyway, fearing that by refusing he might turn away the one most in need. He supplied rent money, fuel and cash for every purpose. There were some for whom he provided on a regular basis, such as an elderly widow who lived alone in a flat on Crosby Street.

Horatio was in the habit of either sending or bringing her foodstuffs twice each month. It was on one of these errands that — with arms loaded — he walked through a darkened street and was set upon by a band of vengeful padrones who, because of his efforts, were now hunted fugitives. They threw him to the ground and, as his groceries scattered about, had just begun to kick and beat him when a group of homeward bound laborers turned the corner, and his attackers quickly disappeared into the shadows.

The incident was reported in several newspapers, making the bruised Horatio a target for raillery when, a few nights later, he attended the monthly dinner meeting of the Harvard Club of

New York, at Delmonico's. The assault was satirically treated, as was almost every other subject, and before the evening ended, one of the members composed lines on the encounter, which were read to everyone's delight.

Horatio's college roommate, Addison Brown, was present, as were Joe and Bill Choate. Joe, currently counsel for the prosecution of the Tweed Ring, also was the subject of humorous banter which was shared by his classmate, Josiah Porter, an ardent Tammany man and Judge of the Harlem Police Court.

The gatherings attracted a number of alumni living in the city, and some members of the Class of 1852 were generally there. As in their days at Cambridge, the Choates, Brown and Horatio remained companions, and Horatio — the only bachelor among them — was a frequent guest at their homes.

He considered Addison Brown among his closest friends, and almost every Saturday afternoon Brown took Horatio from his writing, and the two would stroll up Fifth Avenue to Central Park. Brown, like the Choates, was successfully practicing law but, at every possible opportunity, indulged his hobby, which was botany. On mild Saturdays in spring, Ad Brown enthusiastically searched for blooms he knew could be expected on that date. Finding them in the park's fields or patches of wildwood, he called triumphantly to Horatio to see his discovery, then he plunged into a thicket in search of other species.

Memories of Paris, London and a dozen other places Horatio visited when he crossed the Atlantic a dozen years before kept returning to him, and he impulsively decided to go again. Speedily completing assignments, he advised publishers he would be away from early July until October, and then wrote a letter to his family in South Natick.

He had just booked steamer passage to England for five persons, he told them, "and these are in the names of three Algers, including myself, and two Cheneys." This would be the first trip abroad for his parents, Gusti and Amos, and he relished the prospect of showing them famed attractions of the Old World. They were overjoyed by his invitation, and immediately became deeply involved in agreeably hectic preparation for the journey.

The senior Algers and Cheneys reached New York one drowsy morning in June, and remained a week at The Brevoort, near Washington Square. Horatio abandoned writing tasks to guide them around the city and, after proudly showing his guests through the Newsboys' Lodging House, led them directly to The Battery, then proceeded uptown along Broadway.

In an open carriage they moved slowly through dense traffic, Horatio pointing out various landmarks. Frequently he was greeted, along the way, by news hawkers, errand boys, bootblacks and policemen, and he was proud of this recognition. His father was awed by Trinity and St. Paul's Churches, the ladies more-so by A. T. Stewart's and other great emporiums that lined both sides of the route.

They saw Niblo's Garden, the dignified, brown-fronted Astor House, the block-long Metropolitan Hotel and passed a dozen theaters and new, tall buildings, higher than any in the world. The confused, boisterous intersection at Canal Street — and further north at Fourteenth — bewildered Amos, to the amusement of Olive and Gusti. Reverend Alger asked to pause at Grace Church so he could see its interior and beautiful grounds. This, he said, climbing back into the carriage, was something he must describe to his parishioners when he returned in the fall.

At noon the sight-seers reached Madison Square, and went directly to the Fifth Avenue Hotel for lunch. Later they continued to Central Park, where they spent the afternoon, returning to their hotel in time for dinner and an evening concert.

Their ocean crossing began on calm seas, and was pleasant throughout the voyage to Southampton. They went first to London, then followed the slow-moving River Avon upstream to Stratford. Horatio, who had been to the little Warwickshire town on his first trip to Europe, knew his family would be delighted with the land where Shakespeare spent most of his life. He, himself, was interested in "the humble grammar-school, still standing and still in use," where the immortal writer received his total education.

"His desk is shown," Horatio wrote some time later, "and little as is known of the poet's history, its appearance makes this evident: he owned a jack-knife, and knew how to use it."

They wandered along roads, examining half-timbered houses of centuries past, the thatched cottage in which Shakespeare's wife, Anne Hathaway, was born at nearby Shottery, and the graveyard of the Church of the Holy Trinity, where both lie buried.

Then they continued on the stream's northwesterly course to Rugby, and the school made famous by its late headmaster, Thomas Arnold — who was one of Horatio's personal heroes — and by Thomas Hughes' recollections in "Tom Brown's School-days."

"It was a bright day in mid-summer," Horatio noted. "The spacious playground, shaded by majestic trees, was level as the floor of a room. I could not picture a lovelier scene. Boys of the upper forms — fine, manly fellows of seventeen and eighteen — were playing a match game of cricket with the Free Foresters."

Their travels took them to the World Exposition at Vienna, where Horatio was introduced about the United States Exhibit as a visiting dignitary, and then to Venice, which he had not previously seen.

They climbed the many stairs of the Ducal Palace, from the dungeons to upper galleries, and to the top of the belfry where a great bell tolled the hours. Like other tourists, they saw magnificent villas, ancient streets and alleys from a gondola, Amos exclaiming that traffic on the water roads was as unwieldy as he had seen on Broadway.

They stayed at the Albergo San Marco, a few steps from the wide piazza where pigeons fluttered everywhere and people relaxed to enjoy outdoor concerts at tea-time and through the evening.

"Our hotel contained not many guests, but was a favorite resort for mosquitoes," Horatio complained, continuing, "at the entrance we always were met by an army of beggars, and it is fortunate that the Venetian mendicant is so modest in his expectations. You can buy his blessing for a penny, while an Irish pauper would not think of blessing you under a shilling!"

After Italy, they spent a month in the Swiss Alps, then France, arriving at Paris in late September. It was an ideal season with perfect weather. Leaves were starting to accept the rich hues of autumn, and shiny brown chestnuts, popping from their burrs, fell from trees that lined the avenues and Grand Boulevards.

During final days of their long, happy vacation on the Continent, they spoke of home. The minister was concerned for the welfare of his congregation; Olive fretted that summer dust must have filled the parsonage; Gusti looked forward to returning to her writing and continuing battle for woman suffrage — a cause in which she had become a leader — and Amos was eager to get back to his tree nursery and the free library he was helping to organize in South Natick. Horatio had, during his ramblings, jotted notes for stories, and planned to start them as soon as he got settled in his corner room at the lodging house, which he referred to as his workshop.

When Charles A. Dana took over The New York Sun from the retiring Moses M. Beach, a few years earlier, one of his first wishes was to see the Newsboys' Lodging House which still occupied the top floor of his bulding. Horatio — who reminded the editor of their first meeting at Cambridge some twenty years before — took him through the halls and dormitories, and told him about the institution's ragged clientele. Since that time, Horatio Alger was official greeter and guide to prominent visitors. He escorted many writers through the loft. Harry Castlemon, Mark Twain, John T. Trowbridge, Walt Whitman, Will Adams and others were dinner guests, and Louisa May Alcott — when she came to New York to convalesce from a recent illness — wept at the sight of the homeless orphans.

"Hokey!" a young peddler exclaimed, "but ain't she a real soft puddin'."

Horatio quickly explained to the lady that, in language of the streets, that meant someone who was tender-hearted and gentle.

Dana one day asked Horatio if he would show his friend, Bret Harte, through the place. Harte, who was in the city prior to departing for London, where he planned to make his home, was resting after a cross-country lecture tour. Horatio was thrilled at the opportunity to entertain him, for Harte was one of his favorite authors. He was to most Americans the personification of the Golden Age of California, and Horatio shared the impatient enthusiasm of boys at the lodge as they awaited the arrival of the creator of rugged, loose-jointed, fast-shooting heroes and villains of the mining camps. His reputation had spread from pine forests and snow-capped peaks of Sierra Nevada and San Francisco's Barbary Coast to every corner of the nation.

Before becoming editor of the Overland Monthly, Harte tried his luck as a digger, and later as shotgun rider for Wells Fargo. He had described, and lived, a life of glorious adventure in the Far West, and the Newsboys Lodging House was packed with wide-eyed youths on the evening of his visit. While most had not read his stories, they accepted Horatio's estimate of the colorful writer of "The Luck of Roaring Camp," "The Outcasts of Poker Flat," "The Idyl of Red Gulch" and other tales of life in the gold fields.

When finally the famed story-teller arrived, jaws dropped and all who hoped to meet a reckless frontier gunman were sadly disappointed. He was short, unimpressive in appearance, his dress decidedly on the dandy side. His overcoat had rich fur trimming at collar and cuffs. He wore kid gloves, a silk cravat and elegantly tailored jacket. Four peaks of a lace-trimmed handkerchief were neatly arranged in the breast pocket, and a fresh flower emerged from the button hole above it. Across his vest hung a gold chain attached to which was a beautiful, thin gold watch.

After raising a question in the minds of many, he easily won them over when, at supper, he announced to Horatio and others at the table that this was the kind of grub he used to dream about when he was panning in the hills.

After dinner he was asked to give a short talk. He was willing and, in the chamber used for studies, he soon held his audience spellbound with personal memories presented in a pleasant, informal manner.

"I left New York for California," he began, "when I was scarcely older than you boys, going by way of Panama, and reaching Sonora, in Calaveras County, in 1853.

"It was a land of rugged canyons and magnificent distances. Amid rushing waters, an army of strong men in red shirts and top boots were feverishly in search of buried gold. Weaklings and old men were unknown. It took a stout heart and frame to dare

237

the venture, to brave the journey of three thousand miles, and battle for life in the wilds.

"Strong passions brought quick climaxes, all the better and worse forces of manhood being in unbridled play. Perspiration was so profuse in hot weather, that a bandana was as necessary to the miner as a canteen or a revolver. They wore them clung loosely around their necks, and falling over their chests.

"I took my pick and shovel and asked where I might dig. They said 'Anywhere,' and it was true you could get a few grains from any of the surface earth with which you chose to fill your pan. But in a day's work I got barely enough to live on, and answered a call for a Wells Fargo messenger. As such, I sat beside the driver on the box-seat of a stage coach, in charge of letters and 'treasure' we were taking from mining camps to the nearest town. Stage robbers were plentiful. My predecessor in the position had been shot through the arm, and my successor was killed.

"I held the post for some months, and then gave it up to become the schoolmaster near Sonora."

All listened attentively as his story continued and, when he finished, there was long applause and foot-stamping by the appreciative street boys. Bret Harte's appearance, they concluded, was "Bully!" even though he didn't "look like them miners on the dime novels."

Preparing to leave, Harte invited Horatio to come uptown with him to The Scribblers, where he often stopped in the evening. Although Horatio was not a member, he knew the club, located on Thirteenth Street, off Fifth Avenue. It had been organized a few years earlier by the newspaper men, artists and theatrical folk who used to hang out at Pfaff's before the place was torn down.

It was patterned after an English ale-house, with sanded floor, heavy round oaken tables, stout chairs and a general air of solid comfort. Like the old Charley Pfaff's, it was a place for men with hearty appetites, where roast beef was sliced thick and Welsh rarebit, pork and mutton pies and big, boiled apple dumplings with hard or soft sauce were specialties of the house.

When they were seated, Bret Harte lit a cigar and relaxed. He was known to most of those present, and several came over to greet him.

"I hope I didn't disappoint the kids," he said when they were alone. "Whenever I walk out before a strange audience there is a general sense of dismay and sometimes a gasp of astonishment.

"What people expect in me I don't know. Possibly a six-foot mountaineer with a voice and lecture in proportion. They always seem to have mentally confused me with some of my characters.

"I think if I were more Herculean, with a bright shirt and high boots, many would feel a deeper thrill and a deeper conviction that they had obtained the worth of their money."

They sat and talked late into the night, deciding they had much in common, particularly their interests in writing, travel and translating Greek literature. Harte's father was a tutor in classical languages, so his instruction began at an early age.

Horatio was pleased to hear that "Ragged Dick" and his other books were being read in the camps, copies apparently having arrived by the overland route.

"What you must do now, Alger," Harte advised, "is go to California and write stories with a Western setting. You would find new ideas there. Something is vital about that rugged land, and it cannot help but inspire all who stand amidst the largeness and greatness of its magnificent landscape."

Bret Harte's suggestion appealed to Horatio, often returning to his thoughts months later, even after Harte left America, and had gone to live in London. There were many fine tales still to be told of the Far West, and doubtless they would be well received by Horatio's readers.

The same idea occurred to A. K. Loring. His records showed that, proportionately, sales of Alger books were steadily increasing from Chicago, Westward, but remaining on a fairly even plane in the East. He reasoned that, if youngsters in distant places were interested in the ragged waifs of New York, then Eastern boys would delight in adventures on plains and in mountains beyond the Mississippi. When he mentioned this to Horatio the next time they met, in the summer of 1876, the author readily consented to make the trip, and was anxious to leave at once.

Although he had seen something of Europe, Horatio knew but little of the United States, and now he meant to travel over much of it, all the while collecting material for new stories.

When he returned to the city after his annual stay at South

Natick, he told Francis Smith of his forthcoming journey. Horatio had become one of New York Weekly's top contributors, and Smith enthusiastically approved of his next serial having the gold fields as its setting. It was something he could promote to excellent advantage, he said, and would commence announcements when the first chapters were received.

"Before you leave," Smith suggested, "you'll want to get together with Ed Judson. He's still out on a summer tour with Buffalo Bill and Texas Jack Omohondro, but he'll be back in town next week."

Edward Zane Carroll Judson, best known as Ned Buntline, was another of Street & Smith's great writers, and Horatio was eager to talk with him. He was a true rover of the Indian country, ranging from Dakota Badlands to the Mexican Border in search of blood-thirsty tales and also to escape clutches of present and former wives, at least one of whom he was said to have wed without divorcing the previous spouse.

Horatio squirmed uneasily throughout his meeting with Judson, two weeks later and, before many minutes passed, decided that Ned Buntline definitely was not his choice of companion. Not that Judson wasn't friendly — for he was most willing to assist with advice, letters of introduction, and any other aid asked — but he always seemed on the verge of eruption, and this made Horatio nervous.

Judson was of medium-size and barrel-like structure. A black walrus mustache covered half his florid face; his hair started well back on the pate, hanging as a long fringe over his reddened, wrinkled neck. He spoke and laughed loudly, often stamping a foot or thumping fist upon the table to impress a point.

But it occurred to Horatio, as he watched and listened to Judson, that this probably was exactly the type of man he had expected Bret Harte to be. And Judson's thunderous outbursts, notwithstanding, he probably experienced every adventure he wrote about, and his own exploits easily equalled those of his real and fictional heroes.

He ran off to sea at eleven; at fourteen dove into New York Harbor to save the lives of two children whose boat had capsized. The same year he was commissioned a midshipman in the Navy, deserting at sixteen to join the Army and fight the Seminole War in the Everglades. Discharged as an officer, he travelled West for a fur company. He once killed a man in a pistol duel, was shot three times by an angry mob, hung and abandoned as dead. The flimsy rope broke, however, and he regained consciousness, escaped and rejoined the Army to take part in the Mexican War.

He later made his way to New York, founding a weekly he called Ned Buntline's Own, and doing most of the writing himself. Becoming involved in a riot in which a number of persons were killed and injured, he spent a year imprisoned on Blackwell's Island, there creating novels of piracy on the high seas, as well as rugged tales of the untamed West. He claimed everything he wrote was based upon real experiences — either his own or those of plainsmen with whom he rode the trails.

When the Civil War began, he was released and enlisted in the Union Army, where he fought with distinction having, by the cessation of hostilities, been wounded twenty times and promoted to Colonel. Too restless to resume city life, he returned to the West where he met the famed scouts, Wild Bill Hickok and Texas Jack, and eventually came upon a boastful young hunter named William F. Cody.

Wild Bill, when he wasn't leading cavalry through hostile territory, was a boisterous gunman when drunk, but mild-mannered and respectful when sober. Texas Jack wore Indian scalps tied to his belt, and Cody earned his living slaughtering bison to feed men laying tracks for the Union Pacific Railroad.

He told tall tales of his days as a Pony Express rider and Indian fighter, and looked genuinely heroic in a suit of fringed buckskin. He was a sun-tanned giant with deep blue eyes and blond locks that hung to his shoulders. Judson savored Cody's stories of his exploits — saving a wagon train, halting a cattle stampede and stopping an Indian massacre by taking on and killing the Sioux chief in hand-to-hand combat — and jokingly tagged him "Buffalo Bill." Cody loved it, and Judson made it the best-known name of any hero of the American West.

"Be sure to carry a Bowie knife," Judson advised. "I wouldn't be out there without one. The toughest thing is finding decent whiskey. God, the stuff they brew is horrid," he grimaced at the thought, "and whatever you do, don't drink any liquor the Indians make. It's pure snake venom!"

241

Horatio didn't anticipate any suffering for lack of whiskey, though he didn't say so, but thanked Judson effusively for what the old campaigner believed to be solid advice, sincerely offered.

As it turned out, the first part of the trip would be relatively uneventful, for Horatio agreed to accompany a party of Children's Aid Society boys, and would have no more strenuous duty than occasionally assisting the firm, capable Christian Tracy, who was already in the city, making plans for early departure.

After having written to James, advising he would eventually see him in San Francisco, Horatio bought a small suitcase into which he packed an extra suit, a few other articles of clothing, and a quantity of pencils and note pads. He preferred to travel light, and was soon ready to leave.

Independence, Kansas, was the group's destination and, from the start, the railroad ride was an exciting adventure. For many, it was their first glimpse of the America stretching beyond city limits, but there was no evidence of homesickness on the part of any, nor a desire to return to the life they were leaving more than a thousand miles behind. Except for several Italians and Irish, and one German, this was the first travel experience for most of the street boys on board.

Throughout the first day of the journey, livestock grazing placidly in distant meadows, rivers that were crossed, approaching towns and other unaccustomed sights brought forth loud, spontaneous outbursts from the exhilarated, merry lads. Fortunately, they had the entire coach to themselves, so there were no other passengers to become annoyed. At times Horatio laughingly suggested to Tracy that their rollicking might shake the train from its tracks.

The supervisor, however, explained that, in the throes of these new impressions, it would not be possible to quiet them effectively. But, he added, the hours will take their toll of that exuberance, and the young travelers would be quite docile before the train halted at its dinner siding.

"God bless them," Tracy said. "these poor kids had no rosy time of it. Now they're heading towards a cleaner, better life, but it shan't be without toil and hardship. Let 'em enjoy themselves a spell."

It was early autumn, and the spicy perfume of harvest and burning leaves added to the new pleasures as all inhaled deeply of the season's fragrance. Sensitivities long hidden under the tough covering of privation in New York's gutters and alleyways were coming to the surface — even among the rowdiest — and the waifs were deeply affected by sights and experiences of every passing mile.

They soon were riding swiftly through the Pennsylvania countryside, marvelling at the gaudy array of nature's colors, then into Ohio and next Indiana. They constantly asked questions, wanting to know about stacked stalks of corn, giant pumpkins and all variety of things they never saw before.

They were more sophisticated — and considerably subdued — travelers as the train moved monotonously through Illinois and all across Missouri. Probably without exception, the boys looked forward to their journey's end as, at Kansas City, each young immigrant carried his small parcel of belongings to other cars for the last part of the trip into Southern Kansas.

His task completed upon arrival at Independence, Horatio bade Christian Tracy farewell, wished the boys luck, and set out to make arrangements to continue his Westward course.

Although there had not recently been Indian raids, Horatio was advised against traveling alone across the desolate land. Except for renegades, he need not expect interference from Arapahoes. The Kiowas and Commanches had not been troublesome lately, but he was cautioned about unnecesary wanderings through Cheyenne or Pawnee territory.

After resting for two days, Horatio went to the railroad office to inquire about a large group of homesteaders who would soon be riding West, across the Chisholm Trail, into vast areas the United States bought from the Indians. In preparation for departure, the town was filled with migrating families busily bargaining for teams and wagons, which they hurriedly stocked with food, tools, rifles, and other supplies. Among them were many farmers, but also storekeepers, doctors, teachers and persons of every age, calling and description, hoping for some measure of success and happiness in the newly acquired lands of the Indian Territory. Government observers had been assigned to accompany the rush, primarily to referee disputes and, where possible,

243

to discourage skullduggery by adventurers, gamblers and ruf-
fians.

Horatio — whose reputation as author preceded him — was
referred to a Federal officer, and it was in the commander's
wagon that he moved out one chilly dawn, coughing and choking
in the dust of settlers racing to establish claims to the fertile, rolling terrain of the rich Osage Plains.

Seated beside an Army major, Horatio held tight to his hat
and the bench, as the light ammunition cart, drawn by two
horses, followed close behind the swarming hordes. Occasionally
they stopped to assist a rider whose horse had stumbled, occupants of overturned buckboards, or to occasionally dash toward
sounds of gunfire.

All through the day the frantic drive continued until, late in
the afternoon, they began passing families and individuals setting up shelters alongside claim stakes they pounded into the
ground.

At sundown the Major ordered his cart halted, and an order-
ly was soon preparing supper of salt pork, beans and coffee.
Then, wrapped in a blanket, Horatio slept under the stars, beside
a small, smouldering fire that flickered out long before sunrise.

At daybreak the ride continued, but the pace was slower.
Homesteaders had scattered in all directions, many marking off
acreage and promptly setting to work digging wells and raising
sod huts.

Horatio dismounted at a way station on the banks of the
Arkansas River, where the Army wagon turned to circle back to
Independence. He had no particular travel plan, but wished to
see the country, heading in a northwesterly direction. The weather turned suddenly colder, and the inn-keeper suggested he stay
the night, then continue to Wichita, about twenty miles up-river,
in the morning. There, Horatio was told, he could board either
a train or stagecoach, depending upon where he chose to go.

The stop-over was in charge of a retired soldier who was
called Sergeant, but whether that was a name or rank, Horatio
did not inquire.

"Can ye sit a horse?" Sergeant asked.

"I haven't tried since I was a boy," Horatio replied.

"Well, ye kin try agin t'morra. I got an extra mare here and she'll get ye to town. Just leave 'er to the War Bonnet Livery Stable, and I'll fetch 'er back when I go up in two days or three. I see ye got no rifle. Got a pistol in yer bag?"

"No."

"Yer gonna need something, friend. I'll lend ye me carbeen. Them Pawnees kin smell a feller what's unarmed, an' then it's jes' too bad. If you see any coming at you, take a shot at them and they'll run. They keep a distance if they think yer ready for 'em."

All through the night the wind blew across the prairie outside the one-room mud cabin. The hospitable Sergeant insisted Horatio occupy his bed, while he rolled up comfortably in blankets on the floor and soon was snoring in peaceful slumber. Horatio was tired from the long, rigorous ride, and quickly fell asleep.

He awakened with sun shining through the small windows, and aromas of coffee and frying bacon filling the room.

"Don't you get lonely out here, by yourself?" Horatio wondered, as the two sat down to eat.

"Not on a bet!" Sergeant hastily replied, with emphasis. "Jes' a few years back it was real quiet here. Not one or two folks passin' in a week. Now the stage halts here every three days, and probably a half dozen riders goin' by, mostly headin' West. It's gettin' so, I ain't got time to set an' light me pipe."

Shortly after breakfast, Sergeant bridled his mare, tied Horatio's bag to the saddle and, handing him the loaded carbine and some extra shells, pointed the way.

"Keep by the river," he instructed, "straight north. After fourteen miles ye'll come to a road and that'll carry ye into town."

Thanking the old soldier for his kindness, Horatio urged the horse gently down a knoll to the path that ran along the river. The weary mare knew the way without instruction, and plodded along at barely three miles an hour.

Before noon the morning sun became partly obscured by haze and a mild but steady breeze swept dust and tumbleweed across the plains. The landscape possessed a stern, austere beauty of its own. The terrain ahead was mostly flat and light brown in color, with here and there low hills and sparse vegetation to break the monotonous pattern.

As he rode, Horatio made mental notes as to how this scenery could fit into a story. He meant to use the hardy Sergeant, as well as others he met, as characters, and was now thinking of a predicament in which to embroil a young hero. Meanwhile, the horse continued onward, slowly covering mile after mile on the trail to Wichita.

After riding for hours without seeing any sign of life other than large jack-rabbits hopping in the distance, Horatio glanced across the narrow stream and was surprised and frightened to see four Indians riding on the opposite bank. They appeared to be unarmed, and did not even seem to notice him as each led a pack-horse in a direction parallel to his own.

Were these, he wondered, peaceable Kiowas or Commanches, renegade Arapahoes, or warlike Cheyennes or Pawnees? He, of course, could not recognize one from the other, and didn't know whether to run, shoot or take cover. But, across the river, apparently deep in their own thoughts, they continued onward, without so much as indicating awareness of his presence, and soon had ridden off, out of sight.

Perhaps they wait up ahead to ambush him, Horatio thought. At any rate, he didn't mean to give up his life without a fight, and rode the rest of the way cradling the rifle in the crook of his arm, fully intending to use it if he had to.

But the Indians did not reappear, and Horatio passed no other travellers before, from the crest of a rise, he saw the outskirts of Wichita a mile ahead. Darkness was falling as he approached the town, and lights flickered in windows. He first passed stockyards along the railroad siding, the enclosures filled with lowing cattle. He next rode between a group of warehouses, and beyond these were private homes, first a few then greater numbers, built closer together.

Reaching the main street, Horatio was eyed suspiciously by a rough-looking character of whom he asked the way to the stable. After he passed on, the man spoke hastily to a companion and shortly after Horatio reached the War Bonnet Livery, the two men appeared, accompanied by the sheriff and followed by a group of curious townspeople.

It was a peculiar welcoming committee, and the law officer confronted Horatio.

"How did you come by Marion?" he asked brusquely.

"Who?" Horatio asked, completely bewildered.

"Ain't that Sergeant's mare, Marion," the sheriff demanded.

"Oh, yes," Horatio answered, understanding at last. Then he explained how the way station keeper loaned him the horse, instructing him to leave it at the stable when he reached town. "He'll be in to pick up the horse and his carbine in a couple of days," Horatio added.

The explanation was accepted, and all apologized for the confusion.

"I knew the mare wuz Marion, right off," the rough-looking cowhand — who introduced himself as Truscott — said to Horatio. "You know horse-stealin' is putty serious business out here, and I jes' got sorta s'picious."

He seemed much friendlier now and — eager to make amends — invited Horatio to a nearby saloon for a drink. Horatio declined, saying he was tired after the long ride, and asked where the hotel was.

"Right above the saloon," Truscott said. "C'mon, we'll lead you right to it."

Horatio's room was comfortable, and he slept soundly, despite music and noises in the bar, and the occasional sound of wagons and horsemen moving through the streets.

The following afternoon Horatio took a stage coach north to Nebraska, passing great herds of grazing bison. Two times they saw small parties of Indians riding black and white ponies in the distance.

"They're hunters," a passenger told the others, "out looking for their supper, lucky for us," he said with a smile. "Those are Sioux, and there still are some hostiles running about the hills under Chief Crazy Horse. These days thieving is more what they're after than murder. They got a real yen for livestock, and will go to some risk to steal it. But they find it's unprofitable to attack stage coaches, knowing there's at least a few guns riding, and they don't risk getting killed if they can get what they want sneaky.

"As a matter of fact," the traveler continued, "they're not apt to attack unless they got us so outnumbered that they can't lose. Judging from those small packs of braves, I say we ain't got no worry."

After riding many miles through the hunting grounds of the Oglalas, someone saw a great spire of stone pointing skyward. It was still hours off, above the winding North Platte River, but could be clearly seen. This was Chimney Rock, the driver called down to a man who inquired, for years a familiar landmark on the Oregon Trail. It reached an awesome 400 feet, and could be observed from two travel days distance.

Eventually the weather-beaten monument of sandstone and clay was approached and passed, and the stage coach rolled on to Scottsbluff, where they halted for the night and to change horses.

That evening Horatio visited an encampment of forty families who were heading West along the Trail with its pasture land and good watering places. Although more immigrants were going by rail since the transcontinental lines were joined in Utah, this route was still preferred by farmers who carried with them entire households, livestock and all that could be loaded aboard sturdy Conestoga wagons. There were old and young folks, including a few born on the trail since leaving Missouri weeks before. They rolled slowly all day but, at night, after forming wagons in a circle as protection against marauding Indians, they danced and sang and visited each other's encampments.

Early the next morning the wagon master's whip cracked, prairie schooners wheeled into assigned positions, and the procession started again, to continue until sundown. Horatio stood by, watching busy preparations for departure, and noting it took a half-dozen horses, mules or oxen to pull a heavily loaded wagon. Women and children rode while older boys and men walked alongside, tended herds, and took turns riding lookout posts some distance from the train.

Horatio was thrilled by these hardy pioneers, and impulsively asked if he might go with them part of the way. The train captain found a group willing to accept him, and the author hastily threw his valise on board, and moved out with the rest.

Soon the Rocky Mountains — gray and snow-capped — appeared on the horizon, and the long, thin line of canvas-topped wagons passed between their grassy, sloping foothills. During the days Horatio trekked with the settlers, he spoke with many of them, making notes and making friends, and recording details of everything from the stoves they carried to speech patterns of those from the South and Midwest.

His reputation was known to many, and one evening, as children sat around the campfire, he told stories which were equally enjoyed by the adults. He was pleased with the respect and attention he received, and willingly assumed his share of the chores. He built fires, carried water buckets, and fed and curried horses. It was a hard, inconvenient existence, he decided, but as a temporary experience he found the life invigorating, his companions determined and courageous, and the rugged landscape an unending panorama of indescribable beauty.

When Horatio parted at Fort Laramie, Wyoming, he received from all the hearty farewell of old friends. He bade them God-speed, promising to describe their journey in a book, and made his way directly to the Union Pacific Railroad, where he bought a ticket to Salt Lake City, the next stop on his Westward journey.

He relaxed for several pleasant days in the Mormon Capital, observing the industrious people, their clean, well-planned city, and enjoying a tour through the Tabernacle and Temple, guided by Brother Charles J. Thomas, leader of the Tabernacle Choir and for many years the official escort of prominent visitors. After showing the author about the grounds and interior, he played a number of hymns on the huge organ and then invited the visitor to place his name in the register, alongside signatures of General Phil Sheridan, President Grant, Edwin Booth and other distinguished guests.

In a luxurious parlor car of the Central Pacific Line, Horatio continued his journey to the coast, passing through valleys of Nevada's majestic mountain ranges and eventually into the tall timber country of California.

On an unusually mild, sunny day in February he arrived at San Francisco, where he was met by James and Annie, who was now a winsome little flirt, just seven years old. The delicately-featured blond child looked so like his late sister — for whom she was named — that Horatio was impelled to write immediately to Gusti and his parents to describe the resemblance. A few days later photographs were made, which he sent to South Natick.

After the brothers affectionately embraced after the separation of many years, each laughingly commented how much weight the other gained, and how the hair had thinned.

"At least you've taken on a fine beard," Horatio observed. "I never had the face for one."

James was anxious to hear news of home and family. He was delighted with Horatio's success and with Gusti's marriage. He'd give much to return to South Natick for a visit, he said, and meant to do so soon.

His own career in the West had been interesting and successful. He bought out his partner's share of the optometry practice, and was now sole owner. The business, like himself, was old-established in San Francisco, and prospered at a fine location on Market Street, the city's main thoroughfare. James lived in an elegant two-story mansion atop one of the steep hills that overlooked the sparkling water and white-capped waves of the Bay far below.

Some months earlier he divorced his second wife, and confessed he was lonely in the house, despite servants and luxury. Little Annie was his main interest, he told Horatio, but his occupation kept them apart much of the time.

"I have a chance to remedy that," he continued. "The fact is, I can now sell out at an excellent profit. What I'd net, plus my savings, would make me quite independent. At any rate, Horatio, I believe I'm going to move to Denver. San Francisco used to be fun some years back, but it's become tame. Denver is as civilized as Boston, but still retains a taste of the frontier life I used to love." James' eyes glistened as he recalled his youthful adventures.

Horatio enjoyed every minute of his stay in San Francisco. It was like a new world to him in every respect. With Annie constantly at his side — James accompanying them when he could — Horatio took cable cars up and down the hills and walked over every part of the city from the historic Presidio to the wharves and exotic, noisy Chinese district. From every hilltop the view was magnificent. With most buildings of low construction, because of occasional earthquakes and tremors, there was always fresh air, breeze from the ocean and bright sunshine.

Upon Annie's suggestion they went in her father's carriage across the city to Woodward's Gardens, where they spent a day visiting exhibits at the amusement park. There was an art gallery, a glass structure filled with tropical plants, and an excursion boat that skimmed the surface of an artificial pond stocked with geese, swans, ducks and pelicans.

After lunch, Annie and Horatio visited the bird house, then a menagerie where they saw camels, jaguars, lions, tigers and other wild animals of great variety. Strutting about the lawns were many peacocks attended by a Chinese giant, named Chang Wo Foo, who was eight feet, four inches tall, and dressed in a colorful, long silk mandarin costume.

After weeks of relaxation, sightseeing — and some writing — Horatio told his brother he wished to see the goldfields to gather material for stories.

"I wish I could go along," James said, "But I have to settle up affairs here. I'll show you the best way to travel," he added, unfurling a large map of the state.

When Horatio departed, several days later, he found the journey considerably easier than did his brother in 1857. Now he enjoyed a comfortable ferry ride across San Francisco Bay, then up the Sacramento River, where the greenery of spring was bursting forth upon gently rolling woodlands of the beautiful Central Valley. From the growing town of Sacramento, he went by stage to Marysville. Then he hired a horse and continued along the Yuba River, climbing ever higher toward creeks where middle-aged, bearded men sifted the water for gold dust and nuggets.

These were a different breed from youths who crowded the mountain sides in 1849 and 1850. Their ranks had thinned. Successful miners of the lush years retired or sold out to syndicates; most of the unsuccessful ones having also long since departed. However, there still were those who clung to the wishful idea they'd yet strike a rich vein.

Fortunately for Horatio, he was able to locate a number who remained from the early diggers. Most of these were leathery veterans who panned enough to keep them in grub, and preferred the surroundings to whatever they left behind, a quarter of a century before. They lived simply in huts alongside their claims, working alone or with a partner; often with no other company than a hound or donkey.

These old-timers were a friendly, talkative lot, and hospitably greeted the author, pleased with the chance to relate tales of gold rush days.

"When two or more began," Horatio noted, "why, they swopped bigger lies than Bret Harte claimed he and Sam Clemens used to concoct while sitting around a barroom stove."

In numerous places the air often was filled with the strange, lilting conversation of Chinese prospectors. Most had recently finished jobs as laborers on the transcontinental rail line. Returning on flatcars to San Francisco, they found other Orientals had already established as many laundries as the city could support, and left immediately for the Sierras.

Frugal, industrious and of complacent disposition, some were already prospering while most managed to earn enough to buy supplies of rice, which formed the main part of their diet. Describing two he met, Horatio wrote that they were:

". . . as like as two peas. The same smooth face, the same air of childlike confidence, the same almond eyes, a pigtail of the same length, a blouse and loose pants of the same coarse cloth. . ."

The men of the camps were generally good-natured, hardworking and resourceful. They were at all times ready to help a neighbor, though his shanty may be some miles distant, across rugged, dangerous country. Many cherished company while others were content with their solitude, especially those whose pokes were filled with gold and buried nearby. At such times, strangers might be treated with suspicion, and the miner's Peacemaker .45 or Winchester rifle was loaded and ready for firing.

Thieves and murderers prowled the lonely trails, and the low growl of a miner's dog was depended upon to warn of their approach. Justice was swift and cruel, and the penalty paid by robber and cheating gambler alike often was instant execution, either before a blazing pistol — if caught in the act — or by hanging when tracked down by quickly organized searching parties. There was the occasional tragedy of an innocent wayfarer being hunted and killed, but this form of law was a necessity, Horatio was told, and it sufficed to keep many criminals from the peaceful diggings.

A month later Horatio was on his way again, this time heading North for a brief stay in Oregon — where he crossed lands of the terrorizing Bannock and Paiute tribes — and then over the Columbia River into Washington Territory. Passing through endless evergreen forests, and in the shadows of snow-capped mountain ranges, he travelled as far as Seattle, there boarding a steamer for his return to San Francisco.

Less than a week after he arrived in the city at The Golden Gate, he was again sailing out of its great harbor, homeward bound.

Although James suggested the speedy journey by train, or one of the shorter water routes — crossing either Mexico or the Isthmus by land — Horatio was determined to enjoy a long sea voyage around the Horn.

Learning that a magnificent four-masted schooner was leaving almost immediately, he booked passage, and sailed with the evening tide. He had a splendid cabin, dined at the captain's table and looked forward to some months of relaxation, interrupted only by infrequent calls at strange, enchanting South American ports. There were but few passengers aboard, and after a week at sea Horatio adhered to a schedule that included several hours of writing each day. This was later adjusted so that, while in warmer climates he spent more time on deck and, when cold weather approached, as they neared the Southermost point of their travels, he rarely left his cabin, but wrote constantly, working on two novels and — in-between — a number of short stories, as situations and incidents came to his mind.

When the long, slim vessel eventually nosed slowly into New York Harbor, in September, 1877, Horatio was sun-tanned and feeling better than ever before. In his valise were completed manuscripts of "Joe's Luck," a story of the mining camps that he promised to Francis Smith for serialization in New York Weekly, and "The Young Adventurer; or, Tom's Trip Across the Plains," which he planned as the first of several volumes Loring would publish as The Pacific Series.

"Hokey, Mister Alger," an aggressive young luggage boy shouted as he ran towards the author. "Yer looks so bully I didn't recognize yer. Here, lemme smash yer bag."

Horatio smiled. He knew he was home again.

CHAPTER 24

HOME AGAIN

FROM THE PIER, HORATIO WENT directly to the Newsboys' Lodging House where Mrs. O'Connor kept his room dusted and clean during the months he was away. Among the boys were dozens of new faces, and the place sheltered many more of them than before he left.

The superintendent was delighted to have him back, and a special dinner was served to celebrate Horatio's homecoming. It was heartily joined by a good crowd of youngsters, including those he was meeting for the first time.

At the end of the week he left for South Natick to spend a few days with his family and, upon returning to the city, moved into new quarters at 107 West 44th Street. He occupied sunny front rooms on the second floor of a comfortable three-story brownstone, one of a row on that quiet uptown street off Longacre Square, where were located carriage manufacturers' showrooms, with their adjoining harness shops.

He had fallen far behind in his output, and publishers were calling for more Alger novels. He gave first attention to his Pacific Series and soon was hard at work on "The Young Miner" and "The Young Explorer." Then he completed "The Telegraph Boy," which Loring was eager to issue as the last book in the successful Tattered Tom Series.

In mid-April, 1878, as he was finishing some short stories promised to Gleason's Monthly Companion, Horatio received a telegram from Gusti. It carried the sad news that Francis had suddenly died of pneumonia. What apparently started as an inconsequential cold quickly became a serious infection, and their youngest brother passed away, unattended, in his bachelor quarters in Boston.

Two days later Francis was buried beside his sister, Annie, in the Old Burying Ground behind Reverend Alger's church.

"His passing is all the sadder," his father said, "because he leaves no heirs to carry on his name."

Olive never fully recovered from the shock of her youngest son's death, and became increasingly ill during the weeks ahead. The parson, too, had become distant and spiritless, and spoke frequently of retiring.

"When a minister's lost his fire," he said, "it's time for him to stand aside and let a younger man take over."

He told this to the parishioners, but they unanimously resolved to ask him to stay, at least for another year, by which time he would round out a full half-century in the pulpit.

Reluctantly he agreed, and attempted to continue with his duties. But his mind was occupied only with his beloved Olive's ebbing strength, her frequent lapses of memory, and the attention she required. He stayed near her bedside and, on the evening of September 3d, as they prayed together, she closed her eyes and passed into a deep slumber from which she never awakened. Sadly, the minister told Horatio to advise the others.

"Don't despair, Father," Horatio whispered. "She is at last with Annie and Francis. That is what she wanted."

"Yes," the pastor agreed, "it is also what I want most for myself."

During weeks that followed, the minister frequently regretted his decision to preside over his congregation for another year. He missed Olive terribly, and the world about him now seemed filled with strangers.

Horatio, Gusti and Amos worried constantly, and did everything possible to keep him occupied and interested. Fortunately, the 200th Anniversary of the dedication of the First Unitarian Church at South Natick would take place on November 20th, and it was Reverend Alger's duty to officiate. Half-heartedly, he made plans, but generally agreed to everything his committee recommended. Horatio spent much time assisting, during this period, and composed a special poem which he read at the celebration. Reverend Alger conducted the services and then delivered an address. It was excellent, and everyone congratulated him. The day went off beautifully, under clear blue autumn skies, with many dignitaries present. Even if the minister was not elated, he was gratified with the results, and warmly thanked all who participated.

A week later he received more news to raise his spirits. It was a letter from James, advising that he was returning to South Natick on a long-overdue visit. It had taken much longer than supposed, he wrote, to settle affairs in San Francisco. Now this was done, and he would soon leave, reaching Massachusetts early in December.

Actually, Horatio had written to him weeks previously, urging him to make every effort to come as soon as possible.

Horatio had business to take care of in Boston and New York, but promised to return when James arrived.

He first called on Aaron Loring, and was disturbed by what he saw. Business was not good. The book shop was almost empty, and Loring was devoting insufficient time to publishing. It appeared he had erratically turned full attention to his coffee shop, and even that had become a losing proposition. Some of his best men, including the energetic George Dillingham, left his employ, and he either did not replace them, or had taken on inexperienced or disinterested new assistants. There even were rumors Loring had fallen deeply in debt.

He welcomed Horatio affectionately, as always, but Loring now appeared weary. Everything was going perfectly, he exclaimed, reassuringly, and he was making all manner of elaborate plans for a spring catalogue, new authors, and expansion in every direction. Horatio hoped prospects were as cheering as his publisher allowed, but the picture was not encouraging.

In New York, Horatio went directly to a meeting at the offices of Street & Smith, and was greeted with the good news that they had recently ventured into the book field, having acquired an interest in the publishing concern of G. W. Carleton & Company. One of their first projects would be "The Western Boy," the Alger story previously serialized in New York Weekly. Attending the conference was George Dillingham who later explained to Horatio that he had become a partner in the Carleton organization.

Horatio was, as usual, far behind in his work. He was rushing to complete the Pacific stories and a serialization for Street & Smith. While in New York, he was offered an excellent opportunity by Frank Munsey to write for Golden Argosy. He would receive more than ever before for original installment rights, and was eager to sign the contract. But he could not, at present, due to previous obligations. When new contracts would be drawn-up, however, he intended to have them written in such a way as to allow him to deal with other publishers as well.

He titled the last of his Western novels "Ben's Nugget," and, although he wrote with usual vigor, he hadn't completed a half-dozen chapters before it was time to return to South Natick, as James and Annie were already there, and Horatio was anxious to see them.

Loaded with gifts and bundles, he reached the village on a snowy morning a week before Christmas, having left New York by train the previous evening. He was delighted to see the effect of the little girl on the parson. The old man and his granddaughter were constantly together, and as he gazed upon her — overwhelmed by the striking resemblance to his daughter — Annie sometimes asked her grandfather why there were tears in his eyes.

Gusti and Amos, who despaired never having children of their own, were equally enthralled by the lovely, vivacious child. Her presence in the parsonage gave it new life and cheer, Gusti declared, and she proceeded to spoil and pamper Annie more than all the rest.

It was a gayer Holiday than the household had known for years, and on Christmas morning the parlor was filled with a great assembly of dolls, games and other brightly-colored toys. As she was taught by her mother, Annie selected a number of her presents and set them aside, saying she preferred to give those to poor children whose day wasn't as happy as hers.

Nothing could have given the minister greater pleasure. Later in the morning Amos hitched his horse to the sleigh and, all climbing aboard for the merry ride, they visited and left beautifully-wrapped packages with a number of villagers who could not afford gifts for their children.

When James departed for Denver, in January, 1879, Annie remained in South Natick, and enrolled at the grammar school. During his stay, her father met and fell in love with Ella Frances Hardy, and he vowed to get settled as quickly as possible, and return to marry her in the summer.

Although he could afford to retire, he was unwilling to do so, and re-established his optometry office, which soon became as successful as in San Francisco. Offering latest innovations, he hired competent aides, and quickly trained them to serve his new clients.

Early in July he was back in Massachusetts, his wedding date set for the 27th of that month. It was one of the last ceremonies at which Reverend Alger officiated, for he retired in September, on the fiftieth anniversary of his ordination.

Despite congratulations the pastor received from friends, former parishioners and churchmen who dispersed in many directions over the decades, his thoughts were, as always, of Olive. In September, 1829, she was seated in the Fenno pew, near his pulpit, the Sunday morning he settled over the First Unitarian Church of Chelsea. He recalled their departure, in 1844, when — with their five children — they travelled together to Marlborough, where he was minister of the West Parish Church for more than fifteen years. Then, in 1860, they came to South Natick which, he believed, had been their happiest home. It was here, he declared, that he would live out his days, after which he would be eternally reunited with Olive, and also with Annie and Francis, who already awaited him.

During the following year, 1880, Horatio rarely left New York. He was determined to catch up on his writing, and he continued to tutor Joseph Seligman's children. Some were already at college, and Horatio was busily preparing the others for their examinations.

Although Loring still protested his business operations were in fine shape, word had spread that he was tottering. Horatio was saddened by these reports. Aaron Loring was his good and generous friend, without whom he might not have attained a fraction of his success. Others were eager to engage Horatio, but he disregarded their offers, wishfully thinking Loring would yet survive the crisis everyone in the trade claimed was sinking him.

Although Horatio continued to receive regular royalty payments, others among Loring's creditors were not so fortunate. There was talk that his rent was many months in arrears, and suppliers pressured him for cash. Having held them off as long as possible, praying in vain for a miracle to save him, Loring's bankruptcy was announced in June, 1881. His famous bookstore closed its doors forever and, within a few months, all plates, copyrights and stock were transferred to various bidders.

Stereotypes of the dozens of Algers he printed over more than sixteen years — along with those of "Ben's Nugget," which was ready for the presses at the time of his failure — became property of Porter & Coates, a sturdy publishing house headquartered in Philadelphia.

Horatio tried to find Loring, for he wanted to help him, but the disheartened, broken bookman was nowhere to be found. From time to time there were reports that he was working for a stationer or news-dealer. But by the time Horatio heard about it, and tried to contact him, he was no longer there. He had become a drifter, unable to satisfy any employer.

A year later he reappeared, the one-man operator of a small stationery shop, newspaper and magazine subscription stand, but he was beaten, and avoided contact with old acquaintances. Most of them were equally willing to forget Aaron Loring, but Horatio Alger could not. Simply and unceremoniously, he insisted upon giving gifts of cash. He bought more supplies from him than could be used during a lifetime, subscribed to more magazines than he could read, and persuaded others to do the same, often covering their expense out of his own pocket.

Like most summer mornings in Washington, D.C., July 2, 1881 was sunny, hot and very muggy. President James A. Garfield, on his way to Williams College to attend a class reunion, arrived at Pennsylvania Station with Senator James G. Blaine. He had just remarked how glad he was to escape for a few days to the cool New England countryside when Charles J. Guiteau, a disgruntled office-seeker whom Garfield rejected, stepped into the waiting room and fired two pistol shots at the President. The first bullet grazed his arm, but the second lodged in his back, alongside the spine. For weeks the President clung to a thin thread of life before, in mid-September, all hope was abandoned. He died September 19th.

When newspaper reports made it clear there was no chance for recovery, John R. Anderson, a New York publisher, called upon Horatio and asked if he was available to write a biography of Garfield and, if so, how speedily could it be completed, as he wanted his book to be the first issued after the President's death.

As his contract with Loring was no longer in effect, and he had not yet re-negotiated with Porter & Coates, he was free to do the job, but could not tell exactly how long it would take.

"Perhaps a month," he estimated, "and less if possible."

This was agreeable to Anderson, and the arrangement concluded on the spot. Horatio put aside all other tasks and collected a pile of newspapers that, day after day, were printing the wounded President's life story, from country childhood through his struggle for education, Civil War bravery and entry into politics.

With these as main source of material, he began immediately, writing day and night, pausing only rarely to sleep or refresh himself with cups of tea. Garfield's life conveniently fit the mold of many of Horatio's fictional heroes, so he advanced rapidly, using imagination whenever facts were not available. In the preface to his narrative he acknowledged shortcomings, and suggested to readers two other volumes where more authoritative information could be obtained.

In three weeks the job was finished and delivered, and less than a month later was in circulation, titled "From Canal Boy to President."

Horatio had scarcely returned to manuscripts he put aside in September, when — from Amos — he received the sad news that

Reverend Alger passed away in his sleep during the night. Only the previous day, November 6th, he celebrated his 75th birthday.

Horatio left within the hour for South Natick, arriving that night. At the funeral, the next morning, the church was filled, and many mourners followed the beloved minister's remains to their final resting place in the cemetery across the road.

Gusti and Horatio were grief-stricken, but felt their father now had what he most wanted. Life had become increasingly burdensome to him since Olive died, and his children philosophized that perhaps he was already with her. They hoped Annie and Francis also joined in that happy reunion.

After remaining through the week, Horatio left for New York, and began studying a number of propositions that were set before him. These included some that offered partnership in publishing ventures and speculative business enterprises, in addition to several interesting offers from reliable, well-established printing houses.

He did not claim to be a business man, and discarded all but the writing contracts. These he considered carefully, and eventually came to satisfactory terms with Frank A. Munsey, the owner of Golden Argosy, a popular weekly for young people, and with Porter & Coates. Both firms agreed that, under certain mutually acceptable conditions, he could enter into contracts with other publishers. This was, in essence, the substance of his renewed contract with Street & Smith, and with Golden Days, a Philadelphia story paper on whose pages his tales had already been serialized.

"From Canal Boy to President" became a fast-selling Christmas item, and was reissued in several large editions. Seeing potential for another Alger-treated biography of a famous American, Anderson signed Horatio to write a life of Abraham Lincoln — ultimately published as "Abraham Lincoln, the Backwoods Boy" — and J. S. Ogilvie & Company acquired hard-cover rights to "A Boys' Life of Daniel Webster," which he previously sold to Street & Smith, and they printed it early in 1882 as "From Farm Boy to Senator."

At the same time, Horatio was rapidly completing installments of "Do and Dare" for Golden Argosy, after which Porter & Coates would bring it out as a book.

On January 13, 1882, Horatio shuffled quietly about his rooms in Forty-fourth Street. Streets outside were slushy, and dreary, gray skies indicated it would snow again before evening. It was his fiftieth birthday, and he was alone. There were no callers, and the mail brought no greetings. Although there was much writing to be done, he pushed notes and papers aside and lingered for many minutes at the window, staring down at passersby and carriages. Then he crossed the floor to a dressing mirror and stood looking at his reflection. He saw a short, roly-poly, aging man with very little hair. His face had become fleshy and he needed eyeglasses to examine himself closely.

He could use a shave, his mustache was in want of trimming, and his eyes were dull and red from long hours by the dim lamplight at his work table. His long, heavy housecoat — which reached almost to his carpet slippers — had become frayed and colorless, and he decided it was time to get a new one.

Frequently he returned to his desk, dipped pen into ink and poised to write, but on that day he had neither thoughts nor words. Late in the afternoon he abandoned chores and got ready to go downtown to the Newsboys Lodging House where, that evening, he would give his young friends a lantern slide lecture. His subject was "Crossing the Continent," and he would show brightly colored glass plates depicting railroads, wagon trains, buffalo, cattle, Indian attacks, the Rocky Mountains, U.S. Cavalry, grizzly bears, hunters and gold mining scenes.

He took extra pains with his appearance, for he must set a fine example when addressing the street boys. He was almost ready to leave when there was a knock upon the door. It was a messenger from one of the fashionable mens' furnishing stores, and he handed Horatio a large, handsomely wrapped box.

Quickly opening it, Horatio first found the enclosed card, which was a cordial birthday sentiment from the Seligman family. Horatio was joyous, for he hadn't been completely forgotten, after all. Pulling away the tissue wrapping, he was delighted to find what he sorely needed, a new housecoat. This one was tailored of dark green velvet, with silken collar and cuffs and a braided sash. His initials were embroidered upon the breast pocket.

He tried it on immediately, posing before the looking glass, and was quite satisfied with his image. It was indeed elegant, and he now cut a much snappier figure, he decided, than earlier in the day.

He looked forward to putting it on again as soon as he returned, but now it was late, and he must hurry to William Street. A fine, wind-driven snow was falling as he boarded the Broadway cars and, as the slippery streets slowed traffic, he reached the lodging house fifteen minutes later than planned.

"Your audience is waiting, Horatio," Charley O'Connor said, as he met him at the entrance. "There's a big crowd tonight, so we'll have your show in the dining hall. Let's go right up."

The large room was strangely quiet, as they approached along the corridor, and Horatio remarked that the lads were better behaved than he supposed. He feared a reception of whistles and stamping feet.

But the silence was short-lived and, as O'Connor followed Horatio into the hall, an older boy up front stood and shouted:
"Three cheers for our friend, Mr. Alger!"

Following the boisterous "Hoorays!", the leader sang "Happy Birthday," joined by more than two hundred voices, while O'Connor led the guest of honor to the front of the room. If Horatio was taken by surprise, he was even more astounded when the boys' spokesman — a reformed young tough named Croucher O'Shea — handed him a bulky carton, and all started to yell:
"Open it! Open it!"

This Horatio did, and withdrew a long housecoat of heavy, durable material. It had a large, multi-colored design, and was purchased from a Broadway clothier by The Croucher and a delegation who carried with them the contributions of many newsboys, bootblacks and baggage smashers. Mrs. O'Connor had neatly embroidered Horatio's initials on the breast pocket.

"We figgered this is sum'thin' ye kin use good, sir," The Croucher announced on behalf of his comrades, and he then proceeded to read — with occasional difficulty — a long list of signa-

263

tures the boys had added to a salutation composed by one of them.

The Croucher's recitation was frequently interrupted by snickers and remarks which stopped suddenly every time he looked up and glared in the direction of the loud whispers.

For some minutes he continued calling off names, while boys in the seats commented:

"I didn't know Snitcher could write."

"I writ it for 'im"

"Since when does The Croucher read?"

"He don't. I saw Mr. O'Connor learnin' it to 'im."

"Snipe must'a robbed the shillin' he give."

"Me birthday's t'morra, boys. Don't forget."

After the reading was completed, Horatio removed his jacket and tried on the bulky garment, to the great delight of the donors. He announced it was exactly what he hoped someone would give him, but this gift was far more than he ever expected. Tears welled in his eyes as he spoke, and The Croucher shrilly whistled for more shouts and applause and cheering.

After considerable delay — during which Horatio, parading about in his new housecoat, shook hands with the boys, and personally thanked many of them — order was restored and the evening performance began.

When among his young friends, Horatio was an eloquent speaker, completely at ease, and never faltered or stuttered. The slides and his exciting narration thrilled the lads, and many declared they were ready to retire from blacking boots to travel Westward across the Great Plains.

Later there were refreshments, highlighted by generous portions of birthday cake and pitchers of milk that were refilled several times. In accordance with house rules, lights were extinguished at ten o'clock, the boys went to their rooms and Horatio prepared to hurry home through the storm.

Wrapping a muffler several times around his neck and raising the coat collar, Horatio stepped to the sidewalk, looking up and down the street for a cab. There were none, and he was about to walk to the corner when two policemen stepped from the shadows and blocked his way.

"Mr. Alger?" one of them asked.

"Yes," Horatio answered, surprised, but not particularly concerned.

"Ye're to come with us, sir," the officer said, without giving further explanation.

"I don't understand. Is someone hurt? Are any of the boys in trouble?"

"We wouldn't know that, sir. All we're told is ye're to be brought directly before a judge."

Horatio was puzzled. He was always ready to cooperate with the law, but on this snowy night preferred to go directly home and to bed. He feared someone might be injured and this worried him. On the other hand, it occurred to him, he recently called upon Mother Mandelbaum to thank her for paying medical expenses for one of the newsboys who became seriously ill while he was away. He wanted to reimburse her, but the old woman, who was kind-hearted, though an outlaw, would not hear of it. Perhaps she had been arrested again, and he was somehow implicated.

These were some of the thoughts that raced through Horatio's mind as the policemen hurried him along William Street to the corner of Beaver. This wasn't the direction of either The Tombs or Police Headquarters, and Horatio was completely bewildered when they hauled him through the familiar frosted glass doors of Delmonico's. Before he could ask a question, the officers hustled him upstairs to a private room, thrust him inside and, courteously saying "Good night, Mr. Alger," they hastily departed.

For a brief moment he was alone in the candlelit chamber — which apparently was in readiness for a banquet — but seconds later the large doors at both sides swung open and a dozen of his Harvard Club chums rushed out to surround him and wish him "Happy Birthday!" as they thumped him heartily on the back and shook his hand.

Quickly recovering from his amazement, he laughingly faced the "judge," none other than his dear friend, Addision Brown, who was recently appointed to the bench of the United States District Court for the Southern District of New York. The Choates were there. Henry Denny came from Boston, and Charley Vinal travelled all the way from his parish at Kennebunk,

Maine. William Robert Ware — whom all still called Billy-Bobby — had only a month earlier taken up residence in the city, having been named as Professor of Architecture at Columbia University. It was the first time Horatio saw him in many years, but they immediately recognized each other, and Horatio was jubilant to see him and all the others at this surprise party.

Ad Brown presided and ordered the "gentlemen of the jury" — these were the other celebrants — to take their seats. Horatio was tagged the "defendant," and placed at the head of the table, called the "witness stand." Then supper was served, with intermissions between courses during which each man stood to read poems and dissertations, or to sing a song about the honor guest. Most of the offerings were hilariously funny; some touchingly sentimental. After the last of Horatio's classmates was heard, and the final trays of delicacies served, Ad Brown — with mock severity — instructed Horatio to conduct his own defense with a "rebuttal to the foregoing testimony."

Horatio's remarks were brief, but apparently eloquent, containing recollections of his friends' college tribulations, humorous references to their current stations, and lines of extemporaneous verse describing his apprehension by police and unceremonious delivery to the court of justice. The room filled with laughter and applause as he finished and sat down.

Thereupon, Joe Choate, the "jury foreman," stood to announce the defendant had been judged "not guilty," and it was decided damages should be awarded. Horatio was asked to step forward and received a large, beribboned package.

As he opened it, and took out a luxurious satin housecoat, Ad Brown explained they selected a crimson robe so Horatio would be ever-mindful of his university colors, and the handsomely embroidered initial "H" on the breast pocket would suffice for "Horatio," "Harvard," or both.

It was almost dawn when the merrymakers parted on the corner in front of Delmonico's. The snow had stopped falling, but wind piled high drifts against buildings, and the whiteness that blanketed the city glistened silvery blue in the lamplight. Soon all rode off in hansoms that waited patiently along the curb, and the street was silent and deserted.

As his cab jogged rhythmically uptown, and muffled clopping of the horse's hoof-beats made Horatio sleepy, he yawned in drowsy contentment, agreeing with himself that this had, indeed, turned out to be a very happy birthday. And he received enough housecoats to keep him warm through many long winters.

CHAPTER 25

STRIVE AND SUCCEED

THE STORY OF THE THREE housecoats became one of Harriet Beecher Stowe's favorites, and she insisted that Horatio repeat it at her seventieth birthday party, the following June, when a hundred friends gathered on the lawn of Massachusetts Governor William Claflin's summer home at Newton.

That festival, a great literary gathering, was for Horatio a pleasant reunion with old acquaintances he had not seen in many years. John Trowbridge was there, as was Dr. Oliver Wendell Holmes and Harriet's brother, The Rev. Henry Ward Beecher. John Boyle O'Reilly, the young Irish poet and revolutionary, left his editing duties in Boston to attend, and John Greenleaf Whittier arrived late from Danvers, where he was living with relatives.

Horatio spent only half the season at South Natick, that year, as he promised the Seligmans to join them at Long Branch in August. He had the previous fall completed his tutorship with their children, and had not seen the family in months.

Although he planned to spend several days in New York, he found the mid-summer heat unbearable, and entrained the next morning for the Jersey Shore. Alfred, Edwin, Isabella and a number of their cousins and companions met Horatio at the station and, all talking rapidly at the same time, carried his valise and walked him to their home.

It was the most wonderful summer ever, Isabella exclaimed, enthusiastically, with so many young people, and lots of parties, and all their friends waiting to meet him, and did he bring his newest books for them, and what was he writing now?

As usual, the Seligmans were surrounded by friends, and Horatio came to know most of them. George W. Childs, the distinguished publisher of the Philadelphia Public Ledger, had a palatial home nearby, and was a dinner guest the evening Horatio arrived.

Although each heard of the other, it was the first time they met. The author had followed the ruddy-faced, stocky Childs' adventures and triumphs for some years, as he was the personification of many of the heroes Horatio described. The publisher, on the other hand, was proud of his climb to fame and fortune. He lost no opportunity to relate how, as an orphan, he started his career as a store boy, rising from the ranks, eventually owning a great newspaper, and becoming host to kings and adviser to presidents.

Of small stature, with gray eyes, rosy cheeks and practically bald, he was pleased to be compared with Benjamin Franklin. As a boy he arrived in Philadelphia with little more than a dollar in his pocket and, from the start, based his progress upon Franklin's principles of thrift, industry and temperance.

His first job was with a bookseller who paid him three dollars a week to make deliveries, sweep floors and sidewalk, tend the fire and assist salesmen during busy hours.

Horatio knew this story, but he was thrilled to be hearing it now from Childs, himself.

Like other Alger heroes, Childs eventually saved enough money to open a shop, and began a confectionery business on Market Street, also stocking a line of patent medicines. He sold his stand at a good profit, however, and took a position as clerk in the office of R. E. Peterson, the prominent publisher and bookman. Within a short time he became a trusted and valued employee, married Peterson's daughter and, while still in his twenties, was made a partner in the business.

During recent years he devoted much time and effort to philanthropy, particularly in the direction of financing the education of hundreds of boys and girls. He favored orphans and children of impoverished families, and provided for many the first rungs on their ladders of success. It was his custom to present handsome gold watches to young associates in appreciation for jobs well done.

"It's the greatest gift in the world," he said, "because every time they look at it they ask themselves how much progress they made since the last time they took the timepiece from their vest-pocket. Then they buckle down and work to get further ahead."

The following week, Childs had a garden party in honor of Ulysses S. Grant, who also was a summer resident of Long Branch, and Horatio was invited to attend. It was pleasant, for many people Horatio knew were there. But, from the point of view of spending a scintillating afternoon with the great American military hero and former President, it was something of a disappointment. In build he was rather stockier than Horatio expected, appearing round-shouldered and unkempt. He seemed shy and spoke very little.

There were a number of vacationers from Washington, who knew Grant well, and they greeted him informally as "Lyss." Horatio did not know whether to address him as "General" or "President," and admitted this to the old warrior, when they came face-to-face at the buffet table.

"Suit yourself, sir," Grant answered, in a low, hoarse voice. "My parents named me Hiram, but at school I was Sam. I tell folks I don't care what I'm called, just so's I'm called for meals."

Horatio believed "President" carried the proper respect, and that was what he called him that evening, and on the several other occasions they met.

One evening, a couple of weeks after the party, Horatio and George Childs were strolling along the shore-front, chatting and enjoying the fresh ocean breezes. They passed the Grant cottage, and saw him — with his wife and daughter, Nellie — seated on the porch. He waved to them, and invited the pair to join him for some talk and refreshment.

"What can we offer you, gentlemen?" he asked.

Childs reminded him that both he and Horatio were pledged to temperance.

"Oh, indeed," Grant said, rubbing the side of his beard. "When I was a farm-boy in Ohio I took the pledge, along with my sisters and brothers. Then I got into the Mexican War and forgot about it. When I married, I again joined a total abstinence society, and was steadfast almost a year. My doctor recently prescribed I get steadfast again, so suppose we all have some tea."

He was a cordial host, more talkative than when faced with crowds at a gathering, and considerably more at ease. His early military years was a subject he favored, and he possessed a wealth of anecdotes and memories of days as a lieutenant at Jefferson Barracks, Missouri; of Santa Anna's attack at Buena Vista, and of two homesick years of service on the Pacific Coast.

"That's the place," he said, "where I was probably least steadfast."

＊　　　＊　　　＊

Joseph Seligman's best friend and constant companion, that summer, was Judge Albert Cardozo, a former Justice of the New York State Supreme Court. Cardozo's wife, Rebecca, died three years previously, and he was concerned about the education of his twelve-year-old twins, Emily and Benjamin. His older children, who completed their studies, were Albert, Ellen — capably running the household since her mother's death — Grace and Lizzie, an invalid since birth.

Finding an instructor for his youngest son was uppermost in his mind. There were gaps in Ben's learning, and he desired the boy to continue a family tradition — since 1787 — of attending Columbia University.

Seligman immediately suggested Horatio Alger, but added, doubtfully, that he was so busy writing, he did not know if he could spare the time.

"In any event," Seligman said, "I'll ask him tonight. Even if he's not able, he may know another suitable teacher."

"Master Ben," as Benjamin Nathan Cardozo was called by

his childhood governess, was one of Horatio's favorites among the dozen or more children with whom he spent part of every day. He would be greatly offended, he declared, if he hadn't been offered the position, even though he considered his teaching career as finished. Somehow Horatio would arrange his fall schedule to include several hours of tutoring each week.

The Judge was greatly relieved, and Ben delighted to learn that his friend and favorite author would now be his teacher as well. As a matter of fact, he said, he could hardly wait until September to get started.

Soon after they returned to New York, in the early autumn, Horatio visited the Cardozo home at 12 West 47th Street. It was but a few steps off Fifth Avenue, directly accross from the mansion of Jay Gould.

From their first session, Horatio and the boy became devoted to each other, and the daily lessons were considered more of a period of recreation than work. Ben, a well-poised lad of modest demeanor, had dark hair and brown eyes. Frail of physique, but of a generally playful disposition, he turned desperately serious when studying or practicing at the piano. His technique at the keyboard displayed such talent, his music professor declared, that he predicted for the boy a spectacular concert career.

Ben, nevertheless, preferred to matriculate in law, and in this direction Horatio coached him in the classics. Daily, in the sunny music room on the second floor of the brownstone — surrounded by plants and flowers — they reviewed courses in Greek and Latin; the odes of Pindar, Plato and Aristotle. Ben learned speeches of the great orators of ancient Athens in their original Greek, and soon became proficient in the oratory of Pliny and Cicero, and Epictetus' "Power of Speaking."

Before the spring of 1883, the two proceeded to the works of Shakespeare, Browning and Shelley, soon continuing through Thackery, Dickens and George Eliot.

There never was anything forceful about Horatio's instruction. He still was as easy-going and soft-spoken as during his professional teaching days, years earlier, and represented to Ben Cardozo the same entertaining companion known to students at Potowome and the academy at Deerfield, and to those he tutored at Cambridge. He always was patient, kind and generous, and it was these qualities, perhaps, that earned for him the devotion of all young people, for he understood them so well.

Occasionally, in the evening, Ben and Horatio attended lectures together. The boy was fascinated by Paul du Chaillu, as the suave, spade-bearded Frenchman described his explorations among the pygmies and discovery of gorillas in Equatorial Africa. He told stirring tales of his journey to Ashango-land, illustrating his talk with large, colorful slides.

The audience was larger the night they heard Mark Twain's popular discourse on his youthful ramblings, from boyhood on the Mississippi to unsuccessful prospecting among the gold fields of California. It was a highly entertaining performance, concluding — as always — with his preposterous anecdote of "The Jumping Frog of Calaveras." Dressed in a gleaming white suit — with right hand on his hip and left elbow on lectern — he fixed a sharp, aquiline eye first on one person and then another, before the end of the evening giving each the impression he was engaged with them in a direct, private conversation.

After Sam Clemens walked off the stage, following prolonged, tumultuous applause, Horatio took Ben to meet the author of "Tom Sawyer" in his dressing room. The introduction thrilled the boy, and the humorist asked Horatio if this might be one of his newsboy heroes in the flesh.

"Can I offer you a cigar, sir?" Clemens jokingly asked Ben as he lit one for himself.

"No thank you. But I would like your autograph."

Mark Twain willingly complied, signing both his real name and pen-name on the program, which Ben proudly showed to his father when he got home.

A year later, in June, 1884, as Horatio was intensifying Ben's preparation for forthcoming entrance examinations for Columbia, he received the shocking news that his brother, James, had died suddenly in Denver. He left New York the next morning, arriving in Colorado four days later.

The funeral had already taken place, so he busied himself consoling Annie and James' widow as best he could, and settling his brother's extensive business affairs. Ella told Horatio that, upon returning from an evening at the elegant Unity Club, he suffered a brain hemorrhage, and was dead before the doctor arrived.

Having done all he could, Horatio returned East at the end of the week, bringing Annie to South Natick before travelling on to New York. She was welcomed as their own daughter by Gusti and Amos and, while they deeply mourned James' passing, they felt that they at last had a child of their own. Although she was well provided for by her father's estate, Horatio took immediate steps to adopt her, and she was designated as his legal heir.

Upon his suggestion, Gusti closed the house at South Natick, and she and Amos took Annie to spend the season at a comfortable hotel in Old Orchard, Maine. Then Horatio hurried back to the city, promising to rejoin them, if possible, before the end of August.

Ben continued his studies during his tutor's absence, and Horatio told Judge Cardozo he considered his son eminently ready for the college tests. Nevertheless, Horatio was asked if he would accompany them to Long Branch to occasionally review with his pupil, and spend the balance of the time writing in the cool, relaxed atmosphere of the seashore, or passing the time in any other way he preferred. It was a welcome invitation, after a sad, harrowing experience, and he willingly accepted.

Horatio loved the quiet respectability of Long Branch, and the fact that, through the years, it was virtually unchanging. The same homes were reopened each summer by the same long-time residents who sunned themselves, visited at tea-time and played tennis and croquet in the same manner as in years past. Talk was cheerful, parties cordial, the pace unhurried and the climate superb. Along with his wardrobe he packed the unfinished manuscript of "Helping Himself," and departed with the Cardozos on July 10th.

A tall, serious law student, who came to the resort as a tutor, quickly won the admiration of many of the girls, and was eagerly sought for their parties.

He was Charles Evans Hughes, a Columbia classmate of DeWitt Seligman, and recent winner of a three year fellowship worth five hundred dollars per annum. DeWitt brought his chum, Hughes, to the shore as an instructor for his brother-in-law, Larry Bernheimer. With DeWitt, he often visited the Cardozos and

Seligmans, and was a frequent escort of the young ladies to socials and on evening strolls.

Hughes, when he learned Ben would take the college tests in a month, was most helpful, offering wise guidance and was, in turn, genuinely impressed with the boy's ability and thorough preparation. He was well-equipped, Hughes said, and assured him that he would pass with ease.

Charles Evans Hughes' prediction proved correct, for Benjamin Cardozo finished the examinations with a near-perfect score, and was admitted to Columbia University to attend in the fall of 1885, when he would be fifteen years old. Judge Cardozo was thrilled with the report, as was Horatio, who left Long Branch soon after to spend the rest of his vacation with Gusti, Amos and Annie.

John L. Sullivan, a young man from the Boston slums, became bare-knuckle boxing champion in 1882. Defeating the brawling Paddy Ryan in a bloody contest, he was the idol of streetboys who lived at the Newsboys Lodging House. They kept pictures of him that appeared on the pink pages of the Police Gazette and other sporting journals, and avidly followed his exploits in and out of the ring.

When November 17, 1884 was set as the date he would defend his title against Alf Greenfield, a bruiser from Birmingham, England, with a fine record of having demolished a score of opponents using scientific techniques, the bootblacks and newshawkers talked of little else. The new Marquis of Queensbury rules would be followed, and gloves would be worn, creating the impression that the advantage lie with the contender.

As far as Horatio Alger was concerned, this was a mixture of barbarism, gambling and an unholy display that would fill Madison Square Garden with the worst elements of the city. He would have preferred to steer the boys in the direction of more wholesome entertainment, but did not know how to do it. When he learned the street arabs were buying tickets for the fight, he turned to O'Connor for counsel.

"My advice to you, Horatio," Charley quickly suggested, "is that you come along with me this afternoon when I go to buy my ticket before they're all gone! This is one you mustn't miss. Big John is going to slaughter the Englishman, and I mean to watch."

He went on to persuade Horatio that — as the event was billed — this would be a sparring exhibition devoid of brutality, with contestants wearing padded gloves, and abiding by a set of legally-enforced regulations.

Although Henry Bergh condemned the sport as savagery, The Rev. Henry Ward Beecher — who, himself, was said to be a handy man with his fists — was preaching from the pulpit of his Brooklyn church that this was the emergence of a new era of sportsmanship, and the art of prize-fighting would soon become a gentlemanly pastime. He added he had every intention of attending the match.

Horatio bought a ticket, convincing himself it was in the interest of journalistic research, but was soon caught up in the frenzy. While he refused to bet on the results, and urged others to refrain, he found himself expressing strong preference for the American. He read all he could find on Sullivan's background and on boxing, and in his usual studious fashion, soon became, among his urchins, an expert and arbiter on Queensbury rules.

Together with the superintendent and a group of the boys, he visited the champion's training quarters, on the second floor of Harry Hill's Theater at Houston and Crosby Streets, and was impressed with the huge man's skill and grace.

"Horatio," O'Connor said, "it would be great if we could get him down to our gym. Scientific boxing would be a fine thing for my kids to learn. Maybe you can convince him to come and show them."

Horatio agreed, made his way toward Billy Muldoon, one of Sullivan's handlers, introduced himself, and proposed that the champion spend an evening at the Newsboys' Lodging House to teach the boys his art of self-defense. Someone apparently thought the idea had publicity possibilities, and agreed. John L. Sullivan, himself — when sober — was a generous, good-natured soul, and eager to display a measure of kindness to lads brought up under hardships he recalled from his own youth.

When he appeared in the gymnasium, the room was packed

with ragged waifs, the atmosphere equalling that of a professional ring. Sullivan gave pointers to a number of boys who volunteered, and then sparred gently for some minutes with O'Connor, who was a boxer during his army days.

The champion enjoyed the welcome he received, and returned on other occasions to instruct, and to referee matches that the superintendent carefully arranged. Sullivan was a giant next to Horatio, but the little author decided he possessed an earthy charm as well as personal warmth. Nevertheless, he never mentioned the episode to Gusti, who surely would not consider the champion a suitable guest to address her Sisters of Temperance and Total Abstinence Society.

Every seat in the arena was filled on the night of the 17th, with representatives of every echelon from the press and sporting world to New York society and city administrators present. Many spectators came from out-of-town, and Greenfield brought with him a contingent of supporters from England.

Beecher was there; William K. Vanderbilt, in formal attire, was host to a party of sportsmen, and men with names both famous and infamous shouted along with patrons in the cheap bench sections for the battle to begin.

The din increased when the fighters climbed between the ropes, Horatio and Charley O'Connor cheering with the rest. Sullivan was the larger of the two, but during the first round Greenfield's boxing skill impressed the audience. In the second, Sullivan smashed a sledge-hammer right to his opponent's head, opening a severe gash over the left eye. Greenfield fought back desperately, his face and body — and Sullivan's gloves — soon spattered crimson with blood. With more than a minute to go before the round ended, the champion pressed the Englishman against the ropes, and was mauling him murderously when the police intervened, pulling the fighters apart, and ending the contest.

From the point-of-view of the law, they were trying to slaughter each other and, after the first moments in the ring, it ceased to be the gentlemanly sparring exhibition prescribed in the rules. As far as the audience was concerned, Sullivan was winner and still champion.

✳   ✳   ✳

The demand for Horatio Alger's hero fiction continued to increase, and he wrote steadily to supply his editors and readers. Recalling his long voyage around Cape Horn, he produced "Facing the World," but describing it, instead, as a cruise to Australia. His next was a sequel, "In a New World," an adventure among the gold fields of Australia, that actually was based upon notes made in California, and treated previously in The Pacific Series.

These first appeared as serializations in Golden Argosy during 1885 (the same year his cousin, Senator Russell A. Alger — who attained rank of General in the Civil War — was elected Governor of Michigan) and were followed by "Frank and Fearless" and "Mr. Craven's Stepson" in New York Weekly, the latter continuing into 1886.

Frank Munsey loved every circulation-increasing tale Horatio created for Golden Argosy, but foresaw that installments of a serialization might overlap with final chapters of a previous Alger story and the beginning of the next. He pondered how to avoid confusion, and the possibility of readers tiring of the author's output.

He finally decided to confer upon Horatio a pen-name and, of several suggested, Arthur Lee Putnam was chosen. Henceforth, Munsey instructed his staff, the by-lines of Alger and Putnam would be alternated, and he immediately proceeded to popularize the name as a new literary discovery presented for the pleasure of his subscribers.

The nom-deplume first appeared in 1886, under the title, "Number 91; or, The Adventures of a New York Telegraph Boy." Shortly before that story ended, Munsey embarked upon a paperback book publishing venture, reprinting novels between the soft orange-colored covers of Munsey's Popular Series for Boys and Girls. "Number 91" was one of three Algers produced in this format during 1887 and 1888.

Coincidentally, Street & Smith authorized A. L. Burt to use thrillers that ran in New York Weekly in Burt's paper-wrapped Boy's Home Library. "Joe's Luck" was released as Volume I, Number I, in September, 1887, the group including four more by Alger before suspending about a year later, after which Burt issued Horatio's stories in hard-bound volumes.

Horatio's royalties from pulp editions continued into 1890, during which year United States Book Company selected five of his stories from Golden Argosy and its successor, The Argosy — and one that was not previously serialized — distributing them in their yellow-covered Leather-Clad Tales of Adventure and Romance.

Even before 1882, when their friend, Whitelaw Reid — a Civil War news correspondent and then owner of the New York Tribune — took over a campaign to raise money to send slum children out of the steaming city for summer vacations, the Seligmans were active contributors to the Fresh Air Fund. When they brought Reid together with Horatio, the generous author pledged whole-hearted efforts to the program, and became an active supporter. At a small gathering at the Seligman home, the publisher told Horatio how it began.

In the summer of 1877, The Reverend Willard Parsons, a graduate of Union Theological Seminary and former superintendent of the Home for Little Wanderers, at 40 New Bowery, on New York's East Side, was installed as minister at Sherman, a farming village in Pennsylvania. In sermons, he told his congregation of the pale, undernourished children of his previous parish and asked them to take these boys and girls into their families for brief periods.

"In rickety, over-crowded dwellings," he said, "they actually are dying of malnutrition and contagions. Let us bring them from the streets into the beauty of our blossoming fields. Open your comfortable homes to these poor children" he implored, "for a few weeks of health and happiness."

After services, farmers and their wives crowded around the pastor. They offered to care for little ones, and two weeks later the first group — nine happy, bewildered tots — was met at the station. Then, in buggies and hay ricks, all rode away down dusty roads with their vacation parents.

The experiment was a success. The idea grew. A year later more were entertained, and soon Reverend Parsons was traveling the countryside in search of others willing to give summer to a slum child.

Within five years, interest became so widespread that the minister sought a larger audience for his cause, and aroused the enthusiastic interest of Whitelaw Reid who, with four others — Cleveland E. Dodge, Cornelius Vanderbilt, Morris K. Jessup and Darius O. Mills — organized the Tribune Fresh Air Fund Society.

Horatio gave willingly, enlisting many — including P. T. Barnum — to do the same. He soon had Amos Cheney persuading the people of Natick and other communities to become hosts to the waifs, and his close friend, Lemuel Gardner — a successful importer of woolens — was doing the same among neighbors near his place at Woodstock, Connecticut.

Horatio was always happiest when in the midst of hectic activity in the interest of youngsters. On such occasions his shyness disappeared and he prodded and badgered until he received the aid or promise he sought. And as hard as he worked in behalf of organizations seeking to ease conditions of slum children, he gave even more generously to help those he befriended.

He was known as a one-man employment service, arranging jobs for boys who were outgrowing the Lodging House. He placed scores of them on newspapers, in counting houses, stores, and in firms of out-of-town acquaintances. Regularly, he entered several in the six-month course at Professor Browne's Brooklyn Business College, paying tuition out of his own pocket. After graduation, Horatio set-up two boys as grocers in Biddeford, Maine, two in a profitable furniture business in Boston — in which he was a partner — and a dozen in other enterprises.

His investments, apparently, were not always returned and, although his income was considerable, he ended each year with little cash and a drawer full of promissory notes, most of which he eventually forget, misplaced or discarded. But giving was his pleasure and, as he lived modestly, he was never in want and had sufficient to send extravagant gifts to Annie, and to entertain the young lady in grand style when she visited him in New York.

Horatio also helped his boys when they got in trouble and, for at least two of them he hired lawyers and was active in their defense. When one, convicted of burglary, was sent to Sing Sing, the author interceded and managed to have the term reduced from ten to two-and-a-half years. For another, whose easy disposition, Horatio said, permitted him to be persuaded to sell stolen goods, he employed attorneys, consoled the distressed parents and rounded up character witnesses.

"Of course I shall stand by him," the author wrote in a letter. "I always do stand by a friend in time of trouble."

When the case came to trial, the youth was sternly reprimanded by the lenient magistrate, and sent home with a warning as to consequences of a second appearance before the court.

Among the many lads Horatio was pleased to have about him, five were his favorites, and he remained in close touch with them. These included Tommy Keegan, Louis Schick, Irving Blake and the brothers, John and Edward Down. During Horatio's summer vacations, they sometimes accompanied him to South Natick, Maine coast resorts or the Catskills. In winter they were often at his rooms, especially on Friday evenings, when he traditionally held open house.

Tommy was the youngest of these, and Horatio found for him work in a tailor's establishment, later putting him through school to qualify the boy for something better. Horatio was particularly proud of Schick, a former street-boy who became a clerk and eventually filled an executive position with John Wanamaker, when that Philadelphia merchant took over A. T. Stewart's property at Tenth Street and Broadway. Irving Blake, with whom Horatio corresponded regularly over a period of years, had the ambition of "Ragged Dick," and made the most of opportunities. The youth was virtually self-educated when Horatio asked Whitelaw Reid to hire him as an office boy. Like "Dick," and dozens of other Alger heroes, Irving learned fast, was reliable and soon promoted to the Tribune news staff.

Dearest to him were the Downs who, with their widowed mother, Kate, came from Ireland in 1885, when John was fourteen and Edward twelve. John arrived first, and Horatio met him at the Lodging House, where he stayed, getting started as a messenger while finding a room for his mother and brother, who reached America two months later.

Both boys were slender and dark-haired with blue eyes and

rich brogue. Their mother was a handsome woman in her mid-thirties, with freckles, auburn hair and the lilting voice of her County Kerry people, where she was raised on a hillside farm.

They were a devoted group, and the sons toiled at a variety of jobs to make their mother's life easier than it had been at their impoverished home across the Atlantic. For a while she taught them in the evenings, but then took work as a seamstress so they could attend school near their tenement on Grand Street. Despite their objections, she sewed the day long, saying it helped pass time while her boys were out.

She was a head taller than Horatio, and treated him tenderly, as one of her children. He relished her cooking, taking dinner with them almost nightly, and on Sundays often leading them on picnics to Brooklyn Heights where they relaxed on the grass watching steamers, sailing vessels and swarms of little tugs moving slowly in and out of the harbor below.

He moved them to larger quarters, uptown, insisting upon paying the difference in rent, which he considered his fair obligation in return for meals and the comforts of family life he had not previously known, but which he savored more with each passing day.

Writing under two names — Alger and Putnam — was a demanding occupation and, since early in 1888, when he moved into rather luxurious quarters at 36 West 33d Street, off Fifth Avenue, he steadily increased his daily work load. To satisfy publishers, he turned out serializations faster then ever before, producing "A New York Boy," "A Boy's Fortune," "The Erie Train Boy," "Tom Brace," "Mark Stanton," "Tom Turner's Legacy" and "Walter Sherwood's Probation." During this busy period he also finished "The Odds Against Him" which, after serialization in The Argosy, would be issued as a book by Penn Publishing Company, a new Philadelphia printing house with whom Horatio entered into a very satisfactory agreement.

Early in 1890, Tom Glynn, the editor of New York Weekly, called on Horatio to ask a special favor. Street & Smith was planning a new periodical, to be known as Good News. Horatio's jaw dropped when he was asked if he could be counted upon as a regular contributor.

"I guess you need more assignments like General Custer needed more Indians," Glynn said, apologetically, "but we want to offer the best writers, Horatio, and you are Number One!"

Glynn departed a quarter of an hour later with Horatio's authorization to reprint a number of his old serializations, and the tentative promise to later create new ones, if they are still needed. The next time the author visited Street & Smith headquarters, Glynn introduced him to the young man chosen to edit Good News. Although he would be known by the stock name, "W. B. Lawson," his real name was Edward Stratemeyer.

Slightly-built, and in his late twenties, Stratemeyer — who formerly worked for Munsey — was nervously trying to arrange schedules of adventure tales by Horatio, Oliver Optic, Harry Castlemon, Edward S. Ellis, William Murray Graydon and other top-notchers at the same time he was preparing his first book for publication and getting ready to marry his next-door sweetheart from Newark, New Jersey.

Horatio was overwhelmed by the almost worshipful reception he received from the editor. He was brought up on "Algers," Stratemeyer proudly admitted, first gleaning weekly installments; then re-reading stories when they came out as books. Horatio Alger, he said effusively, was the master whose works were his model.

The next time they met, Stratemeyer asked Horatio for an opinion of his novel — he just received proofs and was eager to show them — titled "Richard Dare's Adventure." There was no doubt he had tremendous ability to work out plots, Horatio thought, and complimented him, offering suggestions for slight revisions.

Over the months they met frequently and became good friends, Horatio enjoying the feeling of paternal warmth he had for younger people, and firm in the belief that the talented, energetic Ed Stratemeyer stood on the threshold of a brilliant career.

Then, in the spring, Horatio caught a cold which, because he was weakened from overwork, caused a severe bronchial infection, and he remained in bed for weeks. His eyes, too, were strained, and he suffered constant headaches.

Kate Down went daily to his rooms to clean and prepare broth and whatever nourishment the doctor prescribed. After school, Edward came to run errands for Horatio, and to take his mother home at night. John, who went from class directly to a job as office boy, visited Sundays, and on occasional evenings during the week.

Horatio recovered by mid-June, but lost considerable weight and the high color was gone from his cheeks. In a week, he declared, he would feel strong enough to go to Maine for a month-long vacation. But his physician didn't approve. He recommended, instead, the drier climate of the West, and urged the weary author to give up meeting deadlines and all forms of exertion for at least six months.

"Don't write," Horatio was ordered, "Don't read. Sit in the sun and relax."

Three weeks later he departed by train, travelling leisurely and making frequent stops at cities and resorts. He was slowly heading in the direction of Helena, Montana, where he would be the guest of his former pupil, Alfred Lincoln Seligman, who settled there and was managing family interests in the copper mining region.

Everything was done to make him comfortable, and the soothing scent of the balsam of ponderosa pine, which filled the forests, cleared his lungs and eased breathing. He slept well, relaxed all day and occasionally attended evening socials with Alfred and his friends.

In November he reached San Francisco, for the first time in more than a dozen years, and was amazed by the city's spectacular growth. Although saddened that James was no longer there, the weather was pleasant, views still magnificent, and his hosts friendly and hospitable. Horatio was greeted as a celebrity, interviewed by newspapers and asked opinions on a variety of topics.

As much as he appreciated everyone's cordiality, he tired easily, became irritable, and realized the need for relaxation his doctor ordered. He resumed his trip, visiting Southwestern regions for the first time, and being constantly thrilled by endless expanses of breathtakingly colorful scenery. All winter he rested in the warm desert sunshine, returning to New York in April, 1891.

He told those who asked that he never felt better, but Horatio's step was slower, his breathing a bit strained. His sparse hair had grayed and clothes hung loosely on his small frame. He smilingly boasted of his trim figure, but Kate Down, seeing him for the first time after his return, was shocked at how he aged, and determined to fatten him up with good cooking. She began immediately, preparing his favorite dishes, and was cheered to see the gusto with which he ate.

"In no time a'tall," she vowed, "the little fellow will be lookin' splendid again, God bless 'im."

Horatio was impatient to resume work, but was warned that a relapse would be worse than the illness he survived. He reluctantly agreed to limit output to two novels a year, working for short periods, and with frequent vacations during which he must not compose a single line.

As the months passed, Horatio increasingly considered the Downs as his own family, and was with them most of the time. He placed the boys in business school, and John had entered a real estate office. Edward greatly desired to become a photographer, and Horatio arranged his apprenticeship with one of the city's finest commercial studios.

Before leaving for Natick, he went one day to Brooklyn with Kate and showed her a lovely house, with a spacious garden behind it, located at 196 Twentieth Street, in a quiet, residential section.

"How do you like it?" he asked. "I'm thinking of buying it."

"'Tis indeed elegant," she said, "but why would ye be needin' such a large place?"

He'd tired of rooming houses, he explained, and wanted something with more permanence and comfort.

"I've decided," Horatio stated simply, "that it's time I had a home rather than a room."

"Ye'll have that here, sure," Kate agreed, "but the boys and me'll miss seeing ye, as I don't suppose ye'll be coming about so often."

"That's not the point at all. We'll still be together; even more so, as I would buy the house only if you and the boys move in, too. It will be better for all of us and I, for one, won't have to give up my lodgings every time I leave the city."

They went inside and Horatio showed the spacious rooms, sunny garden, and section he would arrange as his office and work area. Kate was more impressed with the large, well-equipped kitchen, indoor toilets and fine plumbing.

A week later, Horatio's belongings and contents of the Down's small apartment were wagoned across the Brooklyn Bridge. Kate, happier than she ever remembered being, set to work scrubbing, polishing and furnishing, having promised Horatio he'd find his home ready when he returned in September.

As usual, he first visited with Gusti and Amos, in their quiet village beside the Charles River. He arrived in time for Annie's twenty-first birthday, on July 3d and, as usual, brought her an outrageously expensive gift, a beautifully-jewelled brooch from Tiffany & Company's fashionable store on Union Square. A handsome young lady with soft, light-brown hair, delicate complexion, and the gray eyes of her Fenno ancestors, Annie had recently completed her first year as a school teacher.

While at South Natick, Horatio completed two stories, and sent them off to Munsey. One was "Digging for Gold," a tale of the California miners that followed the pattern of his Pacific Series, but included descriptions of terrain he recently travelled.

The second was "A Fancy of Hers," another of the author's occasional attempts to turn out adult fiction. The tale of a modest New York society girl who takes a teaching job in a small New England community, he used Annie as his model for the lovely heroine, setting the action against a parade of events and characters he remembered from his own childhood at Chelsea. He etched hardships of the underpaid minister and his family; kind and flint-hearted townspeople, gossips, deacons and other rural characters.

Munsey was furious when he read the manuscript. He expected the usual hardy product, but received, instead, a saccharine romance that would start young subscribers writing letters of indignation. On the other hand, he could not risk offending his star contributor.

Always the diplomat, Munsey immediately wrote Horatio a brief memo, complimenting him on the novel. But as it was too mature to offer to children, he reasoned, he would, instead, feature it in Munsey's Magazine, a monthly for adults.

The story eventually appeared, considerably shortened to run complete in one issue. Horatio was pleased when he saw it in print, and decided that, as soon as time permitted, he would write for the appreciative Munsey another romance in a similar vein.

They soon departed for Old Orchard Beach, staying as usual at the dignified Aldine Hotel. Annie was constantly surrounded by beaus. Gusti and Amos relaxed, spending much time in rocking chairs, talking with other boarders on the high, breezy porch, and Horatio often rode to nearby Kennebunkport where John Trowbridge had recently built a house.

Ice cream, tea and checkers were the incentives, and the two men sat through many a warm afternoon, that summer, remembering times past and looking dreamily across the wind-buffeted ledges that divide Wells Bay from the blue waters of the open Atlantic.

CHAPTER 26

THE END OF AN ERA

THE FOLLOWING YEAR, in June, 1892, Horatio and twenty of his college chums gathered at Young's Hotel, in Boston, to celebrate the fortieth anniversary of their Harvard graduation.

"Bald heads and gray beards were in the majority at the table," Horatio noted, and Class Secretary Denny — every inch a gentleman of the old school — jovially greeted each man individually, briskly moving from one to another with the measured, short-stepping gait of a mechanical toy.

It was a festive evening, but touched with sadness as those who attended spoke of others long dead. The Civil War, alone, took eight of their brothers and many who survived the Rebellion also lay buried in nearby and distant graves.

Ad Brown had come up from New York with Horatio. George Cary — Horatio's first roommate — was present, as were Charley Vinal, Williamson, Hurd, Coolidge, Ware and a dozen more who travelled from afar to spend that evening with their friends. Hilliard, the Secessionist against whom Denny used to harangue Abolition, was unable to make the trip from his home in North Carolina. He wrote to Denny of his sorrow at not being there.

"Every now and then," his letter ended, "I catch myself calling the roll as it used to be. So, you see, I am ever true to the dear old Class of '52."

After the sumptuous meal of many rich courses, Horatio — who still was official Class Day Odist — read lines he had prepared, after which Denny, in an uneven, croaking voice, led the group in original choruses to the tunes of "Highland Laddie" and "White Cockade." Then Thorndike was called upon for his traditional rendition of "Our Heroes," which he first sang at the Annual Dinner in 1862.

In the final business of the evening, two men left the room, returning a moment later escorting Horace Hemsley, the venerable colored headwaiter who for many years looked after the comfort of the Class at its dinners. He was invited in to receive, in honor of the event, a gift of cash, after which Denny commended to his special care "our last survivor who, a generation or more from now, will be dining here alone."

∗　　∗　　∗

Kate Down made for Horatio a snug home in Brooklyn. She watched over him like a mother hen, preparing his meals in accordance with physicians' directions, and rapping softly upon his library door at the precise hour he must put aside his writing. She kept his teapot at a boil on cold winter mornings, and flew into the room with medicine at the sound of a cough.

John and Edward had become young giants, both now over six feet tall, and Horatio proudly introduced them as his sons to Edward S. Ellis, Ed Stratemeyer and his wife, Ad Brown, Joe Choate and others who came to visit. Two years later, in 1894, after another winter-long siege of bronchial asthma, he legally adopted both boys, and in his will listed them among his heirs.

That summer, at Martha's Vineyard, he settled back to work after a long period of inactivity, producing "The Young Salesman" for The Argosy and, after completing it in the fall, again embarked on what he planned as a serious adult novel. Inspired by "Ships that Pass in the Night," a popular story by Beatrice Harraden, Horatio quickly finished "The Disagreeable Woman," and presented it to Frank Munsey.

The heyday of weekly fiction sheets was already on the

wane, and the publisher was in a somber, pensive mood the afternoon Horatio handed him the manuscript. He didn't have time to study it at the moment, but asked Horatio to leave the package with him.

A few days later the papers were returned to the author with Munsey's brief request that, for Argosy, he stick to juvenile adventures. Piqued, especially because he was sure his publisher would be pleased, Horatio next mailed his novel to Porter & Coates, but they, likewise, turned it down.

Quite by chance, during Thanksgiving Week, Horatio met George Dillingham, who had ascended to the presidency of G. W. Carleton & Co. After a brief sidewalk conversation they continued on their separate ways but, a week later, Dillingham invited Horatio to lunch the next time he was in the city. When they dined in the Amen Corner of the Fifth Avenue Hotel — a few doors East of the publisher's Twenty-third Street offices — Dillingham asked Horatio to let him publish an Alger story.

Horatio was anxious to accommodate his associate of many years, but such was not easy. He explained that, for reasons of health, he limited output to two novels a year, and these he must supply to Munsey. Then, almost as an afterthought, Horatio mentioned "The Disagreeable Woman," honestly admitting that it had been twice rejected. Dillingham was interested, nevertheless, and, after reading the story, agreed to issue it as a book.

One obstacle remained, Horatio advised, as he still must get a release from Munsey, to whom he was under contract. Munsey, fortunately, was in a more cheerful mood when he received Horatio's request, and agreed, on condition that a pen-name be used, so there could be no conflict with his juvenile tales.

Although Horatio felt this made the proposition uninteresting, Dillingham was still willing. They invented the pseudonym, Julian Starr, and over that by-line the story appeared in a small, green seventy-five cent volume in June, 1895.

Horatio's copies of the book reached him at South Natick where, since early in the month, he had been handling preparations for Annie's wedding, which took place Monday, July 1st in the Unitarian Church where her grandfather was preacher for many years.

The bridegroom was Harry Newell Andrews, sub-master of

the Chapman School at East Boston, and related to the late Henry Wadsworth Longfellow. A number of Longfellows were in the crowded church when "at half-past three," the Natick Bulletin reported, "the bridal party walked up the aisle to the strains of the wedding march from Lohengrin. The bride was given away by her Uncle, Horatio Alger, Jr."

Horatio directed, ordering for Annie the best of everything. Her white silk gown was made in Boston; a string of rare pearls came from Italy. Amos arranged flower decorations and Gusti planned the reception at home following the ceremony.

"After a short wedding trip," the newspaper article concluded, "Mr. and Mrs. Andrews will live in Somerville," where Horatio had bought and furnished a lovely home for his niece.

A week later, thoroughly exhausted, Horatio, Gusti and Amos left for a month in Maine, after which Horatio went on to visit Lemuel Gardner at his friend's new vacation place in the Catskills.

New York was changing in the Nineties and sometimes Horatio felt like a stranger in the city he had for years considered his home. Streets now stretched far to the northern tip of Manhattan and beyond, and there was rapid transportation in every direction. The horse cars and stages were giving way to elevated railroads and trolleys operated by electricity.

The Newsboys' Lodging House was still filled with homeless lads, but Horatio rarely went there, although a room was still reserved for his use. Charles Loring Brace was dead, and so was the lovable Charley O'Connor. When the superintendent passed away, his wife went to live with relatives in the mid-West. The home's new director had made adjustments, and Horatio felt he was getting too old for changes. So he stayed away and, on the occasions he returned to address the boys or take part in a special event, he was unknown to most of them.

So he spent more and more time in Brooklyn, finding work tiresome, but pleasure with Kate and her handsome sons.

Before the end of 1895 — at which time Porter & Coates was

succeeded by Henry T. Coates & Co. — he completed the manuscript of "A Cousin's Conspiracy" for The Argosy, and "Gerald's Mission" for Pleasant Hours, which was one of the periodicals in the Frank Leslie group. Both stories appeared during 1896, but when Pleasant Hours suspended publication in April, the installments continued in Leslie's Popular Monthly.

"Adrift in the City," which Porter & Coates had just gotten into print when the firm's management changed, "has been an exceptional success," Horatio wrote to Irving Blake. Other books were also doing well, with many of his earlier ones selling better in reprint than in their original editions.

Horatio seriously considered retirement, and he told this to Ed Stratemeyer when the young editor came to ask a favor.

He wanted to get into the publishing business himself, Stratemeyer declared, and, having bought the assets of a defunct printing establishment, was starting a weekly story-paper, to be known as Bright Days. He asked Horatio's permission to use an earlier Alger story, and the author gladly allowed him to reissue "The Young Acrobat."

Stratemeyer had already written a number of books, and he wondered whether that might not be a better business than editing. He had just completed the story he considered his best work thus far. It was titled "Shorthand Tom, the Reporter," about a youth with the knack of scribbling notes at high speed. Stratemeyer christened his hero Tom Swift, and was thinking of continuing his amazing adventures in a sequel.

"He is an enterprising man," Horatio wrote of Stratemeyer, "and his stories are attractive and popular. Under favorable circumstances, I think he will win a fine reputation."

During 1896 John Down started his own real estate office in Brooklyn and, with many apartment dwellers crossing the East River to settle in less crowded suburbs of Flatbush and Williamsburg, his business was good. Edward, finishing school and his trade apprenticeship, opened a photography studio on Third Avenue, in New York. Both had married, and they brought their wives to the large house on Twentieth Street, where Horatio insisted there was room for all, and that Kate would enjoy the company and help of her pretty daughters-in-law.

But Kate Down had other plans. She was lonely for Ireland

and her aging parents, and yearned to see them once more.

"They're gettin' along in years," she told Horatio, "and, Lord knows, I am, too. I dream about them and our little cottage on the hillside. Then, when I wake, I think to myself I'll never see them again, and it makes me ever so sad."

Horatio agreed that she should go, and helped her make plans to leave New York in the early spring. By then, Kate promised, her sons' women would learn to manage, and they'd take good care of the author while she was gone.

Kate's preparations for her journey were hectic and joyous. She bought a trunk which she filled with new clothes and many presents for her mother and father, sisters, brothers and numerous other relatives, friends and neighbors. She was packed and ready a week before sailing, and then bustled nervously about, positive something would go wrong and the liner would leave without her.

But the morning of departure dawned at last, and the entire household went with her to the Cunard piers where they accompanied Kate on board, escorting her to the comfortable private cabin that Horatio reserved.

It was a damp, chilly day, with wet fog rolling in from the ocean. There was laughter and tears, last minute instructions from Kate to the girls, and regards and God-blessings from her sons. Porters, ship's crew and passengers were moving quickly in many directions, with voyagers on the decks bidding noisy farewell to those they left on the landing below. Someplace, out of sight, tugboat whistles were heard in the harbor, the shrill blasts followed by deep-throated rasps of many fog-horns.

A gong was heard, and Kate's visitors, after final goodbyes, went down the gangplank and watched sadly as the vessel, with rotors churning gray water into white foam, moved slowly from its dock and out into the bay. They stayed until the ship was out of sight, and then returned to Brooklyn, speaking little during the long ride.

For Horatio, coziness and cheer left the big house with Kate, and his surroundings now were gloomy as the weather. His work lay untouched on his desk while he stood at the window, hands clasped behind his back, staring at the wet street and still-bare trees in neighbors' gardens.

A chill he caught when Kate left for Ireland kept Horatio indoors for several days. With no ambition to create adventure tales, he padded about his rooms lonely and brooding, often wishing he had asked her not to go. But now she was far from him and he felt deserted. The boys and their wives were most attentive, but efforts to comfort him went unappreciated.

By the time he was well enough to go out, the weather became milder, and he rode the cars into Manhattan. He felt better, walking along Broadway, hearing again the cries of newsboys and bootblacks. Perhaps Brooklyn was, after all, too quiet. Perhaps, he surmised, he should have stayed in the crowded city, where inspiration was present, and he could work undisturbed.

Impulsively, he rented and took immediate possession of a spacious chamber in a house he passed on Thirty-fourth Street. He told John and Edward what he had done, saying he wanted the young people to have a home to themselves, without interference of a grumbly old man who sat up coughing all night, and pacing the floor through the day.

They quickly understood the real reason — that he missed Kate terribly — and tried to persuade him to remain, but without effect. The next day he moved his belongings to the new lodgings, and tried to convince himself it was what he should have done sooner.

The sounds of the city revitalized him. He was soon writing again, calling upon old friends, and occasionally visiting the street boys at the Lodging House. Then he would cross to the offices of Street & Smith to spend an hour with Tom Glynn and Henry Ralston, his new office boy. Francis Smith had been dead for some years, and his son, Ormond — still in his thirties — was leader of the organization.

"What ho, Horatio," he greeted the author in the same jovial manner his father did for a generation, "and when can we expect the next Alger story?"

Ormond Smith laughed, Editor Glynn laughed and so did young Ralston. Then Horatio laughed too, feeling that, after all, nothing had changed.

He left for Massachusetts early that year, stopping in Boston to see Aaron Loring. It was a delightful day, Horatio wrote, so after luncheon, they took a trolley car ride to Marblehead, six-teen miles away.

"His work is done now," the letter to Irving Blake continued, "though he still lets books from his library. He is seventy-two or seventy-three years old and, unfortunately, in straightened circumstances."

Soon after Horatio arrived at South Natick, Amos became seriously ill with catarrhal pneumonia, and he remained in bed for three weeks. Annie quickly came from Somerville to help Gusti, with Horatio assisting. The miracle of it all, Amos said later, was that he lived through the ordeal of the three jumping around his bedroom, stuffing him with slops he wouldn't feed a hog, and getting especially rambunctious every time he tried to sleep.

He was well enough, nevertheless, to see part of the Fourth of July celebration. With gray-bearded Civil War veterans in faded uniforms occupying places of honor, the program, which drew as many as 20,000 from nearby towns, featured a parade by local chapters of Antiques and Horribles, a balloon ascension, a sham battle and fireworks after dark.

In August, with Gusti and the recuperating Amos, Horatio went to Mount Washington, New Hampshire, where — the doctor advised — the altitude and climate would benefit both men. It was a relaxing stay at a resort Horatio had not previously visited.

Horatio went to New York in September, but did not remain for long. He found it an empty place without Kate Down, and decided that, until she returned, he would make his home at South Natick, coming back from time-to-time to handle business matters.

He moved into a rooming house at 44 East Tenth Street — a few doors from the lodgings he first occupied in 1866 — and sent out cards to a number of friends advising that he'd be at his quarters Friday evening if they wished to call. A dozen showed up, including John and Edward with their wives, Tommy Keegan, Irving Blake, Louis Schick, Lemuel Gardner and others. The Downs came first and handed Horatio a letter from their mother, which he quickly opened and read.

She was having a fine time, she wrote, and listed the relatives she had seen and those to whose villages she must still travel. The weather was already cold and wet, she added, but in the cottage it's comfortable, so there she sits, keeping the teapot warm for folks who come to visit.

Horatio was glad to have news from Kate, but she mentioned nothing about coming home, and that saddened him.

Horatio entertained the group until after nine o'clock. Then, as was their customary procedure, they adjourned to an ice cream parlor on University Place.

Sometimes in the evening, with Irving or Lemuel, Horatio would hear a concert. He occasionally attended the Metropolitan Opera House, and once went to a travel talk by Theodore Roosevelt at Railroad Hall on Madison Avenue.

Writing had become uphill work, and he accomplished very little before he left in November for Somerville, where he would be the guest of Annie and her husband until after Thanksgiving. Then he continued on to South Natick, staying indoors, except on sunny days. Fortunately, the weather was good on December 3d, when — with Gusti and Amos — Horatio went to Boston for dinner, and then to see Bret Harte's new play, "Lice," which recently opened at the Museum.

Horatio was fussed-over by the ladies, and much in demand as a speaker at evening gatherings. Gusti — probably the most active of Natick's community-minded citizens — drafted him to address the Woman's Christian Temperance Union, of which she was a founder, the Women's Suffrage League (with whose aims Horatio was not in complete accord) and the Natick School Committee, that she headed. Amos, who was the organizer of the Morse Institute Library, also called upon his brother-in-law to read his poetry before the assembled membership at their monthly meetings.

Horatio was pleased with the year-end report he received from Henry T. Coates, indicating his increased earnings in royalties. During 1897 they planned to release two new books — "Frank and Fearless" and "Walter Sherwood's Probation" — and to reissue other titles first printed by his previous publishers.

He read the long letter several times, with mounting exhilaration, and a sudden wish to return to work he abandoned months before. He received additional inspiration from reports, in January, that gold had been found by fur trappers at Bonanza Creek, a tributary of the Klondike River in Yukon Territory.

Gold fever hit hard, just as its discovery in California had done, almost a half-century before, and thousands abandoned homes and jobs to dash toward the Northern wilderness. What had been the land of Indians and a few hunters now was the destination of hordes of prospectors. By steamboat from Seattle, or overland or horseback and on foot, searchers were heading for Dawson, the jump-off point to the nugget-filled creeks.

Enthusiastically, Horatio started writing an adventure of the race to the gold fields, but he tired quickly. His eyes soon became strained and he was forced to put his new story aside.

The winter became severe, and his bronchial ailment returned. Through the long nights he breathed with difficulty, and chest pains were recurring. He gave thanks when spring arrived and his strength returned. With great sorrow he read in newspapers of Will Adams' death, and wanted to attend the funeral, but his doctor insisted he still remain indoors.

There was an atmosphere of sadness at the annual Class Dinner, in June, 1897, for only five of the old Harvard chums were present. Horatio was there, arriving directly from a talk to boys at the Boston YMCA. Denny, of course, presided, and Sam Thorndike sang "Our Heroes." George Cary, recently named as President of Meadville Theological Seminary, and Major Andrew Washburn — the originator of Memorial Day — completed the group.

For months the press had been howling for United States intervention in the bloody rebellion of the oppressed Cuban people against their Spanish rulers. Many Americans agreed that our troops should be sent to clean up the mess, but President McKinley, wanting no unnecessary conflict, warned of being stampeded by the jingoists. Time and again he swept back tides of war, but when, in February, 1898, the American battleship, Maine, exploded and sank in the harbor at Havana, indignation surged. Newspapers blamed the outrage on Spain, and called for immediate action.

McKinley yielded to public furor, and Congress declared war. To Horatio's distant cousin, Russell Alexander Alger, who a year earlier was appointed Secretary of War, fell the task of quickly dispatching a naval squadron to destroy the Spanish fleet, and to transport an army to the Caribbean.

Horatio anxiously wrote to Irving Blake, asking if he was marching off to fight, inquiring which of his other boys had volunteered? Both Stratemeyer and the handsome young journalist, Richard Harding Davis, embarked at Tampa, Florida, with the First Volunteer Cavalry, landed in tangled jungles on the Cuban coast, and advanced with Leonard Wood and Theodore Roosevelt to San Juan Ridge, within easy shelling distance of Santiago.

By mid-summer the Spaniards surrendered, and our forces came home. Although relatively few Americans were killed in combat, many perished of tropical diseases and contaminated food. The scandal that followed shook Washington, and Secretary Alger submitted his resignation.

Horatio again vacationed at Old Orchard Beach, and wrote that "my summer travel is doing me good. I feel brighter and better than I did." Through the autumn his good health continued and to Blake he triumphantly wrote:

"I have twice attended the Boston theatre, delivered a poem before the Women's Suffrage League and went to two entertainments in Natick. . .On Monday night, in Waltham, I gave a talk, interspersed with readings from 'Ragged Dick,' on 'The Street Boys of New York.' Among the audience were about 100 boys. One met me in the street the next day and said, 'Yer done good last evenin'. When are you goin' to lecture agin?' What gratifies me most is that boys, though strangers, seem to regard me as a personal friend.

". . .A new game called 'Authors' will be issued by the U.S. Playing Card Company, in Cincinnati, in the fall. I am in it. I have sent them my photograph, which will appear. . .A boy writes me from a Georgia college that they have my books in the library."

The leaves began to fall, and Horatio turned up his collar when, on sunny afternoons, he took a short walk or crossed the bridge to the village on an errand for Gusti.

"It was cold here this morning," he wrote, "only eighteen degrees at seven o'clock. However, we keep the house warm and comfortable. . .The country is still pleasant. Looking out of the window I see on the lot adjoining a hundred oak and walnut trees. The leaves are beginning to change color. Every day a few children appear whom we allow to pick up the nuts that have fallen. . .Already, the flavor of the Thanksgiving turkey can be scented from the near distance. We make more of this festival in New England than in New York."

He dreaded the coming winter and told friends he feared it would be his last. Kate was still in Ireland and he hoped for news of her return. They corresponded regularly, and of late Horatio took courage and asked when she would come back again, adding that he missed her.

Her aged parents were not well, she replied, and she was needed a while longer to take care of them, all her brothers and sisters being too occupied with their own large families.

"I've been away more than I expected," she wrote, "and I long to see you and my boys again. The weather here is frightful, but if the folks get safely through until spring, please God, I'll come home then."

If only the seasons hurry, Horatio thought. I shall feel better when Kate returns. Then I will go back to Brooklyn. I'll write again — every day, as I used to — and she'll make tea and knock upon my door when it's time to rest.

With these reflections, Horatio often dozed off and, upon awakening, mentally added the months and weeks until he would see her again.

In January, 1899, wracking bronchitis struck again, lasting for weeks and leaving him weak and despondent. When, late in February, he could again sit at his desk, he set to answering letters that piled up while he was sick.

"I write in haste to say I am better from my attack of bronchitis," he wrote to Irving Blake. "There was a strong possibility of pneumonia which, to one of my physique, would probably have been fatal.

". . .I received a letter from Trowbridge a day or two since. He reports himself as well and happy, 'though in his seventy-first year . . . [also one] from Edward S. Ellis, who seems to be hard at work as usual. I wish I could work like him, and in as varied ways . . . He is working on his history, and does considerable besides. I should think this would eventually break him down, but he is very strong and robust, and not at all nervous. . .I envy Ellis his ability to work. My brain is very sluggish at present.

". . .In the November issue of McClure's there is an article by Mark Twain, but it is not up to his 'Innocents Abroad.' We don't improve as we grow older. . .I hear that Edward Bok, of the Ladies' Home Journal, has overworked, and is feeling the effects. He is only thirty-three. I wish you may be as successful.

". . .Have you seen Louisa Alcott's letter in the Ladies Home Journal? Her ideas about the hereafter were original and peculiar. She seems to believe in a series of existences (on earth, probably), and had an idea that she lived before. What a pity she died so soon! She had no competition as a writer for girls. There are plenty of good writers for boys. If there were not, I would occupy a larger field and have more abundant sales.

". . .I am glad you liked the Argosy story. I took special pains with it, so that I hope to leave a good impression on the readers, should that be my last."

*　　*　　*

During Horatio's illness, Joe Choate was appointed by President McKinley as United States Ambassador to the Court of St. James, and would soon leave for England. There was a jolly farewell dinner at the Harvard Club for his old classmate, and Horatio much regretted missing the party.

When, in March, he was invited to serve on a panel to award literary prizes being offered by Woman's World, he accepted and went to New York for the judging. The trip also gave him a chance to spend an evening with Choate before the new envoy departed. He visited Frank Munsey, who recently returned from Europe and, after calling at Street & Smith, he crossed William Street and entered the Newsboys' Lodging House.

It was a world of strangers to Horatio. The superintendent was away. A young clerk in charge at the desk was new, and did not recognize the kindly gentleman who, a quarter of a century earlier, helped Charles Loring Brace and Charles O'Connor move beds and tables from the old Sun Building to their new home.

Dinner time was approaching and the street boys, lining up to register, hurried past the little old man to pay for their room and supper. When Horatio slowly ambled toward the staircase — he wished to see his old corner room once more — the clerk called him back, warning that he wasn't permitted to go upstairs.

With a quiet apology, Horatio turned and left the building.

He hoped to see his young friends but, feeling a cold approaching, wisely left for South Natick instead. Gusti tucked him into bed when he reached home, nursed him for a few days, and he was well enough to stroll with Amos to Bailey's Hotel on a mild evening, a week later.

The robins returned early to South Natick that last spring of the Nineteenth Century, and thin blades of grass soon were emerging from the soil. The rains came, as they always came, bringing with them fragrance and new life.

In June it was time to make summer plans.

"Where will we go this year?" Gusti asked.

"Old Orchard," Amos replied.

"As usual," Horatio added.

Kate finally wrote that she soon would leave Ireland, and every morning Horatio walked to the post office to see if her next letter was there. He wanted to be in New York to meet her when the ship docked.

Horatio wrote to Irving Blake, saying he had started a new story, and that he may spend a week or two in Maine.

"I attended a silver wedding next door last Monday evening," Horatio related. "I am afraid I shall not be able to attend your silver wedding, even if you marry soon.

". . .I wonder, Irving, how it would seem to be as young and full of enthusiasm as you are. I shouldn't dare to go back to nineteen again, lest my share of success prove to be less than it has been. But you will have a chance to see a strange new world with many wonderful inventions and discoveries. If I could come back fifty years from now, probably I should be bewildered. But, in another world, I may have learned things still more wonderful!"

On July 11th, the day before they planned to leave for the Aldine Hotel at Old Orchard Beach, Horatio suffered a severe asthmatic attack. Amos got him upstairs to bed and ran for the doctor. Horatio was struggling to breathe when the physician arrived, but the seizure passed, and his respiration improved. The attacks recurred daily, and the little man's strength was ebbing. A nurse was brought from Boston to stay at his side.

When awake he gasped for air and at other times he slept. His heart and pulse were slowly weakening, and his sister and brother-in-law were told that the end was near. They immediately sent for Annie, who came from Somerville the next day. She held her uncle's hand and he smiled when he opened his eyes and saw her.

During the night Horatio called for Amos, and the nurse hurried to bring him to the bedside.

Almost incoherently, he whispered that the letter he awaited was at the post office, and should be brought to him. He asked Amos to get it. The huge man tried to explain it was still the middle of the night, but promised to be at the post office when it opened.

It was cool and fresh after an early morning thunderstorm, and the sun sparkled on the Charles River as Amos hurried past the garden gate on his way to the post office. The day was Tuesday, July 18th, and the postmaster was still sorting pieces when Amos reached the small building. The mail Horatio had so long awaited was there. Amos ran back down the hill and across the wooden bridge, perspiring and panting as he rushed home to deliver the message from across the sea.

Horatio raised his head when Amos entered, and for some minutes he was alert. Somehow he knew the letter from Kate would come in time. He took the envelope and tried to open it, but didn't have the strength. Annie did it for him. After he read the few lines, Horatio lay back on his pillow and dozed.

A moment later he gulped for air and whispered softly:

"She comes home the 28th. I must be there to meet her. I'll be better then, won't I?"

The nurse quickly agreed.

"Good. Gusti, please prepare my things. I am going to New York."

302

His sister assured him she would.

"Splendid," he continued, with difficulty. "I'm sleepy now. I shall have a nap. Later I can pack and leave on the evening train. But I'm tired. Let me rest."

Still holding the letter, appearing tiny and childlike on the large bed, he closed his eyes to slumber, nevermore to awaken. But on Horatio Alger's face was a relaxed expression of contentment, for he went to sleep knowing that when he joyously greeted his Kate, the first thing he would tell her was that he loved her.

THE WONDERFUL WORLD

OF

HORATIO ALGER'S HEROES

FROM MORAL TALES
TO
DIME NOVELS TO ALGER

CHARLES DICKENS MASTERFULLY DESCRIBED the plights of poverty, but generally without leading his fascinating characters to eventual high reward. Hans Christian Andersen spun charming tales of the poor, but too often left young readers in tears as the story ended. It was Horatio Alger — who had not a small fraction of the talent of either of his well-remembered contemporaries who, nevertheless, did evolve an unfailing formula for bringing his young heroes out of poverty, and — by story's end — well advanced on the road to success and wealth. His product was purely American, uniquely a part of the Mid-Victorian Era in the United States. The final sentence of each of his novels was punctuated with the satisfied sighs of millions of readers who sincerely believed that "If Ragged Dick could do it, so can I!" Then they waited impatiently for Alger's next story.

Horatio Alger distinctly was a phenomenon produced by his times. He also was a prime contributor to the dreams and ambitions of his day. And more copies of his books were issued than those of Dickens and Andersen combined!

Nowadays, however, Alger is too often removed from the

proper environs of the Nineteenth Century, and is incorrectly judged by current standards. Comparing his naive, uncomplicated stories for boys of long ago by modern souped-up criteria is like searching for resemblance between covered wagons and jet-powered aircraft. Both are means of transportation, but there the similarity ends. Nevertheless, in its time, the sturdy covered wagon was accepted as a generally satisfactory way to travel, besides adding a good bit of color and legend to American tradition.

Literary tastes, likewise, have accelerated over the years. That is why it is unfortunate that a number of competent literary assessors overlook or completely forget this when commenting on Alger. They apparently feel that the tongue-in-cheek-with-a-sly-wink treatment (with which many institutions of the Victorian Age are now regarded) is expected and perhaps even appealing to their audience.

The fact is that Horatio Alger's strive-and-succeed stories are as much a part of our literary evolution as is some of today's preferred reading.

During a great part of the Nineteenth Century, our meager literary fare often was as lean and rugged as life on the frontier. Publishers could, if they wished, completely by-pass American authors simply by reissuing (either by arrangement or piracy) the successful works of foreign writers. Even among the early native efforts, there was little to make youthful readers clamor for more.

Some thirty years before Alger's first book, Samuel Griswold Goodrich wrote "The Tales of Peter Parley," probably the earliest of this country's books for children that was not heavily laden with instruction, religious training or moral lessons. It was a start. Several years later, The Rev. Jacob Abbott created his Rollo Series of stories about a good little boy, extraordinarily inquisitive, who apparently never soiled his white starched collar, whether digging a ditch or climbing a tree. The kids read them, but there still was nothing there to make the pulse quicken.

But the juvenile outlook was brightening. Nathaniel Hawthorne, in 1852, had completed the first of his Wonder Books, and three years later, in 1855, Oliver Optic's (William Taylor Adams') "The Boat Club" appeared. This was among the earliest of a long run of success-type stories which, though bearing occasional similarity to the dozens turned out by Alger, never quite achieved Alger's success.

It was in June, 1860, however, that the first uniquely native form of popular literature was published. This was the dime novel, the wretched, sensational "yellow-backs" filled with adventurous exploits of heroes of the frontier.

The first of these, "Malaeska: The Indian Wife of the White Hunter," was written by Ann S. Stephens (already known as a magazine editor as well as a prolific serial writer) and published by the firm of Erastus F. Beadle, of New York. Beadle, originator of the dime novel, had started in Buffalo a couple of years earlier, issuing a dime songster with tremendous success. Arriving in New York, he published a dime joke book with only moderate results prior to printing the first dime novel.

"Malaeska," not intended for a young audience, offered page after page of action. The small paperback volume was loaded with descriptions of Indian-fighting and life in the wilds. The story, which actually was something of a tragedy, related the woes of an Indian princess wed to swashbuckling pioneer. Their son, when he eventually learned he was a half-breed, commits suicide by drowning.

Beadle's Dime Library soon was followed by Beadle's New Dime Novels, Beadle's Half-Dime Library, Frank Starr's American Novels and others. Frank Leslie, Frank Tousey, George Munro, Street & Smith and other publishers — quickly detecting the trend—were soon represented with colorful series of their own.

Edward S. Ellis' "Seth Jones; or, The Captives of the Frontier," probably was among the earliest of dime novel best sellers. Others — recounting blood-and-thunder bravery of Kit Carson, Buffalo Bill, Texas Jack and other famed scouts — were later written by E. Z. C. Judson (Ned Buntline), Col. Prentiss Ingraham, Gilbert Patten (who, as Burt L. Standish, wrote the multi-volume "Frank Merriwell" stories) and an army of swift writers well-equipped with adjectives, heroic phrases and the ability to make readers tingle with excitement.

These lurid tales — their covers invariably spread with scenes of violence — mostly printed in New York and Boston, travelled West with railroad construction crews, and were carried South to Manassas, Shiloh and Vicksburg in the knapsacks of Union troops during the Civil War. They were read on farms and in the teeming, industrial cities of the East.

Long after bed-time, wide-eyed youths hid dime novels under pillow or mattress when parents' footsteps were heard. During the day these tales could only be read in the semi-darkness of the high hayloft or behind the barn, for they were forbidden within the house.

Consider, then — from this point of view — the advent of "Ragged Dick; or, Street Life in New York," Horatio Alger's very successful novel for boys, issued in 1868. "Dick," and the multitude of Alger heroes who followed him, offered the action that young readers hadn't previously found in book form. These were adventures that kids loved and, at the same time, met with the hearty approval of their parents. Not only were Algers welcome indoors, but *they could be read in the parlor!* If further acknowledgement of their wholesomeness was necessary, ministers endorsed Alger's stories, referring to them in sermons and recommending them from the pulpit. They even were awarded as Sunday-school prizes, and for years public library shelves were filled with volumes of the "Tattered Tom" Series, the "Luck and Pluck" Series, "Brave and Bold" and most of the others.

Although every story Horatio Alger wrote contained substantial doses of the didacticism and moral lessons of the earlier writers, he apparently understood young people's needs and delights far better than his predecessors. He served up heroes with which they could identify themselves, bullies they could whip and goals they really believed they could reach. He firmly convinced generations of young Americans that — through honesty, thrift and clean-living by the Golden Rule — wealth and honor were attainable rewards, and that any bootblack or newsboy could become President.

To a great extent, Alger's appeal rested in his unique ability to weave simple, uncomplicated plots, carrying readers breathlessly along with the rapid pace of the narrative. His pages, loaded with dialogue rather than the tedious descriptive prose of that period, quickly gained a hold on the heart of Young America. They believed that the stories, somehow, stuck reasonably close to life and reality. They were clean and inspiring, yet every hero was full of vigor, handy with his fists, invariably combining keen business sense with the coolness of a master detective.

At the same time he was gentle with children and old folks, protected the weak and was respectful to his elders. In any task — no matter how menial — he always gave the employer his money's worth, occasionally going far uptown to return the few cents change a customer forgot to claim.

In order to avoid crowning heroes with a halo, and risk the lads being judged too good to be true, Alger occasionally supplied a flaw to their character. Ragged Dick, during his early bootblack days, gambled and swigged an occasional shot of liquor at two cents a glass. He spent evenings at the notorious Old Bowery Theatre, and also enjoyed a good cigar when he had an extra penny to spare. Tom the Bootblack, as well, admitted that he once was drunk. Mark the Match Boy smoked cigarettes. At the beginning of "Tom Temple's Career," the hero, Tom, is known as The Bully of the Village, and Jack Harding, of "Jack's Ward," continually played heartless pranks upon an old maid aunt. Needless to say, they all reformed long before their stories ended.

Occasionally the author would inject bits of conversation which, although familiar to street-trades practitioners, was excitingly different from his readers' accustomed literary diet, and delighted them. Ragged Dick, whose lifelong home had been streets and alleyways off New York's wicked Bowery, was adept at taking on all-comers in verbal duel. He could tell-off the neighborhood ruffian as readily as the brazen drop-game swindler, but his forte was in humiliating the snobbish fop.

One morning, on lower Broadway, "only a few blocks distant from the Astor House," Dick was addressed by "a rather supercilious-looking young gentleman, genteely dressed, and evidently having a very high opinion of himself." He "turned suddenly to Dick, and remarked, —

"I've seen you before."

"Oh, have you?" said Dick, whirling around; "then p'r'aps you'd like to see me behind."

Tattered Tom — who was a girl — was even rougher!

But in most respects, the Alger hero was a good enough lad.

He was usually about fourteen or fifteen years old, as the stories began, and physically attractive. Hector Roscoe, the hero of "Hector's Inheritance," was "slenderly but strongly made, with a clear skin and dark eyes and a straightforward look. He had a winning smile that attracted all who saw it, but his face could assume a different expression, if need be. There were strong lines around his mouth that indicated calm resolution and strength of purpose. He was not a boy who would permit himself to be imposed upon, but was properly tenacious of his rights." Similarly, Scott Walton, "The Young Salesman," was "the picture of health. He was inclined to be dark, with black hair, bright eyes, and with considerable color in his cheeks." Ben Stanton, "The Young Explorer," was "strong and self-reliant . . . his limbs active, and his face ruddy with health. He looked like a boy who could get along. He was not a sensitive plant, and not to be discouraged by rebuffs."

Alger apparently favored dark-complexioned heroes, frequently describing them as "swarthy." Besides many of his fictional characters, he described both Daniel Webster and Abraham Lincoln as swarthy, in his biographical stories of those men.

Plots were strikingly similar, with only the slightest variations. Most of Alger's heroes — either orphans or the main support of a widowed mother (and occasionally a younger brother or sister) — left their New England or Upper New York State farm homes to seek their fortunes in the city. New York generally was their destination. Then there were the street arabs of the big city, generally a rough lot as the stories opened, sometimes bound to an unsavory task-master who took charge of their small earnings. A number of boys came to America from far-off lands, but they invariably turned out as "reliable . . . wide-awake . . . brave . . . manly . . . self-reliant," basically honest and destined for ultimate success as his native-born stock. Some had, in infancy, been abducted from luxurious surroundings; many were victimized by scoundrels — unconscionable guardians, relatives, step-parents or miserly small-town squires — who used all sorts of vicious and criminal schemes to defraud them of their legacies.

But Alger's young men, endowed with both pluck and luck, moved up the ladder of success in giant strides. While fending off dangerous enemies, they also made generous and powerful

The CAMPAIGN SERIES by HORATIO ALGER JR.

Although, by 1864, Horatio Alger had already written two books, *The Campaign Series* marked his first efforts to turn out full-length adventure stories for boys. This group consisted of "Frank's Campaign," "Paul Prescott's Charge" and "Charlie Codman's Cruise."

First appearance of "Ragged Dick," bootblack who made Horatio
Alger a best-selling author and set pattern for more than a hundred
rags-to-riches tales. Several months before appearing as bound volume,
story was serialized in Student and Schoolmate, a magazine for boys
and girls. A Bowery ruffian, Dick gives up cigars, liquor and gambling,
saves money, studies hard at night and becomes a wealthy man.

RAGGED DICK SERIES

BY HORATIO ALGER JR.

RAGGED DICK.

"Ragged Dick" was on overnight sensation, and publisher A. K. Loring immediately signed Alger to do a series on street life in New York. Surrounding Dick, on decorative title page, are Ben the Luggage Boy; Rufus, newsboy of "Rough and Ready," and Mark the Match Boy.

With few personal belongings tied in a handkerchief, many of Alger's robust lads left the farm to seek fortune. They lived clean and — with luck and pluck — prospered, returning in time to pay off mortgage and save the old homestead from clutches of villainous squire.

In an era of expansion, Alger heroes kept pace with times. Some labored in factories. Others left farms or tenements to travel West in search of gold. Many found adventure on Wall Street, aboard ships or speeding trains.

DARE AND DO RIGHT SERIES

TOM, THE BOOTBLACK.

TONY, THE HERO

By Horatio Alger Jr.

Decorative front page of two books published by J. S. Ogilvie in 1880. Titled the Dare and Do Right Series, both are highly valued by collectors even though "Tom the Bootblack" — one of Alger's best-loved works — was first issued two years earlier as "The Western Boy."

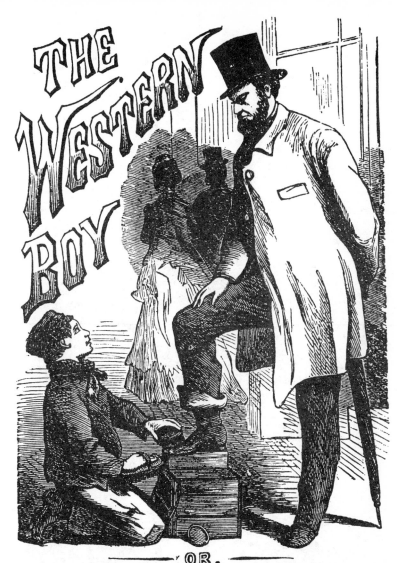

THE WESTERN BOY

OR,

THE ROAD TO SUCCESS.
By Horatio Alger, Jr.

"The Western Boy" appeared only briefly, in 1878, before being reissued as "Tom the Bootblack," title under which it is best known. The hero, a lad "of enterprising disposition," tells that he is "ready to adopt a rich father."

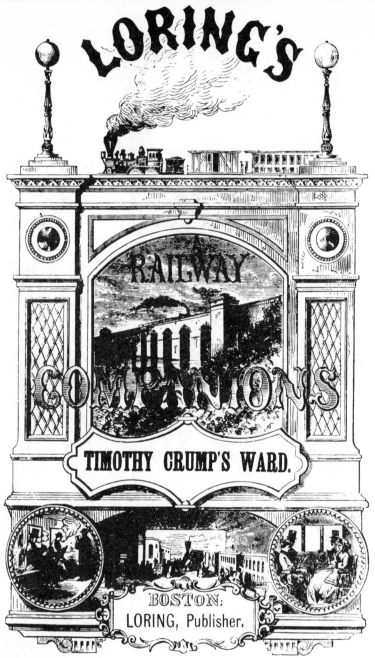

LORING'S

A RAILWAY COMPANIONS

TIMOTHY CRUMP'S WARD.

BOSTON:
LORING, Publisher.

Although issued, in 1866, in hard cover and paperback editions, "Timothy Crump's Ward" remains one of the most elusive of Alger treasures. A story for adults, it was published anonymously. Nine years later Alger rewrote it for children with new title, "Jack's Ward."

friends who helped them on their way. These benefactors most often were acquired by way of a daring rescue. Luke Walton was on the spot to pull a terrified woman from the tracks of a rapidly advancing horse car. Tom Tracy dove into the Harlem River to save a little girl from drowning. Grant Thornton, in "Helping Himself," defends a girl pursued by a drunken tramp, and more than one hero happens on the scene to rescue elderly gentlemen from being set upon by hoodlums intent on robbery. These boys risked their lives to flag-down trains in the nick of time, and stopped teams of runaway horses. In more than one of Alger's Western tales, the lad stands up to masked desperadoes and hostile Indians.

Readily acknowledging that luck played a hand in their destiny, Alger often pointed out that his boys, by being alert and intelligent, were able to take advantage of opportunities that passed others by. And frequently, the author explained, his hero — sensing emergency — was quick to act while others stood by, transfixed by fright or bewilderment.

Horatio's eager youngster was ambitious as well as competitive and, once started, he took every opportunity to improve himself. Although still earning his livelihood as an American District Telegraph messenger or as a luggage carrier along the Fulton Street wharves, he saved his money, studied at night, attended Sunday school and sometimes even took private instruction. Though his shabby clothes were patched and frayed, he was determined to overcome any obstacle and forge ahead.

Neither danger, conspiracy nor the inevitable snob's derision deterred the aspiring street boy from efforts to rise above a humble station. When one dandy sneeringly advised Luke Walton that he doesn't "believe in being friends with the rag, tag and bobtail of society," Luke replied to the slur:

"I don't mean always to be a newsboy or errand boy. I shall work my way upward as fast as I can, and in time I may come to fill a good place in society."

And you can just bet that he did!

During the course of any story, the youth is thrust into a dozen adventures. He is entrusted with funds and sent on secret missions. He tracks down thieves, forgers and assorted felons, and in the process is himself occasionally kidnapped, chloroformed, slugged and robbed.

But all turns out well at story's end. The lad reaps handsome reward, which he shares with loyal friends, and the evildoers have fled, died, are imprisoned or degraded to lowly employment charitably provided by the hero.

Thus, in its final chapters, we find that Ragged Dick has become Richard Hunter, Esq., no longer an ignorant bootblack, but a gentleman and, still later, the owner of a fine piece of land on Forty-second Street not far from Fifth Avenue. Jed, the Poorhouse Boy, likewise, ultimately assumes his rightful place as Sir Robert Fenwick, Baronet, of Fenwick Hall, Gloucestershire, England.

At the conclusion of "Sink or Swim," Harry Raymond — having "seen something of the world" — returns, prosperous, to the town of Vernon just in time to save his mother's mortgaged home, and thwart treacherous designs of the villainous Squire Turner. "Foiled at all points," Alger writes, Turner "dashed his hat angrily upon his head, and rushed from the house in undignified haste. . . Harry, who is now twenty-one, is about to take charge of the New York Branch of Lindsay & Co., which will give him a commanding business position. There are rumors that Maud, whose early preference for him still continues, will, before very long, become the wife of her father's young American representative."

THE AMERICAN HERO ERA

EVEN BEFORE MANY OF ALGER'S books had been produced, A. K. Loring — his first major publisher — during the early 1870's proclaimed him to be "the dominating figure of the new era. In his books he has captured the spirit of reborn America. The turmoil of the city streets is in them. You can hear the rattle of pails on the farms. Above all, you can hear the cry of triumph of the oppressed over the oppressor. What Alger has done is to portray the soul — the ambitious soul — of the country!"

Dozens upon dozens of stories by Horatio Alger, Jr., — which Heywood Broun described as "simple tales of honesty triumphant" — were devoured by virtually every boy who grew up in the United States between the years after the Civil War and the Turn of the Century. As late as 1908, when the magazine, Youth's Companion, offered "any three volumes in the Alger Library for a new subscription," they declared that "the character of these books is exceptional. The author invariably selects as the basis for his writings a boy whose beginning is humble and unpromising, and graphically describes his rise to wealth and fame." Two years later, even as Alger's great popularity was cresting, World's Work, in their issue of June, 1910, estimated that as of that date his books still were selling at the rate of 1,-000,000 copies a year and more. They probably were the most read and re-read books ever published in America!

The "new era" referred to by Loring may just as well have been called the "Alger Era," for the little author was an outstanding influence during the full generation from the late 1860's until his death in 1899. It certainly was The American Hero Era and Horatio Alger, Jr., better than anyone else could, glorified the American Hero.

Those were the exciting years — the restless years — with soldiers of the North and South returning to their homes or seeking new roots. The Nineteenth Century still held more than three decades of adventure and invention, and the nation's frontiers were still pushing Westward across the Great Plains.

In the beginning, thousands of young people flocked to the cities from farms and small towns, their number swelled by boys discharged from the Armies who had no homes to return to, and hordes of abandoned children who had managed to survive by following the troops, carrying water and ammunition for the soldiers in return for occasional rations and the prizes they scavenged from the battlefields of the Rebellion.

Daily reports of gold and silver strikes beckoned to the adventurous from across the wilderness, while others envisioned new lives for their families in the rich farmlands being opened to hardy settlers.

Everywhere there was building and construction. The clanking of sledge hammers against spikes sounded all day, and through the night, as the railroads, reaching Westward to the very horizon, stretched endlessly across the continent. In the new farmlands, the first building to rise was the barn for livestock, then a shack for the family. There was time later — when the harvest was in and stock delivered to market — to put up a better homestead. And by then there may be neighbors to help!

In many communities, new industries were developing. Articles formerly made at home or by small local craftsmen were now being mass-produced in factories. In these unaccustomed surroundings, amid the incessant chatter of machinery, small children toiled, alongside the men and women, from early morning until after dark. Towns quickly grew around these areas, many soon thickly populated by former farm workers who now sought higher wages and steady employment.

During some periods these industries flourished. A number of them expanded and prospered, but many suffered long seasons of inactivity, and greatly reduced their labor forces. Others sooner or later went bankrupt, closing their gates forever, leaving employees destitute and bewildered.

Disappointed, some returned to the farm. Others followed the road to where other industrial plants were going up, but many moved on, past towns, villages and hamlets. They were heading for the great metropolises of the East where, many believed, certain riches waited.

For some, riches and power *were* waiting, for this was the era that created industrial empires, merchant princes and wizards of finance and invention for whom wealth and fame were destined. It was during the period Alger's stories took place that Henry Ford was struggling upward from a mechanic to proprietor of a bicycle shop. John W. Mackay, reaching these shores from Ireland, made his way directly to the gold fields of California, arriving with barely enough to buy a pick and shovel. Thomas A. Edison was a newsboy, and Adolph S. Ochs had just been hired as a printer's devil on the Knoxville Chronicle. John D. Rockefeller roamed the countryside, seeking employment. Andrew Carnegie, arriving in the United States from Scotland, started as a messenger, and Joseph Pulitzer was a penniless immigrant from Hungary.

America was experiencing unprecedented growth and opulence along with the depressions, panics and strife that were the growing pains of a young nation. All the while, through our port cities there arrived — day-after-day, month-after-month — an endless stream of the impoverished and oppressed of other nations.

Incident to the expansion of the post-Civil War decades was economic rivalry and changes wrought by industrial revolution that, in one manner or other, affected the lives of nearly all Americans. These ranged from the complete uprooting of families journeying to where they believed new opportunity lay, to regions entirely converted from the comparative tranquillity known to their ancestors to ones throbbing with new vitality and development. Some communities were altered by the departure of residents — especially the ambitious young — who sought greener pastures elsewhere. Others nearly buckled under the added weight of newcomers, a number of whom were genuinely undesirable, while countless others — because they brought with them ways of living unfamiliar to original inhabitants, and because their presence only aggravated the already vicious competitive scheme — were made to feel equally unwelcome in their new homes.

Threaded throughout this whole fabric were the patterns of change that had become familiar to most Americans. There were the toiling, diligent many and the unscrupulous, tyrannical few. Between the two groups were the weak, the confused and the innocent, sorely in need of a champion.

This was a situation which, as rapidly as the day's changing pace, gave birth to a new theme in American expression. Melodramatic plays filled theaters with audiences intent upon seeing the old homestead saved, justice served to the poor working girl, and ultimate defeat for the villain. Crusading newspapers and magazines took notice of the transition, but nostalgia better recalls wildly exaggerated plots of the sensational popular story weeklies. Novelists, touching upon the subjects of current economic unrest, generally were lachrymose, over-sentimental or heavily slanted toward the relationship between poverty, intemperance and sin.

Until Horatio Alger, Jr., came along with his unfailing success formula, in which the righteous invariably triumphed, and the scoundrel was defeated, no author had as competently or successfully presented this story in style or dosage that more completely delighted Young America. And, certainly, no other writer of that school of rags-to-riches literature is, today, so well-remembered.

Alger's success, apparently, lay in his ability to dramatize — *at his readers' level* — the prevailing scenes of the era in which he composed. Describing the "irresistible attractions" of these stories to boys of generations ago, The New York Times, in an editorial, declared that "they drew pictures of people and places that were part of every boy's experience, whether he lived in New

York or Peoria, and their appeal was not to the spirit of wild adventure so vividly portrayed in the dime novels, but to a kind of hum-drum practical success that most boys clearly saw ahead of them."

In another editorial page commentary, The Times called Alger "the prose laureate" of stories about street life in New York. Almost every one of Alger's tales had as its setting the cobble-stoned streets of Manhattan, with a great deal of the action taking place among seedy tenements a stone's throw from City Hall Park, the rooming houses on Bleecker Street, and in elegant brownstones near Fifth and Madison Avenues. Horatio Alger described, as few other novelists have (and, certainly, no other writer of books for boys has), New York City during the second half of the Nineteenth Century.

These street-by-street Baedekers intrigued the author's New York-dwelling readers, who felt a very close personal participation in adventures taking place so close to home. Boys who lived far from the big city read, in expectant awe, of the haps and mis-haps of the Alger hero in the Bowery pawn-shops, the counting-houses of Wall Street, the Astor House and Barnum's Museum on Broadway, the Fifth Avenue Hotel, Central Park and on the ferry that crossed the East River to Brooklyn.

New York was the live, exciting and eminently appealing sub-hero of many Alger stories. Alger treated the City tenderly, adoring it as an ardent lover; occasionally scolding it with parental indignation. But in any reference, Alger — apparently effortlessly — brought through to his readers its personality with the clarity and resonance of the great bell that used to toll the hours atop the old Jefferson Market Court. When Alger described the busy lower end of the city, the reader must concentrate hard to shut out the rattling of hooves and chains of giant dray teams pulling wagons through noisy, narrow streets. He hears the cries of street peddlers, shrill above the sounds of traffic and the incessant drone and chatter of the crowds.

The frantic cacophony was quickly silenced, however, as Alger showed the way from Broadway to Washington Square. Now, for the reader, there was a hushed atmosphere, only gently disturbed by the gay laughter of children playing on the green, occasionally summoned by vigilant, starch-waisted nursemaids.

Here, the air was gentler and clearer and the reader could, for the moment, relax. He knew that Horatio Alger would permit no violence on Washington Square!

Through a variety of ways, Alger contrived to show off New York to his public. He sometimes accomplished this by having the story's hero hired to tour the town with a visiting stranger. Here was always the opportunity to ride uptown in the horse cars, pointing out A. T. Stewart's big store, Cooper Institute, Grace Church, Fourteenth Street and other interesting sights along the way. There was always time out to rest at Madison Square, before continuing the excursion. Most frequently the boy is called upon to deliver a message or parcel to one of the aristocratic homes on respectable Madison Avenue, or in a nearby side street. Once within, the sounds of the city outside are muted, and the reader steps with the hero luxuriously upon thick carpets, perhaps hearing faintly in the background the receding rustling sound of the servant's long skirt, as she disappears up the staircase to an upper floor to dutifully deliver the message to her mistress.

Alger often reserved 'the' Central Park for the hard-working hero's own pleasure. Here, on a Sunday afternoon, the boy — often accompanied by a companion — would relax on a bench along The Mall, in The Glen or at the grassy border of the Sheep Meadow. They each had indulged themselves to the extent of ten cents, the stage fare from Fulton Street (near where they lived at the Newsboys' Lodging House) to Forty-second Street, the end of the line. From there they strolled, along Fifth Avenue, the distance to the Park entrance at Fifty-ninth Street. The sun shone brightly, on that clear Spring day long ago, and the hero called attention to each of the marble-fronted mansions they passed on route.

New York was smaller then, in the years before the skyline grew, when fewer than 1,000,000 people lived there. The narrow island was most thickly populated between the Battery and Fourteenth Street. The "better neighborhoods" extended from Washington Square to Forty-second Street, but the city already was rapidly expanding to Fifty-ninth Street and far beyond. Third Avenue was lined with houses as far north as 130th Street, which was the terminus of the Harlem Line of horse-cars.

"When the entire island is laid out and settled," Alger wrote in 1866, "probably the numbers will reach two hundred or more. . . It had not been long since work commenced upon [Central Park], and it was still very rough and unfinished. There were no houses of good appearance near it, buildings being limited mainly to rude temporary huts used by the workmen who were employed in improving it.

"The time will undoubtedly come," he predicted, "when the Park will be surrounded by elegant residences, and compare favorably in this respect with the most attractive parts of any city in the world." But at the moment, he concluded, "not much could be said either of the Park or its neighborhood."

After dark, hoodlums roamed the dimly-lit downtown streets. To enter the Five Points or Old Brewery districts — even during daylight hours — was hazardous for unrecognized strangers, and the honky-tonk Bowery was the evil sin-center of New York. Horace Greeley, in his Tribune, campaigned regularly to clean out its dozens of notorious saloons where, in an atmosphere of depravity, drunken seamen and persons of ugly character consorted with abandoned women in the presence of children who — if they had the price — could also buy a drink!

Alger rarely drew his young readers into this atmosphere, except to accompany an oppressed child who had been sent to the corner saloon by a wretched guardian, to get whiskey with money that — the author always suggested — would better have been saved for food or the landlord's visit. Occasionally, however, the hero would guide homeward a drunkard who had just reeled unsteadily through the swinging doors and fallen flat upon his face. "From the cut of his jib," Alger frequently explained, the hero readily recognized the man as a sailor, recently put into port after long months at sea. Sometimes the victim was a young man whose sensitive features and apparent revulsion with his own condition made it clear that here was a gentleman in unaccustomed surroundings, probably fallen in with evil companions.

Whenever possible, Horatio Alger preferred his characters to spend leisure hours in the more genteel parts of the city. Dignified Madison Square and its adjoining streets and avenues were favored settings. It was in residences in this area that the hero visited his distinguished benefactors. When the successful merchant or financier had a young daughter, she invariably invited the lad to a party at her home. If the kindly gentleman had a son, he and the hero soon became fast friends, and together they took evening strolls along Sixth Avenue, the outing generally highlighted by refreshment in an ice cream parlor. In cold weather, the fare included a steaming oyster stew.

It was also in this neighborhood that the story's arrogant snob — generally hastening to meet equally unsavory cronies for an evening at the billiard tables — is surprised to see the humble Bowery Boy socializing with members of some of New York's most prominent families. Sometimes the snob (who more often than not is the hero's cousin, or the son of the dastard who cheated the boy of his inheritance), avoids recognition, lest the shabbily-clad one might greet him, causing embarrassment before stylish friends. The prig usually considers it his obligation to advise the hero's friends that they are, probably unwittingly, permitting into their home a ruffian who, by day, sells newspapers or shines shoes as a livelihood. The usual rebuff is that the poor but honest street boy's society is preferred to that of the snob who, at chapter's end, is sauntering toward Twenty-third Street, swinging his light, gold-headed cane, and plotting new pitfalls for his sworn enemy.

But — it being late in the evening — the unsuspecting hero has already returned to the fourth floor tenement flat in Baxter Street, where he lives with his widowed mother and younger brother. "Tomorrow's troubles," he always says, "can wait 'til tomorrow!"

THE ROAD
TO PROSPERITY

THE TREMENDOUS POPULARITY OF HORATIO Alger's warm, simple stories among readers of generations past, notwithstanding, few kind words for his works are heard today. When critics gather to dissect Alger, their comments often are acid-etched, scathing or — at very least — sarcastic.

Although these appraisals more often are based upon current standards than on those of the author's specific period, audience and purpose, there appears to be at least partial justification for a portion of their complaints.

True, Alger's writing was careless. He occasionally misplaced characters, committed frequent errors and employed a style of writing that may have seemed stilted and archaic, even for Mid-Victorian America. Furthermore, his detractors claim, the Alger Hero possessed more than a fair share of virtues, and his rise to riches too frequently was based upon *luck* rather than effort, skill or know-how.

From the viewpoint of Alger's modern assessors, the author simply added a new twist to the ancient Cinderella theme. His tales were unrealistic, employing a single formula that was developed into more than a hundred stories. "Read one," they invariably say, "and you've read them all."

"The heroes were much too upright; too good to be true," is a common criticism. "Alger's bullies and villains were so evil and conniving you simply couldn't stand them. His characters were made of wood. *And all they ever cared about was money!*"

Besides the fact that most of these heroes (whom Westbrook Pegler called "sanctimonious little heels") started humbly in life, but worked their way upward with the help of an aged benefactor, they all made lots of money. They made it fast! As a matter of fact, it is frequently pointed out, nowadays, that Alger had a predilection for money, and it figures prominently — with cash amounts always indicated to the exact penny — in every one of his books.

Tom Tracy, who sold the Telegram, Mail and Commercial and "all the evening papers" along lower Broadway is, as his story opens, telling a customer that he pays five dollars a month rent for a flat on Bleecker Street. While Tom is engrossed in conversation, his friend, Jimmy O'Hara has sold six newspapers, netting a six-cents profit. Fortunately, Tom's customer buys three papers, generously giving him a silver dollar, so he is not the loser for having tarried.

Ned Newton, blacking boots on the steps of the Astor House, charges five cents for the job. Asked if he can change a quarter, "he drew from the pocket of his ragged vest four nickels, which he handed to the young dude."

Walter Griffith arrived in New York "with a small bundle of clothes tied up in a red silk handkerchief," and "two dollars and a half" in his pocket. Dan, the Detective's mother "makes vests for a man on Chatham Street," earning twenty cents apiece. Many of Alger's boys spent nights at the Newsboys' Lodging House on Fulton Street where the tariff was six cents for a bed; an additional six cents for breakfast. Those who could afford it ate at Pat's, a restaurant in a basement on Nassau Street where, for fifteen cents, they enjoyed a plate of beefsteak and potatoes, bread and coffee. For an extra nickel they could top off the meal with a slice of apple pie.

Almost every Alger story featured at least one daring rescue, for which the hero is handsomely rewarded. In "Frank and Fear-

332

less," Jasper Kent has the opportunity to return little Harry Fitch, who has been kidnapped. The boy's father, in appreciation, gives Jasper a job in his counting house.

Ragged Dick did better. He was standing by the railing of a Brooklyn-bound ferry when six year-old Johnny Rockwell "fell over into the foaming water."

"At the child's scream, the father looked up, and, with a cry of horror, sprang to the edge of the boat. He would have plunged in, but, being unable to swim, would only have endangered his own life, without being able to save his child.

"My child!" he exclaimed in anguish, — "Who will save my child? A thousand — ten thousand dollars to anyone who will save him!"

Dick, being an expert swimmer, dove right in. However, fearing that his readers might judge the young bootblack as being overly mercenary, Alger hastened to point out that "his determination was formed before he heard the liberal offer made by the boy's father. Indeed, I must do Dick the justice to say that, in the excitement of the moment, he did not hear it at all, nor would it have stimulated the alacrity with which he sprang to the rescue of the little boy."

When the lads graduated from the street to the shop or office, they generally started at a weekly salary of about five dollars. However, as gaining the position was often in appreciation for a great service rendered to the employer (such as saving his life, or that of his child), a special arrangement may have been made to pay the lad as much as ten dollars — a substantial sum in those days — and he has taken the first step up the ladder of success.

Because the employer has faith in the shrewdness of a sixteen year-old boy, Luke Larkin, in "Struggling Upward," is commissioned to travel West to the Black Hills to trace a box containing stolen government bonds in the following denominations: "One ten-thousand dollar bond, one five, and ten of one thousand each." Needless to say, it was a successful journey.

On route, however, Luke falls in with a travelling salesman who boasts that his employer allows "a generous sum for hotels, and if I go to a cheap one, I put the difference into my own pocket."

"Is that expected?" asked Luke, doubtfully.

"It's allowed at any rate. No one can complain if I choose to live a little plainer . . . Of course your boss pays your expenses?"

"Yes."

"Then you'd better do as I do — put the difference in your own pocket."

"I shouldn't like to do that."

"Why not? It is evident you are a new traveler, or you would know that it is a regular thing."

"Luke did not answer, but he adhered to his own view. He meant to keep a careful account of his disbursements and report to Mr. Armstrong, without the addition of a single penny."

As tales progressed, the Alger heroes all were blessed with monetary wealth. Chester Rand, coming into an inheritance of five lots of land in Tacoma, Washington, shrewdly sells three "for eight thousand dollars, half cash and the balance on a year's time at twelve per cent interest."

Chester keeps one thousand, investing three in several "lower priced city lots." At story's end, he has sold the remaining two original lots for five thousand dollars each, and could dispose of the others at a handsome profit, but prefers to hold them as an investment.

Upon striking it rich, the lads inevitably share their new riches with faithful friends of leaner days. Accordingly, Mark the Match Boy, after he is established as the long-missing heir of "a rich man, formerly in business in New York, but now a successful merchant in Milwaukie (the spelling of 'Milwaukee' is Alger's)," presents a gift of cash to the kindly Bridget Flanagan.

"Here it is," said Mark, drawing from his pocket a neat pocket-book, containing a roll of bills. "You'll find a hundred dollars inside, Mrs. Flanagan," he said. "I hope they will help you."

"A hundred dollars!" ejaculated Mrs. Flanagan, hardly believing her ears. "Does this good gentleman give me a hundred dollars! . . . It's rich I am with so much money," said the good woman. "May the saints bless you. . ."

While indicating the road to prosperity, Horatio Alger never failed to warn against falling into debt. The first villain encountered in many of his tales is the stingy town squire who holds the mortgage on the old homestead. More than one of the young heroes sees his cottage and its furnishings go under the auctioneer's hammer to pay off his late father's financial obligations. After satisfying the creditors, just enough cash remains for a one-way ticket to New York, where the lad arrives with a few coins in his pocket to start making his way in the world.

With the first money earned — or very shortly thereafter — the boy opens a bank account, making regular deposits. The author carefully recorded the growing bank balance.

Critics today blame the Alger influence for attaching a terrifying connotation to cash-borrowing and money-lending. This was noted some years ago by Paul Gallico, who commented that "it has taken the country banker and rural money-lending institutions a half century to get out from under the stigma placed upon banks, bankers and greedy rich men in general by Horatio Alger. There are still millions of the older generation in the country who are afraid of mortgages and do not know why, but it goes back to their juvenile reading when Alger used it as the plot gimmick whereby the wealthy ground down the poor and took their homes away from them by foreclosure."

It would, indeed, be most interesting if Alger could return today to comment upon our modern system of charge accounts, credit cards, buy now — pay later, installment buying, bank loans designed to help the borrower pay off other debts, etc., etc.

Critics find rich sod for carping in Horatio Alger's small literary merit, his recurring faulty construction and frequent carelessness. Alger wrote rapidly, generally working on two or three stories at the same time, and almost immediately moving on to a new project as soon as a tale was completed. He generally prepared only a single draft, rarely re-writing. The tiny scrawl he employed for manuscripts — with much scratching-out and additions and corrections microscopically written in margins or between the lines — must have been a fright for his editors and type-setters. Considering the urgency for getting his stories into print to satisfy ever-increasing reader demand, the errors are not surprising.

One of the fastest jobs turned out by Alger was "From Canal Boy to President," a biography of James A. Garfield, which his publishers were eager to place in circulation as quickly as possible after the assassination. The author proceeded with determination. But, with little more than newspaper obituary notices for background data, he more or less loosely strung facts together, producing another Alger success-story, but with the hero's name given as James A. Garfield. Being an honest man, Alger suggested to his readers two other books where the straight facts were more readily available.

Horatio also was a very forgetful man. Hence, on Page 206 of "Charlie Codman's Cruise," Miss Bertha (they called her 'Bert') Bowman, "a young lady of ten, with mirthful black eyes and very red cheeks," is referred to as Ida. Ida actually was the foundling of "Timothy Crump's Ward," which Alger was preparing at the same time. And on Page 27 of "Timothy Crump's Ward," Mr. Crump is addressed as Mr. Cooper.

One Page 20 of "The Western Boy," a character introduced as a policeman is, lower on the page, called a physician.

In "The Young Musician," Philip Gray's uncle — who disappears early in the book — is left noticeably unaccounted for at story's end. Hamilton Schuyler, the swindling adventurer of "Mark Mason's Victory," is first known to the reader as Schuyler Hamilton. In "Struggling Upward," Mr. J. Madison Coleman, "attired in a suit of fashionable plaid," wearing "a showy necktie, from the center of which blazed a diamond scarf-pin," starts out to smoke a cigarette, but a few sentences later it becomes a cigar.

Although Tattered Tom (who actually was a girl) claims her name is Jane, Alger states that "her name used to be Jenny, but she has been nicknamed Tom." On Page 183 of the same story, Miss Sue Cameron — "whose father lives on Fifth Avenue" — becomes Mrs. Cameron without explanation nor benefit of clergy.

In the very beginning of "Sink or Swim," Harry Raymond ("a boy of fifteen, well-knit, and vigorous, with a frank, manly expression, and a prepossessing face") is declaiming "in a clear,

"Brave and Bold" was one of the many Alger tales serialized in Street & Smith's New York Weekly. Illustrations show the village belle accepting escort of Robert Rushton, the factory boy, to annoyance of local snob who (inset) receives a thrashing with his own cane.

GOLDEN ARGOSY

Entered according to Act of Congress, in the year 1887, by FRANK A. MUNSEY, in the office of the Librarian of Congress, at Washington, D. C.

Vol. V.—No. 47. | FRANK A. MUNSEY, PUBLISHER. 81 WARREN ST., NEW YORK. | NEW YORK, SATURDAY, OCTOBER 22, 1887. | TERMS $3.00 PER ANNUM IN ADVANCE. | Whole No. 255.

WALTER GRIFFITH FELT A HEAVY HAND ON HIS SHOULDER, AND, LOOKING UP, HE SAW TO HIS DISMAY THAT HE WAS IN THE GRASP OF A POLICEMAN.

✦WALTER✦GRIFFITH;✦
OR,
THE ADVENTURES OF A YOUNG STREET SALESMAN.
By ARTHUR LEE PUTNAM,
Author of " Ned Newton," " Tom Tracy," " Number 91," etc., etc., etc.

CHAPTER I.
WALTER IN BROOKLYN.

A BOY of fifteen, with a healthy brown upon his face, walked down Fulton Street, in Brooklyn, with a small bundle of clothes tied up in a red silk handkerchief. He looked about him with a curious eye, for he had never before been in a city. He was very much impressed by the large and showy stores which line this —the chief business street of New York's sister city.

" I wonder if New York is any bigger than Brooklyn," he said, almost unconsciously giving utterance to the thought.

" Well, I should smile if it wasn't," responded another voice.

Turning his head, Walter Griffith's eyes fell upon a boy dressed in a blue uniform,

*Because installments of two stories in Golden Argosy sometimes over-
lapped, publisher Frank Munsey invented for Alger the pen-name,
Arthur Lee Putnam. Here Walter Griffith, fresh from the country,
is duped by a confidence man and finds himself in trouble with the law.*

GOLDEN ARGOSY

Entered according to Act of Congress, in the year 1887, by Frank A. Munsey, in the office of the Librarian of Congress, at Washington, D. C.

Vol. VI. No. 4.   FRANK A. MUNSEY, 174 WARREN ST., PUBLISHER.   NEW YORK.   NEW YORK, SATURDAY, DECEMBER 24, 1887.   TERMS: $3.00 PER ANNUM, IN ADVANCE.   Whole No. 264.

LUKE WALTON WAS CROSSING ONE OF THE BRIDGES THAT SPAN THE CHICAGO RIVER, WITHOUT NOTICING THAT TWO BOYS WERE FOLLOWING HIM. SUDDENLY THEY SPRANG UPON HIM, AND ONE OF THEM WHISPERED, "HAND OVER YOUR MONEY!"

Luke Walton;
OR,
THE CHICAGO NEWSBOY.
BY HORATIO ALGER, JR.,

Author of "The Young Acrobat," "Bob Burton," "Ragged Dick," "Luck and Pluck," etc.

CHAPTER I.
A CHICAGO NEWSBOY.

"NEWS and Mail, one cent each!"

Half a dozen Chicago newsboys, varying in age from ten to sixteen years, with piles of papers in their hands, joined in the chorus.

They were standing in front and at the sides of the Sherman House, on the cor-

ner of Clark and Randolph Streets, one of the noted buildings in the Lake City. On the opposite side of Randolph Street stands a massive but somewhat gloomy stone structure, the Court House and City Hall. In the shadow of these buildings, at the corner, Luke Walton, one of the largest newsboys, had posted himself. There was something about his bearing and appearance which dis-

---

Alger heroes had to put up with all manner of violence. They were kidnapped, slugged, chloroformed, shanghaied, and dumped into abandoned wells. Here Luke Walton, the Chicago Newsboy, is attacked by hoodlums intent on robbery. Of course, all turned out fine in the end.

A New Story of extraordinary interest by HORATIO ALGER, JR. begins in this issue of The Argosy.

VOL. XIV. No. 486. FRANK A. MUNSEY & COMPANY, PUBLISHERS, 155 EAST 23d STREET. PRICE FIVE CENTS.

THE ARGOSY

NEW YORK, SATURDAY, MARCH 26, 1892.

JED SPRANG FEARLESSLY IN FRONT OF THE WHEELS AND GRASPED THE BRIDLE.

JED,

The Poor House Boy.

By Horatio Alger, Jr.,

Author of "Ragged Dick," "Luck and Pluck," "A Debt of Honor," etc.

CHAPTER I.

JED.

"HERE, you Jed!"

Jed paused in his work with his axe suspended above him, for he was splitting wood. He turned his face toward the side door at which stood a woman, thin and sharp visaged, and asked: "Well, what's wanted?"

"None of your impudence, you young rascal! Come here, I say!"

Jed laid down the axe and walked slowly to the back door. He was a strongly made and well knit boy of nearly sixteen, but he was poorly dressed in an old tennis shirt and a pair of overalls. Yet his face was attractive, and an observer skilled in physiognomy would have read in it signs of a strong character, a warm and grateful disposition, and a resolute will.

"I have not been impudent, Mrs. Fogson," he said quietly.

"Don't you dare to contradict me!" snapped the woman, stamping her foot.

"What's wanted?" asked Jed again.

"Go down to the gate and hold it open. Squire Dixon will be here in five minutes, and we must treat him with respect, for he is Overseer of the Poor."

Jed smiled to himself (it was well he did not betray his amusement) for he knew that Mrs. Fogson and her husband, though tyrannical to the inmates of the poor house of which they had been placed in charge by Squire Dixon three months before, were almost [illegible] in the presence of the Overseer of the Poor, with whom it was their object to stand well.

"All right, ma'am!" he said bluntly, and started for the gate. He did not appear to move fast enough for the amiable Mrs. Fogson, for she called out in a sharp voice: "Why do you walk like a snail? Hurry up, I tell you. I see Squire Dixon coming up the road."

"I shall get to the gate before he does," announced Jed, independently, not increasing his pace a particle.

"I hate that boy!" soliloquized Mrs. Fogson, looking after him with a frown. "He is the most independent young rascal I ever came across—he actually disobeys and defies me. I must get Fogson to give him a horsewhipping some of these fine days; and when he does, I'm going to be there and see it done!" she continued, her black eyes twinkling viciously. "Every blow he received would do me good! I'd gloat over it! I'd flog him myself if I was strong enough."

The amiable character of Mrs. Fogson may be

Jed, the Poorhouse Boy, halted runaway horse to win thanks of rich benefactor. Others rescued children, returned lost wallets, saved old men from thugs. At conclusion, Jed learns he is Sir Robert Fenwick, of England.

ringing voice from the platform of the Vernon High School."
Quoting Daniel Webster, with appropriate gestures, he recites:

"Sink or swim, live or die, survive or perish, I give my hand
and my heart to this vote."

Although it probably passed, unnoticed, neither Alger nor
Harry Raymond gave credit to Webster. Commenting upon this,
Franklin P. Adams said "when I read the book I thought that
Alger himself had made up the high school oration."

✳   ✳   ✳

Poor, naive Horatio was notoriously clumsy when it came
to matters of delicacy or romance. Generally he avoided these
subjects. His readers did not require such morsels and the author, himself, knew pathetically little about them. When, in a
story, he approached them, literary catastrophe resulted. Occasionally he brushed up against intimacy without really meaning to do so and, more often than not, his approach unintentionally produced double-entendre that, even in his day, probably caused some raised eyebrows.

In "Frank and Fearless," Jasper Kent is the prisoner of a
group of criminals in a run-down district of St. Louis. On the
fourth day, he hears someone in the hall and supposes it "to be
the old man with his dinner." But instead "he beheld the fresh
face of a young girl, apparently about sixteen years of age."
After leaving the food, promising to return later with his supper,
and then hurrying downstairs, Alger exclaimed "She left Jasper
eager and excited!"

In "Tom Temple's Career," Imogene Davenport most unwittingly suggests to Tom, who is her dinner guest, "I want to
show you some engravings." A few sentences later, Alger dis-
closes that "Imogene laid herself out to entertain him, and at all
events succeeded in monopolizing his attention."

Miss Pendleton, an elderly spinster in "Sink or Swim," is
about to enjoy a long vacation, and looks forward to "intercourse
which her mode of life for many years had rendered impracti-
cable."

A basket containing an infant girl is left on the doorstep in
an early chapter of "Timothy Crump's Ward." The household —

which includes Jack Crump, his mother, father (Timothy), and Rachel, a dour maiden aunt — is understandably surprised.

"What a dear, innocent little thing!" said Mrs. Crump, with true maternal instinct.

"Ain't it a pretty 'un?" Jack said, admiringly.

"Poor thing!" said the cooper, compassionately.

"It's a world of iniquity!" remarked Rachel, lifting up her eyes dismally. "There isn't any one you can trust. I didn't think a brother of mine would have such a sin brought to his door."

"Good heavens, Rachel!" said the honest cooper, in amazement, "what *can* you mean?"

"It isn't for me to explain," said Rachel, shaking her head; "only it's strange that it should have been brought to *this* house, that's all I say."

"Perhaps it was meant for you, Aunt Rachel," said Jack, with thoughtless fun.

"Me!" exclaimed Rachel, rising to her feet, while her face betrayed the utmost horror at the suggestion.

"She fell back in her seat, and made a violent effort to faint."

While Alger's robust boys could bravely stand up to bullies or bandits, they were — much like Horatio himself — timid and awkward when face-to-face with the opposite sex. Many of the lads' contacts were with older women, ranging from tyrannical wives of almshouse overseers, shrewish step-mothers and Hogarthian rumpots, to the hero's own kindly mother, helpful neighbors and generous benefactresses whom he either rescued from harm or came to know through services performed for them. This group he could meet on fairly even terms, but the bright, handsome little girls — about ten to thirteen years old — whom Alger frequently described as "mischievous," "high-spirited," "flirtatious" and "teasing," were another matter.

These winsome creatures were daughters of employers and benefactors and, from first sight, they impishly announced to daddy that they were setting their caps for his handsome young office boy. They invited the hero to their homes for tea, and he took dancing lessons to acquit himself satisfactorily at their parties. But when they spoke to him, he fumbled for words; when they complimented him, he blushed.

True, he generally wound up marrying one of these girls,

but that was in the future and, rather than hear it in the hero's own words, it always is left for the author to prophesy that "rumors persist that the young lady, whose early preference for him still continues, will, before very long, become his wife."

Alger rarely created a romantic setting but, in his typically unsophisticated — almost Puritanical — manner, he did his best to inject a modicum of juvenile romance into "Sink or Swim."

Harry Raymond, seeking gold in the Victoria Mines, seventy miles northwest of Melbourne, Australia, has come into a fortune of $12,525.00. Maud Lindsay — thirteen years old, "attractive and lovable, warm-hearted and impulsive" — is telling her father, a wealthy English merchant, that she wishes he would return. "It's so lonesome since he went away."

"I begin to think you are in love with Harry, Maud."

"I begin to think so too, papa. Would you object to him for a son-in-law?"

"Just at present I might. I don't think you are old enough to be married."

"Don't be foolish, papa. Of course I don't want to be married till I am old enough . . . If I don't marry Harry Raymond, I'll be an old maid."

"Indeed, Maud had hardly ceased speaking when a knock was heard at the door. Maud rose to open it. She was overwhelmed with delight when, in the visitor, in spite of his rough garb, she recognized our hero, the loss of whose company she had been deploring.

"O Harry, how glad I am to see you!" she exclaimed, actually hugging Harry in her delight. Harry was rather embarrassed at the unexpected warmth of his reception, but felt that it would be impolite not to kiss Maud in return, and accordingly did so."

It was the only romantic kiss recorded by Alger in more than a hundred novels!

NOT GREAT, BUT
DURABLE WRITING

"ALGER, TODAY," HIS CRITICS BELIEVE, "is as dead as the Dodo bird! Nobody reads his stuff anymore and, these days, who struggles upward?"

Who, today, like Carl Crawford, in "The Odds Against Him," labors in a furniture factory for two dollars a week and board? Who, like Luke Larkin, in "Struggling Upward," receives "a dollar a week for taking care of the schoolhouse," and picks up perhaps as much more doing odd jobs in the village? Who, like the enterprising Grit, the Young Boatman, buys a rowboat for a few dollars to establish a ferry service across the Kennebec River, carrying passengers the half-mile from shore-to-shore for ten cents ("but if it were a child or poor person" he would do it for five)? Who, like Harry Walton, the farm boy of "Bound to Rise," would start out as a shoemaker's pegger at three dollars a week, after a period of apprenticeship?

The answer is that few boys in America today would cheerfully start climbing the ladder of success on those terms. Very few would *have* to. Let's face it — even if one such ambitious lad should show up, he would be prevented by a dozen local,

344

state and federal laws from earning a livelihood the way Alger's boys did.

In addition to minimum wage and hour legislation, there are compulsory education statutes, state labor acts, workmen's compensation, federal fair labor standards, income taxes, social security and hospitalization deductions, requirements for labor union membership with dues deductions, full-time and vacation working permits, indoor and outdoor employment regulations, public contracts laws and probably a number of others that the young hero would be violating. Paul the Peddler — selling nickel prize packages — would be shunted off the streets and, very likely, Alger's hordes of shouting, aggressive news-hawkers, bootblacks and baggage smashers would, at very least, be told to keep moving if a policeman should happen along.

The obvious benefits of modern labor legislation fully granted, the ardor to strive and succeed, as Horatio Alger preached it, is a thing of the past. His hero is no longer taken seriously, as he once was, and the boys, themselves, probably are now more inclined toward the image of the organization man with fringe benefits, than to that of the successful merchant or independent entrepreneur that Alger idolized.

The self-made man — as invented by Horatio Alger — apparently is a rapidly-vanishing breed. Office boys will still become corporation presidents, but the chances are they will have college degrees. They will be specialists, their education augmented by the advanced study increasingly required for top posts. The executive outlook for the hustler whose formal schooling didn't go beyond the eighth grade apparently is bleak.

So, with the demise of the self-made man, we also witness the passing of self-made man literature. Perhaps the Alger stories — along with Currier & Ives prints and cigar store Indians (which, while not considered great art, are still eagerly sought by collectors and museums, and bring big prices when offered for sale) — now repose only in that Valhalla known as Americana.

Stories of ragged boys who attained success are no longer popular. The practices of "Helping Himself," "Slow and Sure" and "Risen from the Ranks" are outdated. Nevertheless, the high principles by which Horatio Alger's heroes advanced to leadership still are valid.

Innumerable American leaders of today — and of recent memory — once read Alger and believed in him. Some still do. Many credit the author with providing incentive they may not have otherwise heeded. Not all who today have fond childhood memories of these books started as street boys, and even those for whom early economic struggle was not necessary absorbed Alger's easy-to-take inspiration.

Benjamin Fairless, who rose in life from a part-time school teacher to the head of United States Steel, read Alger in his youth. Former New York Governor Alfred E. Smith treasured them when he was still a newsboy on Manhattan's Lower East Side. Carl Sandburg recalls the good supply of Algers at the Public Library near his boyhood home at Galesburg, Illinois. Herbert H. Lehman, a banker, former Governor of New York and United States Senator, knew the author personally. He "eagerly awaited the publication of every book Alger wrote," and still has a number of copies in his library. Former Ohio Governor Michael V. DiSalle believes "that the Alger theme did have a great deal to do in establishing a pattern for my own mind." He is the owner of a superb Alger collection.

The Most Reverend Francis Cardinal Spellman, Archbishop of New York, as a boy sought them in the Whitman, Massachusetts, Public Library. "I read all that were available," he says, "and enjoyed and, I am sure, benefited from reading them." James A. Farley, Chairman of the Board of Coca Cola Export Corporation, and former United States Postmaster General, read Algers when these books were as much a part of the American scene as county fairs, Sunday outings in the park, and Fourth of July concerts.

Joyce Kilmer, who produced some of our loveliest poetry, read Alger. So did Ernest Hemingway. So did the New York Giants' famed Christy Mathewson and Knute Rockne of Notre Dame. There was, indeed, a time when almost every boy growing up in this country avidly read these simple tales by the most widely read novelist in the history of American literature.

In an effort to update and perpetuate the belief that old-fashioned opportunity still knocks, the American Schools and

Colleges Association in 1947 established their Horatio Alger Awards. Each year medals are given to nine or ten American leaders in all fields whose careers typify the results of individual initiative, hard work and adherence to traditional ideals.

Among those who have been chosen as Annual Horatio Alger Award winners are Dwight D. Eisenhower who performed odd jobs around his boyhood home at Abilene, Kansas, long before he was elected Thirty-fourth President of The United States; Conrad N. Hilton, who began his fabulous career by renting out rooms (in the San Antonio house in which he was born) to travellers at one dollar a night with meals; The Reverend Dr. Norman Vincent Peale, who rose from a grocer's clerk to become one of the nation's great spiritual leaders; Bernard M. Baruch, once a three dollar-a-week clerk, who became a leader in finance, elder statesman and adviser to Presidents.

Dr. Ralph J. Bunche, as a youth, worked as a janitor in Detroit, while completing his education. He became United States Delegate to the United Nations, holds more than thirty-five honorary degrees and sixty major awards, including the Nobel Peace Prize. Thomas J. Watson started as a six dollar-a-week bookkeeper and later became head of IBM. Adolph Zukor arrived in the United States a ragged orphan in 1887, became a pioneer in the motion picture industry and rose to the chairmanship of Paramount Pictures Corporation.

Alfred C. Fuller, the original Fuller Brush Man, was a farm boy of eighteen when he arrived from Nova Scotia. After losing three jobs he started making brushes in the basement of his sister's home at Somerville, near Boston. He manufactured the brushes at night and, like "The Young Salesman," sold them door-to-door during the day. The Fuller Brush Company, which he founded, now has sales in excess of $100,000,000 a year.

Every one of these men has the makings of a genuine Alger Hero!

The name of Horatio Alger, in recent decades, has taken on legendary meaning. It is used as symbol; a figure of speech. As a handy synonym for spectacular rise to fame or success, it has become a colloquialism. When newspapers refer to "a typical Alger story," readers anticipate a report on the uniquely American phenomenon of one who started from scratch and arrived at the top rung of fortune. It has an immediate sight identification that few, if any, other names imply.

Why, then, is Horatio Alger's output rated as trash by modern critics?

A study of virtually every comment and criticism published since 1932 (Alger's centennial year) gives clear indication that many writers are judging him by modern standards. This is wrong. Horatio Alger was a part of his own era. His works should never be measured by today's ultra-sophisticated precepts. While no one can ever claim for him superior quality of writing, his many stories were read and enjoyed by millions of Americans. As has been pointed out, there can be no question about their influence among generations unborn during his own lifetime.

Scoff as his critics may, today, his pen was — during the Alger Era — as powerful as it was popular. His unliterary but, nevertheless, graphic expose of the cruel padrone system broke the back of that racket in New York and in other large cities throughout the country. He dramatically chronicled this shame in "Phil the Fiddler," one of his best-known works.

The story described how children were taken from impoverished homes in Southern Italy — their parents deceived that they were being brought to a better life in America — and, once arrived here, were sent into the streets as beggars or itinerant musicians. Subjected to inhuman treatment by severe masters, their mortality rate was high; the entire outrage scandalous. But, until Alger assumed the initiative and led the drive against this virtual slavery, official policy was to look in the other direction.

It took Horatio only six months, after publication of "Phil the Fiddler," to spell out the end of this criminal traffic. His life was threatened and he even was mauled by irate padrones, but the little minister stuck to his guns, and won. "Phil" provided needed stimulus, and the New York State Legislature enacted into law the prevention of cruelty to children.

At the same time he was drumming up considerable public interest in the Children's Aid Society's project to take homeless waifs off city streets and send them West, where their foster families were establishing new homes along the recently-opened frontier. Several years later he again was hard at work, persuading New Yorkers to contribute to his friend, Whitelaw Reid's drive to provide youngsters from the slums with fresh air vacations in the country.

This, of course, is now all but forgotten. He is remembered — critically by some; with nostalgic reverence by others — for his stories. These often are referred to as "algers," the word being used as an object rather than a name. Few other authors seem to enjoy this distinction, for how often does one hear of "dickenses," "twains," "faulkners" or "steinbecks"?

While mocking Alger is easy, and the spate of articles on the subject — by writers who take him much too seriously — seem to do just that, it is to reckon without the experts. Frederick B. Adams, Chairman of the Selection Committee for The Grolier Club's noted 1946 exhibition of One Hundred Influential American Books Printed Before 1900, called "Ragged Dick" "sufficiently Grade A" for inclusion. Frank Luther Mott, in his "Golden Multitudes; the Story of Best Sellers in the United States," also named "Ragged Dick" in the column of Over-All Best Sellers. Three others, "Fame and Fortune," "Luck and Pluck" and "Tattered Tom," appear on his runner-up list of Better Sellers. Both "Dick" and "Tom" appear again in Jacob Blanck's superb compilation, "Peter Parley to Penrod."

Van Allen Bradley, syndicated Literary Editor of The Chicago Daily News and author of two "Gold in Your Attic" books, advises that Alger correspondence and inquiries ("Where can I buy Algers? I'd love to read one." or "Can you tell me where I can get a few of the old Horatio Alger books for my grandchildren?") reach his desk regularly and in goodly number.

To generalize that young people don't go for Alger's stories is primarily correct. For one thing, few youthful readers have a natural yen for his prose and, unless they are eager enough to enlist the antiquarian book trade to help them (and there is no reason to suppose they should be), they probably will have difficulty finding even a single copy. Of a fair sampling of teen-age students queried, most had heard the name but not many could accurately identify him. Horatio Alger was variously recognized by them as "a poor boy who made good," "the hero of story," "the pen-name of an author who lived many years ago." Still, there were some who knew.

As an experiment, I have, in recent years, presented quantities of Alger's books to children's centers and libraries. The results indicated clearly that they were read, some youngsters asking for more. During 1961, the Chicago Daily News serialized "Luke Walton; or, The Chicago Newsboy." Installments ran over a period of two weeks with considerable mail response — virtually all of it overwhelmingly favorable — resulting immediately and continuing even after the story ended.

It probably would not be entirely unreasonable to suggest that Alger's works could enjoy a certain limited circulation if made available again. They would appeal to sentimental old-timers seeking an evening of temporary relief from international crises and stomach-acidity commercials on the late show. If offered to young readers on equal terms with their present chosen reading, some Algers would be bought. My own sampling has indicated that once started, the kids are inclined to read the book through.

This is written with the full realization that, during the 1950's, a small group of Alger titles were reissued, their availability creating no noticeable dents in then current best-seller lists. Possible explanations for their failure to turn back literary clocks by a couple of generations may have been their presentation, physically, as just another run of paperbacks with modern (rather than period) cover illustrations. Nothing there to arouse nostalgia. There appeared to be nothing attempted in the way of format to appeal to children. Inasmuch as neither myself nor the many avid Alger collectors with whom I am constantly in touch were aware of them at the time, it is also probable that other folks inclined to buy one or two of the titles were likewise uninformed.

Regardless of whether — for one reason or another — someone might be compelled to pick up one of these relics today, we must assume that, like the old oaken bucket, Horatio Alger's tales of triumph are a thing of the past. His heroes were replaced by Frank Merriwell of Yale, soon after by the adventuresome, fun-loving Rover Boys and Tom Swift who, even a half century ago, was beating the competition with television, sky trains, aerial warships and other fantastic gadgets only recently developed or still on the drawing boards. Their dynasties ended, even those stalwarts of the fifty-cent school of literature gave way to new crops which, in their turn, also appear tediously out-moded to new generations of juvenile readers.

But, very likely, even when today's favorites — and tomorrow's — are but dim memories, the *spirit* of Horatio Alger will remain a part of our folklore. Those who may briefly pause to scan the brittle pages of one of these books shall, for a brief moment, see his beloved New York in the dusk of a bygone day. The crowded streets will echo to the rumble and clatter of horse-drawn carriages and the Broadway Stage, to the urgent shouting of vendors, and to the never-ending procession of busy, hurrying, shuffling throngs. And there on the corner, selling newspapers or blacking boots, will be the humble boy whom Alger created into an unforgettable hero; the determined young lad who — much like America — pulled himself up by his bootstraps.

ROAD TO SUCCESS

THE BIBLIOGRAPHY OF THE WORKS OF
HORATIO ALGER

WHERE ARE THEY NOW?

THE DAYS ARE NOT too long past when dusty Algers were picked from the nickel-and-dime sidewalk stalls in front of book shops. Later, they were given a berth of modest respectability in juvenile sections inside the store. Today they are rare books, and do not often make it to the shelves, as many dealers keep at hand want lists of customers hopeful of being first to be notified of a new Alger arrival.

The tremendous revival of interest in the author is not surprising. Its only puzzling aspect is that it took so long to come about! But in America — a nation in which a special place is set aside for nostalgia and "the good old days;" a nation of collectors of things old and charming — a renewed interest in Alger was inevitable. He was, after all, the originator of the strive-and-succeed, struggling upward and bound-to-rise themes that inspired many a youngster that ours is, indeed, the land of opportunity.

Add to the primarily nostalgic interest of the former Alger-reader the discovery by others, as well as by numerous universities, libraries and institutions, that the writings of Horatio Alger, Jr., — if not from a literary point-of-view — were, nevertheless, a mighty force in American literature from the standard of influence of the book on the reader.

If this is not attested to by Alger's inclusion in The Grolier Club's monumental exhibition, in 1946, of One Hundred Influential American Books Printed Before 1900, and if it is not further endorsed by the listing of two Alger stories in "Peter Parley to Penrod," Jacob Blanck's superb bibliographical description of the best-loved American juvenile books, Horatio Alger's popularity surely is proved by the publication and purchase of some 400,000,000 copies of his books!

Alger's first book, "Bertha's Christmas Vision" — a collection of twenty short stories — was published in 1856. In all, one hundred twenty three original titles bear his name. Deduct from this eleven written by Edward Stratemeyer (the famed author of boys books, who claims these tales are completions of outlines left to him by Alger), four that appeared in periodicals but never as books and one unpublished manuscript.

During the decades that the prolific Alger turned out as many as three or four books a year, he also found time to write an unknown quantity of mediocre short stories and a number of poems, some of notable quality. Many of his stories, before appearing in book form, were serialized in the weekly and monthly story papers that were popular at that time.

These generally are the goal of the advanced collector. They are hard to come by, relatively high-priced and generally in poor condition as they are found only in newspapers and magazines, many dating back more than a century.

Pity the innocent beginner who has amassed several books by Alger and believes that he has just about read them all. Then he learns of other titles he does not have. He goes for them and, little-by-little, discovers that prices are rising. If he cannot resist them — despite the higher cost — he's hooked, and will soon be eagerly searching for those he still needs.

At the start he was satisfied with so-called reading copies. These are reprints, and of comparatively little value. Soon through contacts with dealers and some of the several thousand other Alger collectors, he will become aware of — and fascinated by — the existence of Alger first editions. If these are to be his, he must be prepared to spend considerably more for the books than heretofore.

From this point on, it is only a matter of time before he learns that Alger sometimes used a pseudonym, and books carrying his pen-name, Arthur Lee Putnam, are very hard to find, and priced accordingly. His second pen-name, Arthur Hamilton, is even rarer. A third, Julian Starr, is rarest. The aches and pains really set-in when he starts longing for the two books written anonymously, especially "Timothy Crump's Ward," a rarity that countless devotees will envision only in dreams. The second, "Nothing to Do," he may some day possess if he is patient and willing to pay the price.

Later — probably much later — he will learn of the fourteen fabulous paperbacks of which no collection contains all, and even most of the advanced Alger libraries do not include a single copy.

To the book-seller who deals in rare and out-of-print editions, the Alger business has long been an enigma. Even those who, in recent years, have come to realize that a ready market (with good profits) exists for these books, are not always certain of their exact value.

Few dealers are knowledgeable about all the Alger titles, their variant reissue titles, the pseudonyms, paperbacks, minor output and the serializations. Even fewer know the right price to assign to some of these items when they get them. Others are not always able to differentiate between a first edition, a later issue by the original publisher and a comparatively recent reprint.

A knowledge of these facts is essential to collector and dealer alike. It would be tremendously helpful to the rural book-scout or "picker," who regularly attends country auctions and often gets first crack at the contents of old barns, farm attics and cellars. For it is in these areas that Alger treasures can still be found.

Thus, the pressing need for this bibliography. It is intended to answer questions pertaining to Alger-searching and Alger-pricing. For the collector, there is data regarding the abundant, inexpensive reprints — if that is his preference — and as complete information as is obtainable on first editions. Taking into consideration that all Alger items are rapidly becoming scarcer,

and that their worth must increase, an attempt is made to assign to each a fair value.

MANY TITLES,
MANY EDITIONS

STARTING IN 1864, A. K. Loring, Publisher, of Boston, issued some three dozen original stories by Horatio Alger, Jr. Too often the collector — and an occasional book-seller — will assume that any Alger published by Loring is a first edition. This is not necessarily true. While each title certainly had its first edition, many of them were subsequently made available in second, third and some in more editions.

When Loring went bankrupt, in 1881, Porter & Coates, of Philadelphia, took over the printing plates of many Algers set by Loring, and also the author's contract. Accordingly, they published first and subsequent editions of fifteen new Alger stories, but the Porter & Coates reissues of the books originally printed by Loring are simply reprints, and nothing more. This may seem very academic to the sophisticated collector and the experienced dealer or librarian, but many, many Alger reprints from the presses of Porter & Coates are offered and sold as first editions.

Fifteen years after Porter & Coates became heir to the Alger properties, Henry T. Coates & Company succeeded Porter &

Coates, continuing the pattern of originating titles and reissuing old ones.

The fact is that Alger could write tales faster than a single publisher could handle them and he sometimes arranged commitments with two or more houses simultaneously. For this reason we see his books, under the imprints of G. W. Carleton, J. S. Ogilvie, John R. Anderson, Penn Publishing Company and others, offered during the same period.

In 1887, A. L. Burt made an arrangement with Street & Smith to print, in paper wrappers, a number of Alger stories originally serialized in New York Weekly. There were five such original tales in their Boys' Home Library during 1887 and 1888. Towards the end of 1887, Frank Munsey got into the paperback business, listing in his Popular Series for Boys and Girls three Alger stories that had appeared in Golden Argosy.

Golden Argosy, and later The Argosy, continued as a source for paperback material when United States Book Company added six Alger first editions to their Leather-Clad Tales of Adventure and Romance, all in 1890.

These paperbacks — fourteen in all — are among the hardest of any Alger items to acquire.

There existed a legion of publishers who issued only an occasional first edition, and many reprints. The John C. Winston Company, which took over where Henry T. Coates & Company left off, was among the earliest of these, producing only reprints, often with full-color illustrations. Probably the most prolific of the reprint houses were New York Book Company and M. A. Donohue. These turned out cheap hard-cover ten-cent editions by multi-millions, distributing them well into the 1920's. It is probably New York Book Company and Donohue that many of today's Alger readers remember from childhood.

Some publishers attempted only a single book by Alger; some manufactured dozens of titles. The list below includes seventy under whose imprint books by Horatio Alger, Jr., appeared, along with the indication as to whether they published his first editions, reprints, or both. The names are alphabetically arranged. No attempt is made to indicate chronological order, nor the number of books involved.

Aldine Publishing Company. Reprints.
W. L. Allison Company. Reprint.
American News Company. First edition (in cooperation with
Carleton and Street & Smith).
American Publishers Corp. Reprints.
J. R. Anderson & Company. First edition.
J. R. Anderson & Henry S. Allen. First edition.
Bonanza Books. Reprint.
Book Club of California. Reprint.
Brown-Bazin and Company. First edition.
A. L. Burt. First editions and reprints.
H. M. Caldwell Company. Reprints.
G. W. Carleton & Co. First editions.
Chatterton-Peck Company. First edition and reprints.
Cincinnati Publishing Company. Reprint.
Henry T. Coates & Co. First editions and reprints.
Collier Books. Reprints.
Commercial Bookbinding Co. Reprint.
Consolidated Retail Booksellers. Reprints.
Crown Publishers. Reprint.
Cupples & Leon. First editions and reprints.
DeWolfe-Fiske & Co. Reprint.
George W. Dillingham. First edition.
M. A. Donohue & Company. Reprints.
Dramatic Publishing Co. Reprint.
Federal Book Company. Reprints.
James French & Company. First edition.
Frederick Gleason. First edition (?).
Goldsmith Publishing Company. Reprints.
Grosset & Dunlap. Reprints.
Holly Publishing Co. Reprint.
Holt, Rinehart and Winston. Reprint.
Hurst & Company. Reprints.
International Book Company. Reprints.
A. K. Loring, Publisher. First editions.
Frank F. Lovell & Company. First editions and reprints.
John W. Lovell Company. First editions and reprints.
F. M. Lupton. First edition.
MacLellan Publishers. Reprints.
David McKay, Publisher. Reprints.
McLoughlin Brothers. Reprints.
Mershon Company, The. First editions and reprints.
Frank A. Munsey, Publisher. First editions.
Mutual Book Company. Reprints.
New Werner Company, The. Reprints.
New World Book Company. Reprints.
New York Book Company. Reprints.
New York Publishing Company. Reprints.
Odyssey Press. Reprint.
J. S. Ogilvie and Company, First editions and one reissue.
Penn Publishing Company. First editions.
Porter & Coates. First editions and reprints.
Saalfield Publishing Company. Reprints.

John F. Shaw & Co., Ltd. (London). Reprints.
Stitt Publishing Company. First editions and reprints.
Street & Smith. First editions and reprints.
Stuyvesant Press. Reprint.
Superior Printing Company. Reprints.
Thompson & Thomas. First edition and reprints.
Trade Publishing Company. Reprints.
W. S. Trigg. First edition (in cooperation with F. M. Lupton).
United States Book Company. First editions and reprints.
Value Books. Reprints.
Vickery and Hill Publishing Company. Reprint.
John Wanamaker. Reprints.
Ward & Drummond. Reprint.
Arthur Westbrook Company. Reprints.
Whitman Publishing Company. Reprints.
John C. Winston Company, The. Reprints.
World Publishing Company. Reprints.
World Syndicate Publishing Company. Reprints.

THE STRATEMEYER ALGERS

IT ALMOST INVARIABLY COMES as a shock to the collector to learn that a number of books in which Horatio Alger, Jr. is named as the author were not the work of Alger, at all. There are eleven such stories, produced by Edward Stratemeyer — himself a top creator of tales for young people — who styled himself as "Alger's literary executor."

This unique series started in 1900 (a year after Alger's death), with the virtually simultaneous publication of "Falling In With Fortune" and "Out for Business." Beneath Alger's name, on the title pages of both books, was indicated: "Completed by Arthur M. Winfield." Winfield — a well-known Stratemeyer pseudonym, was the name under which he wrote the long-popular Rover Boys Series.

During the six years that followed the issuing of the two "last tales," nine additional stories — crediting Alger as the author — were produced by Stratemeyer. These titles included: "Nelson the Newsboy," "Young Captain Jack," "Jerry, the Backwoods Boy," "Lost at Sea," "From Farm to Fortune," "The Young Book Agent," "Randy of the River," "Joe the Hotel Boy" and "Ben Logan's Triumph."

Did Alger designate his friend, Stratemeyer, to bring to conclusion his unfinished works? Did, indeed, Alger have *anything* to do with the eleven posthumous books? And — if so — exactly where did Horatio Alger, Jr. leave off, and Edward Stratemeyer begin?

The two men first met early in 1890. Stratemeyer — who was then twenty-eight years old — had recently been appointed as editor of Street & Smith's new weekly publication, "Good News." Alger, thirty years his senior, was from the first issue a star contributor, along with a trio of top-notchers that included Oliver Optic (William T. Adams), Edward S. Ellis and Harry Castlemon.

Although Stratemeyer actually later adapted and up-dated the master's technique to the changing pace of the early Twentieth Century, the eleven "completions" appear to be one hundred percent Stratemeyer, with hardly a trace of Alger. "Young Captain Jack's" speech and action contains much of Dick Rover; not a bit of Ragged Dick. "Joe the Hotel Boy" is — from the point of view of writing style — closer kin to Tom Swift (hero of the famed series produced by Stratemeyer under the pen-name Victor Appleton) than to Alger's Tom Brace, Tom Tracy or, for that matter, Tom the Bootblack.

There is, indeed, every inclination to say that Edward Stratemeyer — whose business acumen easily equalled his ability to produce seemingly endless series of books for young readers — was the true author of those "Algers" that appeared only after the author's death. There is the strong temptation to believe that Stratemeyer selected the magic and sales-assuring name of Horatio Alger, just as he invented Winfield and Appleton, and as he gave birth to Clarence Young (pen-name for The Motor Boys Series) and Roy Rockwood (pen-name for the Bomba, the Jungle Boy Series). He devised (and eventually hired as many as fifty writers to create, from his suggestions), literally hundreds of stories using as pseudonyms Capt. Ralph Bonehill, P. T. Barnum, Jr., Carolyn Keene, Laura Lee Hope and others.

People who knew Stratemeyer (who died in 1930) say that

he occasionally spoke of the Alger stories he completed. "If you knew Ed," one gentleman told me "you'd know that he wouldn't say it if it wasn't the truth."

Strongest support of Stratemeyer's claim comes from Henry W. Ralston, a Street & Smith staff member and executive for fifty-two years. He personally knew both men.

"Ed Stratemeyer . . . was a very good friend of Horatio Alger, whom he met during his association with Street & Smith," Mr. Ralston says. "Whether Alger designated Ed as his literary heir, so far as the unfinished volumes were concerned, I do not know. Stratemeyer certainly became legally possessed of them and found a publisher for them after he 'licked them into shape.'

"You would have to have known Stratemeyer to know that he would not pass his work off for that of Alger. He admittedly finished and edited them, as he could do so well. He had a number of boys' books, the sales of which were as large or exceeded some of Alger's best. Remember, we [Street & Smith] bought and published them as by Alger and we simply would not deceive the public."

Additional evidence comes from the old Street & Smith files. An informal memo, of unknown date — referring to paper-back editions of Alger's works — indicates that "101 Alger books appeared, some eight or ten of them completed by Stratemeyer. Alger had them partially written when he died."

Another note concerning the publisher's Alger holdings mentions "the few others we bought from Stratemeyer."

Quentin Reynolds, in his book, "The Fiction Factory," the story of one hundred years of publishing at Street & Smith, notes that "when Horatio Alger died in 1899, he left a few unfinished manuscripts. Stratemeyer picked up where Alger left off and finished them to everyone's satisfaction."

The fine points of 'who-wrote-them?' notwithstanding, these eleven volumes are relatively difficult to obtain. Especially in first editions, they are offered less frequently than Algers published many years earlier. And with the famed author's name appearing on the title page, these books are a proper — and very desirable — part of any Alger collection.

PEN-NAMES,
GHOSTS
AND CONFUSION

THE FACT THAT ANOTHER AUTHOR — Stratemeyer — had a hand in writing a number of Horatio's stories gives considerably less cause for confusion than some of the tougher literary high-hurdles the Alger-seeker must clear. He should, at any rate, be aware of them — or he will stumble.

Consider, for instance, the collector hoping to add editions to his shelf against such unsporting odds as books by Alger that were anonymously published; obscure pen-names, and stories reissued under varying or completely changed titles. Then there are the tales that appeared only in weekly or monthly periodicals, and never issued as bound volumes; serializations that publishers intended to put into book form, but did not, and the irritating (to collector and book-seller alike) hoax of a list of Alger-sounding titles which — though fervently sought for years — do not and never did exist!

Almost as frustrating is the search for stories published under Alger's pseudonyms. As mentioned previously, his pen-name, Arthur Lee Putnam — though not infrequently used both in serializations and bound volumes — is hard to find, and higher-priced than books "By Horatio Alger, Jr." The reason for its use is obvious. Alger was so prolific in his output that frequently two or more of his writings ran concurrently in Munsey's Argosy. The Putnam signature seemed a logical solution to the problem of giving young readers the stories they wanted without overusing the famed Alger name. When these were issued as bound volumes (in paper wrappers or hard covers), early editions generally still credited Arthur Lee Putnam as the author. However, subsequent printings invariably reverted to Alger.

While there is certainty that his second pen-name, Arthur Hamilton, appeared twice, there also is evidence that it could have been used on one other occasion.

Hamilton appears as the author of "A Child of Fortune," which started in Golden Argosy during December, 1885. This was a unique situation of the serialization appearing almost twenty years after the original story — better known as "Helen Ford" — was issued as a book. As this early effort was somewhat shy of the accustomed formula, and the 'hero' was a girl, it may have been decided best that another name should be used. But it is more likely that Hamilton is named as author to eliminate the possibility of confusion with the final parts of "Struggling Upward," and the beginning chapters of "In a New World," the two other Alger stories that were appearing at the same time.

The Arthur Hamilton nom de plume was first used in Gleason's Literary Companion, in 1869, for the serialization of "Ralph Raymond's Heir." As no other Alger stories nor articles appeared in those issues, no reason is given for the use of the pen-name, unless it was a condition imposed by another publication, Student & Schoolmate, to which Alger was then under contract.

During the same year, Gleason either published — or intended to publish — "Ralph Raymond's Heir," By Arthur Hamilton, in paper wrappers. Whether he did or not is unknown, as not even a single copy of this edition has ever been located.

There is only one recorded use of Alger's third pen-name, Julian Starr. It appears in 1895 as author of "The Disagreeable Woman," an effort to produce a sophisticated adult novel. Alger tried unsuccessfully to persuade Frank Munsey — who at that time had first refusal on his writing — to issue the story as a serial. When George W. Dillingham agreed to publish the story as a book, Munsey insisted upon the use of an unfamiliar pen-name so that this story — presumably for grown-ups — should not confound and dismay Alger's tremendous following of Argosy readers.

An obscure fourth pseudonym, Caroline F. Preston, was used only as a signature for short stories. It has been noted in Gleason's Literary Companion, Gleason's Monthly Companion, and in Young Israel, approximately between 1861 and 1878.

Something strange and contradictory about the Preston style mystified me for many years. A careful study of a number of these stories convinced me that it was pure Alger. But others carrying the same by-line, could not possibly come from his pen. As the Alger style is as inflexible as it is familiar, the obvious variations and contrasts were all the more unexplainable.

But the mystery eventually was solved, the key to the answer contained in a brief news item in the June, 1873, issue of Young Israel. The article stated, in part, that "among the many of our good citizens who will this Summer seek recreation and pleasure abroad will be found a trio of Young Israel's able and much-admired contributors — Mr. Horatio Alger, Jr., Miss O. Augusta Cheney [Alger's sister, a successful writer of short stories and dialogues], and Miss Caroline F. Preston. They will tour Italy, Switzerland and Austria, . . . return in October."

The obvious answer immediately became clear: *"Caroline F. Preston" was being used as a pen-name by both Alger and his sister!* Re-checking a number of the stories readily ascertained that those not following Alger's pattern bore the equally recognizable style of Olive Augusta Cheney. Some indicated the hallmarks of both, suggesting probable collaboration.

Some of the Preston-signed short stories — which often appeared in publications in which Alger and/or Cheney items were also featured — include "The Silver Thimble," "Obadia Peabody's Wooing" and "Keeping School at Beanborough" (all in Gleason's Literary Companion, 1861); "Aunt Betsy's Horse," "Mr. Budlong's Courtship" and "Mrs. Houghton's Cat" (all in Gleason's Literary Companion, 1866-1867). No attempt will be made here to give a roster of the Preston writings. The name was more often used by Cheney than by Alger, and only added confusion could result. Suffice it to say that Horatio also made use of that pseudonym.

*   *   *

"Going through some Algers I just bought," a beginning collector wrote to me, "I come across what may be a rare oddity. The book's title is "A Cousin's Conspiracy," but now I see that it's exactly the same story as another Alger book I have, "The Young Bank Messenger." Can you tell me something about it?"

The book is neither rare nor an oddity, but is merely one of the more than two dozen original Alger stories that were later reissued under a different title. Some reissue titles are very similar to the original, just as "Mark Mason," "Mark Mason's Trials and Triumphs" and "Mark Mason's Triumph" are reissues of "Mark Mason's Victory." However, all of these are reissues of the story's original serial title, "A.D.T. 79." Very confusing!

In some instances a story won fame under the reissue title, while the original is little known (except to the advanced collector), and rarely seen. The title, "Dan, the Detective" was abandoned in favor of "Dan, the Newsboy," and the obscure "Western Boy," when changed to "Tom, the Bootblack," became one of Alger's best-known and most beloved works.

The story serialized as "Tony, the Tramp" appeared as a bound volume titled "Tony, the Hero." Years later it was re-issued under the original serial title. This occurred in a number of cases. A complete listing of reissue titles is included in the bibliography.

Four of Alger's stories appeared only in weekly or monthly story-papers, and never as books. "Marie Bertrand," the earliest, was serialized in New York Weekly in 1864. "Silas Snobden's Office Boy" was serialized in The Argosy, starting late in 1889, and "Cast Upon the Breakers" ran in the same periodical during 1893. The fourth story, "A Fancy of Hers," was printed as a full-length novel in the March, 1892, issue of Munsey's Magazine.

Munsey planned to issue "Silas Snobden's Office Boy" as a book, and he, in fact, announced this intention. However, his volume never appeared. Two years later — in 1891 — United States Book Company decided to publish the story, with the title slightly altered to "Mr. Snobden's Office Boy," in their

Leather-Clad Series of Adventure and Romance. They even went so far as to print a title page and deposit it with the Library of Congress. But they never issued the book either.

Over the years, publishers from time-to-time indicated intentions to print an Alger story, but for some reason did not. Nevertheless, these notices in periodicals, catalogues, advance lists of anticipated publications, and title page proofs deposited with the Library of Congress, have started Alger collectors off on false leads and time-effort-and-money-wasting hunts. "Ralph Raymond's Heir," mentioned elsewhere, is a probable example. Two others are "Tom Brace" and "Striving For Fortune" which United States Book Company scheduled for 1892, but their bankruptcy in 1891 prevented publication. Both properties eventually were acquired by Street & Smith, and issued by them in 1901.

From the point-of-view of the antiquarian book-seller, who must lay out hard cash to advertise for the wants of his customers — and whose income depends upon the books he can locate and sell — nothing equals for sheer annoyance a prolonged and expensive search for "ghosts."

These are spurious titles which will not be found because they never existed. There are, unfortunately, enough Alger ghosts to fill a long, phantom shelf. These are titles that sound as though they might be Algers; corruptions of sub-titles; intended and/or serial titles discarded in favor of the title eventually used, and an odd miscellaneous assortment that has no explainable origin.

Many Alger collectors — beginners almost invariably — clutter otherwise valid want lists with these non-existent titles. Listed below are some that have come to my attention over a period of more than thirty-five years. Where I have been able to trace their possible origin, I have done so. Collectors would be wise to remove from their want lists any of these titles for which they may be searching, and concentrate on the real ones. Dealers are advised to scratch them from their ads. There's simply no profit in them!

Adrift in the World. A story by Harriet Lewis, probably confused with Alger's "Adrift in New York," or "Adrift in the City."

Ben Barton's Battle.

Bound to Win. Listed as an Alger title in Hurst edition of "The Cash Boy." Later used as the series heading for a number of books with Alger-sounding titles. Author was indicated as Edwin Alger; publisher, Grosset & Dunlap.

Boy Guardian, The; or, Helping His Mother. Listed in Golden Argosy, 1886, as having been written by Arthur Lee Putnam. Perhaps a confusion with the sub-title of "Jack's Ward."

Cal Cooper's Triumph.

Dean Dexter.

Five Hundred Dollar Legacy. Although listed in a Porter & Coates advertisement, this title apparently was never issued.

For Home and Honor. David McKay reissue of a Street & Smith story by Victor St. Clair. The book's cover and spine clearly — but incorrectly — show Horatio Alger, Jr., as the author. An oddity.

Frank Farnham's Motto. Listed in Golden Argosy, 1886, as having been written by Arthur Lee Putnam.

Frank Mason's Secret. Listed as an Alger title in a Donohue printing of "Luke Walton."

Frank Starr's Purpose. During the late 1860's Erastus F. Beadle issued a dime novel series titled Frank Starr's American Novels. Starr was chief of Beadle's print shop at that time.

Hobart, the Hired Boy.

Last Word, The. An error possibly influenced by Alger's Civil War poem, "Last Words." A story by Stephen Crane carries the same title.

Making of a Man, The. Probably a confusion with "Making a Man of Himself," by Oliver Optic (William T. Adams).

Ned Nestor's Plan.

Plan and Prosper.

Rags to Riches. A commonly used description of Alger stories, but never appeared as a book title.

Rattling Good Story, A. Listed in Street & Smith catalogues, naming Alger as author. This phrase was merely a temporary filler-title assigned to Medal Library releases that, at press-time, remained untitled or unselected. The designation was listed three times, the slots ultimately filled by "Jed, the Poorhouse Boy," "Helping Himself" and "The Tin Box."

Sandy Stone.

Tom Turner. An obvious confusion with "Tom Turner's Legacy."

Toward the Top.

True and Trusty; or, The Boy Hero. Listed in Golden Argosy, 1886, as having been written by Arthur Lee Putnam.

Up the Ladder. This was the serialization title of "Risen From The Ranks," but was never used as an Alger book title. However, it was the title of a book by Lieutenant Murray, a pen-name of Maturin M. Ballou.

Way to Success. Either a confusion with series heading of four Alger volumes published by Porter & Coates, or with "The Way to Success; or, Tom Randall," by Alfred Oldfellow.

Young Entertainer, The. Possibly a remote confusion with "The Young Actor," by Gayle Winterton.

Young Soldier, The. Perhaps a confusion of the Stratemeyer "completion," "Young Captain Jack; or, The Son of a Soldier."

WHAT ARE THEY WORTH?

MANY OF ALGER'S BOOKS regularly bring high prices. Others have little value. Too often, relatively late reprints — discovered during a long-overdue attic cleaning — are offered at disproportionately high figures, the owners believing they have unearthed an imperial treasure. Occasionally, however, these same attics, cellars or barns contain a very rare book.

"What can I get for these old Algers?" the owner frequently asks.

"What should I sell them for?" dealers want to know, because many just don't understand the comparative values of the hundreds of editions issued over more than half a century by dozens of publishers.

Finally, the collector — eager to own them — asks: "What shall I pay?"

The Alger market is a lush one, and will so continue during the years to come, because this material becomes scarcer — while demand increases — every day. Also, in addition to first edition and reprint books, collectors seek the serializations of his novels, and the many short stories and poems that appeared in week-lies and monthlies throughout his long writing career. His man-uscript material, which is hard to come by, also commands im-pressively increasing prices.

Before assigning dollar values to the vast assortment of Alger material, let us try to determine how much of this still is extant, and how to get it.

Although Horatio Alger, Jr., died in 1899, his books re-mained in print, profusely, up to the mid-1920's. Street & Smith maintained their Alger Series, listing some forty of his titles until well into the Thirties. Although his first book was published in 1856, followed by a half-dozen more during the decade that followed, it wasn't until book publication of "Ragged Dick" in 1868 (it had been serialized during 1867), that Alger became a best-selling author. His works maintained this status through the era of World War I, when horizons of young readers ex-panded to the battlefields across the seas, adventure in high-flying airplanes and dirigibles, and to tales of crossing the con-tinent by speedy automobile and motorcycle.

During the generations in-between, uncounted millions of books by Alger were read by the youth of a nation still young, still growing. Some estimates go as high as 400,000,000 copies sold. The most conservative score numbers a mere 100,000,000. Quentin Reynolds, in his book, "The Fiction Factory," puts the figure at 250,000,000, adding "it may well be that his books . . . sold more copies than the works of any American writer before or since."

And some of these books still exist. There may remain more Alger books tucked away in bookcases and storage areas of old homesteads than are presently numbered in the known Alger col-lections, of which there are several thousand. Seeking these old volumes, incidentally, is not limited to private collectors. In ad-dition to such major collections as exist in the Library of Congress, the New York Public Library, New York Historical Society and the Huntington Library at San Marino, California, splendid Al-ger sections also are maintained at Princeton, Harvard, Dart-mouth, the University of Indiana and other universities and famed institutions.

Besides purely Alger accumulations, there is a far greater number of general and specialist collections to which a single specific Alger title — or group of titles — is integral. For instance, Civil War collections value "Frank's Campaign;" Lincoln libraries want "Abraham Lincoln, the Backwoods Boy;" railroad collections include "The Erie Train Boy" and "The Train Boy." Other Alger works fit neatly into such groups as Western U.S., American Indians, New Yorkiana, circusiana, American literature, general hero fiction and many, many other categories. "Ragged Dick" and "Tattered Tom" are regularly sought for inclusion in any number of essentially non-Alger collections.

As these books were read by boys — as well as by a surprisingly large number of their sisters — we can assume that they often received somewhat less than gentle handling. Most volumes, after the original owner had finished, were passed along (often swapped) to waiting friends, the routine continuing until the covers were loose or fallen away, pages torn or missing. To gauge the rate of disintegration of these old books over the greater part of a century, just glance at the children's book-shelf and check the condition of some they received as recently as last Christmas!

Add to the quantities that disappeared through normal use and discard, the tons tossed onto garbage heaps when, occasionally, they were denounced as trash. When this occurred, primarily during the early 1900's, some libraries emptied their shelves of Horatio's stories, and many parents felt obliged to do the same.

Those, then, that were spared are collectors' items. Many are considered rare books, priced accordingly. They are more expensive — and certainly more difficult to find — than the books written by most of the other prominent juvenile writers of Alger's era.

While Algers rarely remain unsold longer than it takes the dealer to notify a customer that he has one, it is a comparatively simple matter to locate any number of books by Oliver Optic, Harry Castlemon, Edward S. Ellis, G. A. Henty, Capt. Mayne Reid and the others who were popular generations back, but today are hardly as well remembered as Horatio Alger, Jr.

Whereas Algers generally turn up singly or in twos it is not unusual for the works of his contemporaries to line dealers' shelves in complete series. For some reason, they often are available in much better condition than the Algers but, even so, they bring lower prices. Optic first editions, with the exception of one or two, can be picked up for a couple of dollars each. Few first editions of any of these authors cost more than $5.00, with a rarity perhaps marked at $10.00 (although there is a fabulous Henty worth several hundred). Algers are worth more, in many instances *much* more.

✻   ✻   ✻

Although first editions are most avidly sought, and bring higher prices, there are collectors who are quite content to build up the most complete set possible of reprints. It is the enjoyable reading that interests them, not intrinsic value nor sturdier bindings.

In the course of amassing an Alger library, the collector must decide how far he wishes to go, and how much he will spend. The specialist desiring shelves filled exclusively with first editions could conceivably spend as much as approximately $6,000 for a fairly complete set. This is based upon dealer and catalogue prices, and necessarily upon a number of estimates. It does not take into consideration that he might be lucky enough to get quite a few bargains at lower costs.

On the other hand, the collector satisfied with reprints may ultimately near completion, spending only between less than $350.00 and $700.00, depending upon whether his reprints were issued by New York Book Company or Donohue, or by publishers whose editions bring more. However, it is necessary to point out that a number of Algers (such as "Grand'ther Baldwin's Thanksgiving," "Timothy Crump's Ward," "Nothing to Do," and perhaps one or two others) appeared only in a first edition and were not later reissued by other publishers.

This bibliography, then, is intended to give the collector — as well as to the book-seller, librarian and literary historian — as much information as I have been able to gather over more than one third of a century.

The list, which contains every original title, as well as the changed reissue titles, also includes clues that make it easy to recognize which is a first edition and which is not. Full background information (serialization dates, peculiarities, pseudonyms, copyright data, etc.) is also supplied.

For many readers, probably the most important and useful feature of this compilation is the cash value assigned to each item. It is most necessary to point out, at the start, that these are prices asked by dealers and/or others who are familiar with the Alger trade. These definitely are *not* prices paid at thrift shops or country auctions.

Nor are these the prices paid by the thousands of book-scouts and 'pickers' — the Alger collector's best friends — who, either as a business or profitable pastime, regularly attend the barn sales in their vicinity. These are the hunters who frequently are called in to survey the treasure or trash discards of spring-cleaning. They get first crack at the contents of a home soon to be abandoned or demolished. Many of these scouts keep and refer to the want lists of their 'clients,' and have been successful in finding the most obscure and valuable Alger items. While many are frankly interested in being book-detectives for the added income it provides, others seek these wants primarily as a sideline to pursuing the rarities of their own hobbies, which may be old buttons, cylindrical phonograph records, antique glassware or the works of other authors.

These, rather, are the prices that knowledgeable, reputable booksellers have asked for their merchandise. They are based upon individual quotations and upon prices listed in catalogues. Also considered in a number of these rates is the amount the book brought at auction. However, auctions are attended by the trade and those figures should be judged as wholesale. The dealer must still add to them his own expenses and fair profit.

Considering the age of Alger's books — and the stern handling to which their youthful owners sometimes subjected them — these prices are based upon books being in a *good, sturdy condition.* They are not based upon what the trade refers to as "mint," "pristine" or "uncut" state, for Alger's works are too rarely found in such condition to warrant that as being set as the standard.

Also keep in mind that these are current prices. Inasmuch as they are substantially higher than they were but a few years ago, they will probably continue to rise.

Considering, for the moment, cash values of *reprints* only (these are the relatively late printings by publishers that, in most instances, did not issue Alger first editions) let us establish an applicable rule-of-thumb listing of their worth. That is, the price paid by the collector. After the price range appears names of publishers whose books fall into each category. There are exceptions noted, just as exceptional reprints are acknowledged in the first edition bibliography.

Valued at $3.00 or less: W. L. Allison Company; Bonanza Books; Cincinnati Publishing Company; Collier Books; Commercial Bookbinding Co.; M. A. Donohue & Co. (except "Wren Winter's Triumph," which is worth $4.00 — $5.00); Federal Book Company; Goldsmith Publishing Company; Holly Publishing Co.; MacLellan Publishers; Mutual Book Company; New Werner Company; New World Book Company; New York Book Company; Odyssey Press; Saalfield Publishing Company; Stuyvesant Press; Superior Printing Company; Trade Publishing Company; Value Books; Arthur Westbrook Company; Whitman Publishing Company; World Publishing Company; World Syndicate Publishing Company.

Valued at $3.00 — $7.50: A. L. Burt (includes the cheaper, generally later, reprints); Chatterton-Peck Company (not to be confused with their first edition Stratemeyer "completion"); Consolidated Retail Booksellers; Cupples & Leon (not to be confused with their first edition Stratemeyer "completions"); Grosset & Dunlap; Holt, Rinehart and Winston; Hurst & Company (not including "Bertha's Christmas Vision," see Bibliography); David McKay, Publisher; McLoughlin Brothers; Mershon Company (not to be confused with their first edition Stratemeyer "completions"); New York Publishing Company; Stitt Publishing Company (not to be confused with their first edition Stratemeyer "completions"); Vickery and Hill Publishing Company; John Wanamaker; John C. Winston Company.

Valued at $7.50 — $15.00: Aldine Publishing Company; A. L. Burt (includes the earlier reprints); H. M. Caldwell Company; Henry T. Coates & Co. (not to confused with Coates' first edition Algers); Crown Publishers; Porter & Coates (this pertains only to Porter & Coates reprints of Alger stories originally published by A. K. Loring); Thompson & Thomas.

Valued at $12.50 — $20.00, or more: American Publishers
Corp.; Book Club of California (their only Alger publication, "The Young Miner" — a fine limited edition — sold
at auction in 1969 for $47.50); DeWolfe-Fiske & Co.; In-
ternational Book Company; Street & Smith (includes
hard cover volumes only. For Medal Library and New
Medal Library first editions see Bibliography. Medal Library and new Medal Library reprints bring about $7.00.
Alger Series paperbacks are worth somewhat less.

It is only slightly more difficult to assign a price-measuring
device to the later printings of Alger titles issued by publishing
houses that also printed the first editions. This group includes
A. K. Loring, Porter & Coates, Henry T. Coates, Penn Publishing, and others that released only one or two Alger books. A
reasonable estimate is approximately one-third to one-half of
the value set for the first edition in the bibliography. This range
is flexible enough to allow for the slightly higher prices asked
for scarcer titles.

About the time that many collectors achieve a good as-
semblage of reprints, and they have acquired a sampling of first
editions — for some are relatively easy to obtain — they may
plunge into the vast, unchartered sea of Horatio Alger's story-
paper output.

While this includes the newspaper and magazine serializations of his stories, it also concerns his many short stories,
articles, poems, ballads and odes.

As indicated in the bibliography, many of Alger's tales first
appeared in the popular story-papers of his era. Some collectors
and dealers consider these to be the *real* first editions, as they
represent the very first printing of the story. While many collectors cherish these clumsy antiques, just as many limit their
hobby to collecting Alger's books.

Fortunately, it was the practice, during the Nineteenth Century, for subscribers to keep each issue of the publication. Then,
at the end of six months or a year, they would return the loose

copies to the publisher who, for a nominal price, permanently bound them between hard covers. The boards generally were either marbled or cloth-covered, the spine frequently made of leather, decorated with raised ribbing and the publication's name and the year stamped in gold.

In addition to being rather bulky, the paper sheets have often become brittle and the pages detached from the binding. Nevertheless, collectors who want them pay the price, and they will accept individual or sheafs of loose copies when the bound volume is not available.

The range of sizes of these periodicals varies from the standard book-size of Student and Schoolmate (in which "Ragged Dick," "Fame and Fortune," and other early tales first appeared) to the giant, old-fashioned newspaper format of New York Weekly ("Brave and Bold," "The Western Boy," etc.).

The prices asked by dealers range between $1.50 and $3.00 for each individual loose number. The bound volumes which, of course, are preferable with the contents usually in better condition, often sell for a disproportionately higher price.

While these prices are not low, it is not difficult to understand the dealer's contention that, in selling the bound volume, he deprives himself of the chance to sell to other customers articles by Ned Buntline, Oliver Optic, Harry Castlemon and other top authors of that period, whose stories were included in the same volume.

The listing of Alger's minor efforts, which is appended to the bibliography, probably is incomplete. While it contains many of his short stories, poems, etc. — perhaps most of them — others, as yet undiscovered, should still come to light.

The price range is wider among these items than with the serializations. It takes more searching to find them and the figure quoted sometimes includes the entire bound volume, although the poem or short story fills less than a page. A book-scout who comes across this type of material is pleased to sell at five dollars, whether it be a page in a loose individual copy or bound in a year's run. A dealer might have to double that price. Remember that he has to buy it (perhaps from the scout, or he could have travelled two hundred miles into the country where he bought it as part of a library). Then he must keep it until a customer comes along. All this is figured into the ultimate cost to the collector.

Probably the most specialized Alger product to entrance collectors is his manuscript material. This includes signatures — all his admirers wanted them and Horatio never disappointed his young friends — letters, short manuscripts, inscribed books, photographs and miscellaneous.

The author's signatures were much in demand and he gave them to all who asked. His daily mail was filled with requests and, as a matter of fact, the majority of autographed letters that are found deal with that subject. Alger invariably answered his own mail and, when his signature was requested, he carefully inscribed it on a small white card and enclosed it with a cordial letter, thanking the writer for asking.

His neat signature he almost invariably wrote as "Yours Faithfully, Horatio Alger, Jr.," followed by the date. In order to save time, while hurrying to appointments or travelling out of town, he would prepare the signed cards in advance, handing them out to all who wanted one.

For those who came to him with autograph albums he inscribed a special sentiment. It was a short verse that he constructed principally of titles of some of his books, admonishing disciples to

Strive and Succeed! The world's temptations flee;
Be Brave and Bold! and Strong and Steady be!
Shift for yourself, and prosper then you must;
Win Fame and Fortune while you Try and Trust!

Another autograph that he wrote in letters, as well as in presentation copies of his books, was the final stanza of his often reprinted poem, "Carving a Name." It apparently was his favorite during later years, for he often wrote

If I would have my name endure,
I'll write it in the hearts of men
In characters of living light
From kindly deeds and actions wrought,
And these, beyond the reach of time,
Shall live, immortal as my thought.

There are no known manuscripts of his published books. The one full story manuscript that still exists, "Mabel Parker" (described in the Bibliography), never was printed. Probably main responsibility for the absence of these articles lay in the practice that the printers setting type for the stories traditionally became owners of the papers they handled. Apparently, most of the typesetters — rather than keep these — let them fall to the composing room floor, only to be swept away. Even if a printer had had the foresight to save the loose sheets, he probably would not have accumulated a full set, as the work invariably was divided among many men.

A simple Horatio Alger, Jr., signature — on card or paper — would be worth about $12.50. Any more extensive autograph, say accompanying a short verse, personalized greeting or other brief message, would cost about $25.00; more if written on a photograph. His letters and private papers are valued at $40.00 to $75.00 and more, depending upon length, interest and importance. A short article or one of his poems would easily bring $150.00 — $200.00 and the manuscript of a complete Alger story, if one were ever to appear on the market, would rate much higher. Such an item, however, would have to be examined before appraisal could be established.

Alger's presentation inscription in one of his books generally is worth the value of the autograph plus the value of the book (such writing generally appeared in first editions), adding about twenty-five percent extra because of the interesting combination.

At best, the prices indicated can only serve as a guide. Just as it was pointed out that a valuable first edition can sometimes be bought for a small fraction of its retail sales value — and, indeed, almost every Alger collector enjoys retelling how he bought a rare-as-hens-teeth first edition for a dime — so is it likely that he would occasionally pay far more for a book than its value (and better judgment) dictates.

It's entirely a question of how badly the edition is wanted, and how much the buyer will pay. When offering a title that has long been sought, the owner may well ask more for it than if he feels his book is not that important to the collector. If the prospective buyer is well-heeled, the asking price could be higher than to one whom the seller knows will only go up to a certain figure, and not a cent higher. If the collector has been searching for a single elusive part of a magazine serialization to complete the run, that chapter may well cost as much (or more) than all the other installments combined. The cost of a hard-to-get item has also been inflated by pitting a number of ardent buyers against each other, and selling to the highest bidder. An annoying practice, certainly, but I have never yet met a top bidder who regretted the price he had to pay. He only treasured his prize all the more!

It is, nevertheless, just as important to point out that the greater majority of book-scouts, dealers and collectors prefer to stick to the square deal. Most scouts I have dealt with — many for a number of years — prefer to add a respectable profit to their cost and make a quick sale. A number of them have occasionally put me on the spot by saying they will accept my appraisal as to the book's worth.

By far, the majority of antiquarian book-sellers try to establish the fair value of the book and offer it on a take-it-or-leave-it basis. Their business depends upon keeping stock moving, and creating trust and esteem among their clientele.

While a number of absurd and infuriating offers (that were more like demands for ransom) quickly come to mind, I recall, just as readily, the reputable West Coast dealer who asked me but five dollars for the rare United States Book Company hardcover edition of "The $500 Check" (with tipped-in title page). Although his specialty lay in another field of literature, he had my want list and could have assumed I would pay more. Then there is the internationally known New York bookman who sold me a group of Lorings — including a few first editions — at a very moderate price. They were part of a library he purchased in order to capture some priceless antique volumes, and he was quite willing to sell these to me at a low figure. He knew I'd have paid more, but 'scalping' just isn't his game.

Then there are the many Alger collectors who delight in helping a fellow-enthusiast add a long-needed volume to his shelf. There was the swapper who — in the early days of my collecting — sent me a crate filled with Alger reprints in return for a set of old lantern-slide scenes of "The Land of the Midnight Sun" that he was equally eager to own. And there is the unknown benefactor who, apparently having read my ads, mailed me his first edition copy of "Helen Ford." The parcel contained no note, and there was no return address. He didn't even give me a chance to say "Thank you!"

SOME TERMS EXPLAINED

TECHNICAL LANGUAGE OF MOST PROFESSIONS is mysterious (or, at very least, unclear) to the layman. Likewise, a number of book terms — like the Latin favored in medicine and law — often are obscure to the non-professional.

As this bibliography is intended for use by all echelons of interest in the writing of Horatio Alger, Jr., effort has been made to avoid the technical jargon wherever possible.

However, a number of words, for which there are no simplifications, must be used. But some of these are self-explanatory, and others may also be familiar, as they appear in book offers and catalogues.

This brief glossary lists these, assigning to each *only the meaning specifically applicable to Alger's works*. These are not necessarily standard nor all-inclusive definitions, and some of their meanings have been omitted when not pertaining to books listed on the following pages.

BLIND-STAMPED: Design or printing stamped onto the cloth binding, but without the use of color.

COLLATION: The order and sequence in which pages, illustrations, etc., are bound into the book.

COVER SIZE: As an aid to identification of first editions, the height and width of books' covers are listed. It serves no purpose to indicate thickness (as often is described in non-professional book offers) as this dimension varies considerably due to climate and shelf conditions.

12mo (duodecimo): Trade term for book size with page height approximately seven to eight inches.

16mo (sextodecimo): Trade term for book size with page height approximately six to seven inches.

DECORATIVE TITLE PAGE: Many of Alger's books, especially those published by A. K. Loring, had an illustrated page (often facing frontispiece) on which variously appeared such matter as the story title, series heading, Alger's by-line and a scene descriptive of either the story or the series of which the story may be a part. This page usually appears immediately in front of the title page.

END-PAPER: The paper lining facing and attached to the front and back covers of the book.

FIRST EDITION: The first printing of the story as a bound volume.

FLY-LEAF: The blank page or pages following and preceding end-papers at front and back of the book.

FRONTISPIECE: Story illustration at front of book, generally facing either the title page or decorative title page.

GHOSTS: Titles that never existed.

HARD COVERS: Among Alger editions, this most frequently refers to the cloth-bound covers. However, the pictorial cardboard bindings of the cheaper Donohue (and similar) issues also fall into this category.

ODDITY: A volume apparently different from the way it was intended to be published. For instance, text bound-in upside-down between the covers (the Library of Congress has a first edition of "Ragged Dick" in this condition); Alger's name erroneously appearing under title of a story he never wrote (the cover and spine of the David McKay edition of "For Home and Honor" — actually written by Victor St. Clair — incorrectly list Alger as author); an Alger story bound between covers produced for another book, indicating another title and author (a number of examples noted, usually among late reprints); an unusual, hitherto unreported state of a book (specimens noted in the bibliography). There are numerous oddities, varying and confusing.

PAPERBACK: The same as *paper wrappers*. The book bound in paper covers.

POINTS: Changes in typography, collation, etc., through which different states or editions can be identified.

REISSUE: Has the same general meaning as *reprint*. An edition published after the original. Many reissues of Alger stories were published with the titles varied or completely different from the original issue.

SERIAL: Many of Alger's stories appeared in parts, as weekly or monthly installments in periodicals.

SERIES: Numerous Alger books were issued in series, or groups of individual titles under a general heading. For instance, A. K. Loring issued six titles under the Ragged Dick Series, three under the Campaign Series, etc. Later however, A. L. Burt issued a random selection of Algers in their catch-all Chimney Corner Series, and Street & Smith included in their Alger Series dozens of titles by Horatio Alger as well as some by other authors.

STATE: In this bibliography, *state* indicates condition caused by early physical changes (typographical, illustration, binding, etc.) in the book.

STORY-PAPER: Weekly and monthly periodicals (issued either in newspaper or magazine format) in which the serializations of Alger's stories — as well as much of his minor output — originally appeared.

TITLE PAGE: Page at front of book (always a right-hand page) on which is listed title, author, publisher and city of publication. The issue (and whether volume is a first edition) can be determined by the date at bottom of title page. Unfortunately, this information appears all too infrequently in Alger's books.

VERSO: The even-numbered (or left-hand) pages of the book.

THE BIBLIOGRAPHY
OF
ALGER'S WORKS

ABNER HOLDEN'S BOUND BOY. See "Try and Trust."

ABRAHAM LINCOLN. See "Abraham Lincoln, the Backwoods Boy."

ABRAHAM LINCOLN, THE BACKWOODS BOY.
John R. Anderson & Henry S. Allen, 1883
TITLE PAGE: (Boyhood and Manhood Series of Illustrious Americans.)/
[Rule]/ Abraham Lincoln,/ The/ Backwoods Boy;/ or,/ How a
Young Rail-Splitter/ Became President./ By/ Horatio Alger, Jr.,/
Author of "The Boyhood and Manhood of James A. Garfield,"/
"Luck and Pluck," Etc., Etc./ New York:/ John R. Anderson &
Henry S. Allen,/ 66 & 68 Reade Street./ 1883.
BINDING: Bound in pictorial stamped cloth. Several colors noted, including
red, green, blue, brown, tan and gray. A study of type wear indicates
red to be the earliest and gray the latest colors used. Cover design,
stamped in black: Illustrious American Series/ Abraham Lincoln
Signing the Emancipation Proclamation (illustration set in circle)/
The Backwoods Boy (illustration set in diamond, shows Lincoln as
a boy)/ [background design of lined rules, leaves, dots, etc.]
Stamped in gold: The/ Backwoods/ Boy/ or How/ A Young/ Rail-
splitter/ Became/ President./ Horatio Alger Jr. Spine: [Line rules]/
Illustrious/ American/ Series/ [grain design with double borders]/
(title stamped in black on gold background: The/ Backwoods/ Boy/
How/ He Became/ President)/ Horatio Alger Jr./ [scroll-and-plume
design]/ [rules]/ (blind-stamped on gold background: J. R.
Anderson/ &/ H. S. Allen)/ [rules]. Blind-stamped border design
on back cover. Cover size: 5" x 7".

COLLATION: Yellow-tinted end-paper; fly-leaf; frontispiece; tissue-covered portrait of Lincoln; title page [p. i]; copyright notice dated 1883 [p. ii]; dedication [p. iii]; page of book advertisements [p. iv]; preface, [pp. v - 6]; contents, [pp. vii - 8]; text pp. 9 - 307; book advertisements, 2 leaves (4 pp.); inserted fly-leaf; yellow-tinted end-paper. In addition to frontispiece and Lincoln portrait are three full-page illustrations.

In the first edition, page of publisher's ads at front of book indicates this title as Number 2 in "The Boyhood and Manhood Series of Illustrious Americans." "From Canal Boy to President" is listed as Number 1, with Number 3, "The Surveyor Boy and President" (not by Alger) projected as "Ready early in October." It also has dedication as insert on a single leaf.

Title page was deposited for copyright early in 1883 with the proposed title designated as "The Backwoods Boy," and re-deposited later the same year as "Abraham Lincoln." The actual book was deposited for copyright September 17, 1883. Later reissued in paperback by Street & Smith as New Medal Library #519, titled "The Backwoods Boy; the Story of Abraham Lincoln." Lists indicate possibility of an even later reissue as "The Young Rail-Splitter," probably a paperback.

Value of first edition is $30.00.

ADRIFT IN NEW YORK; or, Tom and Florence Braving the World.

By the time this enigmatic title appeared between hard covers — the edition published by A. L. Burt Company — towards the end of 1904, the story had already appeared in five separate and varied formats.

The title was first deposited for copyright in 1889. It was registered as a "drama" by Norman L. Munro, and appeared the same year in his Family Story Paper. A dozen years later it reappeared in Golden Hours, the serial starting on September 14, 1901.

"Adrift in New York" was next published in May and June, 1902, as a separate two-part supplement to Comfort Magazine, a publication "devoted to art, literature, science and the home circle." Comfort was published by W. H. Gannett, at Augusta, Maine, and claimed a circulation of 1,250,000. An advertisement at the end of Part I promises "other interesting and ex· citing stories by Horatio Alger, Jr."

The Comfort subscription price was — for some unexplained reason — listed as 10¢ for six months; 25¢ a year. The offer tempted new subscribers with a "free, postpaid copy of the complete story of 'Adrift in New York' in paper book form." If this volume ever was published by Gannett it has long since disappeared, for no copies are known today. These two parts, each 32 pages and printed on rough pulp-stock paper, constitute the authentic first edition of "Adrift in New York."

The following year — on October 31, 1903 — the story, somewhat abridged, was published by Street & Smith in Brave and Bold #45. This was a large-sized, flat five-center with a colorful front cover showing Tom, the hero, rescuing a bearded old man from a club-wielding ruffian. In 1904 "Adrift in New York" started taking on more respectable form as a book when Street & Smith reissued it, on January 30th, as #243 of their paperback Medal Library series.

For the Comfort Magazine two-part supplement, the avid collector would readily pay $17.50 each for the individual sections and proportionately higher if lucky enough to get both parts in reasonable condition. Brave and Bold #45 is occasionally offered at about $7.50. Medal Library #243 is worth $15.00.

ADRIFT IN THE CITY; or, Oliver Conrad's Plucky Fight.
Porter & Coates, 1895

TITLE PAGE: Adrift in the City/ or/ Oliver Conrad's Plucky/ Fight/ By/ Horatio Alger, Jr./ Author of "Ragged Dick" Series, "Tattered Tom"/ Series, "Luck and Pluck" Series/ [publisher's trade-mark device]/ Philadelphia/ Porter & Coates.

BINDING: Tan cloth. Cover design, stamped in blue and black: [Decorative blue ribbon border along top and left side]/ [blue sunburst with title, printed in blue, at center]/ By/ Horatio Alger, Jr./ [black ribbon design at lower right]./ Spine, stamped in blue, black and gold: [Blue ribbon]/ [blue sunburst with title, printed in gold, at center]/ By/ Horatio/ Alger/ Jr./ [publisher's "P & C" monogram]. Cover size: 5⅛" x 7⅜".

COLLATION: Dark brown coated end-paper; two fly-leaves; tissue-covered frontispiece; title page [p. i]; copyright notice dated 1895 [p. ii]; contents, pp. iii — iv; text, pp. [1] — 325; book advertisements, 1 leaf (2 pp.); fly-leaf; dark brown coated end-paper. In addition to frontispiece are three full-page illustrations.

This story first appeared as a serial in Street & Smith's New York Weekly, in 1887, as "Oliver the Outcast." In 1892 Street & Smith again serialized the story — this time as "Adrift in the City" — in Good News. Porter & Coates deposited the title for copyright in 1895 and published a very small first edition before going out of business (the same year) and being taken over by Henry T. Coates & Co. I have, in my library, Horatio Alger's personal copy of this title. It is the Coates edition, dated November 19, 1895, in Alger's handwriting. Close examination of type-wear indicates virtually no difference between the two editions, which are identical in every way except for the publisher's name at bottom of title page. Although not designated as such in the original edition, this story later was listed by Coates as Volume Two of their Victory Series.

The Porter & Coates edition is rare, and easily worth $37.00. The Coates edition brings about $20.00.

A.D.T. 79. See "Mark Mason's Victory."

ADVENTURES OF A NEW YORK TELEGRAPH BOY. See "Number 91."

ADVENTURES OF A TELEGRAPH BOY. See "Number 91."

ANDY BURKE'S FORTUNE. See "Only an Irish Boy."

ANDY GORDAN. See "Forging Ahead."

ANDY GORDON. See "Forging Ahead."

ANDY GRANT'S PLUCK.

Henry T. Coates & Co., 1902

TITLE PAGE: Andy Grant's/ Pluck./ By/ Horatio Alger, Jr.,/ Author of "Ragged Dick Series," "Tattered Tom Series,"/ "Luck and Pluck Series," Etc./ [line rule]/ Philadelphia/ Henry T. Coates & Co.

BINDING: Tan cloth. Cover design, stamped in white, black and brown: [Single black line around border]/ title in white/ [illustration shows hobo halting a horse and carriage driven by boy]/ Horatio/ Alger/ Jr. Spine: [Black line rule at top]/ title in white/ [white line]/ (in white: Horatio/ Alger Jr.)/ [boy standing]/ (in white: Henry T. Coates/ & Co.)/ [black line rule at bottom]. Cover size: 5" x 7½".

COLLATION. Dark brown coated end-paper; tissue-covered frontispiece; title page [p. i]; copyright notice dated 1902 [p. ii]; contents, pp. iii – iv; text, pp. 1 – 335; blank; book advertisements, pp. [1] – 10; fly-leaf; dark brown coated end-paper. In addition to the frontis piece are three full-page illustrations.

"Andy Grant's Pluck" was serialized in Argosy, published by Frank A. Munsey & Company, in 1895. On January 3, 1902, Coates deposited the title for copyright, and later deposited the complete book on July 1, 1902. In the first edition, this title is not listed in the publisher's advertisements at back of the book.

Value of first edition is $20.00.

BACKWOODS BOY, THE. See "Abraham Lincoln, the Backwoods Boy."

BACKWOODS BOY, THE; The Story of Abraham Lincoln. See "Abraham Lincoln, the Backwoods Boy."

BAD LOT, A. See "Bernard Brooks' Adventures."

BEN BARCLAY'S COURAGE. See "The Store Boy."

BEN BRUCE; Scenes in the Life of a Bowery Newsboy.

A. L. Burt, 1901

TITLE PAGE: Ben Bruce./ Scenes in the Life of a/ Bowery Newsboy./ By Horatio Alger, Jr./ Author of "Joe's Luck," "Tom the Bootblack," "Dan the/ Newsboy," "The Errand Boy," etc., etc./ With illustrations by J. Watson Davis./ New York:/ A. L. Burt, Publisher.

BINDING: Dark olive green cloth. Cover design, stamped in red, yellow and black: Black and yellow border divides cover into three panels. Title is stamped in red in the top (horizontal) panel/ below it, [illustration of boy with stick and bundle over his shoulder in left perpendicular panel]/ [red and yellow floral design in right perpendicular panel]. Spine: Title blind-stamped against gold background/ Alger (in gold)/ [floral design]/ A. L. Burt — New York (in red) at bottom. Cover size: 5¼" x 7½".

COLLATION: Light brown floral-designed end-paper; frontispiece; title page [p. i]; copyright notices dated 1892, by Frank A. Munsey, and 1901, by A. L. Burt [p. ii]; contents, pp. iii - iv; text, pp. 1 - 313; book advertisements, pp. [1] - 8; light brown floral-designed end-paper. In addition to the frontispiece are four full-page illustrations.

Book title was registered by Burt on March 11, 1901, and the book deposited for copyright June 19, 1901. "Ben Bruce" had previously been serialized in Argosy in 1892 - 1893, carrying as author's name Alger's pseudonym, Arthur Lee Putnam. Apparently United States Book Company planned to issue it as a paperback in their Leather-Clad Tales of Adventure and Romance series, but went bankrupt before they could do so. In 1908, Street & Smith reissued the story — titled "Ben Bruce; or, Only a Bowery Newsboy" — as Number 462 of the New Medal Library.

The first edition of this book is identified by the imprinting on the spine. Only the first edition has the title blind-stamped against a solid gold background with, below it, the name "Alger." Later editions had the title stamped in gold against the book's dark olive green cloth with, below it, the name "Horatio Alger."

Value of first edition is $15.00.

BEN LOGAN'S TRIUMPH; or, The Boys of Boxwood Academy.
Cupples & Leon Co., 1908

TITLE PAGE: Ben Logan's Triumph/ Or/ The Boys of Boxwood Academy/ By/ Horatio Alger, Jr./ Author of "Joe, the Hotel Boy," "Out for Business,"/ "Nelson, the Newsboy," "Ragged Dick Series," Etc./ Illustrated/ New York/ Cupples & Leon Co.

BINDING: Light tan cloth. Cover design, stamped in red and black: [Black line borders entire cover]./ Title stamped in red in upper right corner/ [illustration of farm boy, holding rake, standing near red barn, with chicken beside him]/ Horatio Alger, Jr. (in black) along bottom of cover. Spine: Ben/ Logan's/ Triumph/ Horatio/ Alger, Jr/ (publisher's name in a circle: Cupples/ & Leon/ Co.). Cover size: 5⅛" x 7½".

COLLATION: End-paper; frontispiece; copyright notice dated 1908; contents, 2 pp.; preface, 2 pp.; text, pp. 1 - 237; book advertisements, 5 pp.; end-paper. In addition to the frontispiece are three full-page illustrations.

Title was deposited for copyright on March 25, 1908, and the book received by the Library of Congress on June 18th of that year. Although Horatio Alger, Jr., is listed as the author, this story is certainly the work of Edward Stratemeyer's fiction syndicate, and "Ben Logan's Triumph" is one of the eleven "Algers" they produced between 1900 and 1908. It is interesting to note that advertisements at the back of this volume list only books turned out by Stratemeyer's writers. The first edition will carry these two obvious clues:

1. The Cupples & Leon Co. name on the spine is printed in a circle. This circle was eliminated from the design in ensuing editions.
2. In a box on the copyright page are listed "Books by Horatio Alger, Jr." "Ben Logan's Triumph" is listed second (after "Joe, the Hotel Boy). There should be no other titles indicated.

Value of first edition is $25.00.

392

BEN'S NUGGET; or, A Boy's Search for Fortune.

Porter & Coates, 1882

TITLE PAGE: Ben's Nugget;/ or,/ A Boy's Search for Fortune./ A Story of the Pacific Coast./ By/ Horatio Alger, Jr.,/ Author of "Ragged Dick," "Tattered Tom," "Luck and Pluck,"/ "Brave and Bold Series," Etc., Etc./ [publisher's trade mark device]/ Philadelphia:/ Porter & Coates.

BINDING: Dark Brown cloth. Cover design, stamped in black: Title at top/ [branch of leaves and berries against line-and-floral panel at center]/ at lower right: Alger. Spine: Lines/ title in black against solid gold background/ [leaves and berries]/ Alger (blind-stamped against solid gold background, with gold grill-work design above and below)/ Porter & Coates (blind-stamped against solid gold background). Cover size: 4¾" x 6⅞".

COLLATION: Dark brown coated end-paper; fly-leaf; frontispiece; tissue-covered decorative title-page [p. 1]; blank, [p. 2]; title page [p. 3]; copyright notice dated 1882 [p. 4]; dedication [p. 5]; blank [p. 6]; preface, pp. 7 - 8; contents, pp. 9 - 12; text, pp. 13 - 275; fly-leaf dark brown coated end-paper.

"Ben's Nugget" is indicated, in a list of book advertisements on the copy-right page, as the fourth and concluding volume of the Pacific Series. This title had been planned for publication by A. K. Loring (Alger's previous publisher), and notice of this actually appeared at the end of "The Young Explorer," the third volume of the series and the last Alger story that Loring was to publish. Apparently Loring already had the manuscript on hand and intended to print the book in October, 1881, but he went bankrupt in June, 1881, and it was Porter & Coates who deposited the title for copyright the following year. "Ben's Nugget," therefore, was the first original Alger story issued by Porter & Coates. Prior to publication, it ran as a serial in the Boston Globe starting with the issue dated February 6, 1882 and ending in issue dated March 11, 1882.

The first edition is identifiable by the fact that no Alger titles, projected for or published at a later date, are listed. Other than the frontispiece and decorative title page, no other illustrations appear in the earliest printings.

Through an arrangement made with Porter & Coates, the story was published in England, in 1883, as "Ben's Nuggets; or, A Boy's Search for Fortune," by John F. Shaw & Co., Ltd., of London.

The first issue of the Porter & Coates edition is worth $22.50. There is no known copy of the London edition.

BEN, THE LUGGAGE BOY; or, Among the Wharves.

Loring, Publisher, 1870

TITLE PAGE: Ben, the Luggage Boy;/ or,/ Among the Wharves./ By/ Horatio Alger, Jr.,/ Author of "Ragged Dick," "Fame and Fortune," "Mark, the Match Boy,"/ "Rough and Ready," "Campaign Series," "Luck and/ Pluck Series," Etc./ [decorative rule]/ Loring, Publisher,/ 319 Washington Street,/ Boston.

BINDING: Bound in blind-stamped cloth. Green and mauve are the two colors noted. Front and back covers are identically blind-stamped with decorative border and center design. Spine, gold-stamped:

[decorative rule]/ Ben/ the/ Luggage/ Boy/ [criss-crossed double line rules]/ [enclosed in six-sided border design: Ragged/ Dick/ Series]/ [illustration of Ragged Dick]/ [decorative rule]. Cover size: 5" x 7".

COLLATION: Yellow-tinted end-paper; fly-leaf; blank leaf, with book advertisements on verso; tissue-covered decorative title page [p. i]; blank [p. ii]; title page [p. iii]; copyright notice dated 1870 [p. iv]; dedication [p. v]; blank [p. vi]; preface [pp. vii] - viii; text [pp. 9] - 290; 1 leaf of book advertisements (2 pp.); fly-leaf; yellow-tinted end-paper. In addition to the decorative title page are three full-page illustrations.

"Ben, the Luggage Boy" was deposited for copyright on May 11, 1870, and probably was in distribution at about that date. The first edition will show title listed as volume V. of the Ragged Dick Series, in the publisher's advertisements at front of the book. The next volume, VI., "Rufus and Rose," is listed for publication "(In December, 1870.)". Under the Luck and Pluck Series, "Sink or Swim" is listed for publication "(In November, 1870.)". There is no frontispiece in the first edition. Later printings moved the illustration that, in the original issue, faces Page 13, to the front position.

Value of first edition is $27.50.

BERNARD BROOKS' ADVENTURES; The Story of a Brave Boy's Trials.

A. L. Burt, 1903

TITLE PAGE: Bernard Brook's (note mis-spelling of Brooks') Adventures/ The Story of a Brave Boy's Trials/ By Horatio Alger, Jr./ Author of "Ben Bruce," "Dan the Newsboy," "A Debt of Honor," "Tom the/ Bootblack," "Mark Mason's Victory," "Tony the Hero," etc., etc./ With illustrations by J. Watson Davis/ New York:/ A. L. Burt Company, Publishers.

BINDING: Identical with "Ben Bruce," except that title on spine is stamped in gold against the dark olive green cloth background, and the full name, Horatio Alger, appears directly below.

COLLATION: End-paper; frontispiece; title page [p. 1]; copyright notice dated 1903 [p. 2]; text, pp. 3 - 306; book advertisements, pp. [1] - 6; end paper. In addition to the frontispiece are four full-page illustrations.

"Bernard Brooks' Adventures" originally was serialized in Munsey's Argosy, in 1893. It was titled "A Bad Lot," and Arthur Lee Putnam was indicated as author. In similar fashion, it was again serialized in Munsey's The Quaker, commencing in issue No. 1, dated November, 1897. The book title was deposited for copyright on February 21, 1903, with the completed book received at the Library of Congress on May 5, 1903.

The hero's last name presents a confusion of apostrophes. On the book's cover and spine, it is incorrectly printed as "Bernard Brook's Adventures." Bernard's name is Brooks, not Brook. The copyright notice carries the correct placing of the apostrophe, as do the running heads on every page of the first edition except page 84, where the apostrophe disappears altogether. The incorrect spelling apparently went undetected until 1907, when — on the title page of the first edition of "In Search of Treasure" — it appeared correctly listed for the first time. However, when — the following year — Street & Smith reissued the story as a paperback (New Medal Library, #468), the name in the title again appeared as "Brook's." The confusion continued until the World War I years when, due to paper shortages, "Bernard Brooks' Adventures" disappeared from the lists of A. L. Burt and also of Street & Smith and other reprint publishers.

Value of first edition is $15.00.

BERTHA'S CHRISTMAS VISION; An Autumn Sheaf.
Brown, Bazin, and Company, 1856

TITLE PAGE: Bertha's/ Christmas Vision:/ An Autumn Sheaf./ [rule]/ By Horatio Alger, Jr./ [rule]/ Boston:/ Brown, Bazin, and Company,/ 94, Washington Street./ 1856.

BINDING: Bound in several colors of cloth; dark brown, black, blue and gray being noted. Probably no priority of issue. Front and back covers identically blind-stamped with border line rules inclosing leafy design. Publisher's monogram at center. Spine, gold-stamped: Three lines/ panel with straight lines at sides and floral design at top and bottom/ (within panel): Bertha's/ Christmas/ Vision/ [rule]/ floral decoration/ scroll/ three lines. Cover size: 4⅞" x 7⅛".

COLLATION: Yellow-tinted end-paper; fly-leaf on which title is printed; frontispiece; tissue-covered decorative title page [p. i]; blank [p. ii]; title page [p. iii]; copyright notice dated 1855, [p. iv]; dedication, [pp. v] - vi; contents, [pp. vii] - viii; text, pp. 1 - 248; fly-leaf yellow-tinted end-paper.

CONTENTS: Little Floy; or, How a Miser was Reclaimed.
My Castle.
Miss Henderson's Thanksgiving Day.
Little Charlie.
Bertha's Christmas Vision.
Wide-Awake.
The First Tree Planted by an Ornamental Tree Society.
The Royal Carpenter of Amsterdam.
Our Gabrielle.
The Veiled Mirror.
Summer Hours.
The Prize Painting.
The Child of the Street.
Lost and Found.
Geraldine.
The Christmas Gift.
My Picture.
Gottfried the Scholar.
Innocence.
Peter Plunkett's Adventure.

The Library of Congress still has the proof of the title page of "Bertha' Christmas Vision," deposited on October 31, 1855. However, it was not until April 11, 1856, that the book was presented for copyright.

This was Alger's first book, and is very rare. It is a collection of twenty short stories, some of which — and possibly all — previously appeared in various story-papers and other periodicals. All of these stories were written somewhat before Alger settled upon his ultimate "strive-and-succeed" pattern, thus making the volume a treasure only for the avid collector. The lover of the author's newsboy and bootblack classics will find little of interest here.

Because of the scarcity of the original edition, a rather late reprint, issued by Hurst & Company, generally brings between $15.00 and $17.50 (a very high price for a reprint). The original, on the rare occasions it is offered, brings about $75.00.

BILL STURDY; or, The Cruise of Kidnapped Charlie. See "Charlie Codman's Cruise."

BOB BURTON; or, The Young Ranchman of the Missouri.
Porter & Coates, 1888

TITLE PAGE: Bob Burton;/ or,/ The Young Ranchman of the/ Missouri/ By/ Horatio Alger, Jr.,/ Author of "Ragged Dick Series," "Luck and/ Pluck Series," "Atlantic Series," Etc./ [publisher's trade mark device]/ Philadelphia:/ Porter & Coates.

BINDING: Identical with "Ben's Nugget."

COLLATION: Dark brown coated end-paper; fly-leaf; tissue-covered frontispiece; title page [p. i]; copyright notice dated 1888 [p. ii]; dedication [p. iii]; verso blank [p. iv]; contents, [pp. v] - vi; text, [pp. 5] - 330; 1 leaf (2 pp.) of book advertisements; fly-leaf; dark brown coated end-paper.

"Bob Burton" was serialized in Golden Argosy during 1886 - 1887, with the title deposited for copyright on November 27, 1886. There is no recorded copyright deposit either of title page or book by Porter & Coates, who issued it in 1888 as Volume One of their "Way to Success Series." The publishers later presented books of this series in slightly larger format, with a picture of a bee-hive on the cover and a beaver on the spine. However, this first edition (and probably a number of subsequent printings) is the smaller-sized book with dark brown covers, as described.

Value of first edition is $22.50.

BOTH SIDES OF THE CONTINENT. See "Mark Stanton."

BOUND TO RISE; or, Harry Walton's Motto.
Loring, Publisher, 1873

TITLE PAGE: Bound to Rise;/ or,/ Harry Walton's Motto./ By/ Horatio Alger, Jr.,/ Author of "Ragged Dick Series," "Tattered Tom Series,"/ "Campaign Series," "Luck and Pluck Series," Etc./ [decorative rule]/ Loring, Publisher,/ Cor. Washington and Bromfield Streets,/ Boston.

BINDING: Covers identical with "Ben, the Luggage Boy." Spine, gold-stamped: Line rules along sides of spine/ arch-like design with lines and leaves at top/ title/ criss-crossed double line rules/ (enclosed design in which is stamped: Luck & Pluck/ Second Series)/ [illustration of young man holding hat in hand]/ [line]/ Loring/ [line].

COLLATION: Yellow-tinted end-paper; fly-leaf; 1 leaf (2 pp.) of book advertisements; tissue-covered frontispiece; decorative title page [p. i]; blank [p. ii]; title page [p. iii]; copyright notice dated 1873, [p. iv]; dedication [p. v]; verso blank [p. vi]; preface, pp. 7 - viii; text, pp. [9] - 331; fly-leaf; yellow-tinted end-paper. In addition to frontispiece and decorative title page are two full-page illustrations.

In 1873, this story was serialized in Young Israel under the title, "Live and Learn." It was intended to publish the book under the same title, and this was announced in the book advertisements and also at the ending of "Try and Trust," the preceding volume of the Luck and Pluck Series. However, the story was published as "Bound to Rise," and retained the title throughout subsequent reissues by other publishers. I mention this because "Live and Learn" has occasionally appeared on lists as a wanted title. It never was used as the title of an Alger book.

Although published (as Volume II of the Second Luck and Pluck Series) in time for the Christmas Season, 1873, "Bound to Rise" — along with some eight other Algers printed between 1873 and 1876 — was not deposited for copyright until early in 1877. No reason is given for this except the logical explanation of a researcher at the Library of Congress: "Maybe they forgot."

Several interesting points clearly define the first edition: In the advertisements at the front of the book, the next book in the series is listed as "III. Up the Ladder; or Harry Walton's Success, in Oct., '74." The same projected title is announced on p. 331. This was almost immediately changed to "Risen From the Ranks," the title under which the next volume was actually released. The first edition does not include the inserted illustration facing p. 16 in later issues, and the engraving facing p. 254 in the first edition was subsequently moved to face p. 256.

Value of first edition is $27.50.

A BOY'S FORTUNE, or, The Strange Adventures of Ben Baker.
Henry T. Coates & Co., 1898

TITLE PAGE: A Boy's Fortune/ or, the/ Strange Adventures of Ben Baker/ By/ Horatio Alger, Jr./ Author of "Adrift in the City," "Grit," "Frank and Fearless,"/ "Dan, the Detective," "Plucky Paul Palmer," Etc./ Philadelphia/ Henry T. Coates & Co./ 1898.

BINDING: Bound in green cloth, stamped in black, gold and a lighter green. Cover design: Black border line all around front cover/ title stamped in gold at top/ black floral design over-printed upon light-green 'blades of grass'/ By Horatio Alger Jr. Spine: Black line/ title stamped in gold/ gold line/ Alger/ black and light-green floral design/ Henry T. Coates/ & Co./ black line. Cover size: 5¼" x 7½".

COLLATION: Slate-colored coated end-paper; fly-leaf; tissue-covered frontispiece; title page [p. i]; copyright notice dated 1898 [p ii]; contents, pp. iii - iv; text, pp. 1 - 325; book advertisements, pp. [1] - 6; fly-leaf; slate-colored coated end-paper. In addition to the frontispiece are three full-page illustrations.

Prior to its appearance in book form, "A Boy's Fortune" was twice serialized. The first appearance was in New York Weekly (starting February 2, 1889) and later in Good News (starting March 11, 1893). Coates deposited the title for copyright on July 29, 1898, and the book was received at the Library of Congress on September 9th of that year. Although not designated as such in the original edition, this story later was listed as Volume Two of Coates' Good Fortune Library.

The first edition is distinguished by the 1898 date at bottom of the title page, but even more significantly by an almost immediate change of frontispieces, thus creating two states of the first edition. The first state frontispiece (which was the one deposited for copyright) depicts two middle-aged men.

The first state of the first edition is worth $25.00, with the early 'freak' copies of the second state worth only slightly less.

BOY'S LIFE OF DANIEL WEBSTER. See "From Farm Boy to Senator."

BRAVE AND BOLD; or, The Fortunes of a Factory Boy.
Loring, Publisher, 1874

TITLE PAGE: Brave and Bold;/ or,/ The Fortunes of a Factory Boy./ By/ Horatio Alger, Jr.,/ Author of "Ragged Dick," — "Tattered Tom" — "Luck and/ Pluck," — "Brave and Bold" Series./ [decorative rule]/ Loring, Publisher,/ Cor. Washington and Bromfield Streets,/ Boston.

BINDING: Covers identical with "Ben, the Luggage Boy." Spine, gold-stamped: [two lines at top]/ [ornament]/ title/ [scrolled ornament]/ Brave and Bold/ Series/ [ornament]/ [illustration of boy flagging train]/ [line]/ Loring/ [line].

COLLATION: Yellow-tinted end-paper; fly-leaf; 1 leaf (2 pp.) of book advertisements; frontispiece; tissue-covered decorative title page [p. i]; blank [p. ii]; title page [p. iii]; copyright notice dated 1874 [p. iv]; dedication (to Francis S. Street, publisher of the New York Weekly), [p. v]; verso blank [p. vi]; preface, pp. 7 - viii; text, pp [9] - 342; 2 fly-leaves, yellow-tinted end-paper. In addition to frontispiece and decorative title page are two full-page illustrations.

Originally published as a serial in New York Weekly, starting August 5, 1872, "Brave and Bold" was issued as a book by Loring in 1874 (although not deposited for copyright until 1877). In his preface, Alger says that this story was also published previously in a London periodical, and that the book "illustrations were suggested by those provided by the English publisher." Unfortunately, no record exists of the British publication.

The first edition is easily identified by advertisements at front of the book. "Brave and Bold" is listed as Volume I of the Brave and Bold Series, with no indication of any other books of this series to follow. At top of page, "Julius" is listed as Volume I of the Second Tattered Tom Series, with no further listings. At center of the page, "Risen From the Ranks" appears as Volume III of the Second Luck and Pluck Series, with no indication of the fourth and final book of that set. On page 16 of earliest printings, the word "frankly" is misspelled as "faankly."

Value of first edition is $27.50.

BULLY OF THE VILLAGE, THE. See "Tom Temple's Career."

CASH BOY, THE. See "Frank Fowler."

CAST UPON THE BREAKERS
Doubleday & Company, 1974.
　　TITLE PAGE: Horatio Alger, Jr./[decorative crossed branches]/Cast Upon/The/
　　Breakers/Foreword By Ralph D. Gardner/1974/Doubleday & Company, Inc./
　　Garden City, New York.
　　BINDING: Gold stamped green cloth. Cover design: Portrait of Alger in an oval with-
　　in rectangle. Spine: Horatio/Alger, Jr./Cast upon/the/Breakers/Foreword/By
　　Ralph D./Gardner/Doubleday. Cover size: 5½″ x 8½″.
　　COLLATION: Decorated green end paper; verso blank; half title page [p. 1]; verso
　　blank [p. 2]; title page [p. 3]; copyright notice (last line reads: First Edition) [p. 4];
　　contents [pp. 5] -7; verso blank [p. 8]; Foreword [pp. 9] - 27; verso blank [p. 28];
　　footnotes [pp. 29] - 33; verso blank [p. 34]; another half title page [p. 35]; verso
　　blank [p. 36]; text [pp. 37] - 258; three blank fly leaves; blank recto of decorated
　　green end paper. There are 8 additional unnumbered pages with 18 illustrations.
　　Dust jacket has pale green front and spine; white on back, printed in dark green,
　　white and black.

The Doubleday publication is the bona fide first edition of this title in bound book
form. Its earliest and only previous appearance was as a serialization in The Argosy.
Starting in the issue #547, dated May 27, 1893, it ran for thirteen weeks, concluding in
issue #559, dated August 19th. A note at the end of the final chapter states that the
story started in #548, but this is incorrect.

"Cast Upon the Breakers" carried the Arthur Lee Putnam pen-name, undoubtedly
because final installments of "Victor Vane" — which carried the regular Alger by-line
— ran concurrently.

The only pre-publication announcement of this story appeared in The Argosy issue
#546, the week preceding the first installment.

Although a complete run of this story is hard to find, even in shabby condition (which
it generally is, due to the quality of paper on which it is printed), the item is of great
interest to the advanced Alger collector.

To such a collector, however, this item is well worth $35.00.

The Doubleday edition is, at this writing, still available in bookstores at its published
price, $6.95. It was issued as a paperback in 1975 by Popular Library with the price
marked $1.50 on the cover.

CHARLIE CODMAN'S CRUISE.

Loring, Publisher, 1866

　　TITLE PAGE: Charlie Codman's Cruise./ A Story for Boys./ By Horatio
　　Alger, Jr.,/ Author of "Frank's Campaign," "Paul Prescott's/
　　Charge," "Helen Ford."/ Loring, Publisher,/ 319 Washington
　　Street, Boston:/ 1867.

　　BINDING: Covers identical with "Ben, the Luggage Boy" ("Charlie Cod-
　　man's Cruise" probably being the earliest Alger first edition to be
　　bound in these covers). Several colors of cloth noted, including red

(the earliest), green, terra cotta and dark brown. Spine, blind-stamped against solid gold background: Charlie/ Codman's/ Cruise (with bottom of letters gold-shaded)/ [illustration of young sailor]/ Loring/ [decorative linked-design]. Cover size: 4¾" x 7⅛".

COLLATION: Yellow-tinted end-paper; 2 fly-leaves; blank side of frontispiece, [p. i]; tissue-covered frontispiece, [p. ii]; title page [. p. iii]; copyright notice dated 1866, [p. iv]; preface, pp. v - vi; text, pp. 7 - 231; fly-leaf; yellow-tinted end-paper.

Although the copyright date of "Charlie Codman's Cruise" — issued as the third volume of the Campaign Series — is February 21, 1867, the title page was deposited on October 18, 1866, and the completed book was presented a month later, on November 20. As it was not expected to place the book in distribution before early 1867, the first edition was printed with that date at bottom of title page. Nevertheless, there is unquestionable proof that copies of the book were on sale by early December, 1866. Therefore, it must be considered as published during that year. My own copy carries a bona fide presentation inscription dated December 25, 1866. A review of the story in "Our Book Table," a department of the January, 1867, Student and Schoolmate, also indicates earlier publication.

The first edition frontispiece — probably the most unusual to appear in any of Alger's books — is a photograph of Boston's Bedford Street corner, to which an artist added a couple of passersby to the scene. It is at this location, incidentally, that the story begins. Look for these points: p. 144, the word 'subtle' is misspelled 'subtile'; p. 165, chapter heading at top of page is incorrectly printed as "Antonio's Plot"; p. 186, the word 'foeman' is misspelled as 'foreman'; p. 206, the name 'Bertha' is incorrectly given as 'Ida'.

This story was released in England under the changed title, "Bill Sturdy; or, The Cruise of Kidnapped Charlie." Issued by Aldine Publishing Company of London, it was among some thirty Algers to appear between 1903 and 1907 in their paperback Garfield Library series.

Value of first edition is $30.00.

CHESTER RAND; or, A New Path to Fortune.
Henry T. Coates & Co., 1903

TITLE PAGE: Chester Rand;/ or,/ A New Path to Fortune./ By/ Horatio Alger, Jr.,/ Author of "Jed," "Ragged Dick," "Luck and Pluck,/ "Tattered Tom," Etc./ [line]/ Philadelphia/ Henry T. Coates & Co./ 1903.

BINDING: Identical with "Andy Grant's Pluck."

COLLATION: Dark brown coated end-paper; tissue-covered frontispiece; title page [p. i]; copyright notice dated 1903, [p. ii]; contents, pp. iii - iv; text, pp. 1 - 383; book advertisements, pp. [1] - 10; fly-leaf; dark brown coated end-paper. In addition to the frontispiece are two full-page illustrations.

"Chester Rand" first appeared as a serialization in Argosy, the first installment appearing in issue #508, dated Saturday, August 27, 1892. The title page of the book was deposited by Coates on May 4, 1903, and the book was received at the Library of Congress on September 3d of the same year.

Two points identify the first edition: On the title page there should be — but isn't — a quotation mark following the word, Pluck. On p. 333, the word 'expensive' is misspelled 'expensvie.'
Value of first edition is $22.50.

CHILD OF FORTUNE, A. See "Helen Ford."

COUSIN'S CONSPIRACY, A. See "The Young Bank Messenger."

DAN, THE DETECTIVE.
    G. W. Carleton & Co. — Street & Smith, 1883
    TITLE PAGE: Dan,/ The Detective./ By/ Horatio Alger, Jr,/ Author of/ "Tattered Tom," "Ragged Dick," "Luck and/ Pluck," "The Train Boy," "The/ Errand Boy," Etc., Etc./ [Carleton's trade mark device]/ New York:/ G. W. Carleton & Co., Publishers./ Street & Smith, New York Weekly./ MDCCCLXXXIV.
    BINDING: Bound in cloth; terra cotta, green and red being noted. Probably no priority of issue. Front cover, stamped in black: At top, double line, starfish design, single line; within an inverted bowl-shaped outline: Dan/ The/ Detective; picket fence design across center; at bottom: floral motif atop five lines. Back cover, blind-stamped: line border around sides with Carleton trade-mark at center. Spine, stamped in black and gold: (in black: double line/ wave design/ single line)/ (in gold: Dan/ The/ Detective/ line/ Alger)/ (in black: line/ floral design/ line/ Carleton trade-mark/ New York). Cover size: 5¼" x 7⅜".
    COLLATION: End paper; fly-leaf on which title and author's name are printed, [p. 1]; verso blank [p. 2]; blank [p. 3]; frontispiece [p. 4]; title page [p. 5]; copyright notice dated 1884 [p. 6]; contents, [pp. 7 - 8]; text, [pp. 9] - 296; 2 leaves (4 pp.) of book advertisements; end-paper. In addition to the frontispiece are four full-page illustrations.

Earliest publication of "Dan, the Detective" was as a serialization in New York Weekly, the first installment appearing in the issue dated August 9, 1880. Eleven years later — in 1891 — it reappeared under the same title in Good News, chapters running from May 23d until August 22d. Its publication as a book was a joint venture between Street & Smith — the publishers of New York Weekly, and holders of the copyright — and J. W. Carleton. Since a number of Carleton's books were reprints of stories originally printed in New York Weekly, it is safe to assume there was a close business connection, and possibly a partial ownership of the Carleton organization by Street & Smith.

The book was deposited for copyright during the latter part of 1883, and appeared before the end of that year, despite the fact that both the book's title page and copyright notice are dated 1884. The Library of Congress copy has a bona fide Christmas, 1883 inscription. "Dan, the Detective" also is listed among the "Author of . . ." titles on the title page of "The Train Boy," a similar Carleton-Street & Smith project published toward the end of 1883. This gives further evidence that, even if "Dan" were not already in distribution, its appearance certainly was imminent.

It was A. L. Burt who, in 1893, first reissued the story as "Dan the Newsboy," the title by which it became one of Alger's best-known tales.

The original Carleton - Street & Smith edition of "Dan, the Detective" is one of the rarest of the Alger treasures. Actually, the title, itself, is virtually unknown even to many long-time Alger collectors. It is rarely seen and almost never offered for sale.

This story appeared briefly in England between 1903-1907, reissued under the title, "Dutiful Dan, the Brave Boy Detective." It was issued by Aldine Publishing Company, London, one of some thirty Algers grouped in their paperback Garfield Library series.

The Carleton-Street & Smith edition is worth $100.00. Many collectors would pay more!

DAN, THE NEWSBOY. See "Dan, the Detective."

DEAN DUNHAM.

United States Book Company, 1890

BINDING: Stiff paper wrappers, grained and tan-colored to give the appearance of leather. Cover design: No. 32/ Price, 25¢/ Leather - Clad Tales/ of Adventure and Romance/ [circular border; within it a man and woman on horseback/ extending beyond perimeter of border are desert flowers, an Indian bow and tomahawk]/ below illustration: Issued Weekly. Annual Subscription $12.00/ July 12, 1890./ Entered at the New York Post Office as second class matter/ Dean Dunham,/ By/ Horatio Alger, Jr./ [line]/ Illustrated/ [line]/ No copyright books by leading authors for boys and girls equaling this series/ in merit and purity were ever before published for less than $1.25 a copy./ United States Book Company,/ Successors to/ John W. Lovell Company,/ 142 to 150 Worth Street, New York. Spine: No. 32/ Dean Dunham./ Price, 25 cents. Back cover: Full-page commercial advertisement.

Story was serialized in Golden Argosy in 1888. Then, on July 12, 1890, it appeared as No. 32 of the Leather - Clad Tales of Adventure and Romance. For some unexplained reason it was not deposited for copyright, by the U.S. Book Company, until March 25, 1891.

Apparently the first hard-cover edition was published in the Berkeley Series of the American Publishers Corporation, from original plates obtained after the U.S. Book Company went bankrupt. It was again serialized, in Army and Navy Weekly, from August 21 to November 6, 1897. In March, 1900, Street & Smith issued "Dean Dunham" in paper wrappers as Medal Library #50, and shortly thereafter in hardcovers.

This title has not been reissued as often as many of the Alger stories. Consequently, it is eagerly sought after (even in reprint editions) by collectors. However, it is the Leather-Clad that is the rarity and for it the purchaser — who is lucky enough to find a copy — will pay about $42.00.

DEBT OF HONOR, A; The Story of Gerald Lane's Success in the Far West.
A. L. Burt, 1900

TITLE PAGE: A Debt of Honor./ The Story of/ Gerald Lane's Success
in the Far West./ By Horatio Alger, Jr.,/ Author of "Joe's Luck,"
"Tom the Bootblack," "Dan the/ Newsboy," "The Errand Boy,"
etc., etc./ With Five Page Illustrations by J. Watson Davis./ New
York:/ A. L. Burt, Publisher.

BINDING: Identical with "Ben Bruce."

COLLATION: Light brown flower-patterned end-paper; frontispiece; title
page [p. i]; copyright notice dated 1900 [p. ii]; contents, [pp. iii] -
iv; text, [pp. 1] - 302; book advertisements, [pp. 1] - 14; light brown
flower-patterned end-paper. In addition to the frontispiece are four
full-page illustrations.

Although the story was serialized in Argosy in 1891, the earliest re-
corded copyright notice is March 6, 1900, when Burt deposited the title.
On July 18, 1900, the completed book was presented at the Library of
Congress for copyright.

The following points identify the first edition: On spine, title is blind-
stamped against gold background, with "Alger" gold-stamped directly below; address on pages of ads at rear must be "97-99-101 Reade Street."
Value of first edition is $15.00.

DIAMOND IN THE ROUGH, A. See "A New York Boy."

DIGGING FOR GOLD; A Story of California.
Porter & Coates, 1892

TITLE PAGE: Digging for Gold/ A Story of California/ By/ Horatio
Alger, Jr./ [publisher's trade-mark device]/ Philadelphia/ Porter
& Coates.

BINDING: Bound in black, yellow and gold-stamped tan cloth. Cover design: Title (stamped in yellow at top)/ Horatio Alger (in black)/
[illustration of mountain scene, two fir trees; sack of coins in fore-
ground against backstrip of yellow coins]. Spine: (Against background of pick, shovel, rifle and rope design: title gold-stamped
within a gold box)/ [lines/ strip of yellow coins/ lines]. Cover size:
5¼" x 7⅞".

COLLATION: Slate-colored end-paper: fly-leaf; tissue-covered frontispiece;
title page [p. i]; copyright notice dated 1892 [p. ii]; contents, pp.
iii - iv; text, [pp. 1] - 352; book advertisements, [pp. 1] - 12; fly-
leaf; slate-colored coated end-paper. In addition to the frontispiece
are three full-page illustrations.

After serialization in Argosy, in 1891, the book was deposited for copyright on August 10, 1892. Through arrangement with Porter & Coates,
the book was published the same year in England by John F. Shaw & Co.,
Ltd., of London. There is no known copy of the London edition. There
is, of course, no connection between this story and the identically-titled
book by R. M. Ballantyne.
Value of first edition is $25.00.

DISAGREEABLE WOMAN, THE; A Social Mystery.

G. W. Dillingham, 1895

TITLE PAGE: The/ Disagreeable Woman/ A Social Mystery/ By/ Julian Starr/ "Our acts show our angels are, for good or ill,/ Our fatal shadows that walk by us still"/ Fletcher/ [Carleton trade-mark device]/ New York/ Copyright 1895, by/ G. W. Dillingham, Publisher/ Successor to G. W. Carleton & Co./ MDCCCXCV/ All rights reserved.

BINDING: Bound in green cloth, stamped in silver. Cover: The Disagreeable/ Woman. By/ Julian Starr. Spine: The/ Disagreeable/ Woman/ [small design]/ Starr/ [Carleton trade-mark device at bottom]. Cover size: 4" x 6½".

COLLATION: End-paper; fly-leaf; blank verso of fly-leaf [p. i]; title page [p. ii]; contents, pp. iii - iv; "Message to My Readers: In reading Miss Harraden's charming idyl, 'Ships That Pass in the Night,' it occurred to me that if there were Disagreeable Men there are also Disagreeable Women. Hence this story." p. v; [there is no p. vi]; text, pp. 7 - 190; fly-leaf; end- paper.

The trail of "The Disagreeable Woman" has long been one of the deepest mysteries of Alger searching (an endeavor deeply-pitted with many dark mysteries). I am in hopes that I can now offer some clues toward its final solution.

This small, slender volume is the first and only one to carry the virtually unknown Alger pseudonym, "Julian Starr." This is an adult story and, as such, has long eluded Alger collectors who — though loaded for bear — have generally kept their sights levelled only at his better-known juvenile output.

The book was deposited for copyright on June 6, 1895. George W. Dillingham, the publisher, was formerly employed by G. W. Carleton, and had been taken into partnership in 1871. Dillingham formally took over control when Carleton retired in 1886 but — in respect and affection for his former employer and partner — he continued using as a trade-mark the old Arabic symbol that Carleton fancied resembled his monogram.

Alger, whose ambition to write adult literature was known, presented his manuscript to Frank Munsey and later to Porter & Coates. It was turned down by both, probably because they feared the novel would disappoint youthful readers who adored Alger.

In 1894, Dillingham approached Alger with the suggestion that the busy author do a book for him. With his current production already promised to Munsey, he offered Dillingham (an old friend since the days they both worked for A. K. Loring) the twice-rejected manuscript. Dillingham accepted it and Alger requested permission of Munsey — to whom he was then under contract — for Dillingham to publish "The Disagreeable Woman." He received Munsey's consent on condition that an entirely new pen-name be used, and that there should be no conflict nor confusion between the adult novel and Alger's regular output of stories for boys. Hence the advent of Julian Starr.

The Dillingham catalogues list "The Disagreeable Woman" by Starr, for the first time in 1896, and continue the title listing at least until 1905 or 1906. The year after Alger's death, his real name appears in the catalogue as author. However, there is no known copy of the book showing the Horatio Alger by-line, although it is most probable that it eventually appeared as such.

When the book was first published, Munsey's Magazine, recommending it in a review as "good, easy reading for a Summer's day," disclosed that "Julian Starr is said to be the nom-de-plume of an author who is widely known in another literary field."

Actually, any reader familiar with the Alger style would immediately have identified him as the true author. All the residents of Mrs. Gray's boarding house on Waverly Place, where the story takes place, are well known to the Alger reader. All situations are identical, with only the young Alger hero absent. Alger's familiar New York settings — the Fifth Avenue Hotel, Sixth Avenue, Fourteenth Street and others — are visited. One of the characters even mentions the "hermit who lived in one of the cottages on the rocks near Central Park." This, of course, could be none other than Noah Outbank, the mysterious recluse of Alger's popular "Tom Tracy."

The Library of Congress owns the only known copy of "The Disagreeable Woman." Doubtless, others are gathering dust on shelves, or are stored away in basements or attics. However, as no copy has — at least for the record — been offered for sale, it is not possible to set a price for this book. I can only guess that there are collectors willing to pay up to $175.00 for the Starr edition, and perhaps double the price for one on which Alger is named as the author.

DISTRICT TELEGRAPH BOY, THE. See "The Telegraph Boy."

DO AND DARE; or, A Brave Boy's Fight for Fortune.
Porter & Coates, 1884

TITLE PAGE: Do and Dare;/ or,/ A Brave Boy's Fight for Fortune./ By/ Horatio Alger, Jr.,/ Author of "Ragged Dick," "Tattered Tom," "Luck and/ Pluck," Etc., Etc./ [publisher's trade-mark device]/ Philadelphia:/ Porter and Coates.

BINDING: Identical with "Ben's Nugget."

COLLATION: Slate-colored coated end-paper; fly-leaf; tissue-covered frontispiece; title page [p. i]; copyright notice dated 1884 [p. ii]; contents, [p. iii] - iv; text, [pp. 1] - 303; fly-leaf; slate-colored coated end-paper. In addition to the frontispiece are three full-page illustrations.

After serialization in Golden Argosy that started in 1882 and continued into the following year, "Do and Dare" was deposited in book form for copyright on August 23, 1884. Sometime after its initial appearance, it was designated as Volume Two of the Atlantic Series. There are no book advertisements in the first edition.

Value of first edition is $22.50.*

DRIVEN FROM HOME. See "The Odds Against Him."

DUTIFUL DAN, THE BRAVE BOY DETECTIVE. See "Dan, the Detective."

*On May 18, 1971, a first edition of *Do and Dare*, inscribed: *William D. Conover —— from his friend Horatio Alger, Jr.* was auctioned at Parke-Bernet Galleries for $120.00, a record for this item.

ERIE TRAIN BOY, THE

United States Book Company, 1890

BINDING: Identical with "Dean Dunham."

Serialized in Argosy, the first installment appearing in the issue dated January 4, 1890. On May 31 of that year the story appeared in paper wrappers as Leather-Clad Tales of Adventure and Romance, No. 26 (although the Library of Congress copy was not deposited for copyright until December 29, 1890). As this title is not listed by U.S. Book Co., as having appeared in one of their hard cover editions, nor by American Publishers Corporation who, having later acquired the original plates, reissued a number of Algers in hard covers, it is very likely that the first hard-bound edition did not appear until about ten years later, when H. M. Caldwell and Company came out with two editions. At least one of these appeared before Street & Smith's hard-cover edition, printed from the same plates as their paperback Medal Library No. 61, issued in 1900.

Although the first edition of "The Erie Train Boy" — which, of course, is the Leather-Clad — is a very rare book, reissues of this title abound, and are among the easiest to find. At least a dozen — and probably more — publishers found this story to be a real money-maker, doubtless because it so rigidly adheres to the Alger strive-and-succeed pattern. Every page, every character and every situation satisfied the young reader of a couple of generations ago. Even the final sentence told them just what they wanted to know: "It looks as if the clouds had passed away, succeeded by the sunshine of permanent prosperity."

The dealer offering this Leather-Clad No. 26 for sale will have no trouble finding a customer willing to pay from $50.00 — up.

THE ERRAND BOY; or, How Phil Brent Won Success.

A. L. Burt, 1888

BINDING: Paper wrappers, printed in red and black. Cover typography (all in red): Volume 1, No. 14. Price 25 Cents, Yearly $2.50. October, 1888/ [long line]/ Boys' Home Library./ The Errand Boy,/ By Horatio Alger, Jr./ A. L. Burt, Publisher, New York./ Published Monthly. Entered at the New York Post Office as second-class matter./ The cover illustration, printed in black, includes — within an uneven rope-like border — a shaded background into which are set three vignettes. The uppermost one shows a hunting scene being observed by an Indian. Mortised into its lower portion is a circle showing the familiar head of a boy (wearing an odd-appearing peakless cap) that appears on the covers of Burt's earliest hard-cover editions. Below the title is a boating scene with lighthouse in the background. Three arrangements of flowers and leaves appear in the corners (except at lower right). Spine (printed horizontally), in black: No. 14/ [line]/ Boys' Home/ Library./ [line]/ The Errand Boy./ [line]/ A. L. Burt,/ New York. Cover size: 5⅛"x7¼".

Story was serialized in Street & Smith's New York Weekly (as were all Alger stories issued in the Boys' Home Library series), the first installment appearing in the issue dated September 10, 1883. Burt deposited the book for copyright on October 8, 1888. A few months later it was distributed in hard covers as a volume of Burt's Home Series, a rather deluxe set in somewhat more-elegant-than-usual cloth covers. Burt later reissued the title in at least six different series, these followed by the cheaper editions of other publishers.

The first edition — the Boys' Home Library No. 14, in paper wrappers — is worth about $42.00.

FACING THE WORLD; or, The Haps and Mishaps of Harry Vane.
Porter & Coates, 1893

> TITLE PAGE: Facing the World/ or/ The Haps and Mishaps of Harry Vane/ By/ Horatio Alger, Jr./ Author of "Ragged Dick Series," "Luck/ and Pluck Series," Etc./ [publisher's trade-mark device]/ Philadelphia/ Porter & Coates.

> BINDING: Identical with "Digging for Gold."

> COLLATION: Slate-colored coated end-paper; fly-leaf; tissue-covered frontispiece; title page [p. i]; copyright notice dated 1893 [p. ii]; contents, pp. iii - iv; text, [pp. 1] - 318; book advertisements, [pp. 1] - 14; fly-leaf; slate-colored coated end-paper. In addition to the frontispiece are three full-page illustrations.

"Facing the World" first appeared as a serialization in Golden Argosy in 1885. Porter & Coates deposited the title for copyright on January 6, 1893 and forwarded the completed book to the Library of Congress on March 24, 1893. Curiously, the story was reprinted as recently as 1940 when, in modern dress, the characters cavorted through the pages of Doc Savage Comics #2.

There is no connection between this story and the Alger serialization in Young Israel (1876) that was titled "Facing the World," but was published in book form (by A. K. Loring, 1876) as "Shifting for Himself."

The first edition lists the sub-title of the next Alger story ("In A New World") as "Harry Vane in Australia." This was subsequently changed to "Among the Gold Fields of Australia."

Value of first edition is $25.00.

FACTORY BOY STORY, THE. See "The Odds Against Him."

FALLING IN WITH FORTUNE; or, The Experiences of a Young Secretary.
The Mershon Company, 1900

> TITLE PAGE: Falling In/ With Fortune/ or/ The Experiences of a Young/ Secretary/ By/ Horatio Alger, Jr./ Author of "Out for Business," "The Young Boatman,"/ "Sink or Swim," "Luck or Pluck," "Paul, the/ Peddler," "Only an Irish Boy," Etc./ Completed By/ Arthur M. Winfield/ Author of "The Rover Boys at School," "The Rover Boys/ on the Ocean," "The Rover Boys in the Jungle,"/ "The Rover Boys Out West," Etc./ [small tulip design]/ New York/ The Mershon Company/ Publishers. [Note: The listing of "Luck or Pluck," above, is an error. It should be "Luck *and* Pluck"].

BINDING: Bound in green cloth with red, white, black and gold stamping. Cover design: [Black border around front cover]/ (stamped in white at top: Falling In With/ Fortune)/ [three vertical panels: left, soldier with rifle, against red background/ at center, white clouds, white tent and black leaves design/ at right, young man in civilian clothes, carrying envelope, against red background]/ in white: By Horatio Alger, Jr. Spine: [black-bordered gold rule]/ [five leaves in a line]/ Falling/ In With/ Fortune/ [black-bordered gold rule]/ Horatio Alger, Jr./ [black-bordered gold rule]/ [red-striped vertical panel, gold sack in a wreath at top of panel, black border]/ in gold: The/ Mershon/ Co. Cover size: 5⅛" x 7⅜".

COLLATION: End-paper; frontispiece; title page [p. i]; copyright notice dated 1900 [p. ii]; preface, pp. iii - iv; contents, pp. v - vi; text, [pp. 7] - 282; book advertisements, 3 leaves (6 pp.); end-paper. In addition to the frontispiece are three full-page illustrations.

"Falling In With Fortune" (deposited for copyright September 29, 1900) is the second "Alger" supposed to have been completed by "Arthur M. Winfield." Winfield is one of the many pen-names employed by the fabulous Edward Stratemeyer. Although the book's preface states that this title and the previously-released "Out for Business" were the last two Alger manuscripts in preparation when the author died a year earlier, another nine "Alger outlines" were discovered and published through 1906.

The first edition does not list — in advertisements at back of the book — any titles by Horatio Alger. Subsequent printings list Algers (Winfield 'completions,' of course) under the heading of "The Rise in Life Series."

Despite the fact that there is little — if anything — of Alger in these Winfields, they are eagerly sought by collectors, and mighty hard to come by (especially in first editions).

Value of first edition is $27.50.

FAME AND FORTUNE; or, The Progress of Richard Hunter.

Loring, Publisher, 1868

TITLE PAGE: Fame and Fortune;/ or,/ The Progress of Richard Hunter./ By/ Horatio Alger, Jr.,/ Author of "Ragged Dick," "Frank's Campaign," "Paul Prescott's/ Charge," "Charlie Codman's Cruise," Etc./ [line]/ Loring, Publisher,/ 319 Washington Street./ Boston.

BINDING: Identical with "Ben the Luggage Boy," except that on the spine there is no "Ragged Dick Series" imprint.

COLLATION: Yellow-tinted end-paper; fly-leaf; blank sheet on verso of which is a listing of Alger book advertisements; tissue-covered decorative title page [p. i]; verso blank [p. ii]; title page [p. iii]; copyright notice dated 1868 [p. iv]; dedication [p. v]; verso blank [p. vi]; preface, pp. vii - viii; text, pp. 9 - 279; fly-leaf; yellow-tinted end-paper. In addition to the decorative title page are three full-page illustrations.

First appearing as a twelve-part monthly serialization in Student and Schoolmate throughout 1868, Alger rushed "Fame and Fortune" into production early in 1867, when it became apparent that "Ragged Dick" was emerging as a tremendous success. Loring designated "Fame and Fortune" as Volume II of the "Ragged Dick Series," depositing the title page for copyright on November 17, 1868, and the completed book on November 11th.

A number of points afford easy identification of the earliest state of the first edition. On the page of ads at front of the book, look for "Mark, the Match Boy," Volume III in the series, to be indicated as ready "[In May, 1869]" and "Rough and Ready," planned as Volume IV, to appear "[In December, 1869]." There must be no frontispiece. A frontispiece was added in the second state by using the illustration that also faces p. 138. In later printings that illustration appeared only as frontispiece, being removed from the p. 138 position. In numbering at top of page 109, there is a space after the number one, with the nine superimposed on the zero. On title page, type on "By" is damaged and under the copyright notice on verso, there is type damage to the "Lo" on "Loring." Don't accept the "319 Washington Street" address on title page as conclusive evidence of a first edition (as even knowledgeable Alger collectors are sometimes inclined to do). This merely indicates that the book was printed before November 15, 1870. By that date, "Fame and Fortune" probably had enjoyed at least a few editions.

Value of first edition is $30.00.

FANCY OF HERS, A.

Frank A. Munsey & Company, 1892

"A Fancy of Hers," one of Alger's few novel-length stories never to appear in book form, was published in the March, 1892, issue of Munsey's Magazine. It was a twelve-chapter adult effort about a New York society girl. Mabel Frost Fairfax, the heroine, is fed up with the social whirl and takes a teaching job in a small New Hampshire community.

The story was advertised as "The strange experiment of a New York girl — A village romance, and a series of sketches of village types — A novel complete in this issue."

Munsey's Magazines — like most family-handled periodicals of about eighty years ago — are not easy to find. The March, 1892, issue is especially rare, as Alger collectors (or book dealers shrewd in the Alger market) quickly remove from circulation the very few that still come along. This is the sort of thing you either pick up, as part of a lot, for a dime at a country auction, or you're tickled to pay today's market price to a bookseller lucky enough to find a copy as a result of extensive searching and advertising.

Valued at about $45.00.

FINDING A FORTUNE.

Penn Publishing Company, 1904

TITLE PAGE: Double-lined blue rules border three compartments in which the type is set, and two in each of which stands an abstract tree-like design. Finding/ A/ Fortune/ by/ Horatio Alger Jr./ Author of/ "Forging Ahead," etc/ Illustrated/ by/ W. S. Lukens/ The Penn/ Publishing/ Company/ Philadelphia/ MCMIV.

BINDING: Tan cloth cover, stamped in red, black, green and gold. In upper panel of cover, two boys sit studying. Behind them, green trees and a gold sky. In lower panel: Finding A/ Fortune/ Horatio

Alger/ Jr. Spine: [Black line]/ Finding A/ Fortune/ Alger/ PPCo./ [black line]. Cover size: 5″ x 7½″.

COLLATION: Illustrated end-paper (drawn in brown on lighter brown background are a boy reading, on the left, and a girl reading at right); fly-leaf; tissue covered frontispiece; title page [p. 1]; copyright notice dated 1904 [p. 2]; contents, pp. 3 - 4; list of illustrations, blank on verso [unnumbered]; text, pp. 5 - 364; 2 fly-leaves; illustrated end-paper, as described. In addition to frontispiece are six full-page illustrations.

Before appearing in book form, this story was serialized in Golden Days. Titled "The Tin Box; or, Harry Gilbert's Fortune," it was issued in 1882. The year after the story first appeared in book form — as "Finding a Fortune" (and as such deposited for copyright May 2, 1904) — it was reissued by Street & Smith (Medal Library No. 326, September 25, 1905) as "The Tin Box." The first hard-cover issue of "The Tin Box" is to be credited to A. L. Burt, and as such it was subsequently reissued by other publishers.

Acquiring a first edition of "Finding A Fortune" is a cut more difficult than many of the other Alger titles, and will probably cost you more. Make sure that the date at the bottom of the title page is MCMIV; make sure the publisher's monogram at bottom of spine is set in an interlocking script-like type. The monogram of two P's — block letters, back-to-back — was not used until a later date. Dealers with Alger clients are having no trouble getting $40.00 for this one.

$500. See "$500; or, Jacob Marlowe's Secret."

FIVE HUNDRED DOLLARS. See "$500; or, Jacob Marlowe's Secret."

$500 CHECK, THE. See "$500; or, Jacob Marlowe's Secret."

FIVE HUNDRED DOLLAR CHECK, THE. See "$500; or, Jacob Marlowe's Secret."

$500; or, JACOB MARLOWE'S SECRET.
  United States Book Company (Successors to John W. Lovell Company, Successor to Frank F. Lovell & Company), 1890

This title first appeared in book form as No. 23 of the Leather-Clad Tales of Adventure and Romance. It was issued, in papers wrappers, on May 10, 1890.

BINDING: Identical with "Dean Dunham."

The first hard-cover, cloth-bound edition appeared the following year, titled: THE $500 CHECK (on cover and spine); THE FIVE HUNDRED DOLLAR CHECK (on title page), and THE $500 CHECK; or, JACOB MARLOWE'S SECRET on Page 1 of the text.

TITLE PAGE: The Five Hundred Dollar/ Check/ By/ Horatio Alger, Jr./ Author of/ "Ragged Dick Series," "Tattered Tom Series," "Luck and/ Pluck Series," "Pacific Series," Etc., Etc./ New York/ United States Book Company/ Successors to/ John W Lovell Company/ 150 Worth St., Cor. Mission Place.

BINDING: Tan cloth, stamped in black, brown and gold. Cover: Brown sunburst (at top), around a wreath in which The/ $500/ Check/ is blind-stamped against black background. On right side of wreath a medical caduceus emblem; at right a bee hive (both stamped in brown). A loosely strung tape hangs from bottom of wreath to (By/ Horatio/ Alger Jr./ stamped in brown). Spine: At top, a brown sunburst upon which is a solid gold-stamped scroll upon which is black-stamped The/ $500/ Check/. Below it, loosely strung tape hangs from leaves, passing through gold-stamped Horatio/ Alger Jr./ and enclosing the word, Illustrated. At bottom, Porter & Coates, stamped in black, and with a slightly wider black strip over-printed. Cover size: 5¼″ x 7⅞″.

COLLATION: Brown coated end-paper; fly-leaf; tissue-covered frontispiece, title page [p. i]; copyright notice dated 1890 [p. ii]; contents, pp. iii - iv; text, pp. 1 - 339; fly-leaf; brown coated end-paper. In addition to the frontispiece are three full-page illustrations.

Prior to publication in book form, the story was serialized — as "$500; or, Jacob Marlowe's Secret" — in Argosy. The first installment ran on December 22, 1888, continuing through the issue dated March 23, 1889. It was again serialized in 1897, starting in Good News on May 1. The publication suspended before the story concluded, and the last two installments (along with other Good News serials) appeared in Ainslee's Army and Navy Weekly, concluding in the issue dated June 26.

It is with the earliest appearance of the story in hard covers that we have one of the most perplexing situations that Alger-collecting has produced. We have some of the answers but — even at this late date — questions still remain to be answered! There is no question that the hard-cover rights to publish this story were the property of Porter & Coates. They signified this by depositing a title page (with the book's title designated as "The Five Hundred Dollar Check") and by eventually, in 1891, being granted copyright #23627. Porter & Coates proceeded with the production, and actually had a small printing off the press sometime in 1891.

The mystery is: Did Porter & Coates ever put their book into distribution? What were the circumstances of United States Book Company taking over the already-printed copies, the plates and subsequent production? That U.S. Book Co. moved rapidly ahead with the publication is unquestioned, as they had an edition in circulation before the end of 1891. This printing had the original Porter & Coates title page removed and their own (printed on a grade of paper different from the other pages) tipped-in, with the U.S. Book Co. copyright date of 1890 — which they obtained for their Leather-Clad edition — printed on the verso. They obliterated, with a wide black surprinted strip, the Porter & Coates name at the bottom of the book's spine. When, shortly thereafter, they replaced the first issue with their own covers, these had the name Lovell stamped in gold at the bottom of the spine.

For years I — along with other Alger collectors — wondered and argued whether or not Porter & Coates actually did print a title page. Despite all odds against it, one has come to light. It was used — and for this there is absolutely no explanation — in an edition published about 1894 by American Publishers Corporation, a short-lived printing house organized as the successor to United States Book Company.

American Publishers actually put out two separate editions of the story. The first is in their deluxe Berkeley Series. However, it was in the later, cheaper Linwood Edition that we strike pay dirt. Although on the spine of the book is gold-stamped "Five Hundred Dollars," the title page presents it as "The Five Hundred Dollar Check." This is the original page prepared by Porter & Coates, and their familiar trade-mark device — the P & C within a wreath, through which a pen and sword are crossed — occupies the center of the sheet. *The back of the leaf even carries the original 1891 Porter & Coates copyright notice!*

Why this edition ever came off the presses is a mystery in itself, unless its purpose was to provide a clue to puzzled book sleuths, generations hence.

We can only guess as to the basic connection between Porter & Coates and the Lovell - United States Book Company combine. It is well-known that the ambitious John W. Lovell planned — and to an extent succeeded — in bringing other publishing houses into his master plan. As a matter of fact, this was the very reason that he arranged to have the firm bearing his name 'succeeded' by U.S. Book Co. He planned for it to become a giant trust, offering to other publishers the choice of joining, or of being swallowed up by it. Inasmuch as this scheme enjoyed short-lived success, and a number of publishers readily fell victims to Lovell's high-pressure persuasion, there is the possibility that Porter & Coates may have been in negotiations to join.

We know they did not join. We know that, nevertheless, "The $500 Check" became a U.S. Book Co. property. We also know, finally, that Porter & Coates and its successor, Henry T. Coates & Company, continued publishing Alger's stories long after Lovell and his United States Book Company were declared bankrupt.

In the years that followed, the story — in some variation of its title — was produced by virtually every one of the reprint publishers who for decades prospered on the works of Horatio Alger, Jr. On November 10, 1900, Street & Smith issued "The $500 Check" as No. 87 of their Medal Library, and quickly followed up with an attractive hard-cover edition. Later editions of other publishers generally seemed to favor as title "$500," or "Five Hundred Dollars." It has not been made clear whether this was in the interest of brevity, or if one of them finally realized that — *since there is no mention of a check in the story* — the earlier title had long been in error! A token step in the right direction may have been taken by A. L. Burt when, in their late reprint group, known as the Chimney Corner Series, they simply used only the original sub-title and called their edition "Jacob Marlowe's Secret."

For the record, there is no connection between the story and a short article titled "Five Hundred Dollars" by Alger, that appeared in the January, 1858, number of Graham's Illustrated Magazine.

It is also interesting to note that in 1887 — more than a year before earliest serialization of Alger's novel — there appeared a volume titled "Five Hundred Dollars." This was a compilation of short stories of New England life (none of them by Alger) that were originally published in a story-paper, The Century.

Because it is a rare oddity, the first state of the first edition of "The $500 Check" presents one of the few instances in which a later-issued hard-cover is more valuable than the earlier Leather-Clad. There are collectors willing to pay up to $125.00 for a copy with the Porter & Coates imprint on the spine; $75.00 for the Lovell imprint. I know of only one copy (my own) of the first state. The Library of Congress keeps the second state in its rare book vault. The Leather-Clad paperback is well worth $45.00.

FORGING AHEAD.

Penn Publishing Company, 1903

TITLE PAGE: Page design same as "Finding A Fortune." Forging/ Ahead/ by/ Horatio Alger Jr./ Author of/ "The Odds Against Him"/ "Making His Mark/ etc./ The Penn/ Publishing/ Company/ Philadelphia/ MCMIII.

BINDING: Identical with "Finding A Fortune."

COLLATION: Decorative end-paper, same as "Finding A Fortune;" fly-leaf; tissue-covered frontispiece; title page [p. 1]; copyright notice dated 1903 [p. 2]; contents, pp. 3 - 4; list of illustrations, blank on verso [unnumbered]; text, pp. 5 - 369; book advertisements, 7 leaves (14 pp.); fly-leaf; decorative end-paper, as described. In addition to the frontispiece are six full-page illustrations.

Prior to publication in book form (the book being deposited for copyright September 4, 1903), the story was serialized two times in Golden Days. Titled "Andy Gordon; or, The Fortunes of a Young Janitor," the first run began March 5, 1881, and continued through the issue dated May 28, 1881. The second run started on January 1, 1898, continuing through issue dated March 26, 1898. As "Andy Gordon," the story was reissued in hard covers by several publishers, the earliest printed by A. L. Burt in 1905. A late paperback edition — Street & Smith Alger Series No. 4 — was distributed with the title misspelled as "Andy Gordan."

First edition points: The date 1903 printed in Roman numerals — MCMIII — at bottom of title page. Publisher's monogram at bottom of spine is set in inter-locking script-like type. Later editions show this as two block-letter P's, back-to-back.

Value of first edition is $40.00.

FRANK AND FEARLESS; or, The Fortunes of Jasper Kent.

Henry T. Coates & Co., 1897

TITLE PAGE: Frank and Fearless/ or/ The Fortunes of Jasper Kent/ By/ Horatio Alger, Jr./ Author of "Brave and Bold Series," Etc./ Philadelphia/ Henry T. Coates & Co./ 1897.

BINDING: Bound in tan cloth, stamped in black and gold. Cover design: Double black lines around border/ ten stalks of leaves and berries/ against which is superimposed title stamped in gold with heavy black border (at top)/ and, stamped in black within a circle (near bottom): By/ Horatio/ Alger/ Jr. Spine: Double black line (at top)/ title (stamped in gold)/ [gold ruled line]/ Alger (in gold)/ [single stalk of leaves and berries]/ (stamped in gold: Henry T. Coates/ & Co.)/ double black line at bottom. Cover size: 5" x 7¾".

COLLATION: Slate-colored coated end-paper; fly-leaf; tissue-covered frontispiece; title page [p. i]; copyright notice dated 1897 [p. ii]; contents, pp. iii - iv; text, pp. 1 - 322; fly-leaf; slate-colored coated end-paper. In addition to the frontispiece are three full-page illustrations.

This story was serialized two times prior to its publication as a book. It first appeared in New York Weekly, starting in the issue dated May 18, 1885 (and was first registered for copyright by Street & Smith on May 4, 1885). Then, starting on February 28, 1891, the story was reprinted in Good News, running serially for twelve weeks. It was on October 11, 1897, that Coates deposited the bound volume for copyright, it appearing shortly thereafter as Volume Three of the Frank and Fearless Series. Some years later, Street & Smith reissued the title two times in paperback form.

The earliest printing of the first edition is dated 1897 at the bottom of the title page and this, for years, has been an enigma to Alger collectors. The original copy of the book — which was submitted to the Library of Congress — bears the dated title page. I have in my own library Horatio Alger's personal copy of the book and it also has the dated title page. Nevertheless, I have seen what would appear to be a very early printing — in which was written a bona fide Christmas, 1897 inscription — but without the dated title page. These factors give some backing to the possibility that the date appeared only in a very small pre-publication edition. Two other points of this edition are slate-colored coated end-papers (later printings had dark brown), and no advertisements at the back of the book.

I know of no other copies of the volume with dated title page, and my search of more than thirty-five years indicates that this version has never been offered for sale either in a book-seller's or auction catalogue. If one were to be offered, I'd judge it to be worth a minimum of $40.00, with the later state — which is not too rare — worth $22.50.

FRANK FOWLER, The Cash Boy.

A. L. Burt, 1887

BINDING: Identical with "The Errand Boy."

First appearance was as serialization in New York Weekly, starting May 10, 1875. The serial title, "The Cash Boy," was suggested by Francis S. Street, for which Alger warmly thanked him in a letter. First edition, in paper wrappers, was by Burt, as Boys' Home Library, Volume 4, issued in December, 1887. The bound book was deposited for copyright in the last days of 1887, receiving entry receipt No. 30732 for that year. Shortly after first publication, Burt reissued the story — printed from the original plates — in their deluxe, cloth-bound Home Series edition. The story — one of Alger's most popular works — was many times reissued, using either the serial title, the book title, or a combination of both.

The original paperback edition is rare, worth $42.00. The first hardcover edition is now worth $12.50-$15.00.

FRANK HUNTER'S PERIL.

Henry T. Coates & Co., 1896

TITLE PAGE: Frank Hunter's Peril/ By/ Horatio Alger, Jr./ Author of

"Ragged Dick Series," "Luck and Pluck/ Series," "Tattered Tom Series," Etc./ Philadelphia/ Henry T. Coates & Co.

BINDING: Identical with "Frank and Fearless."

COLLATION: Slate-colored coated end-paper; fly-leaf; tissue-covered frontispiece; title page [p. i]; copyright notice dated 1896 [p. ii]; contents, pp. iii - iv; text, pp. 5 - 335; fly-leaf; slate-colored coated end-paper. In addition to the frontispiece are three full-page illustrations.

Prior to appearance in book form, the story was serialized, as "Mr. Craven's Stepson; or, Frank Hunter's Peril," in New York Weekly. The first installment appeared in the issue dated December 26, 1885, after having been deposited for copyright on December 19th. Despite the fact that at the end of one of the installments was the announcement that "this story will not be published in book form," Coates did put out the bound volume — the title shortened to "Frank Hunter's Peril" — and deposited it for copyright on September 14, 1896. It was issued as Volume Two of the Frank and Fearless Series. The story was again serialized — in Good News — from November 28, 1891 — February 13, 1892.

The first edition contains no book ads.

Value of first edition is $22.50.

FRANK'S CAMPAIGN; or, What Boys Can Do on the Farm for the Camp.
Loring, Publisher, 1864

TITLE PAGE: Frank's Campaign;/ or,/ What Boys Can Do on the Farm for the Camp./ By Horatio Alger, Jr./ [rule]/ Loring, Publisher,/ 319 Washington Street,/ Boston./ 1864.

BINDING: Bound in mauve, dark brown and green cloth. Front and back covers identically blind-stamped with border rules and close-set vertical lines. Spine, gold-stamped: Frank's/ Campaign/ or/ What A/ Boy/ Can Do/ Loring. Cover Size: 5" x 7".

COLLATION: Yellow-tinted end-paper; fly-leaf; frontispiece; tissue-covered title page [p. i]; copyright notice dated 1864 [p. ii]; dedication [p. iii] verso blank [p. iv]; preface, [pp. v] - vi; contents, [pp. vii] — viii; text, [pp. 9] — 296; fly-leaf; yellow-tinted end-paper. In addition to frontispiece is one illustration.

"Frank's Campaign" — Alger's third book, but the first of the many by him to be published by A. K. Loring — is the first volume of what later was designated as the Campaign Series. The book was deposited for copyright on November 19, 1864.

Loring issued three separate and easily identifiable states of this volume. The first state cover (as described) was not later repeated. The ruled line on the title page was almost immediately replaced (during December, 1864) with the words, "Second Edition." "Frank's Campaign," incidentally, is one of only two Alger books in which the second edition was so indicated ("Paul Prescott's Charge" being the other). An illustration in the first state has been inserted between pages 196 (which is unnumbered) and 197. In the later printings this page was bound-in, facing page 205 (which, for unknown reason, carries the page number 17 throughout all editions examined).

Both the first and second states, but not the third — which was issued after the Civil War ended — carry these points: The Preface begins: "The great struggle in which we are now engaged. . ." The final paragraph on page 295 begins: "I am obliged to leave my story incomplete. The Rebellion is not yet at an end." The third state has a completely changed Preface, and the lines on page 295 are changed to read: "Some years have passed since the above letter was written. The war is happily over and Captain Frost has returned home with an honorable record of service."

The second state binding employs the blind-stamped border-rules described above, but substitutes a rough, pebbled texture for the vertical lines of the first state. The third state front and back covers are in the style of "Ben, the Luggage Boy," and its sub-title shortened to "The Farm and the Camp."

The first state is easily worth $37.50, cherished by Civil War buffs as well as Alger collectors. The second state can bring $27.50, and the third about $15.00.

FROM CANAL BOY TO PRESIDENT, or, The Boyhood and Manhood of James A. Garfield.

John R. Anderson & Company, 1881

TITLE PAGE: From/ Canal Boy to President,/ or the/ Boyhood and Manhood/ of/ James A. Garfield./ By/ Horatio Alger, Jr.,/ Author of Ragged Dick; Luck and Pluck; Tattered Tom, Etc./ Illustrated./ New York:/ John R. Anderson & Company,/ No. 17 Murray Street,/ 1881.

BINDING: Bound in cloth; dark blue, green, brown and terra cotta being noted. Black and gold stamping. Front cover design: black-stamped vignette at top shows Garfield taking oath of office; below, a youth on horseback towing a barge along a canal. Typography: From (black)/ Canal Boy (gold)/ to (black)/ President (gold)/ By Horatio Alger Jr. (black). Back cover has blind-stamped border of classical Greek waves design. Spine: [Top design of lines and dots]/ [branch with leaves]/ (title, blind-stamped on gold background: From/ Canal Boy/ To/ President)/ (gold-stamped: [dot]/ or the/ Boyhood/ and/ Manhood/ of/ James A. Garfield/ [rule]/ Horatio Alger Jr.)/ vignette of palm frond superimposed on fasces (in black)/ [black line]/ (blind-stamped on gold background) J. R. Anderson & Co. Cover size: 4⅞″ x 6¾″.

COLLATION: End-paper; fly-leaf; frontispiece; tissue-covered portrait; title page [p. 1]; copyright notice dated 1881 [p. 2]; dedication [p. 3]; verso blank [p. 4]; preface, pp. 5-6; contents, pp. 7-8; text, pp. 9 - 334; section of 8 leaves of advertisements of books by Charles Dickens; fly-leaf; end-paper. In addition to frontispiece and portrait are three inserted illustrations.

Alger established some sort of a speed record with this story, having completed its writing less than three weeks after the death of President Garfield. Garfield died on September 19, 1881. Alger had completed the story by October 8th (the date indicated on his preface), and the publisher had the first printing off the presses prior to November 3d, the date on which it was deposited for copyright and issued as Volume One of the Boyhood and Manhood Series of Illustrious Americans.

So great was the rush to get the story into print that the pressmen inadvertently transposed pages 266 and 268. An erratum slip, advising the reader of this error, was tipped onto page 267 of the first edition. This was, of course, corrected in all subsequent printings.

Most Alger collectors agree that "From Canal Boy to President" is one of the easiest Algers to obtain in an early edition (although the first state, with tipped-in erratum slip is rare as hens' teeth!), and copies offered are frequently found to be in sturdier condition than most of the author's other works.

There are two logical reasons for this. The first is that the book apparently was issued in huge quantities, probably with an eye toward cashing-in on the tremendous public interest in the late President's recent assassination. Although Anderson may have been able to foresee the great sale of his books, it appears that the young people who received them did not devour the story as avidly as they did fiction based upon Alger's typical success formula. This, perhaps, is the reason that so many of the copies remaining until today give the crisp appearance of having never been taken from the library shelf.

The first issue, with erratum slip, is rare and well worth $30.00. Later printings are worth about half that price, although a $20.00 tag is not unusual.

FROM FARM BOY TO SENATOR; Being the History of the Boyhood and Manhood of Daniel Webster.

J. S. Ogilvie & Company, 1882

TITLE PAGE: From/ Farm Boy to Senator;/ Being the History of the/ Boyhood and Manhood/ of/ Daniel Webster./ By Horatio Alger, Jr.,/ Author of "From Canal Boy to President," "Ragged Dick/ Series," "Tattered Tom Series," etc., etc./ New York:/ J. S. Ogilvie & Company,/ No. 31 Rose Street.

BINDING: Bound in cloth; brown, green and blue having been noted. Stamping, design, typography and size similar to "From Canal Boy to President," with these exceptions: Cover: vignette at top shows Daniel Webster making a speech; below is illustration of boy driving team of oxen. Spine: vignette is of plow superimposed upon a branch of olive leaves; below it the Ogilvie trade-mark, an eight-pointed star blind-stamped upon a gold shield. Back cover: Blind-stamped border with decorative design at center.

COLLATION: Yellow-tinted end-paper; frontispiece; title page [p. 1]; copyright notice dated 1882 [p. 2]; dedication [p. 3]; verso blank [p. 4]; contents, [pp. 5] - 6; preface, [pp. 7] - 8; one leaf (blank page with portrait of young Webster on verso [unnumbered]; text, [pp. 9] — 310; one leaf (2 pp.) of book advertisements; yellow-tinted fly-leaf. In addition to frontispiece and portrait are two illustrations.

Street & Smith, in 1870, copyrighted this story under the title of "A Boys' Life of Daniel Webster." The book title was deposited in 1880, but was not published until 1882, probably as a result of the popularity of "From Canal Boy to President." Judging by the similarity of format and binding, one gets the impression that this was to have been a part of the

Boyhood and Manhood Series of Illustrious Americans. However, if there had been any such plan between the Anderson and Ogilvie organizations, it came to an end with the formation of Anderson & Allen, which firm published "Abraham Lincoln, the Backwoods Boy" in 1883 as the second volume of the series. They later followed this up with a third volume, a life of George Washington, not written by Alger.

Value of first edition is $25.00.

FROM FARM TO FORTUNE: or, Nat Nason's Strange Experience.

Stitt Publishing Company, 1905

> TITLE PAGE: From/ Farm to Fortune/ Or, Nat Nason's Strange Experience/ By/ Horatio Alger, Jr./ Author of "Lost at Sea," "Nelson the Newsboy,"/ "Out for Business," "The Young Book/ Agent," "Ragged Dick/ Series," Etc./ [decorative device]/ New York/ Stitt Publishing Company/ 1905.

> BINDING: Identical with "Falling In With Fortune," except that white stamping is substituted for the gold on spine, and publisher is Stitt, not Mershon.

> COLLATION: End-paper; frontispiece; title page [p. i]; copyright notice dated 1905 [p. ii]; preface, pp. iii - iv; contents, pp. v - vi; text, [pp. 1] - 248; fly-leaf; end-paper. In addition to the frontispiece are three full-page illustrations.

Although "From Farm to Fortune" is, of course, one of the eleven "Winfield" (Edward Stratemeyer) completions, Alger's name alone appears as the author. The book was received for copyright at the Library of Congress on October 3, 1905.

The first edition has the 1905 publication date indicated at bottom of the title page, and contains no listing of book advertisements at the back of the book. Later printings list the title as a volume of The Rise in Life Series (it is the second title listed although actually was the seventh to be published).

Although there is nothing of Alger's writing to be identified with this story, it is, nevertheless, a wanted item — and a hard one to come by — for the collector's shelf.

Value of first edition is $25.00.

FROM RAILSPLITTER TO PRESIDENT. See "Abraham Lincoln, the Backwoods Boy."

GEORGE CARTER'S LEGACY; or,   The Inventor's Son. See "Herbert Carter's Legacy."

GERALD'S MISSION. See "Making His Mark."

GRAND'THER BALDWIN'S THANKSGIVING; With Other Ballads and Poems.

Loring, Publisher, 1875

> TITLE PAGE: Grand'ther Baldwin's/ Thanksgiving/ with/ Other Ballads

and Poems/ by/ Horatio Alger, Jr/ [decorative rule]/ Loring, Publisher/ Corner Bromfield and Washington Streets/ Boston.

BINDING: Bound in green, brown, terra cotta and possibly other colors of cloth, probably with no priority of issue. Front and back covers have a blind-stamped border-rule. Front cover has sheaf of wheat gold-stamped at center. Spine (gold-stamped): [Doubleline rule]/ Grandfather/ Baldwin's/ Thansgiving/ [decorative rule]/ Horatio/ Alger/ Loring/ [double-line rule]. Cover size: 4⅞" x 7".

COLLATION: Dark brown coated end-paper; fly-leaf; title page [p. 1]; copyright notice dated 1875 [p. 2]; contents, [pp. 3-4]; leaf on which is printed "Ballads," [p. 5]; verso blank [p. 6]; text, pp. 7 - 125; dark-brown coated end-paper.

CONTENTS: Ballads:
Grand'ther Baldwin's Thanksgiving.
St. Nicholas.
Barbara's Courtship.
The Confession.
Rose in the Garden.
Phoebe's Wooing.
The Lost Heart.
John Maynard.
Friar Anselmo.

Miscellaneous Poems:
In the Church at Stratford-on-Avon.
Mrs. Browning's Grave at Florence.
My Castle.
Apple Blossoms.
Summer Hours.
June.
Little Charlie.
The Whippoorwill and I.
Carving a Name.

In Time of War:
Gone to the War.
Where is My Boy Tonight?
A Soldier's Valentine.
Last Words.
Song of the Croaker.
King Cotton.
Out of Egypt.
The Price of Victory.

Harvard Odes:
Fair Harvard, Dear Guide of Our Youth's Golden Days.
As We Meet in They Name, Alma Mater, Tonight.
Fair Harvard, the Months have Accomplished their Round.
There's a Fountain of Fable, whose Magical Power.

Occasional Odes:
Bi-Centennial Ode.
For the Consecration of a Cemetery.

Like Alger's first book ("Bertha's Christmas Vision"), "Grand'ther Baldwin's Thanksgiving" is a collection of his writings, most — possibly all — of which had previously been published earlier in various periodicals.

419

Several, such as "Carving a Name," "Where is My Boy Tonight?", "Last Words," "Song of the Croaker," and others, achieved considerable vogue and were reprinted in school readers and also in the 'reciters' that were so popular for home entertainment during Alger's era. "John Maynard," a ballad of a heroic sailor that first appeared in the January, 1868, issue of Student and Schoolmate, was tremendously popular and quickly became a standard presentation at scholastic oratory contests.

An early hand-written draft of "Carving a Name" — which hangs framed in my library — contains several words and lines (and one stanza less) at variance with the version as it was eventually published.

Although hardly as popular with Alger's readers as his standard output of that period, "Grand'ther Baldwin's Thanksgiving," (which Loring didn't get around to depositing for copyright until 1879) is treasured by collectors and is gold in the pockets of book sellers. It is one of the higher-priced, rare Algers that does appear on the market from time-to-time, generally in sturdier condition than most of the author's editions.

This volume has appreciated considerably in recent years. Valued at about $75.00; from $100.00-up if inscribed by Alger.

GRIT. See "The Young Boatman."

GRIT; or, The Young Boatman Of Pine Point. See "The Young Boatman."

GRIT, THE YOUNG BOATMAN. See "The Young Boatman."

HARRY VANE. See "In a New World."

HECTOR'S INHERITANCE; or, The Boys of Smith Institute.
Porter & Coates, 1885
   TITLE PAGE: Hector's Inheritance;/ or,/ The Boys of Smith Institute./ By/ Horatio Alger, Jr.,/ Author of "Ragged Dick," "Tattered Tom," "Luck and Pluck,"/ Etc., Etc./ [publisher's trade-mark device]/ Philadelphia:/ Porter & Coates.
   BINDING: Identical with "Ben's Nugget."
   COLLATION: Dark brown coated end-paper; fly-leaf; tissue-covered frontispiece; title page [p. i]; copyright notice, dated 1885 [p. ii]; contents, [pp. iii] - iv; text, [pp. 5] - 307; 8 pp. of book advertisements; fly-leaf; dark brown coated end-paper. In addition to frontispiece are three full-page illustrations.

The story was first serialized in Golden Argosy in 1883. It was serialized again in the Boston Globe during February-March, 1885. Porter & Coates deposited the book for copyright on September 1, 1885. Although as popular in its day as were most of Alger's stories, "Hector's Inheritance" is a succession of the stereotyped situations, benefactors, villains and prose that — in recent decades — has been subject to more cynicism than praise. A typical example of the criticized Alger style is noted in this standard dialogue, as Hector is interviewed by Titus Newman, a wealthy merchant whose small daughter the boy saved from being "crushed beneath the hoofs of the horses and the wheels" of a rapidly-approaching carriage on Madison Avenue near Twenty-third Street:

"Have you any taste for any kind of liquor?"

"No, sir," answered Hector, promptly.

"Even if you had, do you think you would have self-control enough to avoid entering saloons and gratifying your tastes?"

"Yes, sir."

"That is well. Do you play pool?"

"No, sir," answered Hector, wondering whither all these questions tended.

"I ask because playing pool in public rooms paves the way for intemperance, as bars are generally connected with such establishments."

The first edition is identified most readily by the indication of this title as the last on the list of Alger stories, on Page 7 of the advertisements at the back of the book. Later editions show "Hector's Inheritance" listed as third volume of the Atlantic Series, with the fourth title ("Helping Himself") already in print. Also, the "Boy Pioneer Series" (three titles by Edward S. Ellis) will be the final entry in the ad section. Later issue shows "Footprints in the Forest" as final entry.

Value of first edition is $20.00.

HELEN FORD.

Loring, Publisher, 1866

TITLE PAGE: Helen Ford./ By Horatio Alger, Jr./ Loring, Publisher./ 319 Washington Street,/ Boston./ 1866.

BINDING: Bound in terra cotta, mauve and green cloth. Probably no priority of issue. Front and back covers identically blind-stamped around border with repeated diamond-design enclosed between two double rules. Spine, gold-stamped: [Heavy ornamental line with thin line beneath it]/ ([scroll, with in it] Helen/ Ford)/ Loring/ thin line with heavy ornamental line beneath it. Cover size: 5¼" x 7⅞".

COLLATION: Yellow-tinted end-paper; fly-leaf; title page [p. 1]; copyright notice dated 1866 [p. 2]; text, pp. 3 - 297; one leaf (2 pp.) of book advertisements; fly-leaf; yellow-tinted end-paper.

"Helen Ford" is unusual in more ways than one. It is Alger's first and only effort to write a story for older girls; it is one of his few works to be serialized after being published in book form. The serialization is the only Alger item extant that carries his rare pseudonym, Arthur Hamilton.

Although the title page was deposited on August 29, 1866, and the book submitted on October 9th of that year, copyright was not granted until February 21, 1867, some months after the book was put into circulation.

The story which, in itself, is not a specimen of Alger at his best, nevertheless is unique. Helen Ford is a young singer who is the main support of her unworldly father, an inventor whose ambition it is to build an airplane. Alger doesn't believe this can be done, commenting that "no man of a well balanced mind would have labored with such sanguine expectations of success on a project so uncertain as the invention of a flying machine." At the story's end, the author concludes: "Mr. Ford has long since given up his invention as impractical."

In December, 1885 — almost two decades after Alger wrote the book — the story was serialized as "A Child of Fortune" in Golden Argosy. The observation has been made that the pen-name, Arthur Hamilton, was employed either because Alger was not proud of this early work, or that it was best to disassociate his name from the authorship of a story for girls. The more likely explanation is that Frank Munsey (a publisher quick to establish a pen-name for an author, and the originator of Alger's Arthur Lee Putnam pseudonym) had the story carry the Hamilton by-line so that there would be no conflict with two other Alger stories, the ending chapters of "Struggling Upward," and the beginning of "In a New World," with which "A Child of Fortune" ran concurrently. Arthur Hamilton is first supposed to have been used by Alger in 1869, in connection with early publication of another story (see "Ralph Raymond's Heir").

The first edition of Helen Ford carries the date, 1866, at bottom of the title page. There are no advertisements for Alger books. The covers of later editions carried a somewhat different blind-stamped design that included a sunburst within a decorative diamond-shape at center.

Value of first edition is $30.00.

HELPING HIMSELF; or, Grant Thornton's Ambition.

Porter & Coates, 1886

TITLE PAGE: Helping Himself/ or/ Grant Thornton's Ambition./ By/ Horatio Alger, Jr.,/ Author of "Ragged Dick," "Tattered Tom," "Luck and/ Pluck," Etc., Etc./ [publisher's trade-mark device]/ Philadelphia:/ Porter & Coates.

BINDING: Identical with "Ben's Nugget."

COLLATION: Brown coated end-paper; fly-leaf; tissue-covered frontispiece; title page [p. i]; copyright notice dated 1886 [p. ii]; contents, [pp. iii] - iv; text, [pp. 5] - 320; fly-leaf; brown coated end-paper. In addition to frontispiece are three full-page illustrations.

Before appearing in book form, "Helping Himself" was serialized in Golden Argosy, the installments appearing during the last part of 1884 and continuing through the first part of 1885. Porter & Coates deposited the title page for copyright on April 26, 1886, and presented the completed volume on July 31st. My copy has, pasted onto the front fly-leaf, a presentation card on which appears Alger's signature and the date, May 8, 1886, indicating either the possibility of the book being in distribution at that early date, or that the copy at hand is a pre-publication edition.

The first edition contains no book advertisements, and the letter J is damaged in the word "Justice" at top of page 193.

Value of first edition is $20.00.

HERBERT CARTER'S LEGACY; or, The Inventor's Son.

Loring, Publisher, 1875

TITLE PAGE: Herbert Carter's Legacy;/ or,/ The Inventor's Son,/ By/ Horatio Alger, Jr.,/ Author of "Tattered Tom" Series; "Luck and Pluck" Series; "Brave/ and Bold" Series, Etc., Etc./ [rule]/ Loring, Publisher, Cor. Washington and Bromfield Sts.,/ Boston.

BINDING: Identical with "Bound to Rise."

COLLATION: Yellow-tinted end-paper; fly-leaf; 2 leaves (4 pp.) of book advertisements; frontispiece; tissue-covered decorative title page; title page [p. i]; copyright notice dated 1875 [p. ii]; dedication [p. iii]; verso blank [p. iv]; preface, [pp. v] - vi; (Note: there is no leaf for [pp. vii - viii]); text, [pp. 9] - 327; yellow-tinted end-paper. In addition to frontispiece and decorative title page are two full-page illustrations.

Prior to appearing in book form, "Herbert Carter's Legacy" was serialized in Young Israel during 1875. Loring had the book on sale by the end of the same year, but did not deposit the volume for copyright — for reasons unknown — until 1877, at which time a number of other previously published Alger stories were presented at the same time. This title is Volume IV of the Second Luck and Pluck Series.

The first edition will show, in ads at front, "Sam's Chance," Volume III of the Second Tattered Tom Series, to be published in "April, '76." It will also show "Jack's Ward," Volume II of the Brave and Bold Series, as being already in print, and — on the facing page — a full-page ad for "Seeking His Fortune."

With the title changed to "George Carter's Legacy; or The Inventor's Son," the story was issued in England by Aldine Publishing Company about 1903.

Value of first edition is $25.00.

HERMIT'S HEIR, THE. See "Mark Manning's Mission."

IN A NEW WORLD; or, Among the Gold-Fields of Australia.
Porter & Coates, 1893

TITLE PAGE: In A New World/ or/ Among the Gold-Fields of Australia/ By/ Horatio Alger, Jr./ Author of "Facing the World," "Do and/ Dare," "Ragged Dick Series," "Luck/ and Pluck Series," Etc./ [publisher's trade-mark device]/ Philadelphia/ Porter & Coates.

BINDING: Identical with "Digging for Gold."
COLLATION: Slate-colored coated end-paper; fly-leaf; tissue-covered frontispiece; title page [p. i]; copyright notice dated 1893 at bottom of page of book advertisements [p. ii]; contents, pp. iii - iv; text, [pp. 1] - 323; book advertisements, [pp. 1] - 8; fly-leaf; slate-colored coated end-paper. In addition to frontispiece are three full-page illustrations.

Prior to appearance in book form, "In a New World" was serialized in Golden Argosy, installments starting at the end of 1885. Porter & Coates deposited the book for copyright on June 16, 1893.

In 1894, a year after publication in the United States, the story was re-issued in England, titled "The Nugget Finders; A Tale of the Gold Fields of Australia," with the author indicated on title page only, and as "H. Alger." This unusual (for Alger books) reprint was issued by John F. Shaw & Co., 48 Paternoster Row, London. A frontispiece, in full color, is very similar to the illustration that faces Page 188 in the Porter & Coates edition. The binding is green, with blind and gold-stamping. The title is gold-stamped in panels on cover and spine. Cover size: 5⅜" x 7⅞".

A later state of the British edition gives the publisher's address as 3 Pilgrim Street, London, E.C.

"The Nugget Finders" is one of the three Algers published by Shaw. The other two (previously noted) were "Ben's Nuggets; or, A Boy's Search for Fortune" (1883), and "Digging for Gold" (1892).

Yet another London publisher, Aldine, reissued this story (between 1903 and 1907) as "Val Vane's Victory; or, Well Won." It was a paperback in their Garfield Library series.

First edition of "In A New World" is identified by the title appearing as final volume of the New World Series, on [p. ii], and by the fact that "Digging for Gold" is the last Alger title listed in the advertisements at back of the book.

This is the rare case of the reissue, "The Nugget Finders," being more valuable than the original first edition. The scarce British item — which rarely appears — is easily worth $45.00. The first edition of "In A New World" is worth $22.50.

IN SEARCH OF TREASURE; The Story of Guy's Eventful Voyage.

A. L. Burt Company, 1907

> TITLE PAGE: In Search of Treasure/ [double line]/ The Story of Guy's Eventful Voyage/ [single line]/ By Horatio Alger, Jr./ Author of "Ben Bruce," "Bernard Brook's Adventures,"/ "A Debt of Honor," "Mark Manning's Mission,"/ etc., etc./ [publisher's trade-mark device containing words: Burt's Library of the World's Best Books]/ Illustrated by/ J. Watson Davis/ [double line]/ A. L. Burt Company,/ Publishers, New York.

> BINDING: Bound in brown cloth, stamped in black, white, orange and blue. Cover design: In Search/ of/ Treasure/ by/ Horatio Alger Jr./ [illustration of boy digging up a chest of coins]. Spine: [line]/ In/ Search/ of/ Treasure/ [line]/ [figure of boy waving hat]/ A. L. Burt Company/ New York/ [line]. Cover size: 5⅜" x 7⅝".

> COLLATION: End-paper; frontispiece; title page; copyright notice dated 1894 by Frank A. Munsey & Company, and 1907 by A. L. Burt Company; text, [pp. 1] - 301; end-paper. In addition to frontispiece are three full-page illustrations.

Prior to the appearance in book form, the story was serialized in Argosy, the first installment appearing in the April, 1894, edition, under title of "The Island Treasure." "In Search of Treasure" is among the last two Alger first editions published by Burt ("Wait and Win" was the last), and is quite rare, despite its comparatively late date. In 1911, Street & Smith issued the title in paper wrappers as Number 622 of their New Medal Library. At about the same time Burt reissued an edition in their Chimney Corner series.

Value of first edition is $35.00.

ISLAND TREASURE, THE. See "In Search of Treasure."

JACK'S WARD; or, The Boy Guardian.

Loring, Publisher, 1875

TITLE PAGE: Jack's Ward;/ or,/ The Boy Guardian./ By/ Horatio Alger, Jr.,/ Author of "Ragged Dick" Series; "Luck and Pluck" Series; "Tattered/ Tom" Series, Etc., Etc./ [rule]/ Loring, Publisher,/ Cor. Washington and Bromfield Sts.,/ Boston.

BINDING: Identical with "Brave and Bold."

COLLATION: Yellow-tinted end-paper; fly-leaf; 1 leaf (2 pp.) book advertisements; frontispiece; tissue-covered decorative title page [p. 1]; verso blank [p. 2]; title page [p. 3]; copyright notice dated 1875 [p. 4]; dedication [p. 5]; verso blank [p. 6]; preface [p. 7]; verso blank [p. 8]; text, pp. 9 - 331; fly-leaf; yellow-tinted end-paper. In addition to frontispiece and decorative title page are two full-page illustrations.

Issued in 1875 (although not deposited for copyright until 1877) as Volume II of the Brave and Bold Series, "Jack's Ward" is a re-written version of the supremely rare "Timothy Crump's Ward," which had been published anonymously in 1866. Nevertheless, this story has been (as Alger puts it, in his preface) "wholly rewritten, considerably enlarged, and, it is hoped, improved." It must, therefore, be considered as a new and separate work.

More closely following Alger's literary style of twenty years earlier, when the parent book was written, Jack Harding differs from the heroes of the author's 1875 period in two major respects. The first is that both Jack's mother and father are alive; their household even includes a melancholy maiden aunt. The second difference is that moderate good fortune befalls the Harding family relatively early in the tale, and Jack is spared the privation endured by most of Alger's heroes.

The first edition will indicate — in the ads at front — no further listing of titles in the Brave and Bold Series, after "Jack's Ward." "The Young Outlaw" will be listed as Volume II of the Second Tattered Tom Series, with the Roman numerals III and IV printed below, but without any ensuing titles announced.

Value of first edition is $35.00.

JACOB MARLOWE'S SECRET. See "$500; or, Jacob Marlowe's Secret."

JED, THE POORHOUSE BOY.

Henry T. Coates & Co., 1899

TITLE PAGE: Jed,/ The/ Poorhouse Boy/ By/ Horatio Alger, Jr./ Author of "Ragged Dick," "Luck and Pluck," "Tattered Tom,"/ Etc., Etc./ Philadelphia/ Henry T. Coates.

BINDING: Bound in light brown cloth. Cover design (stamped in darker brown): Jed The/ Poorhouse/ Boy/ two crossed branches. Spine (stamped in darker brown, black and gold): Single branch running full-length of spine with, surprinted upon it in black: Jed The/ Poorhouse/ Boy (against gold background)/ Alger (against gold background)/ Coates (against gold background). Cover size: 5" x 7½".

COLLATION: Dark brown coated end-paper; tissue-covered frontispiece; title page [p. i]; copyright notice dated 1899 [p. ii]; contents, pp. iii - iv; text, pp. 1 - 363; dark-brown coated end-paper. In addition to the frontispiece are two full-page illustrations.

Prior to appearing in book form, "Jed, the Poorhouse Boy" was serialized in Argosy, the first installment appearing on March 26, 1892. Although the title was not deposited for copyright until January 22, 1900, the first edition apparently was in distribution shortly before Christmas, 1899.

The hero of this story attains even greater heights than most of Alger's plucky youngsters. Not only does Jed — who started life in the Scranton Poorhouse — achieve his fortune but, at story's end, we learn that the slavey once abused by the tyrannical Overseer of the Poor is really Sir Robert Fenwick, Baronet, of Fenwick Hall, Gloucestershire, England.

There are no book advertisements in the first edition.

Value of first edition is $17.50.

JERRY, THE BACKWOODS BOY, or, The Parkhurst Treasure.

The Mershon Company, 1904

TITLE PAGE: Jerry, The/ Backwoods Boy/ Or/ The Parkhurst Treasure/ By/ Horatio Alger, Jr./ Author of "Young Captain Jack," "Nelson, the/ Newsboy," "Out for Business," "Lost at/ Sea," "Ragged Dick Series," Etc./ [small tulip decoration]/ The Mershon Company/ Rahway, N.J. [space] New York.

BINDING: Identical with "Falling In With Fortune."

COLLATION: End-paper; frontispiece; title page [p. i]; copyright notice dated 1904 at bottom of list of books "By the same author," [p. ii]; preface, pp. iii - iv; text, [pp. 1] - 248; 1 leaf (2 pp.) book advertisements; end-paper. In addition to frontispiece are three full-page illustrations.

This is another of the eleven volumes Stratemeyer "completed," although only Alger's name appears. There is a good possibility that "Jerry, the Backwoods Boy" may have been issued simultaneously with "Lost at Sea." Both books were received for copyright at the Library of Congress on the same date, October 20, 1904. This, in itself, is not conclusive, but I have at hand a copy of the former, bearing a November, 1904 gift inscription, but with the list of book ads showing "Lost at Sea" as already being in print.

Two years after book publication, the story was serialized in Comfort Magazine, running from November, 1906, through October, 1907.

Despite the fact that it is most questionable that Alger had anything to do with this story, his name is given as the author, the book is hard to come by, and the collector seeking to add it to his shelf will have to pay for it at least $22.50-$25.00.

JOE'S LUCK; or, A Boy's Adventures in California.

A. L. Burt, 1887

BINDING: Identical with "The Errand Boy."

After being serialized in New York Weekly, the first installment appearing in the issue dated March 4, 1878, Burt issued the story in paper wrappers as Volume I of the Boys' Home Library, dated September, 1887. The book had been deposited for copyright on August 29th of that year. Earliest printing shows publisher's address as 162 William Street. Shortly thereafter (possibly the same year) Burt reissued the story in their deluxe clothbound edition. After 1899, Burt issued reprints in a variety of bindings of other designs and — still later — cheap reprints were put out by other publishers.

The original paperback edition is rare, worth about $42.00. The first hard cover issue brings about $15.00.

JOE THE HOTEL BOY; or, Winning Out By Pluck.

Cupples & Leon, 1906

TITLE PAGE: Joe The Hotel Boy/ Or/ Winning Out By Pluck/ By Horatio Alger, Jr./ Author of "Ragged Dick," "Tattered Tom," "Nelson/ The Newsboy," "Out For Business" Etc./ [rule]/ illustrated/ New York/ Cupples & Leon.

BINDING: Bound in tan cloth with red, black and blue stamping. Cover design: [Black rule around border]/ Joe/ The/ Hotel/ Boy/ [illustration of bellboy in blue uniform, standing beside red trunk]/ Horatio Alger, Jr. Spine: Joe/ The/ Hotel/ Boy/ [rule]/ Horatio/ Alger, Jr./ Cupples/ &/ Leon. Cover size: 5¼" x 7⅝".

COLLATION: End-paper; tissue-covered frontispiece; title page; copyright notice dated 1906; preface, [2 pp.]; contents, [2 pp.]; text, pp. 1 - 268; 2 leaves [4 pp.] of book advertisements; fly-leaf; end-paper. In addition to the frontispiece are three full-page illustrations.

"Joe The Hotel Boy" is the tenth of the series of books attributed to Alger, but actually the work of Edward Stratemeyer. Like a number of others, this volume lists Alger's name only, as author. Prefaces of others of this group indicate that they were started by Alger, but completed after his death by Arthur M. Winfield (a Stratemeyer pseudonym). Nevertheless, there is little, if anything, of Alger's style and technique to be found in "Joe The Hotel Boy" or, for that matter, in any of the eleven "completions."

Title of the story was registered on July 7, 1906, and the book deposited for copyright July 23, 1906.

Two first edition points are noted: There is no circle around the Cupples & Leon name at bottom of spine; there is no ad listing for "Ben Logan's Triumph," the eleventh and final "Winfield-Alger."

Value of first edition $22.50.

JULIUS. See "Julius; or, The Street Boy Out West."

JULIUS THE STREET BOY. See "Julius; or, The Street Boy Out West."

JULIUS; or, The Street Boy Out West.

Loring, Publisher, 1874

TITLE PAGE: Julius;/ Or,/ The Street Boy Out West./ By/ Horatio Alger, Jr.,/ Author of "Ragged Dick Series," "Tattered Tom Series,"/ "Luck and Pluck Series," "Campaign Series," Etc./ [rule]; Loring, Publisher,/ Cor. Washington and Bromfield Streets,/ Boston.

BINDING: Covers are identical with "Ben, The Luggage Boy." Spine (gold-stamped): [line]/ [decorative canopy]/ Julius,/ The/ Street Boy/ Out West/ [decorative device]/ Tattered Tom/ Books./ Second Series/ [vignette of boy with hand in pocket]/ [line]/ Loring/ [line].

COLLATION: Yellow-tinted end-paper; fly-leaf; 1 leaf (2 pp.) of book advertisements; frontispiece; tissue-covered decorative title page [p. i]; verso blank [p. ii]; title page [p. iii]; copyright notice dated 1874 [p. iv]; dedication [p. v]; verso blank [p. vi]; preface, pp. 7 - viii; text, [pp.9] - 276; fly-leaf; end-paper. In addition to the frontispiece and decorative title page are two full-page illustrations.

"Julius; or, The Street Boy Out West" is Volume I of the Second Tattered Tom Series. Although published in 1874, the book was not deposited for copyright until early 1877 (along with several other Algers whose copyright formalities Loring had previously neglected).

This was one of Alger's most popular books, and Julius one of his most beloved characters. The story was variously reissued by numerous other publishers under titles of "Julius," "Julius the Street Boy," and perhaps other slight variations.

The book is Alger's tribute to the Children's Aid Society which, during the post-Civil War years, resettled many of New York's street boys, war orphans and assorted homeless waifs on farms in the newly-opened Western Territories.

Any of the Loring editions of this title are rare; a bona fide first edition especially so. The first edition is easy to detect, to the frequent consternation of the collector who thought he had one, but discovered that — lacking one or more important and obvious points — he owned a later issue. Look for these: The first page of book ads will indicate that the First Series of both the Tattered Tom and Luck and Pluck Series are "now ready," but the Second Series of both "preparing." On the second page of ads, "Julius" is listed as Volume I of the Second Tattered Tom Series, but Volume II must show that "The Young Outlaw" will be ready in "Oct., '74." The Volume III title of the Luck and Pluck Series must be listed as "Up the Ladder; or, Harry Walton's Success, in Oct., '74 [no period]". There must be no listing of any volumes of the Brave and Bold Series. A copy of the book having a gift inscription of early date (not later than June 15, 1874) will surely have all the indicated points. The inscription, of course, merely being a double-check on points, and of no "point value" itself.

The first edition, as described, brings up to $35.00. Later Loring issues are priced at about $20.00.

KIT WATSON'S TRIUMPH. See "The Young Acrobat."

LESTER'S LUCK.

Henry T. Coates & Co., 1901

TITLE PAGE: Lester's Luck./ By/ Horatio Alger, Jr.,/ Author of "Ragged Dick Series," "Tattered Tom Series,"/ "Luck and Pluck Series," Etc./ [rule]/ Philadelphia:/ Henry T. Coates & Co.,/ 1901.

BINDING: Identical with "Jed, The Poorhouse Boy."

COLLATION: Dark brown coated end-paper; tissue-covered frontispiece; title page [p. i]; copyright notice dated 1901 [p. ii]; contents, pp. iii - iv; text, pp. 1 - 362; fly-leaf; dark brown coated end-paper. In addition to the frontispiece are three full-page illustrations.

This story was serialized in Argosy, the first installment appearing in the issue dated August 26, 1893. Coates deposited the title with the Library of Congress on March 12, 1901, and forwarded the bound volume on August 10th of the same year.

There are no book advertisements at the back of the first edition. Later printings listed Alger ads up to and including "Digging For Gold." Also offered are books by Harry Castlemon, Edward S. Ellis, C. A. Stephens and J. T. Trowbridge.

Value of first edition is $20.00.

LIVE AND LEARN. See "Bound to Rise."

LOST AT SEA; or, Robert Roscoe's Strange Cruise.

The Mershon Company, 1904

TITLE PAGE: Lost At Sea/ Or/ Robert Roscoe's Strange/ Cruise/ By/ Horatio Alger, Jr.,/ Author of "Nelson the Newsboy," "Out for/ Business," "Falling in With Fortune,"/ "Young Captain Jack," "Ragged/ Dick Series," Etc./ [tulip design]/ The Mershon Company/ Rahway, N.J. (space) New York.

BINDING: Identical with "Falling In With Fortune."

COLLATION: End-paper; frontispiece; title page [p. i]; copyright notice dated 1904, below list of books "By the same author," [p. ii]; preface, pp. iii - iv; contents, pp. v - vi; text, [pp. 1] - 250; end-paper. In addition to the frontispiece are three full-page illustrations.

Another of the stories "completed" by Stratemeyer and claimed by him to originally have been outlined by Alger before his death. Very doubtful, judging by the pure Stratemeyer style. Deposited for copyright, the book having been received at the Library of Congress on October 20, 1904.

The first edition has but one identifying point: The list of books on the copyright notice page [p. ii], shows "Lost at Sea" in top position. There must be no later titles listed above it.

The Alger-lover will not regard this as required reading, but he'll yearn to add it to his collection, and — most likely — will be required to pay for it about $22.50.

LUCK AND PLUCK; or, John Oakley's Inheritance.

Loring, Publisher, 1869

TITLE PAGE: Luck and Pluck; Or, John Oakley's Inheritance./ By/ Horatio Alger, Jr./ Author of "Ragged Dick," "Fame and Fortune," "Mark, the Match/ Boy," "Rough and Ready," "Campaign Series," Etc./ [rule]; Loring, Publisher,/ 319 Washington Street,/ Boston.

BINDING: Identical with "Bound to Rise," except that the present volume does not carry the "Second" series imprint on spine.

COLLATION: Yellow-tinted end-paper; fly-leaf; blank leaf on verso of which is page of book advertisements; frontispiece; tissue-covered decorative title page; title page [p. i]; copyright notice dated 1869 [p. ii]; dedication [p. iii]; verso blank [p. iv]; preface, pp. v - vi; (no presence of [pp. vii - viii]); text, [pp. 9] - 343; fly-leaf; yellow-tinted end-paper. In addition to frontispiece and decorative title page are six full-page illustrations (probably more than in any of the other Alger books issued by Loring).

Prior to publication in book form, "Luck and Pluck" was serialized in the "Our Young People's Story Teller" section of Ballou's Monthly Magazine, and adult publication. The first installment ran in the January, 1869 issue, continuing through December. Loring issued the title as Volume I of the Luck and Pluck Series, which eventually was comprised of eight stories. The title page of the present volume was deposited on November 22, 1869. There is no record of the book being presented for copyright, although it definitely was in distribution in time for Christmas, that year.

The first edition clues are all in the page of ads at front of the book. The Luck and Pluck Series will show only this volume as being in print, with "Others in preparation." Above, the listing of the Ragged Dick Series must show "V. Ben, The Luggage Boy. (In April, 1870.)" and "VI. Rufus and Rose; or, The Fortunes of Rough and Ready. (In December, 1870.)" Value of first edition is $25.00.

LUKE WALTON; or, The Chicago Newsboy.

Porter & Coates, 1889

TITLE PAGE: Luke Walton/ or/ The Chicago Newsboy/ By/ Horatio Alger, Jr./ Author of "Ragged Dick Series," "Luck and/ Pluck Series," Etc./ [publisher's trade-mark device]/ Philadelphia:/ Porter & Coates.

BINDING: Identical with "Ben's Nugget."

COLLATION: Dark brown coated end-paper; fly-leaf; tissue-covered frontispiece; title page [p. i]; copyright notice dated 1889 [p. ii]; contents, pp. iii - iv; text, pp. 5 - 346; book advertisements, pp. 1 - 6; fly-leaf; dark brown coated end-paper. In addition to the frontispiece are three full-page illustrations.

"Luke Walton" was serialized in Golden Argosy, installments running from late 1887 into 1888. Porter & Coates deposited the book for copyright on August 9, 1889.

This volume is the last to be published in the dark brown cloth binding with the black, gold and blind-stamped decorations. Shortly after the publication of this story, Porter & Coates decided to issue it, along with their next Alger project, "Struggling Upward," and the previous two, "Bob Burton" and "The Store Boy," into the four-volume Way to Success Series. Accordingly, shortly after first publication, "Luke Walton" was reissued in slightly larger format, between gray covers featuring a bee-hive illustration (see "Struggling Upward"), and was designated as Volume Three of the Way to Success Series.

None of the above evidence appears in the first edition. The earliest issue lists "Bob Burton" — in book ads at rear — as the last title to be issued. "Luke Walton" is not listed until the later edition.

It will be of interest to students of Alger's writing to note that, in 1865, a similar story titled "Luke Darrell, The Chicago Newsboy" was published by Tomlinson Brothers, a Chicago publishing house. While "Luke Walton" definitely is one hundred percent Alger, there is a good possibility that he was familiar with the earlier publication.

The dark brown-covered "Luke Walton" is worth $25.00.

MABEL PARKER; or, The Frontier Treasure. A Tale of the Frontier Settlements.

Unpublished manuscript, exact date unknown.

"Mabel Parker" is an adult story, submitted to Street & Smith about 1880, but never published in any form. This is the only known Alger manuscript of a complete novel existing to this date.

The story is hand-written on 203 pages, divided into seven installments. Each chapter has been separated by Alger, who pasted around the sheets a paper band on which he wrote the installment number and his name. Each packet contains about 30 sheets, upon each of which Alger wrote twenty-eight lines of small, fine script.

This would ordinarily give the impression of being a first draft, with much scratching-out, and many changes and corrections indicated in margins and between the lines. However, as I am satisfied that Alger virtually never rewrote a story manuscript, I am quite positive that the condition of the "Mabel Parker" papers is that of most of those he presented to his publishers.

The setting of the story is Western New York State, apparently near where Buffalo is now located. Alger indicates that his tale took place about "60 years ago," placing the action during the first two decades of the Nineteenth Century.

There is no scale nor precedent by which the value of this manuscript may be established.

MAKING HIS MARK

Penn Publishing Company, 1901

TITLE PAGE: Making His Mark/ [rule]/ By/ Horatio Alger, Jr./ Author of "The Odds Against Him,"/ "The Young Boatman," etc./ [rule]/ Illustrated By Robert L. Mason/ [publisher's trade-mark device]/ The Penn Publishing Company/ Philadelphia MCMI.

BINDING: Dark blue cloth stamped in red and white. Cover design: A combination scroll-and-framework at center with fruit basket at top and acorn design toward bottom (all in white). Within frames (in red): Making/ His/ Mark/ Horatio/ Alger, Jr. Spine (with typography in red and vignette in white): Making/ His Mark/ [rule]/ Horatio/ Alger/ [basket of fruit]/ [script-like monogram] P P Co. Cover size 5¼" x 7½".

COLLATION: Brown flowered end-paper; fly-leaf; tissue-covered frontispiece; title page [p. 1]; copyright notice dated 1901 [p. 2]; contents, pp. 3 - 4; text, pp. 5 - 307; book advertisements, pp. 1 - 12; fly-leaf; brown flowered end-paper. In addition to the frontispiece are four full-page illustrations.

This story apparently was first published as a serial in Pleasant Hours. It was titled "Gerald's Mission," the first parts appearing early in 1896. Chapters ran until publication ceased with the issue dated April, 1896. Thereafter, it continued — in small installments — in Leslie's Popular Monthly, ending in the number of October, 1897. I have not been able to confirm this, but am relying upon undoubtedly valid references that appear frequently in Alger's letters of that period. He stated, in a note dated October 26, 1896, that Penn Publishing Company wants the book rights, but that he was still bound exclusively to H. T. Coates.

It is interesting to note that the story's hero is Gerald Lane, the identical name Alger gave to the hero of "A Debt of Honor." This is mere coincidence, however, as no connection exists between the two stories.

"Making His Mark," the book being deposited for copyright on April 3, 1901, is one of the seven Algers published by Penn Publishing Company over the sixteen-year period between 1890 and 1906. The first edition must have the publication year in Roman numerals — MCMI — at bottom of title page. On the last page of ads, at back of the book, "The Young Boatman" and "The Odds Against Him" are the only two Alger titles listed. The first few copies contain an oddity in that a double set of endpapers were bound-in at the front of the book. This, conceivably, could have been part of a trial or pre-publication run.

Value of first edition is $30.00.

MAKING HIS WAY. See "The World Before Him."

MARIE BERTRAND; or, the Felon's Daughter.
Street & Smith, 1864

"Marie Bertrand" is a short novel that was serialized in New York Weekly. The first installment appeared in the issue dated January 7, 1864, and continued through the following five numbers, the final part appearing February 4, 1864. This story, one of Alger's early attempts at adult fiction, never was published in book form.

A great part of the story is about Jacques Bertrand, a French convict escaping from the prison galleys at Brest. His daughter, Marie — who enters the story in the second installment — ekes out a meager living as a seamstress in Paris. But by story's end, Marie (whose real name is Rose), is reunited with her mother, the Baroness de Conray — from whom she was kidnapped years before — and married to handsome Victor Delacroix, nephew of the dowager with whom she found employment as a companion.

Although the author selected a foreign setting, the characters and action very much approximate those prominent in his later, better-known works.

In his books to come, many a hero's mother augments the family income sewing for a penurious slave-driver. Alger's Baedeker-like descriptions of Paris are as exact and exciting as his later landmark guides to New York. For full-run, advanced collectors would pay $45.00.

MARK MANNING'S MISSION; or, The Story of a Shoe Factory Boy.

A. L. Burt Company, 1905

> TITLE PAGE: Mark Manning's/ Mission/ [double line]/ The Story of a Shoe Factory Boy/ [single line]/ By Horatio Alger, Jr./ Author of "Mark Mason's Victory," "Ben Bruce,"/ "Bernard Brook's (note misspelling of "Brooks'") Adventures," "A Debt of Honor,"/ etc., etc./ [publisher's trade-mark device]/ With Five Page illustrations by J. Watson Davis/ [double line]/ A. L. Burt Company,/ Publishers, New York.

> BINDING: Blue-gray cloth, stamped in red, black, yellow and gold. Cover design: Yellow border all around cover. At top are two circles. In circle at left is head of a boy carrying shoe-blacking box; at right, boy with stick and bundle over his shoulder. In panel below: Mark Manning's Mission/ By Horatio Alger, Jr./ At bottom of cover is a circle within which is illustration of young executive writing in book; row of books behind him. Beyond the circle is the New York skyline. Spine: (in gold) Mark/ Manning's/ Mission/ [line]/ [black line]/ (in gold) Horatio Alger/ [black line]/ [design, yellow with black outline]/ [yellow line]/ A. L. Burt Company/ New York/ [yellow line]. Cover size: 5¼" x 7½".

> COLLATION: End-paper; frontispiece; title page [p. i]; copyright notice dated 1905 [p. ii]; contents, pp. iii - iv; text, pp. 1 - 268; book advertisements, [pp. 1] - 8; end-paper. In addition to frontispiece are four full-page illustrations.

This story first appeared as a serial — titled "The Hermit's Heir; or, Mark Manning's Mission" — in the Boston Globe, beginning November 24, 1894 and ending December 21, 1894.

Burt deposited the title for copyright on February 2, 1905, and the completed book was received July 21 of the same year.

Later editions of this story substitute brown for yellow on cover and spine design. Otherwise, no significant difference.

Value of first edition is $12.50.

MARK MASON. See "Mark Mason's Victory."

MARK MASON'S TRIALS AND TRIUMPHS. See "Mark Mason's Victory."

MARK MASON'S TRIUMPH. See "Mark Mason's Victory."

MARK MASON'S VICTORY; or, The Trials and Triumphs of a Telegraph Boy.

A. L. Burt, 1899

TITLE PAGE: Mark Mason's Victory/ The Trials and Triumphs of/ A Telegraph Boy./ By Horatio Alger, Jr.,/ Author of "Joe's Luck," "Tom the Bootblack," "Dan the News-/ boy," "The Errand Boy," etc., etc./ Illustrated./ New York:/ A. L. Burt, Publisher.

BINDING: Identical with "Ben Bruce."

COLLATION: Tan-tinted end-paper with flower design; fly-leaf; frontispiece; title page; copyright notice dated 1899; contents, [2 pp.]; text, [pp. 1] - 308; book advertisements, [pp. 1] - 14; fly-leaf; tan-tinted end-paper with flower design. In addition to the frontispiece are four full-page illustrations.

Prior to appearing in book form under the present title, the story was serialized in Argosy in 1892 (the first installment appearing in the issue of May 7th) under the title of "ADT 79." Arthur Lee Putnam was indicated as the author. United States Book Company planned to issue the story in paper wrappers — probably under the original title — but their bankruptcy in 1893 prevented this.

While the story never again was issued as "ADT 79," it was reprinted, after the Burt publication, by a number of publishers, under a variety of generally similar titles. Some of these include "Mark Mason," "Mark Mason's Trials and Triumphs," "Mark Mason's Triumph," "Trials and Triumphs of Mark Mason," and possibly others. I have more than once noted the story listed as "Trials and Triumphs of a New York Telegraph Boy," but am unable to verify this. I frankly believe this to be a confusion with the sub-title of "Number 91" (or, "The Adventures of a New York Telegraph Boy," under which that story was reissued).

The first edition of the Burt publication must have the title blind-stamped against gold panel, and only the name "Alger" appearing on spine. On the first page of book ads the publisher's address must be 97-99-101 Reade Street, New York.

The first edition is worth $12.50, but — to the avid collector — a complete run of the serialization, "ADT 79," with the Putnam by-line, is worth twice that sum.

MARK STANTON; or, Both Sides of the Continent.

United States Book Company, 1890

BINDING: Identical with "Dean Dunham."

Title page of this story was deposited by the United States Book Company towards the end of 1890, and the book was received for copyright on February 7, 1891. Nevertheless, the volume — issued in paper wrappers as Number 25 of the Leather-Clad Tales of Adventure and Romance — was apparently in circulation on or about May 24, 1890, which is the cover date.

Ten years later, Street & Smith deposited for copyright their reissue of the story and, on September 8, 1900, released it as Number 78 of their Medal Library series under the altered title of "Both Sides of the Continents or, Mark Stanton." Shortly thereafter (or quite possibly, simul taneously), they put out the story in more respectable hard covers, reverting to the original "Mark Stanton" title. This is the first hard cover edition.

For some reason, "Mark Stanton" did not attract the attention of many of Alger's other stories and was not as profusely reprinted. Therefore, not too many copies of this story — under either variation of title — are to be found. Accordingly, we have here the situation of reissues having somewhat more than their usual value.

Incidentally, through a printing error, the 1890 date on the cover of the earliest Leather-Clad edition appears as "890." Nevertheless, any copy of this issue is worth at least $45.00. Street & Smith's "Both Sides of the Continent" brings $20.00, and their hard cover "Mark Stanton" about $12.50. Surprisingly, I've noted instances of the David McKay reissue — made from the Street & Smith plates — being sold for almost as much. The story also was printed as "Mark Stanton," by H. M. Caldwell Company, in 1905, and some years later was once more published in paperback, by Street & Smith, as Alger Series Number 20, again titled "Both Sides of the Continent." Even these later appearances disappear quickly from dealer's shelves at prices ranging from $7.50, up.

MARK, THE MATCH BOY; or, Richard Hunter's Ward.

Loring, Publisher, 1869

TITLE PAGE: Mark, The Match Boy;/ Or,/ Richard Hunter's Ward./ By/ Horatio Alger, Jr./ Author of "Ragged Dick," "Fame and Fortune," "Frank's Campaign,"/ "Paul Prescott's Charge," "Charlie Codman's Cruise," Etc./ [rule]/ Loring, Publisher,/ 319 Washington Street,/ Boston.

BINDING: Identical with "Ben, the Luggage Boy."

COLLATION: Yellow-tinted end-paper; fly-leaf; blank leaf, on verso of which is page of book advertisements; tissue-covered decorative title page [p. i]; verso blank [p. ii]; title page [p. iii]; copyright notice dated 1869 [p. iv]; dedication [p. v.]; verso blank [p. vi]; preface, pp. vii - viii; text, pp. 9 - 276; fly-leaf; yellow-tinted end-paper. In addition to the decorative title page are three full-page illustrations.

The title page of "Mark, The Match Boy" was deposited for copyright on March 20, 1869. According to the April date at the end of Alger's preface, the books probably were in distribution early in May, 1869.

This is one of the easiest Lorings to pick up in later printings, but hard to find in the bona fide first edition. The story was issued as Volume III of the Ragged Dick Series. The first issue must show, as the listing for Volume IV: "Rough and Ready; or, Life among the New York Newsboys [in December.]" and below: "Others in preparation." Only the first state carries the imprint of Rockwell & Rollins, Printers and Stereotypers, on copyright page. The address at bottom of title page will be indicated as 319 Washington Street, but this — lacking the other points — would not guarantee first edition. That address was used for several months after "Mark" first appeared, during which time the book enjoyed a number of printings. Later editions — probably beginning with those printed after November, 1870 — have as a frontispiece the illustration facing Page 85 of the earlier issues. These also will have the later state of decorative title page, showing a group of four boys instead of the earlier state, which depicted only the figure of Ragged Dick.

In 1940, "Mark, The Match Boy" appeared as a cartoon strip in Shadow Comics, issued by Street & Smith.

The first edition is worth $30.00. Later states, $15.00.

THE MERCHANT'S CRIME. See "Ralph Raymond's Heir."

MR. CRAVEN'S STEPSON. See "Frank Hunter's Peril."

MR. SNOBDEN'S OFFICE BOY. See "Silas Snobden's Office Boy."

NED NEWTON; or, The Fortunes of a New York Bootblack.
United States Book Company, 1890
BINDING: Identical with "Dean Dunham."

First published on May 17, 1890, as Volume Number 24, Leather-Clad Tales of Adventure and Romance, with Arthur Lee Putnam indicated as author. The story had earlier appeared as a serialization in Golden Argosy, in 1887, also by Putnam, but the copyright of record is for the Leather-Clad edition in paper wrappers, deposited on February 2, 1891.

The first hard cover edition — still bearing the Putnam by-line — appeared about 1894 (?), issued by American Publishers Corporation from original plates acquired after the demise of United States Book Company. Horatio Alger's name is noted for the first time on cover of the edition issued — also from the original plates — on June 15, 1901, by Street & Smith as their Medal Library No. 118. Shortly thereafter, Street & Smith released their hard cover edition with Alger as author.

Although no connection whatsoever is implied, it is interesting to note that a Ned Newton turns up in the early 1900's as the great chum of Tom Swift, the ingenious hero of Edward Stratemeyer's famous series.

The Leather-Clad "Ned Newton" is worth $45.00. The American Publishers Corporation hard cover edition is worth $25.00, but many collectors will pay more to get a book with Arthur Lee Putnam as author. They appear only rarely. The Street & Smith paperback is worth $12.50.

NELSON THE NEWSBOY; or, Afloat in New York.
The Mershon Company, 1901
TITLE PAGE: Nelson The Newsboy/ Or/ Afloat in New York/ By/ Horatio Alger, Jr./ Author of "Out For Business," "Falling In With Fortune,"/ "Young Captain Jack," "Tattered Tom,"/ "Ragged Dick," Etc./ Completed By/ Arthur M. Winfield/ Author of "The Rover Boys at School," "The Rover/ Boys on the Ocean," "The Rover Boys in the/ Jungle," "The Rover Boys Out West," Etc./ [small sunburst design]/ New York/ The Mershon Company/ Publishers.

BINDING: Identical with "Falling In With Fortune."

COLLATION: End-paper; frontispiece; title page [p. i]; copyright notice dated 1901 [p. ii]; preface, pp. iii - iv; contents, pp. v - vi; text, [pp. 1] - 276; 3 leaves (6 pp.) of book advertisements; end-paper. In addition to the frontispiece are three full-page illustrations.

"Nelson the Newsboy" is another of the Winfield completions, with the Stratemeyer pseudonym appearing on the title page. The title was deposited on September 23, 1901, and the book received at the Library of Congress on October 5th. The present story is a volume (with no particular sequence designated) of the Rise In Life Series, all books in the set having passed through the Stratemeyer fiction factory.

"Winfield," in his preface, states that "in its original form Mr. Alger intended this story of New York life for a semi-juvenile drama." I strongly doubt this, and can find nothing in the book of which Horatio Alger would have been proud.

In the first edition, the present title is not listed among the advertisements at the rear of the book; under ad for Flag of Freedom Series, by Captain Ralph Bonehill, "With Custer in the Black Hills" must not be listed.

Despite the relatively late date of issue, these "Winfield completions" are not frequently offered. The collector who feels he must have a first edition of "Nelson the Newsboy" will pay for it about $27.50.

NEW YORK BOY, A.

United States Book Company, 1890

BINDING: Identical with "Dean Dunham."

"A New York Boy" first appeared as a serialization in Golden Argosy, with thirteen installments published during 1888, and with Arthur Lee Putnam as author.

Although their copyright notice is dated 1891 (properly, as the book was deposited at Library of Congress on March 14, 1891), United States Book Company released the story as No. 30 of their Leather-Clad Tales of Adventure and Romance, on June 28, 1890. The book was bound in paper wrappers, with Putnam still listed as the author.

Starting on January 15, 1898, the story was again serialized, this time in Army and Navy Weekly. The title was changed to "A Diamond in the Rough; or, How Rufus Rodman Won Success." Putnam still listed as author. After three installments had appeared, the publication suspended, changing its name to Half-Holiday. In the new periodical, the story continued to completion during the following eight weeks, concluding in the issue dated March 26, 1898.

Apparently the first hard cover edition of "A New York Boy" was issued by American Publishers Corporation as Number 30 of their Berkeley Series. Still carrying Putnam as the author, the book was printed from the original United States Book Company plates.

The Alger by-line appeared for the first time in Street & Smith's Medal Library No. 93, a paperback edition issued on December 22, 1900. Early in 1901, they published the story in hard covers and — some years later — as Number 23 of their (paperback) Alger Series. In both of these editions, Horatio Alger, Jr., was credited with authorship.

The Leather-Clad is worth $45.00; the American Publishers Corporation hardcover, $30.00; the Street & Smith Medal Library No. 93, $12.50.

NOTHING TO DO: A Tilt at our Best Society.

James French & Co., 1857

TITLE PAGE: Nothing To Do:/ A Tilt at our Best Society./ To do nothing is to be a great part of your title./ Shakespeare./ Illustrated./ Boston:/ Published by James French & Co./ 1857.

BINDING: Gold and blind-stamped on dark brown, red, blue and green cloth (and possibly other colors), with no priority of issue. Cover design: Blind-stamped line and scroll-work border, identical on front and back. Gold-stamped at center of front panel: Nothing To Do/ A Tilt at our Best Society. Spine: No stamping, type, nor design of any kind. Cover size: 4¾" x 7⅛".

COLLATION: Dark brown coated end-paper; fly-leaf; fly-leaf on which is printed: Nothing To Do., verso blank; tissue-covered frontispiece; title page [p. 1]; copyright notice dated 1857 [p. 2]; dedication to William A. Butler, author of "Nothing To Wear") [p. 3]; verso blank [p. 4]; text, [pp. 5] - 45; fly-leaf; dark brown coated end-paper. There are no illustrations other than the frontispiece, despite the fact that "illustrated." is prominently printed on the title page.

The "Nothing" series is an enigmatic literary complex of not less than six slim volumes of poetry. Horatio Alger can definitely take credit for only one of them — "Nothing To Do: A Tilt at our Best Society" — although it is an anonymous work with no author listed. The Alger "Nothing" was published by James French & Co., Boston, in 1857, after having deposited the title for copyright on August 7th of that year.

The first, or keystone, volume of the series is "Nothing To Wear, An Episode of City Life," published in 1857 (as were all six books) by Rudd & Carleton, of New York. The satirical poem first appeared in Harper's Weekly, written by William Allen Butler, a prominent New York business man and lawyer and himself a very social figure. His father was a partner of Martin van Buren, and he could trace ancestors right back to Oliver Cromwell.

Although "Nothing to Wear" hadn't the merit of some of Butler's other works of that period, it caught the fancy of a public sorely in need of a smile during that depression and panic year of 1857.

When Harper decided not to issue Butler's poem in book form, believing there could be no further demand, Rudd & Carleton assumed the risk. From the date of publication, books sold by the thousands, in effect creating a fad that kept sophisticates, pseudo-sophisticates and just plain folks grinning over its pages for many months. An edition published by A. Crowquill, Ltd., of London, and sub-titled "An Episode of Fashionable Life," was equally popular around England's Victorian firesides.

Replies in verse were not long in coming. The first of these was Alger's "Nothing To Do," but it is most interesting to note that another volume — with the identical title — was published almost simultaneously by Wiley & Halsted, of New York. Alger certainly had nothing to do with the New York edition, which is described on the title page as "An Accompaniment to 'Nothing To Wear.' By A Lady."

"Nothing To Eat," described as "NOT By the Author of 'Nothing to Wear'," was next on the scene, published by Dick & Fitzgerald, of New York. I have at hand a list of the Alger Collection of the Princeton University Library. Next to the title, "Nothing To Eat," is the notation "(By

Alger?)." The New York Public Library card file indicates Alger as "supposed author." The author definitely was not Alger, although it could have been Judge Haliburton, creator of the humorous Sam Slick stories, and available to Dick & Fitzgerald, his publishers at that time.

As though to prevent the series from expiring, a claim against Rudd & Carleton was filed by a Miss Peck, daughter of an Episcopal clergyman of Greenwich, Connecticut, to the effect that the poem — which she said was hers — was lost on the Madison Avenue stage, where it was found by Butler. Although Miss Peck apparently received little satisfaction from her suit, the publishers capitalized upon the publicity by engaging Mortimer Thompson — the immortal "Doesticks" — to quickly put into frivolous verse a burlesque on the subject. His product, which was titled "Nothing To Say: A Slight Slap at Mobocratic Snobbery, which has 'Nothing To Do' with 'Nothing To Wear.' by Q. K. Philander Doesticks, P.B."

For a short while it appeared that Doesticks had had the last word, that the idle rich had returned to their "brownstone palaces on Fifth Avenue," to nibbling "a duck, or a grouse, or a pheasant," and to "Atlantic crossings" in search of "dresses in which to do nothing at all." However, it was Wiley & Halsted who ended the season with "Nothing To You; or, Mind Your Own Business. In answer to 'Nothings' in general, and 'Nothing to Wear' in particular. By Knot-Rab."

These six volumes were, of course, prepared for adult audiences. Alger wrote his during the period prior to taking the decisive step towards a lifelong career of writing stories for boys. Of little meaning today, the "Nothing" series was filled with thinly veiled references to events and personalities of that era. They were written at a time, when for an evening's entertainment, the family would gather in the parlor and, while one would read, the others would listen.

The question has arisen, "What proof is there that Alger wrote 'Nothing To Do'?" There are two simple answers: 1. Anyone familiar with Alger's poetry would immediately recognize this work as his. 2. Alger has admitted he wrote it.

As confusing as is the "Nothing" series is the tremendous range of prices for which Alger's "Nothing To Do" is being offered. There is no question of "first edition" in this case. Every copy noted bears the same points. Condition of the books offered is generally indicated to be good-or-better; understandably better than much of Alger's juvenile output.

Although offered for as much as $145.00 (some years ago) proper range would be $80.00-$85.00. This item has appreciated impressively in recent years.

NUGGET FINDERS, THE. See "In A New World."

NUMBER 91; or, The Adventures of A New York Telegraph Boy.
Frank A. Munsey, 1887
  BINDING: Orange colored paper wrappers with black printing. Cover:
    No. 5./ 25 Cts./ Munsey's Popular Series/ For Boys/ [small illus-
    tration of a viking ship]/ And Girls/ [line]/ Copyright, 1887,/ By
    Frank A. Munsey./ December, 1887./ Subscription Price,/ Per Year,
    12 Numbers, $3./ [double line]/ Entered at the Post Office at New
    York as Second Class Mail Matter./ Number 91/ Or,/ The Adven-

tures of a New York/ Telegraph Boy./ By/ Arthur Lee Putnam./ Illustrated./ [line]/ No copyright books by leading authors for boys and girls equaling this series/ in merit and purity were ever before published for less than $1.25 a copy./ — The Publisher./ [line]/ Copyright, 1887, By Frank A. Munsey./ New York:/ Frank A. Munsey, Publisher./ [line]/ 1887. Spine: Number 91. Cover size: 4½" x 6½".

As "Number 91," the story was serialized in Golden Argosy in 1886, with Arthur Lee Putnam as the author. Munsey then issued it as one of the three Algers to appear in his paper wrapper Popular Series for Boys and Girls. This story was No. 5, with the cover dated December, 1887. At bottom of both cover and title page the 1887 date appears, but the copyright notice is dated 1888. To add to this confusion, the book actually was deposited for copyright on June 7, 1889.

Shortly thereafter, when John W. Lovell took over Munsey's book publishing operation, he issued "Number 91" simultaneously in the Leather-Clad Tales series and in a deluxe hard cover edition. Both products still listed Arthur Lee Putnam as author. The cloth-bound publication can be considered to be the first hard cover edition of this title. In appearance, it was covered with blue cloth (red also noted), and was gold, black and blind-stamped. "Number 91" was stamped in black against a solid gold panel at center of the cover, with floral design behind the panel. Below it, "Putnam" was printed diagonally, between heavy black lines. The spine also has the title stamped in black against gold panel. Below it the floral design is continued from the front cover. At bottom, in a circle, "Lovell." Outside the circle, "Rugby Edition."

Sometime in 1894, the hard cover edition was reissued by American Publishers Corporation, who acquired the original plates from the receivers of the by then-bankrupt United States Book Company. Putnam still appeared as author.

On March 17, 1900, Street & Smith — who had by this time come into possession of the original plates — reissued the story between their typically colorful paper wrappers. The title — which was issued as Medal Library No. 53 — was changed to "The Adventures of a New York Telegraph Boy." The first printing still featured the name of Arthur Lee Putnam on cover, spine and title page, but this was quickly revised and all ensuing editions listed Horatio Alger as the author. The title, on the title page, had been inverted so that "Number 91" appeared as the sub-title. The first page of text still carried the original "Number 91" heading, as did the running heads throughout. However, at the same time that the Alger name was substituted for Putnam, the title on the first text page became "Adventures of a New York Telegraph Boy." Within the year, Street & Smith released their own hard cover edition, still using Munsey's original plates, but having further shortened their reissue title to "Adventures of a Telegraph Boy."

The first edition of "Number 91," the Munsey's Popular Series for Boys and Girls, in paper wrappers, is worth $45.00. The Lovell hard-cover issue is worth $30.00, and any ensuing editions — if they show Arthur Lee Putnam as author — bring about $25.00.

ODDS AGAINST HIM, THE; or, Carl Crawford's Experience.

Penn Publishing Company, 1890

TITLE PAGE: The Odds Against Him/ Or/ Carl Crawford's Experience/ By/ Horatio Alger Jr/ [rule]/ Philadelphia/ The Penn Publishing Company/ 1890.

BINDING: Bound in green cloth, with black and gold stamping. Cover design (with all stamping in black): The Odds/ Against Him/ [ten straight, closely-set lines across the width of the cover]/ Horatio Alger Jr. Spine (all gold-stamped except for the lines, which are black): The Odds/ Against/ Him/ [ten straight, closely-set lines]/ Horatio/ Alger/ Jr/ [publisher's monogram device, containing the letters, P-P-Co.]. Cover size: 5¼" x 7½".

COLLATION: End-paper with over-all design of green vines; fly-leaf; frontispiece; title page [p. 1]; copyright notice dated 1890 [p. 2]; contents, pp. 3, 4, 5; blank verso of p. 5 [p. 6]; text, pp. 7 - 349; fly-leaf; end-paper with over-all design of green vines. In addition to frontispiece are ten full-page illustrations (more than in any other Alger first edition).

Before issuance in book form, "The Odds Against Him" was serialized in Argosy, the first installment appearing in the issue dated October 5, 1889, and continuing through the edition of December 28, 1889. It is interesting to note that, on at least one occasion, the story was titled on the magazine's cover as "The Factory Boy Story" and, at another time during the serialization, as "The Story of a Factory Boy." The story never appeared under either of these titles although it was reissued some years later by A. L. Burt, entitled "Driven From Home."

Penn Publishing Company deposited the bound volume for copyright on July 21, 1890. The first edition is distinguished by its binding, cover design and by the 1890 date appearing at the bottom of the title page. This book — like all Penn firsts — brings a relatively high price on the rare occasions it is offered for sale.

Value of first edition is $30.00.

OLIVER THE OUTCAST. See "Adrift in the City."

ONLY AN IRISH BOY; or, Andy Burke's Fortunes and Misfortunes.

Porter & Coates, 1894

TITLE PAGE: Only An Irish Boy/ Or/ Andy Burke's Fortunes/ And Misfortunes/ By/ Horatio Alger, Jr./ Author of "Ragged Dick," "Fame and Fortune,"/ "Sink or Swim," "Tattered Tom,"/ "Brave and Bold," Etc./ [publisher's trade-mark device]/ Philadelphia/ Porter & Coates.

BINDING: Identical with "Adrift in the City."

COLLATION: Dark brown coated end-paper; fly-leaf; tissue-covered frontispiece; title page [p. i]; copyright notice dated 1894 [p. ii]; contents, pp. iii - iv; text, [pp. 1] - 324; book advertisements, [pp. 1] - 8; fly-leaf; dark brown coated end-paper. In addition to the frontispiece are three full-page illustrations.

Prior to appearing in book form, "Only An Irish Boy" was serialized in New York Weekly, the first installment appearing in the issue dated May 18, 1874. It later was again serialized, this time in Good News, running from May 15, 1890 through the issue dated July 31, 1890. Porter & Coates deposited the title for copyright on April 24, 1894, and submitted the bound book on July 17th of the same year. This probably is among Alger's most often reprinted stories. It subsequently was issued in paperback form as Street & Smith Medal Library 198; later as Number 10 of their Alger Series and also as Number 88 of the Brave and Bold series. The title was released by viritually all of Alger's reprint publishers, with the sub-title generally being shortened to "Andy Burke's Fortunes." There is evidence that the story was distributed, both in England and Ireland, under the title of "Andy Burke's Fortune," but I have been unable to verify this.

The first edition will show "Digging for Gold" as the last Alger title to be published, with "On the Trail of the Moose" last under the listings by Edward S. Ellis.

Value of first edition is $22.50.

OUT FOR BUSINESS; or, Robert Frost's Strange Career.

The Mershon Company, 1900

TITLE PAGE: Out For Business/ Or/ Robert Frost's Strange Career/ By/ Horatio Alger, Jr./ Author of "Falling In With Fortune," "Luck or Pluck" (note that this is an incorrect listing of "Luck and Pluck"),/ "The Young Boatman," "Only an Irish Boy,"/ "Young Miner," Etc./ Completed By/ Arthur M. Winfield/ Author of "The Rover Boys at School," "The Rover Boys/ on the Ocean," "The Rover Boys in the Jungle,"/ "The Rover Boys Out West," Etc./ [small tulip design]/ New York/ The Mershon Company/ Publishers.

BINDING: Identical with "Falling In With Fortune," except that the color of cloth is brown instead of the green found in every other volume of this series.

COLLATION: End-paper; frontispiece; title page [p. i]; copyright notice dated 1900 [p. ii]; preface, pp. iii - iv; contents, pp. v - vi; text, [pp. 7] - 287; end-paper. In addition to the frontispiece are three full-page illustrations.

"Out For Business" is the first of the eleven "Winfield completions." Mershon deposited the title for copyright on June 16, 1900, and the completed volume was received at the Library of Congress on September 20, 1900. This story was issued simultaneously with — or perhaps one week earlier than — "Falling In With Fortune." The two titles were claimed to be (according to the book's preface) "the last tales begun by that prince of juvenile writers, Mr. Horatio Alger, Jr. . . The gifted writer was stricken when on the point of finishing the stories, and when he saw that he could not complete them himself, it was to the present writer that he turned . . ." The preface, which is dated March 1st, 1900, is signed "Arthur M. Winfield." This is, of course, one of Edward Stratemeyer's most prominent pennames, and the one he used for many years under the multi-volume Rover Boys Series.

The first edition has, as noted above, brown rather than the usual green cloth covers. There are no advertisements at the back of the book.

Value of first edition is $25.00.

PADDLE YOUR OWN CANOE; or, Harry Raymond's Resolve. See "Sink or Swim."

PADDLE YOUR OWN CANOE; or, The Fortunes of Walter Conrad. See "Strong and Steady."

PAUL PRESCOTT'S CHARGE.
Loring, Publisher, 1865

TITLE PAGE: Paul Prescott's Charge./ A Story for Boys./ Horatio Alger, Jr./ Author of "Frank's Campaign."/ [rule]/ Loring, Publisher,/ 319 Washington Street,/ Boston./ 1865.

BINDING: Bound in green, mauve, terra cotta and dark brown cloth. Front and back covers identically blind stamped with border rules. Spine (gold-stamped): [Rule]/ [arch]/ Paul/ Prescott's/ Charge./ [vignette of old man, seated, with boy at his feet]/ Loring/ [heavy rule]. Cover size: 4¾″ x 7″.

COLLATION: Yellow-tinted end-paper; fly-leaf; tissue-covered frontispiece; title page [p. 1]; copyright notice dated 1865 [p. 2]; dedication [p. 3]; verso blank [p. 4]; preface [p. 5]; verso blank [p. 6]; contents, [pp. 7] - 8; text, [pp. 9] - 224; fly-leaf; yellow-tinted end-paper. In addition to frontispiece is one full-page illustration.

The title of "Paul Prescott's Charge" was deposited for copyright on July 26, 1865, shortly before Alger finished writing the story in August. Curiously, the bound book was not received for copyright until two years later in 1867, although the copyright page indicated the year as 1865.

Loring issued four separate states of this story, and probably at least several editions of each.

The first state is distinguished by the necessary combination of frontispiece and — on title page — a ruled line, 319 Washington Street address and 1865 date at bottom.

The second state is similar, except that the line, "Second Edition," is substituted for the ruled line on title page. This, incidentally, is one of the two Alger books showing the Second Edition notice. "Frank's Campaign" is the other. All other points match those of the first state.

The third state, issued two years after the first, employs the familiar blind-stamped covers noted on all of the various Alger series published by Loring. The indication, "Campaign Series" (of which this is the Second Volume), has been added to the spine. A second fly-leaf substitutes for the frontispiece, which has been relocated and inserted to face Page 25. A tissue-covered "Campaign Series" decorative title page also has been inserted in front of the title page. Beneath Alger's name, on the title page, the line has been changed to read: Author of "Ragged Dick Series."

The fourth state, apparently issued towards the end of 1875, has a somewhat different spine design. The vignette of the old man with the young boy is eliminated and the typography and design of the remaining elements is altered. Two leaves (4 pp.) of book advertisements appears at the front; the tissue-covered frontispiece has again been given a forward position, followed by the Campaign Series decorative title page already referred to. At bottom of title page, the publisher's address has been changed to: Cor. Bromfield and Washington Streets.

The first and second states are rare, and are of equal value, $30.00.

443

PAUL THE PEDDLER; or, The Adventures of a Young Street Merchant.
Loring, Publisher, 1871

TITLE PAGE: Paul The Peddler;/ Or,/ The Adventures of a Young Street Merchant./ By/ Horatio Alger, Jr./ Author of "Ragged Dick Series," "Tattered Tom Series," "Luck and/ Pluck Series," "Campaign Series," Etc./ [decorative rule]/ Loring, Publisher,/ Cor. Bromfield and Washington Streets,/ Boston.

BINDING: Covers identical with "Ben, the Luggage Boy." Spine (gold-stamped): [Decorative rule]/ (within panel: Paul/ The/ Peddler)/ Tattered Tom/ Series/ [vignette of Tom]/ [decorative rule].

COLLATION: Yellow-tinted end-papers; fly-leaf; blank leaf on verso of which is a page of book advertisements; frontispiece; tissue-covered decorative title page [p. 1]; verso blank [p. 2]; title page [p. 3]; copyright notice dated 1871 [p. 4]; dedication [p. 5]; verso blank [p. 6]; preface, pp. 7 - viii; text, [pp. 9] - 281; yellow-tinted end-paper. In addition to frontispiece and decorative title page are two full-page illustrations.

After appearing in Student and Schoolmate as a serial, starting in the January, 1871, issue, "Paul The Peddler" appeared in book form in the Fall of that year, although it was not deposited for copyright until early in 1872. The story was issued as Volume II of the Tattered Tom Series.

The standard first edition is identified by a study of the ads at front of the book. Volume III of the Tattered Tom Series must be listed as "Phil, The Fiddler; or, The Young Street Musician. (In April, 1872.)" Below this line will be the announcement of Volume IV: "Slow And Sure; or, From the Sidewalk to the Shop. (In November. 1872) Others in preparation." Under the ads for the Luck and Pluck Series, Volume IV must be listed as "Strive And Succeed; or, The Progress of Walter Conrad. (In October, 1872.)"

The term, "standard first edition," is used above because I have at hand a curious copy of this title which, I am positive, pre-dates the standard issue. This book is bound in marbled boards, the spine being red morocco with gold-stamped title and ruled lines. On the back cover is a blind-stamped oval medallion and within it — also blind-stamped — the words, "Peterson's/ Uniform Edition/ of the/ Complete Works/ By/ The Best Authors." A minute examination of type-wear indicates that this edition unquestionably was printed prior to the standard first edition. Although I strongly suspect that the Peterson named on the cover (but not elsewhere) is T. B. Peterson and Brothers, a magazine and book publisher and distributor located in Philadelphia at about that time, the regular Loring imprint appears on the title page. There are no book advertisements, as do appear in the regular Loring publication, and the frontispiece, decorative title page and two additional illustrations also are absent.

In 1903 an Augusta, Maine, story-paper, Sunshine, serialized the story under the title, "Successful Paul."

Although it is not possible to establish the value of the Peterson oddity, that book is surely worth as much as the standard first edition — $30.00.

PHIL, THE FIDDLER; or, The Story of a Young Street Musician.
Loring, Publisher, 1872

TITLE PAGE: Phil, The Fiddler;/ Or,/ The Story of a Young Street Musician./ By/ Horatio Alger, Jr./ Author of the "Ragged Dick Series,"

"Tattered Tom Series,"/ "Campaign Series," "Luck and Pluck Series," Etc./ Illustrated By Laura Caxton./ [decorative rule]/ Loring, Publisher,/ Cor. Washington and Bromfield Streets, Boston.

BINDING: Identical with "Paul the Peddler."

COLLATION: Yellow-tinted end-paper; fly-leaf; blank leaf on verso of which is a page of book advertisements; frontispiece; tissue-covered decorative title page [p. 1]; verso blank [p. 2]; title page [p. 3]; copyright notice dated 1872 [p. 4]; dedication [p. 5]; verso blank [p. 6]; preface, pp. 7 - viii; text, pp. 9 - 265; fly-leaf; end-paper. In addition to the frontispiece and decorative title page, there are two full-page illustrations.

"Phil, the Fiddler," one of Alger's best known stories, candidly chronicled the shame of the Padrone system in New York. The book was deposited for copyright at mid-year, 1872, and issued at about the same time.

In the first edition, the ads at front will indicate, for Volume IV of the Tattered Tom Series: "Slow and Sure; or, From the Sidewalk to the Shop. (In November. 1872.) Others in preparation." Under the heading of the Luck and Pluck Series, Volume IV must be listed as: "Strive and Succeed; or, The Progress of Walter Conrad. (In October, 1872.) Others in preparation."

Due to the popularity of the book, the first edition brings a somewhat higher than average price. Worth about $40.00.

PLUCKY PAUL PALMER. See "The Train Boy."

RAGGED DICK; or, Street Life in New York.

Loring, Publisher, 1868

TITLE PAGE: Ragged Dick;/ Or,/ Street Life In New York/ With The Boot-Blacks./ By/ Horatio Alger, Jr.,/ Author of "Frank's Campaign," "Paul Prescott's Charge," Charlie/ Codman's Cruise," "Helen Ford."/ [decorative rule]/ Loring, Publisher, 319 Washington Street,/ Boston.

BINDING: Virtually identical with "Fame and Fortune," except for slight variation of design pattern of ruled lines on spine.

COLLATION: Yellow-tinted end-paper; fly-leaf; blank leaf, on verso of which appears a page of book advertisements; tissue-covered decorative title page [p. i]; verso blank [p. ii]; title page [p. iii]; copyright notice dated 1868 [p. iv]; dedication [p. v]; verso blank [p. vi]; preface, pp. vii - viii; text, pp. 9 - 296; fly-leaf yellow-tinted end-paper. In addition to the decorative title page are three full-page illustrations.

"Ragged Dick" was not Alger's first book, as is widely believed (it was his eighth), but it is the story that launched him as an all-time best-selling author of books for boys.

Prior to appearing in book form, the story of "Ragged Dick" was serialized, in 1867, in Student and Schoolmate, a monthly magazine for young people edited by William T. Adams who, as Oliver Optic was, himself, a well-known author. Loring deposited the book for copyright on May 20, 1868, and released it to the trade at about the same time.

The first edition of "Ragged Dick," a very rare book, is distinguished by a number of points. The page of ads at front of the book should show — under the Ragged Dick Series — that the present title (Volume I) is the only one in print. Volume II must be listed thus: "Fame and Fortune; or, The Progress of Richard Hunter. (In December.) Others in preparation." Below, the three volumes of the completed Campaign Series will be listed. The decorative title page must show Dick, with his shoe-blacking box, standing alone in New York's City Hall Park. Sometime later this illustration was changed to depict four young street boys with the tools of their trades. On the title page, the address must be 319 Washington Street. This, by itself, is not conclusive, as it merely means that the book was printed prior to November, 1870. However, if another address is shown, the book definitely is not a first edition. It is not generally known that a small printing of "Ragged Dick" appeared with the title page address given as 205 Washington Street. Loring established temporary headquarters there (and earlier, for a short period, at 35 School Street) while readying his new plant and book store at the Corner of Bromfield and Washington Streets.

Jacob Blanck tells me that, among earliest issued, some were printed on lighter-weight paper than others. He believes the lighter stock copies (making a slightly slimmer volume) to be the first, with other points identical.

Of bona fide first editions of "Ragged Dick," very few exist to this day. There probably are fewer than one dozen copies accounted for, to the great despair of the majority of Alger collectors.

When this bibliography was first published in 1964, a real first of "Dick" was valued at about $100.00. Since then it has been catalogued by reputable booksellers at about $150.00, later at $175.00 and a copy described as "a little rubbed" was recently sold at Parke-Bernet, New York, for a record at auction of $210.00.* The price will doubtless increase as the known copies find their way into universities, public collections and institutions from which they are not likely to return to circulation. Other Loring editions of "Ragged Dick" — non-firsts — bring relatively high prices ($35.00 and more) and even the relatively late output by Alger's many reprint publishers are eagerly sought by collectors who lack the earlier issues.

RALPH RAYMOND'S HEIR.

F. M. Lupton, 1892

The above-indicated date — 1892 — is an arbitrary one, but as suitable as any to serve as a starting point in one of the most perplexing Alger-hunts known to collectors of hero fiction!

The story first was published, as "Ralph Raymond's Heir," in Gleason's Literary Companion, in 1869. It was serialized, and the author's name given as Arthur Hamilton. This was the first occasion upon which Alger is known to have employed this pseudonym, although he could have used it previously, and he surely did use it again some sixteen years later (see "Helen Ford").

During the same year, Gleason intended to — or perhaps actually did — issue the novel in paper wrappers. Although offered for sale "as a pamphlet," for 25¢ (in the issue of August 14, 1869), no copy of this publication has been produced. It is not present in any collection and — although collectors, dealers and librarians have searched and advertised for it for

---

*Compare these figures with the $10.00 for *Ragged Dick*, listed by the old established Boston booksellers, Edward Morrill & Son, in 1941. That superb catalogue, *American Children's Books*, included a dozen additional Alger first editions (all but one issued by A. K. Loring) at proper-for-that-time prices ranging between $3.00-$6.00. Samuel Morrill, the present owner, recalls that Dr. A. S. W. Rosenbach enthusiastically congratulated his father on this catalogue.

many years — not a single positive clue has as yet been established that the paperback volume ever existed. Perhaps it *was* printed and, over the generations, the last fragile copies deteriorated and disappeared. Perhaps — as was not infrequent — the publisher intended to issue the book, but subsequently changed his mind. On the other hand, a copy may — at this moment — be hidden in an attic, a long-forgotten trunk or in the corner of a bookshelf, covered with a century's accumulation of dust. If this item shall ever be uncovered, its owner can convert it into a tidy sum of cash.

Lacking the Gleason publication, we turn next to The Leisure Hour Library, Vol. III, No. 201, dated July 28, 1888. Here, with the original title changed to "The Merchant's Crime," and the author's name correctly identified as Horatio Alger, Jr., the complete story filled the pages of a sixteen-page pamphlet that sold for three cents. The copyright notice lists the name of F. M. Lupton, but W. S. Trigg is shown as the publisher. Although this new title was soon laid aside, it did reappear once more, in April, 1897, when the story (apparently printed from the old Leisure Hour Library plates) was included in a quarterly, Lupton's Famous Fiction by the World's Greatest Authors. This was a large, magazine-size performance that sold for twenty-five cents.

The earliest known issue that contends for recognition as a first edition is "Ralph Raymond's Heir," By Horatio Alger, Jr., published by F. M. Lupton as No. 11 of The Idle Hour Series, dated March 30, 1892. This was a ten cent book in paper wrappers, published semi-weekly. The actual story runs 108 pages (a short story is appended to fill out the volume), and it is from these plates that the subsequent Lupton editions were printed.

The book's cover is of light brown paper, with dark brown printing. The title page: Ralph Raymond's Heir./ A Novel./ By Horatio Alger, Jr.,/ Author of "Ragged Dick," "Fame and Fortune," "Rough/ and Ready," Etc./ [rule]/ New York:/ The F. M. Lupton Publishing Company,/ No. 65 Duane Street.

The sixteen page short story at the back of the book is entitled "Dr. Winscombe's Sacrifice." Although this is probably not Alger's work, it is interesting to note that that article accompanies "Ralph Raymond's Heir" through all its future printings by Lupton.

Some months after its Idle Hour Series publication, Lupton graduated "Ralph Raymond's Heir" to its deluxe twenty-five cent Bijou Series, reissuing the story in the July 13th edition.

Having already deposited the story for copyright on March 23, 1892, Lupton proceeded with the production of a hard-cover, cloth-bound book. The earliest of these was the Stratford edition, apparently appearing during late Summer, 1892. At least two — and quite possibly more — Lupton editions were forthcoming and, years later, the title was added to the lists of a number of publishers who reissued dozens of Alger stories until well into the 1920's.

Lacking indication that the 1869 Gleason paperback ever existed, Lupton's Idle Hour Series No. 11 is the acknowledged first edition of "Ralph Raymond's Heir." Any of the few known copies would easily bring $45.00 if offered for sale. Leisure Hour Library No. 201 is worth $30.00.

RANDY ON THE RIVER; or, The Adventures of a Young Deckhand.
Chatterton-Peck Company, 1906

TITLE PAGE: Randy of the River/ or/ The Adventures of a Young Deckhand/ By/ Horatio Alger, Jr./ Author of "Nelson the Newsboy"

"Out for Business,"/ The Young Book Agent," "Lost at Sea,"/ "Ragged Dick Series," Etc./ [small tulip design]/ Chatterton-Peck Company/ New York, N.Y.

BINDING: Identical with "From Farm to Fortune," except publisher's monogram on spine is C. P. Co.

COLLATION: End-paper; frontispiece; title page [p. i]; copyright notice dated 1906, with list of book advertisements [p. ii]; preface, pp. iii - iv; contents, pp. v - vi; text, [p. 7] - 274; fly-leaf; end-paper. In addition to the frontispiece are three full-page illustrations.

The title of "Randy of the River" was deposited for copyright October 25, 1906 by Stitt Publishing Company. However, by the time the bound volume was received, on November 16, the firm had become Chatterton-Peck. "Randy" was issued as a volume of The Rise in Life Series, of which most or all were written by Edward Stratemeyer, although Horatio Alger's name appears as the author.

The first edition must show the publisher's "C.P.Co." monogram at bottom of spine. Chatterton-Peck must appear at bottom of title page, and the present title must appear at bottom of the list of stories on copyright page. There must be no book ads following the text. Value of first edition is $25.00.

RISEN FROM THE RANKS; or, Harry Walton's Success.

Loring, Publisher, 1874

TITLE PAGE: Risen From The Ranks;/ Or,/ Harry Walton's Success./ By/ Horatio Alger, Jr.,/ Author of "Ragged Dick," — "Tattered Tom," — "Luck and/ Pluck," — "Brave and Bold" Series./ [decorative rule]/ Loring, Publisher,/ Cor. Washington and Bromfield Streets,/ Boston.

BINDING: Identical with "Bound to Rise."

COLLATION: Yellow-tinted end-paper; fly-leaf; one leaf (2 pp.) book advertisements; frontispiece; tissue-covered decorative title page [p. 1]; verso blank [p. 2]; title page [p. 3]; copyright notice dated 1874 [p. 4]; dedication [p. 5]; verso blank [p. 6]; preface, pp. 7 - viii; text, [pp. 9] - 349; yellow-tinted end-paper. In addition to frontispiece and decorative title page are two full-page illustrations.

Prior to appearance in book form, this story was serialized in 1874 in Young Israel, entitled "Up the Ladder; or, Harry Walton's Success." This also was the anticipated book title, as Loring book advertisements that appeared prior to publication will indicate. In the early edition of "Bound to Rise" (the preceeding volume) the forthcoming title also is announced as "Up the Ladder." Nevertheless, apparently due to a last-minute change, the book was titled "Risen From The Ranks," and issued as Volume III of the Second Luck and Pluck Series. Although the book was in circulation well before Christmas, 1874, it was not deposited for copyright until 1877.

The first edition must show, in the book ads: "Julius; or The Street Boy Out West" as Volume I of the Second Tattered Tom Series, with no later title announced; "Risen From The Ranks; or, Harry Walton's Success" is listed as Volume III of the Second Luck and Pluck Series with no later title announced, and "Brave and Bold; or, The Fortunes of a Factory Boy" is Volume I of the Brave and Bold Series, with no further listing.

Value of first edition is $30.00.

ROBERT COVERDALE. See "Robert Coverdale's Struggle."

ROBERT COVERDALE'S STRUGGLE; or, On the Wave of Success.
Street & Smith, 1910

TITLE PAGE: [Decorative rule]/ Robert Coverdale's/ Struggle/ Or/ On
The Wave Of Success/ By Horatio Alger, Jr./ [decorative rule]/
Author of "Tom Temple's Career," "The Train Boy,"/ "The Errand
Boy," "Bernard Brook's (note misspelling of Brooks') Adventures,"/
"Ned Newton," "From Farm Boy to Senator,"/ "Dan, the Newsboy,"
and many other first-/ class stories for boys, the most complete/
line of which is published in the/ Medal and New Medal Librar-
ies./ [publisher's trade-mark device]/ [decorative rule]/ Street &
Smith, Publishers/ 79 - 89 Seventh Ave., New York City/ [decora-
tive rule].

BINDING: Paper wrappers, black typography and multi-colored illustrations. Cover design: New Medal Library No. 555/ 15 Cents/ Robert
Coverdale's/ Struggle/ By Horatio Alger, Jr./ [within a red frame,
illustration of boy on a raft]/ [four circles within which are depicted
skating, running, baseball and sailing scenes]/ Street & Smith: Publishers: New York. Spine (black print on solid red background):
New/ Medal/ Library/ Robert Coverdale's Struggle/ By Horatio
Alger, Jr./ Number/ 555. Cover size: 5" x 7¼".

COLLATION: Seven leaves (14 pp.) of book advertisements; title page
[p. 1]; verso blank, with no indication of copyright [p. 2]; publisher's note [p. 3]; publisher's price announcement [p. 4]; text,
[pp. 5] - 303; book advertisements on verso; 1 leaf (2 pp.) of book
advertisements.

Prior to appearing in book form, this story — entitled "Robert Coverdale;
or, The Young Fisherman of Cook's Harbor" — was serialized three separate
times in Golden Days. It first appeared, starting in the issue dated October
30, 1880, and ending in the issue dated January 15, 1881. The second run
started on February 11, 1888, continuing through the issue dated May 5,
1888. The third and last serialization began on December 3, 1904, with the
final installment in the issue of February 25, 1905.
   "Robert Coverdale's Struggle" is the last of Horatio Alger's works to
appear in book form. Street & Smith issued their edition — in paper wrappers — on February 15, 1910. The Library of Congress printed catalogue of
cards lists the title, followed by the symbol [191-?], indicating that the
book may never have been desposited for copyright. No copyright notice
appears in the Street & Smith paperback, nor is it printed in the later A. L.
Burt hard-cover edition.
   The Burt edition appeared shortly before Christmas, 1910. The cover
illustration depicts a hunting scene, a boy in red-striped turtle-neck sweater,
a rifle on his shoulder and a dog beside him. This was Burt's standard sixty-
cent edition of that period. They apparently never printed the book in
their deluxe "dollar" format. Although the Street & Smith Medal Library
printing was relatively limited, Burt continued issuing the title in their
Chimney Corner Series for several years. The Burt hard-cover reprints are
not difficult to find.

However, the Street & Smith first edition is the rarest of all Alger paperbacks. Only one copy is known to exist. Prior to its discovery, Alger experts seriously questioned whether it ever really was issued, as the listing of a title in a publisher's catalogue is not, in itself, sufficient proof. Publishers have frequently decided against printing titles included in the catalogues they prepared many months in advance. The single known copy of New Medal Library No. 555 is worth at least $350.00.

ROLLING STONE, A; or, The Adventures of a Wanderer.

Thompson & Thomas, 1902

TITLE PAGE: A Rolling Stone/ Or/ The Adventures of a/ Wanderer./ rule/ By/ Horatio Alger, Jr./ Author of the "Western Boy," "Slow and Sure," "Phil the/ Fiddler," "Paul the Peddler," Etc./ [flower]/ Thompson & Thomas/ Chicago. [A double-line border completely encloses the type].

BINDING: Blue cloth with black and white stamping. Cover design: A Rolling/ Stone/ [illustration of a boy walking with stick and bundle; city skyline at background]/ By/ Horatio/ Alger. Spine: A/ Rolling/ Stone/ Alger/ Thompson/ and/ Thomas. Cover size: 5¼" x 7½".

COLLATION: End-paper; frontispiece; title page [p. 1]; copyright notice dated 1894 (Munsey) and 1902 (Thompson & Thomas) [p. 2]; contents, [pp. 3 - 4]; text, [pp. 5] - 294; fly-leaf; end-paper. In addition to the frontispiece is one full-page illustration.

Prior to publication in book form, "A Rolling Stone" was serialized in Argosy, by Arthur Lee Putnam. The first installment appeared in the issue dated February 24, 1894, and continued through the issue (by then published monthly) dated June, 1894.

Early in 1902, the title was deposited for copyright by Thompson & Thomas, of Chicago. They issued "A Rolling Stone" with Alger listed as the author and — later in the same year — they reissued the story under a new title, "Wren Winter's Triumph."

The first edition of "A Rolling Stone" will show the type on Page 43 to be in normal good condition. After early issue the type at upper right side of the page became noticeably damaged. It is in this battered condition that it appears in Thompson & Thomas' "Wren Winter's Triumph," and also in later reprints by Donahue, made from the original plates. The story was never reissued under the original title.

The first edition of "A Rolling Stone" and the earliest issue of "Wren Winter's Triumph" are equally valued at $22.50.

ROUGH AND READY; or, Life Among the New York Newsboys.

Loring, Publisher, 1869

TITLE PAGE: Rough and Ready;/ Or,/ Life Among the New York Newsboys./ By/ Horatio Alger, Jr./ Author of "Ragged Dick," "Fame and Fortune" "Mark the Match/ Boy," "Campaign Series," "Luck and Pluck," Series, Etc./ [decorative rule]/ Loring, Publisher,/ 319 Washington Street,/ Boston.

BINDING: Identical with "Ben, the Luggage Boy."

COLLATION: Yellow-tinted end-paper; fly-leaf; blank leaf on verso of which is a page of book advertisements; frontispiece; tissue-covered decorative title page [p. 1]; verso blank [p. 2]; title page [p. 3]; copyright notice dated 1869 [p. 4]; dedication [p. 5]; verso blank [p. 6]; preface [p. 7]; verso blank [p. 8]; text, pp. 9 - 300; fly-leaf; yellow-tinted end-paper.

"Rough and Ready" was serialized in Student and Schoolmate during 1869, before being issued in book form at the end of that year. On November 22, 1969, Loring deposited the title page for copyright.

The present title was published as Volume IV of the Ragged Dick Series. The first edition will indicate, below "Rough and Ready": "V. Ben, The Luggage Boy. (In April, 1870)/ VI. Rufus And Rose; or, The Fortunes of Rough and/ Ready. (In December, 1870.)." At the bottom of the list of book advertisements, "Luck And Pluck; or, John Oakley's Inheritance" will appear as the only title of the Luck and Pluck Series that is already in print.

The first edition also will show an illustration facing Page 217. In later issues, the illustration is inverted to face Page 216.

Value of first edition is $27.50.

RUFUS AND ROSE; or, The Fortunes of Rough and Ready.

Loring, Publisher, 1870

TITLE PAGE: Rufus and Rose;/ Or,/ The Fortunes of Rough and Ready./ By/ Horatio Alger, Jr./ Author of "Ragged Dick," "Fame and Fortune," "Mark, the Match Boy,"/ "Rough and Ready," (front quotation mark missing) Ben, the Luggage Boy," "Campaign/ Series," "Luck and Pluck Series," Etc./ [decorative rule]/ Loring, Publisher,/ 319 Washington Street,/ Boston.

BINDING: Identical with "Ben, the Luggage Boy."

COLLATION: Yellow-tinted end-paper; fly-leaf; blank leaf on verso of which appears book advertisements; frontispiece; tissue covered decorative title page [p. I]; verso blank [p. II]; title page [p. III]; copyright notice dated 1870 [p. IV]; dedication [p. V]; verso blank [p. VI]; preface, pp. VII - VIII; text, pp. 9 - 292; fly-leaf; yellow-tinted end-paper. In addition to the frontispiece and decorative title page are two full-page illustrations.

It was in Student and Schoolmate that the story of "Rufus and Rose" first appeared, from January through December, 1870. Toward the end of that year, that monthly publication offered Loring's cloth-bound edition, postpaid, for $1.05 per copy, which was a reduction from the regular $1.25 bookstore price. At the same time, the magazine offered free portraits of Horatio Alger as an inducement to readers to remit subscription payment at an early date.

Loring deposited the volume for copyright on November 10, 1870, and it was probably placed in distribution at about that time, as its publication is noted in the December issue of Student and Schoolmate.

The first edition of "Rufus and Rose" is the last Alger first edition to carry the 319 Washington Street address at bottom of title page, and very few copies of the story will be found with that address. In the advertisements at front, the present title is listed as Volume VI (and the last) of the Ragged Dick Series. However, under the Luck and Pluck Series, the last title listed must be "III. Strong and Steady; or, Paddle your own canoe. (In October, 1871.)" Below the listing of the forthcoming Tattered Tom Series, titles are anticipated as follows: "I. Tattered Tom; or, The story of a Street Arab. (April, 1871.)" and "II. Paul, The Peddler; or, The Adventures of a Young Street Merchant. (In November, 1871)".

The early editions show, as frontispiece, Rufus — with Rose and their friend, Miss Manning — accosted by the villainous James Martin. Possibly feeling that the appearance of the two young ladies might not appeal to the boys who clamored for each new Alger story, this illustration was later relegated to a position facing page 122. As the replacement, the picture of a bootblack thumbing his nose at Mr. Martin (in front of the Tribune office) was moved up from its original position, facing page 40.

Although issued as the last volume of its series, "Rufus and Rose" is the first of the group to use the revised decorative title page. Until the appearance of "Rufus and Rose," this illustration showed Ragged Dick, with his boot-blacking box, standing alone in front of New York's City Hall. The revised version shows Dick surrounded by the three young men (Ben, the Luggage Boy, Rufus and Mark, the Match Boy) who were heroes of the six stories of this series.

Value of first edition is $27.50.

RUPERT'S AMBITION.

Henry T. Coates & Co., 1899

TITLE PAGE: Rupert's Ambition/ By/ Horatio Alger, Jr./ Author of "Chester Rand," "Lester's Luck," "Ragged Dick Series,"/ Etc., Etc./ Philadelphia/ Henry T. Coates & Co./ 1899.

BINDING: Identical with "Jed, The Poorhouse Boy."

COLLATION: Dark brown coated end-paper; tissue-covered frontispiece; title page [p. i]; copyright notice dated 1899 [p. ii]; contents, pp. iii - iv; text, pp. 1 - 366; fly-leaf; dark brown coated end-paper.

"Rupert's Ambition" appeared as a serialization in Argosy, the first installment issued on December 23, 1893, and the final chapter on March 10, 1894. Henry T. Coates deposited the title page for copyright on May 17, 1899, and supplied the bound volume on August 16, 1899.

The first edition's identification is its dated title page.

Value of first edition is $22.50.

SAM'S CHANCE; and How He Improved It.

Loring, Publisher, 1876

TITLE PAGE: Sam's Chance;/ And/ How He Improved It./ By/ Horatio Alger, Jr.,/ Author of "Ragged Dick" Series; "Tattered Tom" Series; "Luck and Pluck" Series; Etc., Etc./ [decorative rule]/ Loring, Publisher,/ Cor. Bromfield and Washington Sts.,/ Boston.

BINDING: Identical with "Julius; or, The Street Boy Out West."

COLLATION: Yellow-tinted end-paper; fly-leaf; one leaf (2 pp.) book advertisements; frontispiece; tissue-covered decorative title page; title page [p. i]; copyright notice dated 1876 [p. ii]; dedication [p. iii]; verso blank [p. iv]; preface, pp. v - vi; (there is no leaf for pp. vii -

viii); text, [pp. 9] - 271; fly-leaf; yellow-tinted end-paper. In addition to the frontispiece and decorative title page are two full-page illustrations.

A. K. Loring deposited the bound volume for copyright sometime during March (exact date unavailable), 1876.

All of the first edition identification is in the book ads. Under the Tattered Tom Series, "Sam's Chance" will be listed as already in print with, below it, only the Roman numeral "IV" with no indication of the next title. A later edition listed it as "IV. 1879." Still later, "IV. The Telegraph Boy. In 1879". On the second page of advertisements, the Brave and Bold Series will show the first three volumes as already being in print.

Value of first edition is $30.00.

SEEKING HIS FORTUNE, and Other Dialogues.

Loring, Publisher, 1875

TITLE PAGE: Seeking His Fortune,/ And/ Other Dialogues./ By/ Horatio Alger, Jr.,/ And/ O. Augusta Cheney./ Loring, Publisher,/ Cor. Bromfield and Washington Streets./ Boston.

BINDING: Covers identical with "Ben, The Luggage Boy." Spine (gold-stamped): [Rule]/ [decorative panel]/ (within which is stamped: Seeking/ His/ Fortune)/ By/ Horatio Alger/ and/ O. A. Cheney/ [vignette of man holding a traveling bag]/ [rule]. Cover size: 4¾" x 7".

COLLATION: Yellow-tinted end-paper; fly-leaf; 1 leaf (2 pp.) book advertisements, [pp. 1 - 2]; title page [p. 3]; copyright notice dated 1875 [p. 4]; dedication [p. 5]; verso blank [p. 6]; preface [p. 7]; verso blank [p. 8]; contents [p. 9]; verso blank [p. 10]; text, pp. 11 - 270; 2 fly-leaves; yellow-tinted end-paper.

CONTENTS: Seeking His Fortune.
One Week an Editor.
Keeping Genteel Boarders.
Mrs. Skinflint's Bargains.
Mrs. Grundy's Tyranny.
Aunt Hannah's Valentine.
Mr. Bliss' Vision.
High Life Below Stairs.
Boarding on a Farm.
Taming a Wife.
John Smith's Trials.
Aunt Rachel's Fright.
The Hypochondriac Cured.
Aunt Patience's Ear-Trumpet.
The Ghostly Visitation.
Practical Husbandry.
Mr. Smith's Day at Home.
The Country Cousin.
Taking Poison.
Deacon Robinson's Present.
Mrs. Marden's Lesson.
The Magic Mirror.

Although issued in 1875, "Seeking His Fortune" — a collection of twenty-two dialogues — was not deposited for copyright by A. K. Loring until early in 1877.

The book is a collaboration between Horatio Alger and his younger sister, Olive Augusta Cheney, who was a prolific writer of short stories. In his preface, Alger acknowledges that only the first dialogue, "Seeking His Fortune," was written by him. All the others were written by Mrs. Cheney, with Alger serving as editor. "Nearly all the dialogues in the present collection," Alger writes, "were originally contributed to a juvenile magazine in New York. Many of them have been used at exhibitions in different parts of the country." The juvenile magazine was Young Israel, and that publication offered "Seeking His Fortune" as a prize to winners of its various writing competitions.

"Seeking His Fortune," Alger's contribution, originally appeared as a two-part feature in the March and April, 1866, issues of Student and Schoolmate. Mrs. Cheney's "Taming of a Wife" appeared in the September, 1872, issue of the same magazine.

"Seeking His Fortune" ranks second only to the fabulous "Timothy Crump's Ward" in value and desirability to Alger collectors. There probably are fewer than six known copies. First edition points are inconsequential in the case of this rare book. Grab any that may be offered.

A curious reprint of this title was published in 1882 by Ward & Drummond, of New York. Issued between cardboard covers, this edition — which is virtually unknown, even to advanced collectors — is as rare as the original. However, it is worth only a fraction of the Loring, perhaps $50.00. The Loring edition of "Seeking His Fortune" has been catalogued at $425.00, but its real value is nearer $375.00.

SHIFTING FOR HIMSELF; or, Gilbert Greyson's Fortunes.
Loring, Publisher, 1876
  TITLE PAGE: Shifting for Himself;/ Or,/ Gilbert Greyson's Fortunes./ By/
       Horatio Alger, Jr.,/ Author of "Ragged Dick," — "Tattered Tom," —
       "Luck and/ Pluck," — "Brave and Bold" Series./ [decorative rule]/
       Loring, Publisher,/ Cor. Washington and Bromfield Streets,/ Boston.
  BINDING: Identical with "Brave and Bold."

  COLLATION: Yellow-tinted end-paper; fly-leaf, 2 leaves (4 pp.) of book
       advertisements; frontispiece; tissue-covered decorative title page;
       title page [p. i]; copyright notice dated 1876 [p. ii]; dedication
       [p. iii]; verso blank [p. iv]; preface, pp. v - vi; there is no leaf for
       [pp. vii - viii]; text, [pp. 9] - 356; 2 fly-leaves; yellow-tinted end-
       paper. In addition to the frontispiece and decorative title page are
       two full-page illustrations.

"Shifting For Himself" appeared as a bound volume, early in November, 1876, after it had been serialized — earlier the same year — in Young Israel. The serialization title was "Facing the World," but was in no way connected with the Alger book of that title, published by Porter & Coates in 1893. Loring eventually deposited his book for copyright early in 1877, some months after it was issued.

The first edition is identified by these points: In the book ads, "Sam's Chance" is the last title indicated under the Second Tattered Tom Series. It is followed by "IV. (In April, 1877.)". Under the Brave and Bold Series,

"Shifting For Himself" is listed as Volume III, with no indication of the next volume.

On Page 115, the letter "u" in "upon" is mis-printed upside-down. On Page 337, the word "abundant" is mis-spelled as "baundant." On Page 343, the words "an end" are joined, forming "anend." On Page 356, the final volume of the Brave and Bold Series is announced as "Work and Hope; or, Ben Bradford's Motto." This later was changed to "Wait and Hope," the title under which the story actually appeared.

Value of first edition is $30.00.

SILAS SNOBDEN'S OFFICE BOY.

Doubleday & Company, 1973

TITLE PAGE: Horatio Alger, Jr./[decorative crossed branches]/Silas Snobden's/ Office Boy/Foreword by Ralph D. Gardner/1973/Doubleday & Company, Inc./ Garden City, New York.

BINDING: Gold stamped brown cloth. Cover design; Portrait of Alger within blind-stamped rectangle. Spine: Horatio/Alger, Jr./Silas/Snobden's/Office/Boy/Fore-word/By/Ralph D./Gardner/Doubleday. Cover size: 5½" x 8½".

COLLATION: Brown end paper (white verso); half title page [p. 1] blank verso [p. 2]; title page [p.3]; copyright notice (last line reads "First Edition" — later editions omit this line) [p. 4]; Foreword [pp. 5] - 24; footnotes [pp. 25] - 26; text [pp. 27] - 240; white recto of brown end paper. There are 16 additional unnumbered pages with 32 illustrations. Dust jacket has brown front and spine; white on back, printed in mauve, white and black.

"Silas Snobden's Office Boy," with Arthur Lee Putnam as author, ran for thirteen weeks as a serialization in The Argosy. The first installment appeared in No. 365, dated November 30, 1889. The last part concluded in No. 377, dated February 22, 1890.

The Putnam pseudonym was used to avoid confusion with "The Odds Against Him," which was running when "Silas Snobden's Office Boy" began, and "The Erie Train Boy" (both carrying the Alger by-line), which started some weeks before the present story ended.

It apparently was intended to release the story as "Mr. Snobden's Office Boy," and it was thus announced. However, it was not printed under that title. On the cover of the issue of December 21, 1889, the title was incorrectly listed as "The Story of an Office Boy." That was the only time that confusing title was used. However, that once was sufficient to start collectors searching for what can be considered a "ghost" title.

In 1891, United States Book Company indicated its intention to issue the story in their Leather-Clad Tales of Adventure and Romance Series. They dug up Munsey's unused title, "Mr. Snobden's Office Boy," printed a title page and deposited it with the Library of Congress (copyright #34855), but never issued the book.

Incidentally, Jacob Blanck has come up with the interesting discovery that the title, "Mr. Snobden's Office Boy," was originally copyrighted — about 1858 — by Moses M. Beach, Editor of The New York Sun. Mr. Blanck considers it likely the story first appeared as a serial in The Sun, as Alger's output was then being anonymously published by that newspaper.

This is one of the unique items that the advanced Alger collector searches for after he has a good row of the author's bound volumes on his shelf. A complete run does not often turn up. I picked them up, issue by issue, over a long period of years, and paid top prices for the last few numbers, needed to fill final gaps in the serialization. The complete run of thirteen issues, bound or loose, is worth $65.00 and more.

Bound volume issued by Doubleday February 2, 1973. "Silas Snobden's Office Boy" had gone into a fourth printing as of July 1973, all editions totaling 12,500 copies. Chapters I – IV were previously printed in The Literary Guild's "Works in Progress;

Selections From the Best in Books to be Published in Coming Months," Number 8, [January, 1973]. A condensation appears in Argosy Magazine, June, 1973, and a paperback edition by Popular Library was published in February, 1974.

The book, currently in print, is priced at $5.95 (although collectors and o.p. booksellers are reportedly offering somewhat more for the 4,500 first edition copies, all of which were sold out in advance of publication).

SINK OR SWIM; or, Harry Raymond's Resolve.

Loring, Publisher, 1870

TITLE PAGE: Sink Or Swim;/ Or,/ Harry Raymond's Resolve./ By/ Horatio Alger, Jr.,/ Author of "Ragged Dick," "Fame and Fortune," "Mark, The Match Boy,"/ "Rough and Ready," "Ben, the Luggage Boy," "Rufus and Rose,"/ "Campaign Series," "Luck and Pluck," Etc./ [decorative rule]/ Loring, Publisher,/ 319 Washington Street,/ 35 School Street,/ Boston.

BINDING: Identical with "Luck and Pluck."

COLLATION: Yellow-tinted end-paper; fly-leaf; leaf with page of book advertisements and verso blank; frontispiece; tissue-covered decorative title page [p. i]; verso blank [p. ii]; title page [p. iii]; copyright notice dated 1870 [p. iv]; dedication [p. v]; verso blank [p vi]; preface, pp. vii - viii; text, pp. 9 - 388; fly-leaf; yellow-tinted end-paper. In addition to the frontispiece and decorative title page are four full-page illustrations.

Prior to appearing as a bound volume, "Sink or Swim" was serialized in Ballou's Monthly Magazine, from January through December, 1870. Ballou's, primarily an adult publication, ran the installments in Our Young People's Story Teller, a department for children. All of the illustrations that later appeared in the bound volume were originally published in Ballou's.

A. K. Loring deposited the volume for copyright on November 15, 1871, almost a year after it was first issued. The first edition lists two addresses — 319 Washington Street and 35 School Street — at bottom of title page. It is the only Alger first edition to carry both addresses, and possibly the only printing of any Alger story published by Loring to list 35 School Street (a temporary headquarters while awaiting completion of the new offices and book store at the Corner of Bromfield and Washington Streets).

There must be only one page of book ads. These will show, under Luck and Pluck Series, "III. Strong and Steady; or, Paddle your own Canoe. (In October, 1871.)" Under the Tattered Tom Series the listings are "I. Tattered Tom; or, The story of a Street Arab. (April, 1871.)" and "II. Paul, the Peddler; or, The Adventures of a Young Street Merchant. (In November, 1871.)"

This story was reissued by Aldine Publishing Company, London, between 1903-1907 as "Paddle Your Own Canoe; or, Harry Raymond's Resolve." It was a paperback in their Garfield Library series. Note that there is no connection between this reprint and the similarly titled early serialization of "Strong and Steady."

Value of first edition is $30.00.

SLOW AND SURE; or, From the Street to the Shop.

Loring, Publisher, 1872

TITLE PAGE: Slow and Sure;/ or,/ From the Street to the Shop./ By/

Horatio Alger, Jr./ Author of "Ragged Dick," "Fame and Fortune," "Mark, the Match/ Boy," "Rough and Ready," "Campaign Series," Etc./ [decorative rule]/ Loring, Publisher,/ Cor. Washington and Bromfield Streets,/ Boston.

BINDING: Identical with "Paul the Peddler."

COLLATION: Yellow-tinted end-paper; fly-leaf; 1 leaf (2 pp.) of book advertisements; frontispiece; tissue-covered decorative title page [p. 1]; verso blank [p. 2]; title page [p. 3]; copyright notice dated 1872 [p. 4]; dedication [p. 5]; verso blank [p. 6]; preface, pp. 7 - viii; text, [pp. 9] - 280; fly-leaf; yellow-tinted end-paper. In addition to the frontispiece and decorative title page are two full-page illustrations.

Prior to appearing as a bound book, "Slow and Sure" was serialized in Student and Schoolmate during 1872. A. K. Loring issued the volume in November of that year, but did not deposit it for copyright until February 13, 1873.

In the first edition, the book advertisements at front must show the following listings: Under the Tattered Tom Series, after the listing for "Slow and Sure," "Second Series in preparation. I. Julius; or, The Street Boy out West, — in Nov., '73." The listings under the Second Luck and Pluck Series must include "I. Try and Trust; or, The Story of a Bound Boy, — in April, '73." and "II. Live and Learn; or, How Harry Walton rose in the World, — in October, '73."

On the title page, the letter "c" in "Etc." must be perfect. All later printings examined show this letter to be damaged.

Value of first edition is $30.00.

STAR OF THE CIRCUS, THE. See "The Young Circus Rider."

STORE BOY, THE; or, The Fortunes of Ben Barclay.

Porter & Coates, 1887

TITLE PAGE: The Store Boy;/ or,/ The Fortunes of Ben Barclay/ By/ Horatio Alger, Jr.,/ Author of "Do and Dare," "Hector's Inheritance,"/ "Ragged Dick" Series, "Tattered Tom"/ Series," Etc./ [publisher's trade-mark device]/ Philadelphia:/ Porter & Coates.

BINDING: Identical with "Ben's Nugget."

COLLATION: Dark brown coated end-paper; fly-leaf; tissue-covered frontispiece; title page [p. i]; Copyright notice dated 1887 [p. ii]; contents, [pp. iii] - iv; text, [pp. 5] - 314; 3 leaves (6 pp.) of book advertisements; fly-leaf; dark brown coated end-paper. In addition to the frontispiece are three full-page illustrations.

Prior to appearing in book form, "The Store Boy" was serialized in Golden Argosy, the first installment appearing late in 1883 and continuing into 1884. The following year, 1885, it was serialized in the Boston Globe. Porter & Coates deposited the book for copyright on October 15, 1887, and had it in distribution during the following month.

Years later, on December 24, 1904, Street & Smith reissued the story — entitled "Ben Barclay's Courage; or, The Fortunes of a Store Boy" — as Number 105 of their five cent Brave and Bold Series. This was a large-sized, 32-page publication in colorful paper wrappers. The cover showed

Ben Barclay bravely rescuing three girls from the roof of a burning building.

The first edition of "The Store Boy" will show — in the ads at back of the book — that "The Young Circus Rider" is the last Alger title listed. On the title page, an unnecessary quotation mark follows the word "Series," after "Tattered Tom."

Strangely enough, Brave and Bold No. 105 is harder to find than the first edition of the hard-covered Porter & Coates edition. However, the later paperback reissue is of value only to serious collectors seeking all variations of the Alger titles.

Brave and Bold No. 105 is worth $15.00. Value of the Porter & Coates first edition is $25.00.

STORY OF A FACTORY BOY, THE. See "The Odds Against Him."

STORY OF AN OFFICE BOY, THE. See "Silas Snobden's Office Boy."

STRIVE AND SUCCEED: Or, The Progress of Walter Conrad.

Loring, Publisher, 1872

TITLE PAGE: Strive and Succeed;/ Or,/ The Progress of Walter Conrad./ By/ Horatio Alger, Jr./ Author of "Ragged Dick," "Fame and Fortune," "Mark, the Match/ Boy," "Rough and Ready," Campaign Series," Etc./ [decorative rule]/ Loring, Publisher,/ Cor. Washington and Bromfield Streets,/ Boston.

BINDING: Identical with "Luck and Pluck."

COLLATION: Yellow-tinted end-paper; fly-leaf; 1 leaf (2 pp.) book advertisements; tissue-covered frontispiece; decorative title page [p. i]; verso blank [p. ii]; title page [p. iii]; copyright notice dated 1872 [p. iv]; dedication [p. v]; verso blank [p. vi]; preface, [p. vii] - viii; text, pp. 9 - 355; 2 leaves (3 pp. book advertisements, 1 p. blank); fly-leaf; yellow-tinted end-paper. In addition to the frontispiece and decorative title page are three full-page illustrations.

"Strive and Succeed" was originally serialized in Young Israel, during 1872, and issued in bound book form by A. K. Loring in October of the same year. Loring deposited the title page as late as December 16, 1872 and the bound volume on January 2, 1873. Nevertheless, the book's first edition was on sale in sufficient time for the 1872 Christmas Season.

The first edition lists the Alger book ads as follows: The Second Tattered Tom Series must list "I. Julius; or, The Street Boy out West, — in Nov. '73." The Second Luck and Pluck Series must list "I. Try and Trust; or, The Story of a Bound Boy, — in April, '73." and "II. Live and Learn; or, How Harry Walton rose in the World, — in October, '73."

Following the last page of text, only the first edition will list the following (non-Alger) advertisements: "Veronica; or, The Light House Keeper," "Countess Kate," by Miss Yonge; "The Boys at Chequasset," by Mrs. A.D.T. Whitney; "The French Robinson Crusoe," "Milly; or, The Hidden Cross," "Judge Not, or Hester Powers' Girlhood," and four volumes of The Breakwater Series, by Virginia F. Townsend. This first edition is something of an oddity, as it was most unusual for Loring to place book advertisements both in the front and back of a volume.

The second state changed the anticipated publication date of "Try and Trust" to "May, '73," and carried no book advertisements after the last page of the text.

Value of first edition is $30.00.

STRIVING FOR FORTUNE; or, Walter Griffith's Trials and Successes. *Street & Smith, 1901*

This story was first published as a serialization in Golden Argosy. Entitled "Walter Griffith; or, The adventures of a Young Street Salesman," by Arthur Lee Putnam. The first installment appeared in the issue dated October 22, 1887, and concluded in the issue dated January 14, 1888.

United States Book Company copyrighted the story in 1892, intending to issue it in their Leather-Clad Tales of Adventure and Romance, titled "Striving For Fortune; or, The Adventures of a Young Street Salesman." Although they apparently never issued the volume, they had already prepared the plates, for it is from these engravings that the Street & Smith editions were printed.

Street & Smith published what can be considered the first edition of the caption title as Number 138 of their Medal Library series, with Horatio Alger listed as the author. The ten cent publication, in paper wrappers, was released on November 23, 1901 (but was not deposited for copyright until January 20, 1902).

In my library there is a curious version of the book. Although it carries the proper Street & Smith title page, with title indicated as "Striving For Fortune; or, Walter Griffith's Trials and Success," the title on the first page of text is set in the unique style of the Leather-Clads, being slightly varied as "Striving For Fortune; or, The Adventures of a Young Street Salesman." To add to the mystery, the slim volume is bound in dark blue hard-covers. As none of the Medal Library series were issued in hard covers — and it is most unlikely that a contemporary reader would go to the expense of binding a ten cent paperback novel — there is the likelihood that this was a pre-publication issue, cloth-bound to give permanence for filing and storage. While this is mere supposition, it must be pointed out that the earliest distributed edition noted has the original first page of text altered, and the heading reset in the Street & Smith style.

Apparently simultaneously (for it was received at the Library of Congress on November 4, 1901) Street & Smith issued the story in hard covers. On the cover and title page, the title was printed as "Walter Griffith." But on the first page of text it ran as "Walter Griffith; or, The Adventures of a Young Street Salesman."

Some years later, Street & Smith reissued "Striving For Fortune" — again as a paperback — in their Alger Series.

As this story was not reissued as profusely as most of the other Algers, it is a relatively hard item to come-by. The Medal Library 138, "Striving For Fortune," is rare and worth $25.00. The hard-cover "Walter Griffith" — in the Street & Smith edition — now brings about $15.00. A full run of the serialization in Golden Argosy is well worth $30.00.

STRONG AND STEADY; or, Paddle Your Own Canoe.

Loring, Publisher, 1871

TITLE PAGE: Strong and Steady;/ or,/ Paddle Your Own Canoe./ By/ Horatio Alger, Jr./ Author of "Ragged Dick Series," "Tattered Tom Series," "Luck and/ Pluck Series," "Campaign Series," Etc./ [decorative rule]/ Loring, Publisher,/ Cor. Bromfield and Washington Streets,/ Boston.

BINDING: Identical with "Luck and Pluck.

COLLATION: Yellow-tinted end-paper; fly-leaf; leaf with blank page and a page of book advertisements on verso; tissue-covered frontispiece; decorative title page [p. i]; verso blank [p. ii]; title page [p. iii]; copyright notice dated 1871 [p. iv]; dedication [p. v]; verso blank [p. vi]; preface, [pp. vii] - viii; text, pp. 9 - 362; yellow-tinted end-paper. In addition to frontispiece and decorative title page are four full-page illustrations.

Prior to appearing as a bound book, the story was serialized in Young Israel during 1871, entitled "Paddle Your Own Canoe; or, The Fortunes of Walter Conrad." "Strong and Steady" was issued by Loring (as Volume III of the Luck and Pluck Series) late in October, 1871, but it was not deposited for copyright until mid-1872.

The first edition will show, under the book ads at front, that "Strive and Succeed; or, The Progress of Walter Conrad," will be issued as Volume IV of the Luck and Pluck Series "(In October, 1872.)" Below the heading of the Tattered Tom Series, "Phil, The Fiddler; or, The Young Street Musician," will appear "(In April, 1872.)." In first state, the final page of text is a single leaf, inserted. Second state has final page of text as a part of a two-leaf insert, with the second leaf blank.

Value of first edition is $30.00.

STRUGGLING UPWARD; or, Luke Larkin's Luck.

Porter & Coates, 1890

TITLE PAGE: Struggling Upward;/ or, /Luke Larkin's Luck/ By/ Horatio Alger, Jr.,/ Author of "The Ragged Dick Series," "Tattered Tom Series,"/ "Luck and Pluck Series," "Pacific Series," Etc., Etc./ [publisher's trade-mark device]/ Philadelphia:/ Porter & Coates.

BINDING: Rough, blue-gray cloth. Cover design, stamped in black and yellow. Way to Success/ Series/ [vignette of beehive within a wreath, against a palm frond]/ Horatio Alger Jr. Spine, stamped in black, yellow and gold: [Black and gold rules]/ Struggling/ Upward (title being blind-stamped against gold panel) [black and gold rules]/ [vignette of beaver within a wreath against a palm frond]/ Labore/ Et/ Honore/ [black and gold rules]/ Horatio/ Alger /Jr./ [black and gold rules]/ Porter & Coates (blind stamped against gold panel). Cover size: 5¼" x 7⅞".

COLLATION: Dark brown coated end-paper; fly-leaf; tissue-covered frontispiece; title page [p. i]; copyright notice dated 1890 [p. ii]; contents pp. iii - iv; text, pp. 5 - 333; 1 leaf (2 pp.) book advertisements; fly-leaf; dark brown coated end-paper. In addition to the frontispiece are three full-page illustrations.

Prior to its appearance as a bound volume, the story was serialized in Golden Argosy. The first installment appeared in the issue dated March 13, 1886, concluding with the issue dated June 19, 1886.

With the publication of this volume, Porter & Coates abandoned their smaller (16mo) dark brown binding in which their earlier Algers had been issued. It must have been a last-minute decision to adopt the new (12mo) binding, as it had already been announced in the Porter & Coates catalogue for 1890 that the standard format would be used.

Curiously, this story is occasionally offered as the "Way to Success," because that title (with the word "Series" in smaller type, below) is prominently stamped in black on the cover. It is in a much larger and more prominent type-face than "Struggling Upward," which only appears blind-stamped in smaller type on the spine. No individual Alger story ever appeared under the title of "Way to Success," although Porter and Coates issued four titles under this series. Shortly after the appearance of "Struggling Upward" (the fourth and final book in the group), the three earlier titles ("Bob Burton," "The Story Boy" and "Luke Walton") were converted to the new format.

As recently as 1946, "Struggling Upward" was rewritten for dramatic presentation by Rilla Carlisle (pen-name of Anne Coulter Martens). The three-act play was published, in paper wrappers, by the Dramatic Publishing Company, of Chicago.

The first edition is identified by the rough, blue-gray covers (as described). Later editions were bound in a smooth, light gray cloth. Also, the dark brown coated end-papers were abandoned after the first issue, and gray papers substituted.

Value of first edition is $25.00.

SUCCESSFUL PAUL. See "Paul the Peddler."

TATTERED TOM; or, The Story of a Street Arab.

Loring, Publisher, 1871

TITLE PAGE: Tattered Tom;/ or,/ The Story of a Street Arab./ By/ Horatio Alger, Jr.,/ Author of "Ragged Dick Series," "Luck and Pluck Series," "Campaign Series."/ [decorative rule]/ Loring, Publisher,/ Cor. Bromfield and Washington Streets,/ Boston.

BINDING: Identical with "Paul the Peddler."

COLLATION: Yellow-tinted end-paper; fly-leaf; leaf with blank side and book advertisements on verso; frontispiece; tissue-covered decorative title page [p. I]; verso blank [p. II]; title page [p. III]; copyright notice dated 1871 [p. IV]; dedication [p. V]; verso blank [p. VI]; preface, pp. VII - VIII; text, [pp. 9] - 282; 2 leaves (3 pp. book advertisements, 1 blank); fly-leaves; yellow-tinted end-paper. In addition to the frontispiece and decorative title page are two full-page illustrations.

A. K. Loring deposited "Tattered Tom" for copyright on August 12, 1871, a couple of months after the first edition was issued. Readers generally are surprised to learn that Tom — one of Alger's most rugged characters — is a girl. On Page 47 Tom recalls that her real name is Jane. However, due to a lapse on the author's part, her name (when it next appears on Page 97) is incorrectly given as Jenny.

Despite the fact that the story has a heroine instead of a hero "Tattered Tom" is among the most typical of Alger's works, and definitely one of the most popular. Although it was reissued by many publishers, a first edition is rare.

In the first edition, the book ads at front must show, under the Tattered Tom Series, "II. Paul, the Peddler; or, The Adventures of a Young Street Merchant. (In November, 1871.)" The last listing under the Luck and Pluck Series will be "III. Strong and Steady; or, Paddle your own Canoe. (In October, 1871.)"

Due to its rarity and relatively great demand, a first edition of "Tattered Tom" is worth at least $45.00.

TELEGRAPH BOY, THE.
Loring, Publisher, 1879

TITLE PAGE: The/ Telegraph Boy./ By/ Horatio Alger, Jr./ Author of "Ragged Dick" Series; "Luck and Pluck" Series;/ "Brave and Bold" Series, Etc., Etc./ [decorative rule]/ Loring, Publisher,/ Corner of Bromfield and Washington Sts.,/ Boston.

BINDING: Identical with "Julius; or, The Street Boy out West."

COLLATION: Yellow-tinted end-paper; fly-leaf; 2 leaves (4 pp.) of book advertisements; frontispiece; tissue-covered decorative title page [p. i]; verso blank [p. ii]; title page [p. iii]; copyright notice dated 1879 [p. iv]; dedication [p. v]; verso blank [p. vi]; preface, [pp. vii] - viii; text, [pp. 9] - 262; fly-leaf; yellow-tinted end-paper.

According to the Library of Congress records, "The Telegraph Boy" was deposited for copyright on March 25, 1882, and was issued Copyright Number 4713N. This is curious, because Loring went bankrupt in June, 1881.

The story later was reissued in paper wrappers as "The District Telegraph Boy."

The first edition of "The Telegraph Boy" will show — in the book ads — "III. Sam's Chance, and How He Improved It" as the last listing under the Tattered Tom Series. There must be no listing of any volumes of The Pacific Series.

Value of first edition is $30.00.

TIMOTHY CRUMP'S WARD; or, The New Years Loan, And What Came of it.
Loring, Publisher, 1866

TITLE PAGE: Timothy Crump's Ward;/ or,/ The New Years Loan,/ And What Came of it./ [rule]/ Loring, Publisher,/ 319 Washington Street,/ Boston.

BINDING: Bound in purple cloth. Cover design is identical with "Helen Ford." Spine, which also is similar to "Helen Ford," differs only in that the title, Timothy/ Crump's/ Ward, is stamped in the purple cover color against fringed scroll, which is stamped solid gold. Cover size: 5"x7⅞".

COLLATION: End-paper; fly-leaf; title page [p. 1]; copyright notice dated 1866 [p. 2]; contents, pp. 3 - 4; text, pp. 5 - 188; fly-leaf; end-paper.

"A. K. Loring, 319 Washington St., sends us 'Timothy Crump's Ward'." So began a brief notice in the September, 1866, issue of Student and Schoolmate. The item continued, calling the anonymous tale "a spirited story for summer reading, evidently written by a practiced pen."

This is our only clue to the Alger collectors' most perplexing and favorite mystery. It is apparent that the hard-cover book was issued in August, 1866, probably simultaneously with its appearance in paper wrappers, as a volume of Loring's Railway Companions series.

There are but *three* known copies of "Timothy." These include two hard-cover editions in private collections, and one paperback in the rare book vault of the New York Public Library. The extreme value — for this book is, by far, more valuable than any other by Alger — is created not by literary quality, but by rarity and the great desire on the part of a number of institutions as well as private collectors to capture this prize. While"Timothy Crump's Ward" is not the scarcest of Algers (there exists only *one* known copy of the first edition of "Robert Coverdale's Struggle"), it definitely is the one most fervently desired.

The publication apparently was not too successful a venture for Loring, so few were printed. The story lies half-way between a juvenile and an adult novel and, in style, represents the Alger formula only partially ripened. Nevertheless, both author and publisher apparently had enough faith in the product for Alger to revise and rewrite it, in 1875, and issue the story anew as "Jack's Ward."

Although most dealers are well aware of "Timothy's" value — and it appears on every collector's 'want list' — its identity is probably not so well known to the many book scouts who often get first crack at the contents of a rural attic or barn. They are quick to recall inquiries for items on which the author's name is clearly printed, but an anonymous performance, even if present under a dust-covered pile of books in a dark corner, could easily be overlooked.

But "Timothy Crump's Ward" is well worth intensive searching, for the finder may well find himself the possessor of a book worth as much as $1,000.00.

TIN BOX, THE. See "Finding A Fortune."

TOM BRACE; Who He Was and How He Fared.
Street & Smith, 1901

Prior to appearing in paper wrappers as Medal Library No. 122, issued by Street and Smith on July 13, 1901, "Tom Brace" had already appeared as a serialization in Argosy. The story, by Arthur Lee Putnam, began in the issue dated February 23, 1889, and concluded in the issue of May 25, 1889.

In 1892, the United States Book Company deposited the title for copyright, thereby indicating their intention to publish the story in book form, probably in their Leather-Clad series. However, they went bankrupt before this could be done and it wasn't until October 1, 1901 (apparently after publication) that Street & Smith deposited the title. On October 9th the book was received for copyright at the Library of Congress.

The Medal Library paperback, therefore, must be considered the true first edition. It carries Alger's name as author, and the colorful pictorial cover shows a young man talking with a seated gentleman who looks exactly like Theodore Roosevelt. The character is a Mr. Archer, the New York attorney who had been searching for Tom. This oddity has apparently been noted by every collector owning and every dealer offering this edition.

Another curious confusion is the listing, in Street & Smith's 1911 catalog (under The Medal Library series) of "51 — Tom Bruce, By Horatio Alger, Jr." Number 51 actually was titled "Tom Tracy," which is not included in that catalog, but "Tom Brace" does appear, correctly listed as Number 122. Alger never wrote a story known as "Tom Bruce," although Toms were the leading characters of several of his books and as many short stories.

Shortly after issuing the paperback, Street & Smith issued "Tom Brace" in hard covers, printed from the original plates.

"Tom Brace," in the paper wrappers, is worth $20.00. The hard-cover edition brings $15.00.

TOM TEMPLE'S CAREER.

A. L. Burt, 1888

BINDING: Identical with "The Errand Boy."

Originally appearing as a serialization in New York Weekly, entitled "The Bully of the Village; or, Tom Temple's Career," the story began in the issue dated June 30, 1879. Francis S. Street, publisher of the periodical, suggested the serial title to Alger.

A. L. Burt published the story in March, 1888 (depositing book for copyright March 29, 1888), as Volume I, No. 7, of their Boys' Home Library series, with title changed to "Tom Temple's Career." Almost simultaneously, they issued a hard-cover edition — in their deluxe Boys' Home Series — that sold for $1.00.

The rare first edition, in paper wrappers, is worth $42.00. The hard-cover issue will bring about $15.00.

TOM THATCHER'S FORTUNE.

A. L. Burt, 1888

BINDING: Identical with "The Errand Boy."

The story first appeared in New York Weekly, serialized under the title, "Tom Thatcher's Quest; or, Following a Clue." The first installment appeared in the issue dated January 9th, 1882.

It was in July, 1888, that Burt issued the bound volume as Volume I, No. 11 of their Boy's Home Library series, with the title changed to "Tom Thatcher's Fortune." They had deposited the book for copyright on July 16, 1888.

Shortly after appearing in paper wrappers, the Burt hard-cover edition appeared, printed from the original plates.

The paperback is the first edition and, like all Alger stories published as parts of the Boys' Home Library, it is rare and worth about $42.00. The earliest hard-cover edition brings about $15.00.

TOM THATCHER'S QUEST; or, Following a Clue. See "Tom Thatcher's Fortune."

TOM THE BOOTBLACK. See "The Western Boy."

TOM TRACY; or, The Trials of a New York Newsboy.

Frank A. Munsey, 1888

BINDING: Identical with "Number 91."

After appearing in Golden Argosy, during 1887, with Arthur Lee Putnam as author, Frank A. Munsey issued "Tom Tracy" in paper wrappers as Number 10 of his Popular Series for Boys and Girls. The issue was dated May, 1888, and still carried Putnam as author. The copyright is dated June 7, 1889, but by that date Frank H. Lovell had taken over the Munsey book publishing operation. The earliest edition of "Tom Tracy," therefore, will have the Munsey imprint on the title page. Later printings name Lovell as publisher. On April 26, 1890, Lovell reissued "Tom Tracy" as Number 21 of his Leather-Clad Tales of Adventure and Romance having deposited the title for copyright on May 16, 1890.

Shortly after the Leather-Clad issue — and by this time John W. Lovell had succeeded his brother as publisher — the story appeared for the first time in hard covers in Lovell's attractive Rugby Edition. This, and later reprints by International Book Company and American Publishers Corporation, still carried Putnam as author.

The original plates eventually came into the possession of Street & Smith, who published "Tom Tracy" on March 3, 1900, as Number 51 of their paperback Medal Library series. Although the earliest printing still listed Putnam, this was quickly changed, being replaced by Alger. Before the end of 1900, Street & Smith issued the story in a hard-cover edition, with Alger regularly credited as the author. It was, apparently, during 1900 that the last of the Arthur Lee Putnam by-lines was retired, and that pseudonym never was used again.

The original Munsey's paperback edition is worth $42.00. The Leather-Clad and the Rugby hard-cover each will bring $30.00. Any other editions with the Putnam by-line are worth $25.00. The Medal Library issue and the Street & Smith hard-cover each bring about $15.00.

TOM TURNER'S LEGACY; The Story of how He Secured It.

A. L. Burt, 1902

TITLE PAGE: Tom Turner's/ Legacy/ The Story of how He Secured It/ By Horatio Alger, Jr./ Author of "Joe's Luck," "Tom the Bootblack," "The Errand/ Boy," "Dan the Newsboy," etc., etc./ With Illustrations By J. Watson Davis/ A. L. Burt Company, Publishers/ 52 - 58 Duane Street, New York.

BINDING: Identical with "Bernard Brooks' Adventures."

COLLATION: Flowered end-paper; frontispiece; title page; copyright notice dated 1890 (By Frank A. Munsey Co.), and 1902 (By A. L. Burt); contents, pp. i - ii; text, pp. 3 - 316; book advertisements, [pp. 1] - 8; flowered end-paper. In addition to the frontispiece are four full-page illustrations.

"Tom Turner's Legacy" first appeared as a serialization in Argosy, in 1890. On April 3, 1902, Burt deposited the title and forwarded the bound volume for copyright on June 24 of the same year.

The first edition must list Burt's address (on title page and ads at back of book) as 52 - 58 Duane Street, New York. In the advertisements, "Ben Bruce" must be the last Alger title shown as already in print.

Value of first edition is $15.00.

TONY, THE HERO.

J. S. Ogilvie & Company, 1880

TITLE PAGE: Tony, The Hero./ By/ Horatio Alger, Jr./ Author of "Abner Holden's Bound Boy;" "Tom, the Bootblack;"/ "Dare and Do Right Series;" Etc., Etc./ New York:/ J. S. Ogilvie and Company,/ 29 Rose Street.

BINDING: Bound in cloth, green and maroon having been noted. Cover design (stamped in black): An archway of flowers, within lines, at top, arrangement of ferns and flowers from bottom, left, to top, right. Spine (stamped in black and gold): [Black line]/ [gold border]/ [black line]/ [black flowered design]/ [line]/ Tony/ The/ Hero (title blind-stamped against gold panel)/ [black line]/ Alger/ [black line]/ [vignette of ferns]/ [publisher's trade-mark device]/ [black line]/ [gold border]/ [black line]. Cover size: 5⅛" x 7⅜".

COLLATION: Yellow-tinted end-paper; fly-leaf; decorative title page; title page [p. i]; copyright notice dated 1880 [p. ii]; dedication [p. iii]; verso blank [p. iv]; contents, [pp. v] - vi; text, pp. 7 - 253; 8 leaves (16 pp.) catalogue of Ogilvie publications; yellow-tinted end-paper.

Prior to appearing as a bound volume, this story — entitled "Tony, the Tramp" — was serialized in New York Weekly, the first installment in the issue dated June 26, 1876.

Ogilvie deposited their altered title for copyright in mid-1880, and issued "Tony, the Hero" shortly thereafter as the second volume of their Dare and Do Right Series (Volume I was "Tom, the Bootblack," a reissue of "The Western Boy"). This Ogilvie issue is the first edition, and a very rare book.

In March, 1890, A. L. Burt issued the title in paper wrappers as Number 23 of their Boys' Home Library series. This was an unusual occasion upon which the hard-cover book preceded the paper wrappers. Burt followed up their initial performance with their own hard-cover edition, issuing "Tony" as a volume of their deluxe Boys' Home Series.

Years later — probably after 1910 — reissue publishers started printing the story under its original serialization title. The Hurst and Company im-

print is the earliest of these noted, but priority of issue is of little con-
sequence in this case.

The Ogilvie edition is worth at least $50.00 and a collector who needs it
(as most do) probably would pay more. The Burt Boys' Home Library
paperback is worth $25.00, and the Burt hard-cover, $15.00. A complete
run of the serialization in New York Weekly brings $35.00.

TONY, THE TRAMP. See "Tony, the Hero."

TRAIN BOY, THE.

 G. W. Carleton & Co., 1883

 TITLE PAGE: The/ Train Boy./ By/ Horatio Alger, Jr.,/ Author of/
 "Tattered Tom." "Tom Thatcher's Quest,"/ "Ragged Dick," "Luck
 and Pluck,"/ "Dan, the Detective," "The/ Errand Boy," Etc., Etc./
 [publisher's trade-mark device]/ New York:/ G. W. Carleton & Co.,
 Publishers./ MDCCCLXXXIII.

 BINDING: Identical with "Dan, the Detective."

 COLLATION: Brown-tinted end-paper; 2 fly-leaves; leaf on which is
 printed title and author's name [p. 1]; verso blank [p. 2]; blank
 side of frontispiece [p. 3]; frontispiece [p. 4]; title page [p. 5];
 copyright notice dated 1833 [p. 6]; contents, [pp. 7 - 8]; text,
 [pp. 9] - 298; 1 leaf (2 pp.) book advertisements; fly-leaf; brown-
 tinted end-paper. In addition to the frontispiece are five full-page
 illustrations.

The earliest appearance of "The Train Boy" was as a 36-page pamphlet
distributed as a free sample by Street & Smith in 1892. This booklet contained the first nine chapters of the story. A notice at the end invited readers
to continue the serialization in New York Weekly, "from where it stops
here." Because of its rarity, it is worth describing the cover of the pamphlet:
The Train Boy/ By Horatio Alger, Jr.,/ Author of/ "Tom Thatcher's
Quest." "Brave and Bold,"/ "Abner Holden's Bound Boy," Etc./ [line
rule]/ New York;] Street & Smith/ 31 Rose Street.

The serialization appeared in New York Weekly during 1883. Before
the end of that year, Carleton had published the bound volume in some
sort of a cooperative arrangement with Street & Smith.

Some years later the story was again serialized, this time in Good News,
entitled "Plucky Paul Palmer." The first installment appeared in the issue
dated August 29, 1891, concluding in the issue of November 21, 1891.

The Street & Smith pamphlet is worth $30.00. The Carleton first edition
brings $35.00.

TRIALS AND ADVENTURES OF HERBERT MASON; or, Try and Trust.
See "Try and Trust."

TRIALS AND TRIUMPHS OF A NEW YORK TELEGRAPH BOY. See
"Mark Mason's Victory."

TRIALS AND TRIUMPHS OF MARK MASON. See "Mark Mason's
Victory."

TRY AND TRUST; or, The Story of a Bound Boy.

Loring, Publisher, 1873

TITLE PAGE: Try And Trust;/ or,/ The Story Of a Bound Boy/ By/ Horatio Alger, Jr.,/ Author of "Ragged Dick Series," "Tattered Tom Series,"/ "Campaign Series," "Luck and Pluck Series," Etc./ [decorative rule]/ Loring, Publisher,/ Cor. Washington and Bromfield Streets,/ Boston.

BINDING: Identical with "Bound to Rise."

COLLATION: Yellow-tinted end-paper; fly-leaf; 1 leaf (2 pp.) book advertisements; frontispiece; tissue-covered decorative title page [p. 1]; verso blank [p. 2]; title page [p. 3]; copyright notice dated 1873 [p. 4]; dedication [p. 5]; verso blank [p. 6]; preface, pp. 7 - viii; text, [pp. 9] - 355; fly-leaf; yellow-tinted end-paper. In addition to the frontispiece and decorative title page are three full-page illustrations.

As "Abner Holden's Bound Boy," this story originally was serialized in New York Weekly. The first installment appeared in the issue dated April 6, 1871. Loring issued the book (as Volume I of the Second Luck and Pluck Series) and deposited it for copyright, in April, 1873.

The first edition must show, in the book advertisements at front, that "Try and Trust," Volume I of the Second Luck and Pluck Series, will be published "in May, '73." This was almost immediately corrected to show the title as already being in print. The projected title for Volume II is "Live and Learn" (the book ultimately was titled "Bound to Rise"), due "in October, '73." Under the Second Tattered Tom Series, Volume I is listed as "Julius; or, The Street Boy out West, — in Nov., '73."

On Page 355, the next volume in the series must be indicated as "Live and Learn; or, How Harry Walton Rose in the World."

Between 1903-1907 this story was reissued by Aldine Publishing Company, London, as "Trials and Adventures of Herbert Mason; or Try and Trust."

The earliest state, as described, is worth $30.00. The second state, indicating "Try and Trust" as already published, brings up to $25.00.

UP THE LADDER; or Harry Walton's Success. See "Risen From the Ranks."

VICTOR VANE, The Young Secretary.

Porter & Coates, 1894

TITLE PAGE: Victor Vane,/ The/ Young Secretary/ By/ Horatio Alger, Jr./ Author of "Ragged Dick," "Tattered Tom," Etc./ [publisher's trade-mark device]/ Philadelphia/ Porter & Coates.

BINDING: Identical with "Adrift in the City."

COLLATION: Dark brown coated end paper; fly-leaf; tissue-covered frontispiece; title page [p. i]; copyright notice dated 1893, by Frank A. Munsey & Co., and 1894, by Porter & Coates, [p. ii]; contents, pp. iii - iv; text, [pp. 1] - 346; 1 leaf (2 pp.) book advertisements; fly-leaf; dark brown coated end-paper. In addition to the frontispiece are three full-page illustrations.

Prior to publication as a bound volume, "Victor Vane" appeared as a serialization in Argosy, the first installment in the issue dated April 1, 1893, and concluding in the issue of June 24, 1893.

Porter & Coates deposited the title on May 12, 1894, and submitted the book for copyright on August 16, 1894.

In the first edition there will be no advertisements for books by Horatio Alger (only for books by Harry Castlemon, with "The Mail Carrier" the last title listed). There must be an interlocked "P & C" monogram at bottom of spine, and the Porter & Coates imprint on title page. When, some months after publication of "Victor Vane," the publishing firm became Henry T. Coates & Company, these two elements were altered, all others remaining identical with the original edition.

Value of first edition is $25.00.

WAIT AND HOPE; or, Ben Bradford's Motto.

Loring, Publisher, 1877

TITLE PAGE: Wait And Hope;/ or,/ Ben Bradford's Motto./ By/ Horatio Alger, Jr./ Author of "Ragged Dick," "Tattered Tom," "Luck and Pluck,"/ "Brave and Bold" Series./ [decorative rule]/ Loring, Publisher,/ Corner of Bromfield and Washington Sts./Boston.

BINDING: Identical with "Brave and Bold."

COLLATION: Yellow-tinted end-paper; fly-leaf; 1 leaf (2 pp.) book advertisements; frontispiece; tissue-covered decorative title page; title page [p. 1]; copyright notice dated 1877 [p. 2]; dedication [p. 3]; verso blank [p. 4]; preface, [pp. 5] - 6; [no leaf for pp. 7 - 8]; text, [pp. 9] - 352; fly-leaf; yellow-tinted end-paper. In addition to the frontispiece and decorative title page are two full-page illustrations.

After appearing in Young Israel during 1877 as two separate but related stories, the first part titled "Wait and Hope" and the second part "Wait and Win" (a different story from the "Wait and Win" later published by A. L. Burt), the two were combined as "Wait and Hope" and issued as a bound volume by A. K. Loring, late in October, 1877. The original copyright date is April 3, 1882, but the Library of Congress has another copy of this title — also a first edition — dated June 7, 1883. Both carry the identical copyright number (5242N). It is curious that both copies are dated after Loring went bankrupt in 1881.

Most significantly, the first edition of "Wait and Hope" must show no listing for the Pacific Series. Under the Second Tattered Tom Series, there should be no listing of "The Telegraph Boy" following the number "IV." The type is broken in the number "159," at the top of that page.

Relatively few copies of "Wait and Hope" were printed by Loring, making the volume a rather difficult one to locate. It is not hardly as simple a matter to find a copy of this or other volumes of the Brave and Bold Series as it is to track down most numbers of the earlier Ragged Dick or Luck and Pluck Series.

Value of first edition is $35.00.

WAIT AND WIN; The Story of Jack Drummond's Pluck.

A. L. Burt, 1908

TITLE PAGE: Wait And Win/ [double line]/ The/ Story of Jack Drum-

mond's Pluck/ [line]/ By Horatio Alger, Jr./ Author of "In Search
of Treasure," "Ben Bruce," "Bernard/ Brooks' Adventures," "A Debt
of Honor," etc., etc./ [publisher's trade-mark device]/ with four
page Illustrations/ By J. Watson Davis/ [double line]/ A. L. Burt
Company,/ Publishers, New York.

BINDING: Bound in blue cloth with brown and black stamping. Cover
design: [Black border around cover]/ Wait and Win/ Horatio Alger
Jr/ [illustration of three boys in a boat]. Spine: [Line]/ Wait/ and/
Win/ Alger/ [illustration of boy waving flag]/ A. L. Burt/ Com-
pany/ [line].

COLLATION: End-paper; frontispiece; title page; copyright notice dated
1908; text, pp. 1 - 279; 3 blank leaves; end paper. In addition to
the frontispiece are three full-page illustrations.

The story originally appeared as a serialization in Golden Argosy, entitled "Work and Win," during 1884. The following year — 1885 — it was
published in the Boston Weekly Globe, installments running from August
11th through September 8th, under a new title, "Wait and Win; or, Jack
Drummond's Pluck." Under this heading it was copyrighted, by Horatio
Alger, on September 2, 1885.

There is, of course, no connection between this novel and Alger's "Wait
and Win; or, Ben Bradford's Motto," which was printed in Young Israel
during the second half of 1877, and which eventually was issued in book
form by Loring as "Wait and Hope."

It was not until 1908 that A. L. Burt published "Wait and Win," depositing the title on January 15, 1908, and submitting the bound volume a
month later, on February 15th.

The first edition of "Wait and Win" — the last Alger first edition to be
issued by Burt — is among the rarest of Burt's hard-cover books. Soon after
publication they reissued the title in at least two cheaper editions. This
was followed by the publication of the story under its original serialization
title — "Work and Win" — by a number of reprint publishers in paper-
wrappers and hard-covers.

Value of first edition is $30.00.

WALTER GRIFFITH. See "Striving For Fortune.

WALTER SHERWOOD'S PROBATION.
Henry T. Coates & Co., 1897

TITLE PAGE: Walter Sherwood's/ Probation/ By/ Horatio Alger, Jr./
Author of "Ragged Dick Series," "New World Series," Etc./ Phila-
delphia/ Henry T. Coates & Co./ 1897.

BINDING: Identical with "A Boy's Fortune."

COLLATION: Navy blue coated end-paper; tissue-covered frontispiece;
title page [p. i]; copyright notice dated 1897 [p. ii]; contents, pp.
iii - iv; text, pp. 1 - 351; navy blue coated end-paper. In addition
to the frontispiece are three full-page illustrations.

The story originally was serialized in Argosy during 1890. Henry T.
Coates published "Walter Sherwood's Probation" in hard-covers, depositing

the volume for copyright on November 11, 1897, and issuing it as Volume I of his Good Fortune Library series.

The first edition is distinguished by the 1897 date at bottom of title page, and there must be no advertisements in the book. Later printings carried ads for the works of Alger, Harry Castlemon, Edward S. Ellis and J. T. Trowbridge.

Value of first edition is $22.50.

WAY TO SUCCESS. See "Struggling Upward."

WESTERN BOY, THE, or, The Road to Success.
  G. W. Carleton & Co. in cooperation with Street & Smith and American News Co., 1878

TITLE PAGE: The/ Western/ Boy/ [illustration (same as cover design) of boy blacking a man's boots]/ Or,/ The Road to Success./ By Horatio Alger, Jr.

BINDING: Bound in various colors of cloth, blue, terra cotta and green having been noted (with no priority of issue). Cover design (stamped in black): [Double-line border around cover]/ The Western Boy./ By/ [same illustration as on title page, as described]/ Horatio Alger, Jr. Spine (stamped in black and gold): [Black line]/ [gold line]/ [black line]/ [sun-ray design]/ [black line]/ [gold line]/ [black line]/ [thin gold line]/ The/ Western/ Boy (blind-stamped against gold panel)/ [thin gold line]/ [black line]/ [gold line]/ [black line]/ [bullseye with arrow below it]/ [black line]/ Illustrated/ [black line]/ [three black lines]/ American News Co./ [black line]/ [gold line]/ [black line]. Cover size: 5¼" x 7½".

COLLATION: Yellow-tinted end-paper; leaf on which is printed: The Western Boy/ [line]/ By Horatio Alger, Jr. [p. 1]; book advertisements on verso [p. 2]; title page [p. 3]; copyright notice dated 1878 [p. 4]; dedication [p. 5]; book advertisement [p. 6]; contents, [pp. 7 - 8]; text, [pp. 9] - 258; fly-leaf; yellow-tinted end-paper.

Prior to appearing as a bound volume, "The Western Boy" was serialized in New York Weekly, the first installment appearing in the issue dated June 30, 1873, and concluding in the issue dated September 15, 1873.

In every respect, the extremely rare first edition of "The Western Boy" is probably the most unusual Alger book ever published. Even the very first question — Who published it? — is a most difficult one to answer. The book's copyright notice indicates that it was Street & Smith who copyrighted the story in 1878. However, the Library of Congress records do not substantiate this. The story is dedicated to the readers of New York Weekly "By the Publishers, Street & Smith." A Carleton advertisement at the front of the book, announces that "Messrs. Street & Smith, publishers of the New York Weekly, having been for many years requested by their readers to issue some of their best and most popular Stories in Book Form, have at last consented, and have now made arrangements for such publications with the well-known New York House of G. W. Carleton & Co., Publishers."

To add to the confusion, the imprint of the American News Company is gold-stamped at the bottom of the book's spine.

Perhaps a logical assumption is that Street & Smith, owners of the story, made a deal with Carleton, a book publisher, to produce the job, and with American News Co. — primarily a mass-circulation house — to handle distribution. At any rate, between the three, they produced a very rare book, and a mystery to vex Alger collectors of generations yet unborn.

The cover and title page illustrations — which are identical — are the only ones in the book. They show Tom, the hero, polishing the boots of James Grey who (although he looks strikingly like Abraham Lincoln with a beard and tall silk hat) has conspired to deprive the young bootblack of a fortune left to him by his late father. Incidentally, by story's end, Tom has made a powerful ally of a man he saves from drowning, recovers his fortune, marries the belle of Cincinnati society, becomes a lawyer and moves further westward to Wisconsin, where a distinguished future is predicted for him.

The book is a prime example of sloppy editing. A character introduced as a policeman at the top of Page 21 is referred to as a physician a few lines below. The reader will note innumerable typographical errors throughout, with words misspelled, letters inverted, and meaningless anagrams formed by misplaced letters.

In 1880, Street & Smith deposited for copyright the reissue title, "Tom, the Bootblack," by which the story became one of Alger's most popular (and today, best-remembered) works. In that year — via another cooperative scheme similar to the earlier arrangement with Carleton — J. S. Ogilvie produced "Tom, the Bootblack" as Volume I of their Dare and Do Right Series. This first issue under the new title also is a very rare book. The binding of Ogilvie's "Tom" is identical with "Tony, the Hero," which appeared as the second volume of the series.

On March 1, 1889, A. L. Burt indicated their intention of printing the story by depositing the title for copyright. Accordingly, during that month they published "Tom, the Bootblack" as Volume I, Number 19, of their Boys' Home Library series. While this cannot under any condition be rated as a first edition, it nevertheless is — like every number of the Boys' Home Library — as rare as hens' teeth, and a most desirable acquisition.

For some unexplainable reason, Thompson & Thomas (a Chicago firm that for a brief period hit a small bonanza issuing Alger stories) in 1902 revived the original title, and published what was to be the last edition to be titled "The Western Boy." From that time forward, virtually every one of the dozens of publishers reissuing Alger's stories — and they were literally turning them out by the millions — added "Tom, the Bootblack" to his permanent list. It ranked in popularity with Ragged Dick, Tattered Tom, Julius, Dan and the few others of that golden group.

While a first (Carleton) edition of "The Western Boy" is tantalizingly difficult to find, it, nevertheless, appears every few years. I know a half-dozen collectors who have the book, and it has been offered for sale a number of times in the not too distant past.

The Ogilvie issue of "Tom, the Bootblack" — while it cannot compete with the Carleton performance for first edition honors — is so rare that, until relatively recently, collectors believed it either never did, or no longer, existed. Nevertheless, about three copies have come to light in recent years, and its existence is firmly established. Although not the first edition, the collector will have to pay for it almost as much as he must for the Carleton publication.

Some years ago a mid-western dealer catalogued the Carleton first edition for $125.00 and immediately sold it — to another dealer. A collector I know more recently paid the same price to a private quoter. The Burt's Boys' Home Library paperback brings $35.00.

WORK AND WIN. See "Wait and Win."

WORLD BEFORE HIM, THE.
Penn Publishing Company, 1902

TITLE PAGE: Page design same as "Finding A Fortune." The/ World/ Before/ Him/ by/ Horatio Alger Jr./ Author of/ "The Odds Against Him"/ "Making His Mark"/ etc./ The Penn/ Publishing/ Company/ Philadelphia/ MCMII.

BINDING: Identical with "Making His Mark."

COLLATION: Brown flowered end-paper; fly-leaf; tissue-covered frontispiece; title page [p. 1]; copyright notice dated 1902 [p. 2]; contents, pp. 3 - 4; text, pp. 5 - 383; 1 leaf (2 pp.) book advertisements; brown flowered end-paper. In addition to the frontispiece are six full-page illustrations.

Prior to appearing as a bound volume, the story was serialized two times in Golden Days, entitled "Making His Way." The first run started in the issue dated May 22, 1880, continuing through August 7, 1880. Its second appearance began on November 21, 1896, concluding with the issue dated February 6, 1897.

Penn Publishing Company deposited the volume for copyright on June 26, 1902. Some years later the story was reissued under its serial title as "Making His Way."

The first edition is identified by the 1902 date in Roman numerals at bottom of title page. There must be no listing of Alger stories in the book advertisements.

Like all of the Alger stories issued by Penn, this item runs slightly higher than the general output of a number of the other publishers.

Value of first edition is $35.00.

WREN WINTER'S TRIUMPH. See "A Rolling Stone."

YOUNG ACROBAT, THE, of The Great North American Circus.
Frank A. Munsey, 1888

BINDING: Identical with "Number 91."

Prior to appearing in book form, "The Young Acrobat" was serialized, during 1887, in Golden Argosy. The following year — in March, 1888 — Munsey issued the story in orange-colored paper wrappers as Number 8 of his Popular Series for Boys and Girls. This was the first edition, deposited for copyright on June 7, 1888.

When Frank W. Lovell took over Munsey's book publishing operation, he reissued "The Young Acrobat" as Number 20 in the Leather-Clad Tales of Adventure and Romance series, also in paper wrappers. The publication was dated April 19, 1890. That same year, Lovell published the story in hard covers in his Rugby Edition. Some years later, H. M. Cald-well used the same plates for a subsequent cloth-bound edition.

The story next appeared as a serialization (for the second time) in Bright Days — a weekly edited and published by Stratemeyer — starting September 5, 1896, and ending in the number of December 12th. It enjoyed a third run in Half Holiday, entitled "Kit Watson's Triumph; or, The Adventures of a Boy Acrobat." The first part ran in the issue dated February 5, 1898; the last on April 30, 1898.

On December 30, 1899, Street & Smith published "The Young Acrobat" as Number 42 of their Medal Library Series. This was the first of many Alger stories to be published in paper wrappers by Street & Smith. Their earlier Medal Library issues were mainly the works of Oliver Optic, Gilbert Patten, James Otis, Edward Ellis and a number of writers for young people who, although popular at the turn of the century, have long since been forgotten. Somewhat later, Street & Smith also published a hard-cover edition but, with so many previous editions, it is of relatively little worth. Likewise of comparatively small value is its appearance in Street & Smith's Brave and Bold No. 68, dated April 9th, 1904.

Like all of the three Alger stories originally appearing in Munsey's Popular Series for Boys and Girls, the present edition is worth at least $45.00. The Leather-Clad, while not the first edition, still will bring $30.00, and the Lovell hard-cover $25.00. The full run of the serializations are equally valued at $25.00, and the Street & Smith Medal Library No. 42 brings $15.00. Other issues are of small value, of collector-interest primarily as a gap-filler on the shelf until one of the rare early editions come along.

YOUNG ADVENTURER, THE; or, Tom's Trip Across the Plains.
Loring, Publisher, 1878

TITLE PAGE: The/ Young Adventurer;/ or,/ Tom's Trip Across The Plains./ By/ Horatio Alger, Jr.,/ Author of "Ragged Dick" Series; "Tattered Tom" Series;/ "Luck and Pluck" Series; Etc./ [decorative rule]/ Loring, Publisher,/ Corner of Bromfield and Washington Sts./ Boston.

BINDING: Bound in cloth, green and mauve having been the only colors noted. Cover design (stamped in black): Two identical wide black horizontal bands containing blind-stamped design. Behind them, two thin vertical lines with fancy design at the ends. The same design is completely blind-stamped on the back cover. Spine (stamped in black and gold, with all lettering in gold); [Black line]/ [gold line]/ [black decorative line]/ The/ Young/ Adventurer/ [gold decorative rule]/ Horatio Alger Jr/ The Pacific/ Series (blind-stamped against gold panel with decorative black border at top and bottom)/ [illustration of boy riding a horse]/ [double black line]/ Loring/ [black line]/ [gold line]/ [black line]. Cover size: 4¾" x 7".

COLLATION: Yellow-tinted end-paper; fly-leaf; 2 leaves (4 pp.) book advertisements; frontispiece; tissue-covered decorative title page; title page [p. 1]; copyright notice dated 1878 [p. 2]; dedication [p. 3]; verso blank [p. 4]; preface, [pp. 5] - 6; (there is no leaf for

474

[pp. 7 - 8]); text, [pp. 9] - 293; fly-leaf; yellow-tinted end-paper. In addition to the frontispiece and decorative title page are two full-page illustrations.

Before publication as a bound volume, "The Young Adventurer" appeared as a serialization in Young Israel during 1878. Loring published his book in the Fall of 1878, although it was not deposited for copyright until early (probably January) 1879.

Loring issued the book as Volume 1 of the Pacific Series. In the preface, Alger says it is the first of "four stories relating to the Pacific coast." Actually, Loring published only the first three volumes. He went bankrupt before the fourth volume (scheduled for publication in October, 1881) could be issued. Volume IV — "Ben's Nugget" — therefore, became the earliest Alger first edition issued by Porter & Coates.

The first edition must show no listing of any volumes of the Pacific Series in the book advertisements. The frontispiece must show Tom Nelson and his father talking with Squire Hudson. In later editions this illustration has been moved to face Page 50. This was done to substitute a considerably more action-packed frontispiece — Tom, on horseback, being pursued by Indians — that appears facing Page 286 of the first edition.

The first edition must indicate, on Page 293, that the following volume of the series will be "The Young Pioneer; or, Tom Nelson in California." In the following edition this was changed to "The Young Miner; or, Tom Nelson in California," the title under which the book was published.

Early editions carry a misprint in the date at the end of Alger's preface. It is printed as 1876. It should be 1878.

Value of first edition is $30.00.

YOUNG BANK MESSENGER, THE.

Henry T. Coates & Co., 1898

TITLE PAGE: The/ Young Bank Messenger/ By/ Horatio Alger, Jr./ Author of "Ragged Dick Series," "New World Series," Etc./ Philadelphia/ Henry T. Coates & Co./ 1898.

BINDING: Identical with "A Boy's Fortune."

COLLATION: Slate gray coated end-paper; tissue-covered frontispiece; title page [p. i]; copyright notice dated 1898 [p. ii]; contents, pp. iii - iv; text, pp. 1 - 325; 3 leaves of book advertisements, numbered [pp. 1] - 6; fly-leaf; slate gray coated end-paper. In addition to the frontispiece are three full-page illustrations.

Prior to appearing as a bound volume, the story, entitled "A Cousin's Conspiracy," was serialized in Argosy during 1896. It was the last original story by Horatio Alger to be published in that periodical.

Henry T. Coates & Co., deposited the title for copyright on July 29, 1898, and submitted the bound volume on September 10th of that year. The book was issued as the third volume of the Good Fortune Library, although there must be no such listing in the present first edition.

The first edition must have the 1898 date at bottom of title page, and the last Alger title listed in the ads is "Digging For Gold."

I have in my library an earlier edition of "The Young Bank Messenger" than the one described. However, I am positive that it was prepared as a pre-publication sample, and probably never was commercially distributed. Nevertheless, it is well-worth describing its variances with the first distributed edition (which is the one described above). Instead of the green cloth binding, the pre-publication state has a leather spine and marbled boards. There are no coated end-papers, but there is a front fly-leaf (which the regular edition lacks). There is no frontispiece, but the illustration used as frontispiece in the regular edition faces Page 127. There are only four (instead of six) pages of advertisements at the back of the book, with the last listing for Alger items being The Tattered Tom Series. The book-size is 16mo (like the early Porter & Coates Algers), rather than the 12mo dimensions of the usual Henry T. Coates products. Title page is dated, and a close examination of type wear verifies the earlier publication.

The first edition is worth $22.50. The pre-publication edition is worth at least that amount, but must be considered as unique and unlikely to reappear.

YOUNG BOATMAN, THE.

Penn Publishing Company, 1892

TITLE PAGE: The Young Boatman/ of/ Pine Point/ By/ Horatio Alger Jr./ [line]/ Philadelphia/ The Penn Publishing Company/ 1892.

BINDING: Bound in tan cloth. Cover design (stamped in brown and red): The/ Young/ Boatman/ [over-all illustration of boy rowing boat on a lake, with trees and hills in background]/ Horatio Alger Jr. Spine (stamped in brown, red and gold): The/ Young/ Boatman/ Alger/ [illustration of boat-hook, oars and lantern]/ [publisher's monogram of letters] PPCo. Cover size: 5¼" x 7½".

COLLATION: Brown flowered end-paper; 2 fly-leaves; blank side of frontispiece [p. 1]; tissue-covered frontispiece [p. 2]; title page [p. 3]; copyright notice dated 1892 [p. 4]; contents, pp. 5 - 6; text, pp. 7 - 369; on verso of p. 369 is an advertisement for "The Odds Against Him"; 2 leaves (4 pp.) book advertisements; fly-leaf; brown flowered end-paper. In addition to the frontispiece are four full-page illustrations.

Prior to publication in book form, the story was serialized — as "Grit; or, The Young Boatman of Pine Point" — in New York Weekly. The first installment appeared in the issue dated May 19, 1884. In 1890 it was again serialized — in Good News — starting September 4th and ending in the number of November 20th.

Penn Publishing Company deposited the book for copyright on July 18, 1892, placing it in distribution during the same month. Shortly after publication, Penn issued the book in a second state cover of brown cloth, described as follows: Cover design: The Young/ Boatman (stamped in green on two scrolls)/ [boy's head outlined against red background, with winding green scroll-work design around his shoulders, extending toward lower left corner of cover]. Spine: Title stamped in green against a gold panel. Similar to first state in other respects.

The book is rare in first and second states, but not too hard to find in the Penn third issue, identified by blue cloth covers with silver stamping. The book is very easy to find in any of the later hard-cover or paper-back reprints, the reissue titles including "Grit," "Grit, the Young Boatman," "Grit the Young Boatman of Pine Point," "The Young Boatman," "The Young Boatman of Pine Point," and possibly other variations.

First edition is worth $30.00. The second state, $25.00.

YOUNG BOATMAN, THE, OF PINE POINT. See "The Young Boatman."

YOUNG BOOK AGENT, THE; or, Frank Hardy's Road to Success.
Stitt Publishing Company, 1905
   TITLE PAGE: The Young/ Book Agent/ Or, Frank Hardy's Road to Success/ By/ Horatio Alger, Jr./ Author of "Lost at Sea," "Nelson the Newsboy," "Out/ for Business," "Young Captain Jack," "Ragged/ Dick Series," "Tattered Tom Series," Etc./ [small decorative device]/ New York/ Stitt Publishing Company/ 1905.
   BINDING: Identical with "From Farm to Fortune."
   COLLATION: End-paper; frontispiece; title page [p. i]; copyright notice dated 1905 [p. ii]; preface, pp. iii - iv; contents, pp. v - vi; text, [pp. 1] - 272; fly-leaf; end-paper. In addition to the frontispiece are three full-page illustrations.

According to an announcement in the May, 1906, issue of American Boy Magazine, a serialization of " 'The Young Book Agent,' By Horatio Alger, Jr." would soon be published in that periodical. The notice was accompanied by a photograph of the author. The first installment appeared in June, continuing until November, 1906.

It is safe to say that the present title was written by the Edward Stratemeyer syndicate, and that Alger had little or no part of it, although his name is indicated as the author. "The Young Book Agent" is one of the eleven novels issued after Alger's death that Stratemeyer claims were completions of manuscripts or outlines given to him by the famous writer of books for boys.

The first edition is identified by the "Stitt" at bottom of spine, and also by that name accompanied by a 1905 date at bottom of title page. There are no book advertisements in the first edition.

Value of first edition is $30.00.

YOUNG CAPTAIN JACK; or, The Son of a Soldier.
The Mershon Company, 1901
   TITLE PAGE: Young Captain Jack/ Or/ The Son Of A Soldier/ By/ Horatio Alger, Jr./ Author of "Out for Business," "Falling in with Fortune,"/ "Adrift in New York," "Tattered Tom,"/ "Ragged Dick," Etc./ Completed By/ Arthur M. Winfield/ Author of (no front quotation mark) The Rover Boys Series," Etc./ [small sunburst design]/ New York/ The Mershon Company/ Publishers.
   BINDING: Identical with "Falling in with Fortune."
   COLLATION: End-paper; frontispiece; title page [p. i]; copyright notice dated 1901, with book advertisements above, [p. ii]; preface, pp. iii - iv; contents, pp. v - [vi]; text, [pp. 1] - 262; 2 leaves (4 pp.) of book advertisements; end-paper. In addition to the frontispiece are three full-page illustrations.

Shortly before the release of the hard-cover edition, the story of "Young Captain Jack" started a serialization in Golden Hours. The first installment appeared in the issue dated July 6, 1901, concluding in the issue dated September 7, 1901. The issue of the week preceding the first installment included an announcement, listing Horatio Alger, Jr., as author, but "Completed by Arthur M. Winfield, author of "The Rover Boys Series," etc.,

etc." The notice continued: "We have obtained at great expense the right of first publication in serial form of the last manuscript, left in an incompleted state, by the late Horatio Alger, Jr. It has been completed by Mr. Winfield, who is not only one of the most popular authors, but was Mr. Alger's intimate friend and his literary executor. No other writer could have done this work so well."

Arthur M. Winfield is, of course, a pseudonym of Edward Stratemeyer.

Mershon deposited the title for copyright on April 30, 1901, and submitted the bound volume on August 13, 1901. The book was in distribution shortly before the serialization ended.

The first edition must show "Nelson the Newsboy" at the top of the listing of books "By the Same Author" on the copyright page. No titles must be indicated for stories issued by Mershon after 1901. There should be no Alger book advertisements following the last page of text. Value of first edition is $27.50.

YOUNG CIRCUS RIDER, THE; or, The Mystery of Robert Rudd.
Porter & Coates, 1883

TITLE PAGE: Atlantic Series./ [rule]/ The/ Young Circus Rider;/ or,/ The Mystery of Robert Rudd./ By/ Horatio Alger, Jr./ [publisher's trade-mark device]/ Philadelphia:/ Porter & Coates.

BINDING: Identical with "Ben's Nugget."

COLLATION: Dark brown coated end-paper; fly-leaf; tissue-covered frontispiece; title page [p. 1]; copyright notice dated 1883 [p. 2]; preface, [pp. 3] - 4; contents, [pp. 5] - 6; text, [pp. 7] - 273; book advertisements, pp. 1 - 8; 3 fly-leaves; dark-brown coated end-paper. In addition to the frontispiece are two full-page illustrations.

Porter & Coates deposited the title — as "Star of the Circus," the title under which it was serialized in the Boston Globe from May 22, 1882 until June 24, 1882 — toward the end of that year and submitted the bound volume July 3, 1883, probably after the book was in distribution. It was after the pages of text were printed that it was decided to change the title to "The Young Circus Rider." The cover and spine list "Young Circus Rider," and the title page lists the full title and sub-title. However, the first page of text — and all the running page heads that follow — give the title as "The Star of the Circus." The story was issued as Volume I of the Atlantic Series.

The first edition is identified by inclusion of "The Star of the Circus" titling as indicated above.

Value of first edition is $22.50.

YOUNG EXPLORER, THE; or, Among the Sierras.
Loring, Publisher, 1880

TITLE PAGE: The/ Young Explorer;/ or,/ Among The Sierras./ By/ Horatio Alger, Jr./ Author of "Ragged Dick," "Tattered Tom," "Luck and Pluck,"/ "Brave and Bold," Series; Etc., Etc./ [decorative rule]/ Loring, Publisher,/ Corner of Bromfield and Washington Sts.,/ Boston.

BINDING: Identical with "The Young Adventurer."

COLLATION: Yellow-tinted end-paper; 2 leaves (4 pp.) book advertisements; frontispiece; tissue-covered decorative title page [p. i]; verso
blank [p. ii]; title page [p. iii]; copyright notice dated 1880 [p. iv];
dedication [p. v]; verso blank [p. vi]; preface, [pp. vii] - viii; text,
[pp. 9] - 285; yellow-tinted end-paper.

Volume III of the Pacific Series, the bound volume was deposited for
copyright on October 4, 1881. This is curious, as Loring went bankrupt in
June, 1881. We can assume that it was Porter & Coates — who bought all
of the stereotype plates for the Alger stories in October, 1881 — who arranged the copyright.

Although on Page 285 of the text there is the announcement that "the
fourth and concluding volume of the Pacific Series will be called 'Ben's
Nugget; or, A Boy's Search for Fortune'," that book was not published by
Loring. "The Young Explorer" was the publisher's last book by Horatio
Alger. When "Ben's Nugget" eventually came off the presses, two years
later, it bore the Porter & Coates imprint.

The first edition will show, in the book ads, only Volumes I and II of
the Pacific Series as being already in print. "The Young Explorer" is not
listed.

As Loring's activities already were waning during 1880, editions were
small. Accordingly, "The Young Explorer" — along with its companion volumes of the Pacific Series — does not appear frequently.

Value of first edition is $30.00.

YOUNG MINER, THE; or, Tom Nelson in California.

Loring, Publisher, 1879

TITLE PAGE: The/ Young Miner;/ or,/ Tom Nelson In California./ By/
Horatio Alger, Jr./ Author of "Ragged Dick," "Tattered Tom,"
"Luck and Pluck,"/ "Brave and Bold," Series; Etc., Etc./ [decora-
tive rule]; Loring, Publisher,/ Corner Bromfield & Washington
Streets,/ Boston.

BINDING: Identical with "The Young Adventurer."

COLLATION: Yellow-tinted end-paper; fly-leaf; 1 leaf (2 pp.) book advertisements; frontispiece; tissue-covered decorative title page; title
page [p. 1]; copyright notice dated 1879 [p. 2]; dedication [p. 3];
verso blank [p. 4]; preface, [pp. 5] - 6; (no leaf for pp. 7 - 8);
text [pp. 9] - 288; fly-leaf; yellow-tinted end-paper.

Issued by Loring as Volume II of the Pacific Series, "The Young Miner"
was deposited for copyright as late as October 4, 1881. This probably was
arranged by Porter & Coates after they purchased the Alger plates, following Loring's bankruptcy.

The first edition will contain no listing of volumes of the Pacific Series
in the book advertisements.

Value of first edition is $30.00.

YOUNG MUSICIAN, THE.

Penn Publishing Company, 1906

TITLE PAGE: Page design same as "Finding A Fortune." The/ Young/
Musician/ by/ Horatio Alger Jr./ Author of/ "Finding a Fortune"

etc./ Illustrated/ by/ Clyde O. Deland/ The Penn/ Publishing/ Company/ Philadelphia/ MCMVI.

BINDING: Identical with "Finding A Fortune."

COLLATION: Decorative end-paper (identical with "Finding A Fortune"); fly-leaf; tissue-covered frontispiece; title page [p. 1]; copyright notice dated 1906 [p. 2]; contents, pp. 3 - 4; list of illustrations [p. 5]; verso blank [p. 6]; text, pp. 7 - 341; fly-leaf; decorative end-paper, as described. In addition to the frontispiece are six full-page illustrations.

Prior to publication as a bound volume, "The Young Musician" was twice serialized in Golden Days. The first run started in the issue dated September 17, 1881, continuing through the issue of December 10, 1881. The second serialization started on October 29, 1898, concluding in the issue of January 14, 1899.

Penn Publishing Company deposited the volume for copyright on April 2, 1906, and it was in distribution by the middle of that month. The first edition is identified mainly by the 1906 date in Roman numerals (MCMVI) at bottom of title page. There must be no book advertisements, and the publisher's monogram at bottom of spine must show the two "P's" back-to-back, with the "Co" superimposed.

Value of first edition is $42.00.

YOUNG OUTLAW, THE; or, Adrift in the Streets.

Loring, Publisher, 1875

TITLE PAGE: The Young Outlaw;/ or,/ Adrift In The Streets./ By/ Horatio Alger, Jr.,/ Author of "Ragged Dick," — "Tattered Tom," — "Luck and/ Pluck," — "Brave and Bold," Series./ [decorative rule]/ Loring, Publisher,/ Cor. Washington and Bromfield Streets,/ Boston.

BINDING: Identical with "Julius; or, The Street Boy out West."

COLLATION: Yellow-tinted end-paper; fly-leaf; blank page on verso of which appears a full-page advertisement for "Seeking His Fortune"; 1 leaf (2 pp.) book advertisements; frontispiece; tissue-covered title-page [p. 1]; verso blank [p. 2]; title page [p. 3]; copyright notice dated 1875 [p. 4]; dedication, [p. 5]; verso blank [p. 6]; preface, pp. 7 - viii; text, [pp. 9] - 256; fly-leaf; yellow-tinted end-paper. In addition to frontispiece and decorative title page are two full-page illustrations.

Although the book — issued as Volume II of the Second Tattered Tom Series — was published in 1875, it was not until two years later, in 1877, that A. K. Loring deposited it for copyright.

The first edition must include a full-page advertisement for "Seeking His Fortune." In the listings, the present title is Volume II, under the Second Tattered Tom Series, with numbers III and IV below it, but not followed by titles nor anticipated dates of forthcoming books. Under the Brave and Bold Series, Volume I, "Brave and Bold," is already in print, and below it: "II. ——, in October, 1875."

Value of first edition is $30.00.

YOUNG RAILSPLITTER, THE. See "Abraham Lincoln, the Backwoods Boy."

YOUNG SALESMAN, THE.
Henry T. Coates & Co., 1896
TITLE PAGE: The/ Young Salesman/ By/ Horatio Alger, Jr./ Author of "Ragged Dick Series," "Tattered Tom/ Series," "Luck and Pluck Series," Etc./ Philadelphia/ Henry T. Coates & Co.

BINDING: Identical with "Frank and Fearless."

COLLATION: Slate-gray coated end-paper; fly-leaf; tissue-covered frontispiece; title page [p. i]; copyright notice dated 1896 [p. ii]; contents, pp. iii - iv; text, pp. 5 - 352; fly-leaf; slate-gray coated end-paper. In addition to the frontispiece are three full-page illustrations.

Prior to appearing in a bound volume, "The Young Salesman" was serialized in Argosy, the first part appearing late in 1894, and the installments continuing into 1895.

The first edition, which Coates deposited for copyright on September 14, 1896, is identified by the binding, which must be as described, and should contain no book advertisements.

Value of first edition is $22.50.

POEMS, BALLADS AND ODES.

The Pictorial National Library:	
Voices of the Past	June, 1849
Written While a Student at Harvard:	
Come Brothers, Lift the Song of Gladness (a song)	1851
Fair Harvard, the Ties that Have Bound Us So Long (Class Day Ode)	June 25, 1852
Boston Evening Transcript:	
A Chant of Life	April 11, 1853
Peterson's Magazine:	
A Welcome to May	May, 1853
Gleason's Pictorial Drawing Room Companion:	
The Death of Little Alice	March 26, 1853
The Cottage by the Sea	May 7, 1853
A Child's Prayer	August 6, 1853

Bertha's Christmas Vision: 1856
    My Castle
    Little Charlie

    Bertha's Christmas Vision (a combination of
        verse and prose).
    The First Tree Planted by an Ornamental Tree
        Society
    Our Gabrielle
    Summer Hours
    The Child of the Street
    Geraldine
    My Picture
    Innocence (Alger lists this in his book as being
        "contributed by a friend").

Gleason's Weekly Line-of-Battle Ship:
    The Fountain of Love   November 6, 1858

Bi-Centennial Ode:
    Sung at the Bicentennial Celebration of the in-
        corporation of Marlborough, Mass.   June 13, 1860

Hymn   September 15, 1863
    Written for the consecration of Glenwood Cem-
        etery, South Natick, Mass.

Student and Schoolmate:
    A Very Young Old Man (Alger wrote in a letter   Date Unknown
        that this was his first contribution to the
        publication edited by his friend, William
        T. Adams. I have been unable to confirm
        this).
    Song of the Croaker   October, 1864
    Where is My Boy Tonight?   November, 1864
    Introductory Poem for a May Festival   May, 1867
    John Maynard, A Ballad of Lake Erie   January, 1868

New York Sun:
    John Maynard (anonymous)   1866
        This poem has a common source with John
        Hay's "Jim Bludso." In a letter to Henry
        Denny, dated March 6, 1893, Alger said
        " . . . The poem, John Maynard, the pilot
        of Lake Erie, is, as I have reason to believe,
        an account of an actual incident . . . The
        name and all the details are real. Only the
        name of the vessel I furnished. I called it

Ocean Queen, not a very fitting name for a Lakes steamer, but I had no idea when I wrote the ballad that it would become so popular or I would have tried to find a better one. It is to be found in at least twelve collections, including readers and speakers, and I received letters of appreciation from Longfellow, Stedman, Prof. William Mathews, B. P. Shillaber and others. . ."

Shenstone Laurel:
The First Tree Planted by an Ornamental Tree Society (anonymous)   March 31, 1861
Who Will Miss Me? (signed "A.")   July 18, 1861

The Living Age:
One Year Ago (a Civil War poem reprinted from the Christian Register)   June 21, 1861

Rebellion Record:
Song of the Croaker   1863

Anecdotes, Poetry and Incidents of the War: North and South, 1860-1865:   1866
Song of the Croaker

Gleasons Literary Companion:
New Year's Day   January, 1869

The Five Harvard Odes (sung at annual dinners of the Harvard Club, in New York):
I. Fair Harvard, Dear Guide of our Youth's Golden Days   February 23, 1869
II. As We Meet in Thy Name, Alma Mater, Tonight   February 11, 1870
III. This Night We Would Rest   February 22, 1871
IV. Fair Harvard, the Months Have Accomplished their Round   February 21, 1872
V. There's a Fountain of Fable whose Magical Power   February 21, 1873

New York Weekly:
Fair Harvard, the Months Have Accomplished their Round   March, 25, 1872
Friar Anselmo, A Medieval Legend   August 5, 1872
There's a Fountain of Fable whose Magical Power   March 24, 1873

An introductory paragraph stated: "At the Seventh Annual Dinner of the Harvard Club, given at Delmonico's, in the City, on the 21st of February, the following felicitous and meritorious ode, from the pen of our valued contributor, Horatio Alger, Jr., was sung with immense applause."

Marlborough Mirror:
    This Night Let Us Rest   September 30, 1874

Grand'ther Baldwin's Thanksgiving: 1875
    Grand'ther Baldwin's Thanksgiving
    St. Nicholas
    Barbara's Courtship
    The Confession
    Rose in the Garden
    Phoebe's Wooing
    The Lost Heart
    John Maynard
    Friar Anselmo
    In the Church at Stratford-on-Avon
    Mrs. Browning's Grave at Florence
    My Castle
    Apple Blossoms
    Summer Hours
    June
    Little Charlie
    The Whippoorwill and I
    Carving a Name
    Gone to the War
    Where is My Boy Tonight?
    A Soldier's Valentine
    Last Words
    Song of the Croaker
    King Cotton
    Out of Egypt
    The Price of Victory
    Fair Harvard, Dear Guide to our Youth's Golden Days
    As We Meet in Thy Name, Alma Mater, Tonight
    Fair Harvard, the Months have Accomplished their Round
    There's a Fountain of Fable whose Magical Power
    Bi-Centennial Ode
    For the Consecration of a Cemetery

More than thirty years after their first appearances in print, Alger claimed that—during the Civil War period — a number of these were published anonymously in the Boston Transcript and New York Sun.

Hymn   November 20, 1878
>   Written for celebration commemorating the
>   founding of Unitarian Church at South
>   Natick.

Golden Argosy:
>   The Primary School   October, 1885

Fortieth Anniversary Poem
>   Read at the Annual Dinner of the Harvard Class   June 29, 1892
>   of 1852.

Songs of the Psi Upsilon Fraternity   1857
>   Greeting Song

Charles Hudson's History of Marlboro: 1862
>   Original Ode (the BiCentennial Ode presented
>   at Marlborough's 200th Aninversary Cele-
>   bration in 1860).

Lyrics of Loyalty: 1864
>   Gone to the War
>   Last Words

Pen Pictures of the War: 1864
>   Last Words

The Harp and the Cross (a collection of religious
poetry compiled by Stephen G. Bulfinch):   1867
>   Little Charlie

Character Building: (no date)
>   Carving a Name
>   John Maynard

Ever New and Never Old: 1870
>   John Maynard

One Hundred Choice Selections in Poetry and Prose: 1872
>   John Maynard

The Iveson, Blakeman and Taylor Fifth Reader: 1873
>   Carving a Name

Ballads of Bravery: 1881
    John Maynard

Standard Recitations No. 2:   1883
    John Maynard

Crown Jewels; or, Gems of Literature, Art and Music: 1887
    Carving a Name
    John Maynard

The Civil War in Song and Story: 1889
    Song of the Croaker

University of Life: 1900
    John Maynard

Iliff's Select Readings for Public and Private Enter-
    tainment: 1893
    Carving a Name

The Peerless Reciter or Popular Program: 1894
    John Maynard

The Elocutionist; or, Pearls for the Speaker: 1895
    John Maynard

The Peerless Reciter: 1908
    John Maynard

Bartlett's Familiar Quotations (Eleventh Edition)   1938
    John Maynard

A Victorian Keepsake: 1941
    Carving a Name

The Family Book of Best Loved Poems (Edited by
    David L. George, Published by Hanover House):   1952
    John Maynard

SHORT STORIES, ARTICLES, ETC.

The Pictorial National Library:
    Chivalry   March, 1849
    Cervantes   November, 1849

Written While a Student at Harvard:

Disquisition on the Immortality of Boot Soles   September 7, 1850

A Greek Version: From Lacey's "Address in Behalf of the Greeks."   October 15, 1850

A Dissertation: The Poetry of the Troubadors   October 21, 1851

First Prize Bowdoin Dissertation: Athens in the Time of Socrates (Alger submitted this under the pen-name of "Athenaceus," but later wrote his real name on the cover).   1851

A Greek Version: The State of Athens Before the Legislation of Solon (Alger signed this Bowdoin competition entry "By Zeta, a a Member of the Junior Class," but later signed his real name. At the end of the manuscript a faculty examiner noted: "There are several errors in this version, partly in the use of words and some in inflections; but it is, on the whole, deserving of the prize, being generally correct, and showing a good deal of attention and labor").   1851

An English Oration: Cicero's Return From Banishment   July 21, 1852

Gleason's Pictorial Drawing Room Companion:

Margaret's Test; or, Charity its own Reward	December 17, 1853
The Veiled Mirror; or, Pictures of the New Year	January 7, 1854
Three Games at Chess; a Legend of Venice	March 11, 1854
The Double Elopement; A Sketch	April 29, 1854
Peter Plunkett's Journey	July 1, 1854
The Christmas Gift	December 30, 1854
Mark Easton's Valentine	January 29, 1859
The Face at the Window	January 7, 1860
Old Gray	January 14, 1860
The Royal Game	February 19, 1860
Walter Gordon's Resolution	February 26, 1860
The Managing Wife	March 17, 1860
Robert Morton's Heirs	March 31, 1860

The Flag of Our Union:

Delays are Dangerous	January 14, 1854
The Uncle's Return	February 4, 1854
The Twenty Franc Piece	March 25, 1854
Marguerite and Her Parrot	May 27, 1854
Peter Plunkett's Journey	July 8, 1854
The Sybil's Prediction	July 15, 1854
Little Floy	July 29, 1854
The Artist's Apprentice	August 26, 1854
The King and the Neatherd	September 9, 1854
The Miller of Nottingham	October 7, 1854
The Saracen Dwarf	November 18, 1854
Miss Henderson's Thanksgiving Day	December 2, 1854

Miss Henderson's Thanksgiving Day: 1855
    Printed as a space filler at the end of "The Sea
        Witch," a book by Maturin M. Ballou.
The Two-Acre Lot: 1855
    Printed as a space filler at the end of "The
        Maniac's Secret," a book by Sylvanus Cobb,
        Jr.

Ballou's Dollar Monthly:

The Saracen Dwarf	January, 1855
Miss Henderson's Thanksgiving Day	February, 1855
The Two-Acre Lot	February, 1856
Cousin John	April, 1856
Tommy's Adventure	October, 1886
A Snowball Fight, and What Came of it.	February, 1889

Bertha's Christmas Vision: 1856

    Little Floy; or, How a Miser was Reclaimed
    Miss Henderson's Thanksgiving Day
    Bertha's Christmas Vision (a combination of
        verse and prose)
    Wide Awake
    The Royal Carpenter of Amsterdam
    The Veiled Mirror
    The Prize Painting
    Lost and Found
    The Christmas Gift
    Gottfried the Scholar
    Peter Plunkett's Adventure

Graham's Illustrated Magazine:

Five Hundred Dollars	January, 1858

Gleason's Weekly Line-of-Battle Ship:

Matthew Pendleton's Wager	November 13, 1858
The Schoolmaster	November 20, 1858
Kitty Ray's Perplexity	November 27, 1858
Jacob Blount's Will	December 11, 1858
The Divining Rod	December 25, 1858
Diamond Cut Diamond	January 8, 1859
Kathleen's Trials	January 15, 1859
The King and Abbot	January 22, 1859
Mark Easton's Valentine	January 29, 1859
Beauty Versus Money	February 12, 1859
The Gold Piece; or, The Newsboy's Tempta- tion	February 26, 1859
The Lottery Ticket	March 12, 1859
The Hasty Match	March 26, 1859
A Woman's Stratagem	April 16, 1859

Bread Upon the Waters	April 30, 1859
The Miser of Nottingham	May 14, 1859
Tim, the Blacksmith	May 21, 1859
Small Savings	June 18, 1859
Keep Your Engagements	June 25, 1859
The Old Maid's Cat	July 9, 1859
The Miser's Dream	July 30, 1859
John Grover's Lesson	August 6, 1859
A Duke in Disguise	August 27, 1859
The Secret of Success	September 3, 1859
The Counterfeit Half-Dollar	October 1, 1859
The Blue Chest	October 8, 1859
The Test of Character	October 22, 1859
The Refractory Scholar	November 12, 1859
The Turning Point. A Temperance Sketch	November 19, 1859
Five Hundred A Year	December 3, 1859
Mr. Morrison's Investment	December 17, 1859
Mr. Buffington's Lesson	December 24, 1859

New York Sun: 1859

The Discarded Son; or The Cousin's Plot
The Secret Drawer
The Cooper's Ward
The Gypsy Nurse
Madeleine the Temptress

Gleason's Literary Companion:

Job Bradshaw's Luck	January 7, 1860
The Fallen Bridge	January 14, 1860
The Rival Archers	January 21, 1860
Mark Henderson's Failing	January 28, 1860
The Fair Servitor	February 4, 1860
Nicholas Elwin's Tragedy	February 11, 1860
Charles Dean's Success	February 18, 1860
The Cook's Perplexity	February 25, 1860
Don't Give Up	March 3, 1860
Timothy Boltwood's Horse	March 10, 1860
Mrs. Gordon's Lot	March 17, 1860
A Blessing in Disguise	March 31, 1860
The First Patient	April 7, 1860
The Golden Prize	April 21, 1860
Henry Trafton's Independence	April 28, 1860
The Lost Receipts	May 5, 1860
John Beckwith's Reverses	May 19, 1860
The Boarding School Drudge	May 26, 1860
Norah Burke's Trial	June 2, 1860
Two Ways of Investment	June 9, 1860
Old Simon's Victory	July 14, 1860
Carl Hansen's Luck	August 4, 1860
The Little Image Merchant	August 25, 1860

John Golding's Mirror	September 15, 1860
Sybil Hampton's Test	October 13, 1860
Living for Others	November 10, 1860
Miss Plympton's Thanksgiving	December 1, 1860
Little Paul's Christmas Gift	December 29, 1860
Herbert's Dream; a New Year's Story	January 5, 1861
The Little Outcast	January 19, 1861
The Tin Savings Bank; a Tale for Hard Times	October 12, 1861
Edward's Temptation	1864
John Hayden's Cigar	1864
Milly's Oranges	July 29, 1865
Mrs. Cordner's Reformation	August 19, 1865
The Sybil's Prediction	November 18, 1865
The Saracen Dwarf	December 30, 1865
Mrs. Burbank's Governess	January 20, 1866
Robert Graham's Valentines	February 24, 1866
The Uncle's Return	March 24, 1866
Job Plympton's Ghost	March 31, 1866
Miss Graham's Mistake	June 2, 1866
The Clifton Mortgage	August 25, 1866
Henry Fletcher's Luck	September 29, 1866
Philip Allison's Lesson	October 27, 1866
The Golden Test	December 15, 1866
The Christmas Watch	December 29, 1866
John Stevenson's Good Fortune	January 5, 1867
Mrs. Grover's Grand Piano	March 16, 1867
Thomas Minturn's Failure	April 13, 1867
A Neighbor's Quarrel	August 3, 1867
Adam Holcomb's Will	August 24, 1867
Ruth Henderson's Pride	September 28, 1867
Mrs. Murray's Lesson	November 9, 1867
Mrs. Grantley's Guests	November 30, 1867
John Rawson's Christmas Gift	December 28, 1867
New Year's Calls	January 4, 1868
The Prima Donna	January 18, 1868
Capt. Seymour's Housekeeper	February 15, 1868
Mrs. Montcalm's Pride	March 14, 1868
James Cornell's Good Fortune	April 11, 1868
The Brother's Return	May 16, 1868
Mrs. Crampton's Experiments	June 13, 1868
The Uncle's Ordeal	July 25, 1868
A Narrow Escape	August 22, 1868
Sir Herbert's Pride	September 26, 1868
Slow and Sure	October 31, 1868
John Walton's Revenge	November 21, 1868
The Dark Hour	December 26, 1868
The Disguised Heiress	January 9, 1869
A Chance Meeting	February 27, 1869
The Missing Necklace	March 6, 1869
A Critical Case	March 27, 1869
Dock Thieves	April 10, 1869
Katy's Sacrifice	April 24, 1869
The Artist's Bride	May 1, 1869

Miss Aubrey's Fortune	May 15, 1869
The Old Silver Watch	May 22, 1869
Under an Umbrella	June 5, 1869
Count von Heilbrun	July 24, 1869
Maud's Mistake	August 21, 1869
The Jewel Case	August 28, 1869
Agnes Fleming's Choice	September 18, 1869
The Husband's Secret	October 2, 1869
Mrs. Fenton's Mystery	October 9, 1869
The Carlton Legacy	October 23, 1869
Mrs. Chandler's Little Plot	October 30, 1869
Atonement	January 1, 1870
The Lottery Ticket	March 19, 1870
The Miser's Dream	April 16, 1870
The Lucky Meeting	June 25, 1870
Thomas Macy's Plot	July 23, 1870
Alice's Fortune	September 3, 1870

Gleason's Home Circle:

Nicholas Elwin's Tragedy	February 11, 1860
The Carlton Legacy	October 23, 1869
The Schoolmaster	1870
Blanche Trevor's Love	1871
Norah Burke's Trial	1871
Walter Gordon's Resolution	1871
Jacob Blount's Will	1871
Robert Morton's Heirs	1871
A Woman's Strategem	1871
Paul's Picture	1872
The Browns; or, Boarding in the Country	November, 1874
The Boarding School Drudge	1879
New Year's Calls	1879
John Beckwith's Reverses	1879
The Brother's Return	1880
Carl Hansen's Luck	1880
The Dark Hour	1880
The Frightful Caricature	1880
Henry Trafton's Independence	1880
Herbert's Dream	1880
The Lost Receipts	1880
The Uncle's Ordeal	1880

Marlborough Mirror: May 5, 1860

A Visit to the Falls at Montmorenci
Report on an Address by Napoleon III — March 9, 1861
Address to Graduates at Reunion of Gates Academy and Marlborough High School — September 30, 1874

491

492

Gleason's Monthly Companion:

John Golding's Mirror	January, 1872
Delays are Dangerous	July, 1872
A Helping Hand, A Temperance Sketch	March, 1873
Herbert Dexter's Ordeal	April, 1873
The Match Boy	April, 1873
The Uncle's Return	June, 1873
The Two Paths	June, 1873
The Artist's Apprentice	August, 1873
Aunt Jane's Ear Trumpet	October, 1873
Thomas Mordaunt's Investment	November, 1873
Miss Henderson's Thanksgiving Day	December, 1873
The Saracen Dwarf	January, 1874
Milly's Oranges	March, 1874
Mrs. Cordner's Reformation	May, 1874
The Miller of Nottingham	July, 1874
The King and the Abbott	October, 1874
The Uncle's Return	January, 1875
Mr. Tipton's Fate	June, 1875
The Clifton Mortgage	November, 1875
Henry Fletcher's Luck	December, 1875
The Christmas Watch	August, 1876
Adam Holcomb's Will	October, 1877
Ruth Henderson's Pride	November, 1877
Albert Grafton's Speculation	December, 1877
Mrs. Grantley's Guests	July, 1878
The Rival Archers	July, 1878
The Prima Donna	October, 1878
Timothy Boltwood's Horse	November, 1878
Mrs. Crampton's Experiments	December, 1878

Young Israel:

A Glimpse of Venice	January, 1874

Golden Days:

Who Shall Win?	March 6, 1880
Tom's Temptation, A Story for Boys	March 13, 1880
The New Schoolmaster	March 27, 1880

The Home Companion:

Who Shall Win? A Story of School Life	June, 1881

New York Weekly:

The Boy Scout; A Tale of Virginia in 1861	February 6, 1882
A Brave Irish Boy; A Story of Kentucky	February 13, 1882
The Boy Substitute; or, The Young Wisconsin Volunteer	February 20, 1882

The Boy Guide of Rich Mountain; A Story of
  West Virginia   February 27, 1882
Johnny Wilson; or, The Little Drummer Boy
  in 1861   March 6, 1882
A Street Arab at the Seat of the War in 1861   March 13, 1882

Gleason's Monthly Magazine:
  Frederic Manheim's Suit   September, 1882
  The Uncle's Ordeal   October, 1882
  Miss Simpson at Saratoga   October, 1882

New York Waverly:
  Ben's Atonement   May 8, 1886

Golden Argosy:
  Mr. Wilton's Office Boy   August 21, 1886
  Little Nan   May 16, 1887

Leisure Hour Library:
  Aunt Jane's Ear Trumpet   January 15, 1887

The Boston Globe:
  Sybil Hampton's Test   December 29, 1887

The Yankee Blade:
  A Frightful Caricature   November 23, 1889
  The Christmas Watch   December 7, 1889

Ladies Home Journal:
  Are My Boys Real?   November, 1890

The Shining Hour:
  The Two Daisys; a Christmas Sketch   December, 1890

Good News:
  A Snowball Fight, and What Came of it   July 3, 1890
  Johnny Wilson   August 14, 1890
  The Little Drummer Boy   August 14, 1890
  A Street Arab   August 21, 1890
  A Brave Irish Boy   August 28, 1890
  The Boy Substitute   November 27, 1890
  Tommy's Adventure   December 11, 1890
  The Errand Boy's Christmas   December 20, 1890
  The Boy Scout   February 20, 1892
  The Clifton Mortgage   July 9, 1892
  Philip Allison's Lesson   July 9, 1892
  The Brother's Return   November 26, 1892
  New Year's Calls   January 14, 1893
  Robert Grabariou's Resolution   March 13, 1897

The Golden Magnet:
 John Walton's Revenge   April, 1891

The Writer:
 A Letter by Alger (apparently one of a series
  by prominent authors, telling how they got
  started).   January, 1892

Argosy:
 Tom Parker's Strange Visitor   **December 17, 1892**

Vickery's Fireside Visitor:
 The Clifton Mortgage   August 15, 1893
 The Lost Receipts   December, 1896

Happy Days: 1896
 Mr. Wilton's Office Boy
 John Beckwith's Reverses
 The Lost Receipts

Lupton's Famous Fiction by Great American
  Authors: 1897 (?)
 John Beckwith's Reverses
 The Lost Receipts
 Mr. Wilton's Office Boy

Good Reading Magazine:
 John Beckwith's Reverses   1900
 Mr. Wilton's Office Boy   1900

Sunshine for Youth:
 Ben's Atonement   **June, 1902**

People's Literary Companion:
 Ben's Atonement   June, 1902

Tip Top Weekly:
 Tommy's Adventure   April 18, 1908
 One Good Indian (Note: This is a reissue title of
  "Tommy's Adventure"):   November 4, 1911
 The Clifton Mortgage   August 23, 1913

Harper's Magazine:
 Obituary of Horatio Alger, Jr.   **August, 1899**

INDEX